Moderates

Moderates

The Vital Center of American Politics,
from the Founding to Today

. . . .

DAVID S. BROWN

University of North Carolina Press   Chapel Hill

© 2016 The University of North Carolina Press
All rights reserved
Set in Charis Regular By Westchester Publishing Services
Manufactured in the United States of America

The paper in this book meets the guidelines for permanence and durability
of the Committee on Production Guidelines for Book Longevity of the
Council on Library Resources.

The University of North Carolina Press has been a member
of the Green Press Initiative since 2003.

Library of Congress Cataloging-in-Publication Data
Names: Brown, David S. (David Scott), 1966– author.
Title: Moderates : the vital center of American politics, from the Founding
    to Today / David S. Brown.
Description: Chapel Hill : University of North Carolina Press, [2016] |
    Includes bibliographical references and index.
Identifiers: LCCN 2015042383| ISBN 9781469629230 (cloth : alk. paper) |
    ISBN 9781469629247 (ebook)
Subjects: LCSH: Moderation—Political aspects—United States—History. |
    Politicians—United States. | Political culture—United States. | Politics,
    Practical—United States. | United States—Politics and government.
Classification: LCC E183 .B89 2016 | DDC 306.20973—dc23
    LC record available at http://lccn.loc.gov/2015042383
    ISBN 978-1-4696-2923-0 (cloth: alk. paper)
    ISBN 978-1-4696-2924-7 (ebook)

For
Leslie, Sharon, and Julie,
my beautiful
sisters

I stood there holding my sturdy shield over both parties;
I would not let either side win a victory that was wrong.

—Solon

Contents

Part III
Pragmatists

Acknowledgments

I am pleased to recognize those individuals and institutions that have aided and sustained the writing of this book. Helping me track down and access documents were a number of archivists and research librarians at Elizabethtown College's High Library, the Massachusetts Historical Society, the George Bush Presidential Library and Museum, the State Historical Society of Missouri, the Columbia University Center for Oral History, and the Library of Congress. A timely research stipend and much-appreciated release time were provided by Elizabethtown College; the Scowcroft Institute of International Affairs and the Thomas J. Dodd Research Center at the University of Connecticut furnished opportune travel grants. Beyond institutional support, several people kindly lent their expertise. With his own work percolating, Jeff Ludwig spent part of a long, snowy Rochester winter going over the manuscript—I hope he knows it's much the better for his discerning comments. Kimberly Adams dissected an embryonic draft of an uncooperative introduction, raising the right points and coaxing a lazy author into a clearer accentuation of his ideas. I am further indebted to my friend and former colleague Paul Gottfried for countless conversations, typically with dog in tow, on the curious circus that is American politics. Much to my benefit John Milton Cooper Jr. generously read the manuscript twice and allowed me to prevail upon his patience in a marathon phone session devoted to style and expression. I'm grateful as well for the really helpful readings of the manuscript by an anonymous reviewer for the University of North Carolina Press. The reviewer's suggestions strengthened the work both structurally and stylistically. My editor, Chuck Grench, early on saw the possibility of this project, and I am pleased that he took it on. His assistants, first Iza Wojciechowska and then Jad Adkins, kept the wheels turning and the questions coming.

Moderates

Introduction

Searching for the Center

· ·

A sane person . . . someone whose political beliefs seem quiet and mild, and as such always ignored by the media, which seeks out people from the screechy Left and shrill Right because they make for better sound bites.

—The web-based *Urban Dictionary*'s definition of "Moderate," 2003

One could be excused for thinking that moderation has no place in today's polarized political culture. It has long been fashionable for such periodicals of note as the *Boston Globe*, the *New York Times*, and the *Washington Post* to trumpet some variation of what one *Post* headline called in 2014, "The End of Moderates." The presumed historical trajectory that informs these stories dates back to the 1960s when liberal Rockefeller Republicanism began to give way to what would later be called conservative Reagan Republicanism. A half-century on, we remain captive to this clean, neat narrative. For beyond the occasional header, "the end of . . ." argument has become the dominant paradigm in modern American political thought, embraced by liberals and conservatives alike. Unabashedly presentist, it suggests that moderates make up little more than a faltering wing of the contemporary GOP, as if centrism had no history outside of that party or prior to our times.

One might expect to find richer and more reflective treatments of the country's moderate persuasion in the scholarly literature, yet on the whole that has not been the case. Although we have several excellent studies that explore moderation in a particular era or context—John Patrick Diggins's biography of John Adams, Daniel Walker Howe's study of the American Whigs, and Geoffrey Kabaservice's recent assessment of the Republican Party since Eisenhower are examples of the genre—we lack a synthetic treatment of centrism as a vital and inclusive tradition reaching back to the nation's eighteenth-century partisan roots. As a result, much of the historiography relegates moderates to mere factions within parties and thus lacking a cohesive identity or "largeness" of purpose.

Aside from documenting a scattering of middle-grounders and deal makers—Henry Clay, architect of three important antebellum compromises, comes perhaps most readily to mind—our conventional political narrative marches to the beat of a mechanical liberal-conservative consensus. For several decades after its postwar inception, that consensus skewed liberal as a rising cohort of scholars, themselves the children of the New Deal, praised the emerging welfare-warfare state and made something of a patron saint of FDR. At Harvard alone two historians, Arthur Schlesinger Jr., and Frank Freidel, labored throughout the 1950s on sympathetic multivolume treatments of Roosevelt and his era. Though challenged during the tumultuous 1960s, the case for liberalism as the "normative" American ideology continued to rule the interpretive roost.

This began to change in the 1980s with the onset of Reaganism. Though historian Alan Brinkley could argue as late as 1994 that "twentieth century American conservatism has been something of an orphan in historical scholarship," this certainly is no longer the case. For some years now the right has received more attention than perhaps any field in American political history. Books and articles weighing conservatism's impact on everything from Christianity to capitalism, social policy to suburbanization, have claimed the historiographical high ground. In a 2011 "state of the field" essay published in the *Journal of American History*, Kim Phillips-Fein argued that until the past two decades, "it was still possible to see the story of the twentieth century in terms of the triumph and expansion of liberalism, from the New Deal through the civil rights movement, feminism, the gay rights movement and environmentalism. Today, most historians accept that significant parts of the American population always dissented from the liberalism of the mid-twentieth century."[1]

What Phillips-Fein describes is a shifting focus in the scholarship rather than a fundamental reassessment or rethinking. Whether emphasizing a kind of Rooseveltian or Reaganite essentialism, the imperfect liberal-conservative idiom remains stubbornly entrenched as the operative approach to translating American politics—as so, it dominates our discussions and limits our vision. One need not dismiss its real if conditional descriptive power to notice its inherent limitations. Perhaps most problematic is the assumption that an unbridgeable ideological chasm divides liberals and conservatives—the nation read, that is, through a Fox

News vs. MSNBC lens. We know, however, that historically there has been far more flexibility, "play," and pragmatism in our partisanship than this rigid binary model suggests. Taking that truism as its starting point, this book examines the moderate tradition in American politics running from the Founding to Today.

Contra contemporary opinion, the delicate art of deal making was once widely respected in America. Up to the Civil War, parties, sections, and statesmen expected to compromise and burnished their reputations by doing so. As something of an object lesson, the Constitutional convention stood as the great and ever looming model of how concessions and accommodations could bring together disparate interests. More than drafting a framework of government, the "Fathers" established a practice of conciliation that allowed the Clays of future congresses the freedom to seek, beyond partisan or regional loyalties, common ground in times of crises. Subsequent compromises in 1820 (concerning the congressional balance of power between free and slave states), 1833 (testing the constitutionality of the federal tariff), and 1850 (regarding the status of slavery in the western territories) built upon this sturdy structure. Conversely, the reputation of moderates and mediators sunk after failing to reach yet another settlement in 1860. As historian Peter B. Knupfer has observed, "the secession winter produced not only a strong reaction in both sections against any further compromise but also an outpouring of abuse against past compromises and compromisers. The old rhetoric of compromise had lost its appeal to a significant number of Americans; the tie between union and compromise had been broken."[2]

Since that time, political moderates have suffered the slings and arrows of both left and right. Their reputation reached a nadir of sorts when Barry Goldwater famously declared at the 1964 Republican national convention that "extremism in the defense of liberty is no vice. And . . . moderation in the pursuit of justice is no virtue." Turning his back on history, Goldwater portrayed centrism as timid and indecisive, ignoring completely its constructive and time tested qualities. This study offers a much different and, I hope, more capacious reading on the subject. Though sensitive to the limitations of the moderate middle, I underscore pragmatism's positive impact in a political culture all too eager to emphasize ideologues and idealists. To be clearer still, my conception of centrism chimes with John Milton Cooper Jr.'s description of Theodore Roosevelt's politics, which he defined some years ago as "inspired moderation."[3] It is this side and this sensibility I wish to recover.

· · · · ·

The question of political moderation today is of special importance to the Republican Party. For despite notable success in recent "wave" congressional elections (2010 and 2014), it has for over a generation experienced considerably less success in national elections. Put simply, the heyday of modern conservatism has long since passed. The fiscal, evangelical, and foreign policy right met its moment in the 1980s under Ronald Reagan. His promises to unleash the U.S. economy from the shackles of government regulation, stem the "moral decline" let loose by the divisive sixties, and roll back the Soviet empire encouraged a powerful governing consensus that extended beyond the conservative faithful. Thirty years on, however, the GOP, popularly outpolled in five of the last six general elections, is a minority party in search of a majority. Many regard it as out of touch with contemporary culture, an ideological dinosaur awaiting a demographic Armageddon. For their part, GOP hardliners seem ill disposed to make peace with their centrist colleagues and forge a more "current" identity. In a 2009 appearance on the Sunday news show *Face the Nation*, former vice president Dick Cheney denied that the moderate Colin Powell even belonged in the GOP. "If I had to choose in terms of being a Republican," he told host Bob Schieffer, "I'd go with Rush Limbaugh. My take on it was Colin had already left the party."[4]

Limbaugh, and any number of Limbaugh-like media pundits aside, the *beau idéal* of the political right remains Ronald Reagan, although one might wonder why. Reagan left, after all, a far more complex and less ideologically ironclad legacy than a surface impression suggests. Domestically, he signed into law the Immigration Reform and Control Act of 1986, which effectively amnestied millions of illegal immigrants; that same year he signed the Tax Reform Act, which eliminated a number of deductions, increased corporate taxes, and broadened the tax base— congressional Democrats Richard Gephardt and Bill Bradley sponsored the bill. In foreign affairs Reagan dealt successfully with the Soviet Union through a series of give-and-take summits, even proposing to Secretary-General Mikhail Gorbachev at their 1986 Reykjavík talks that both countries destroy all of their ballistic missiles within ten years. At the time, many on the American right thought he had gone crazy. And on the issue of fiscal conservatism, Reaganomics proved a spectacular bust.

Government grew notably larger during the 1980s while the country's national debt rocketed to an unprecedented $3 trillion as the United States became the world's largest debtor nation.

One could argue that the open secret of Reagan's success lay in his ability to conciliate both the right and the center. By no means a liberal Republican, neither was he a particularly good Reaganite. Roll back "Roe v. Wade?" Resist raising taxes? Shrink the central government? None of it happened. For his first Supreme Court nominee, Reagan chose Judge Sandra Day O'Connor, a former Arizona state senator who had supported both the Equal Rights Amendment and legalized abortion. Today the right has recast Reagan as an uncompromising cold warrior who led a moral revival at home. Practicing a kind of sentimental conservatism, it has become intellectually constrained in a gilded memory cage of its own making.

Former Florida governor Jeb Bush knows this. In a 2012 address before a group of editors and reporters at Bloomberg L.P. in Manhattan, he doubted whether Reagan would find much support in today's GOP: "Ronald Reagan would have, based on his record of finding accommodation, finding some degree of common ground . . . would [now] be criticized for doing the things that he did."[5] A year later, Bush, speaking at the Ronald Reagan Dinner at the Conservative Political Action Conference in Washington, more formally called for a more inclusive GOP. "Way too many people believe Republicans are anti-immigrant, anti-woman, anti-science, anti-gay, [and] anti-worker," he warned his audience. "And the list goes on and on and on. Many voters are simply unwilling to choose our candidates even though they share our core beliefs because those voters feel unloved, unwanted, and unwelcome in our party."[6]

Thinking historically, one might compare the present condition of the GOP to that of the Jeffersonians in the 1850s or to the supporters of the conservative Ohio senator Robert Taft in the 1950s. In the first instance agrarianism, states' rights, and slavery—long the DNA of national development—neared their end. Driven out of power, the Democracy subsequently engaged in a major overhaul in concepts and convictions that prefaced its appeal to a twentieth-century urban-industrial nation: the party of Jefferson became the party of FDR. The Taft analogy speaks perhaps even more directly to the particular challenges facing today's conservatives. For much like the current right, Taftites nurtured a vision of unreflective capitalism combined with a unilateral foreign policy that appealed to small town America. But the market crash and subsequent global war demonstrated the irrelevancy of a GOP locked in a quasi-Victorian mindset of classical liberalism and splendid isolationism. Voters informed Republicans of that in 1932, and for a long time after.

· · · · ·

More than a rumination on the contemporary GOP's identity crisis, this book assays a series of moderate coalitions touching several centuries. The first, the Adams-Federalists, fell ideologically between the poles of Jeffersonianism (the advocates of states' rights) and Hamiltonianism (the supporters of a strong activist state). Both John Adams and Alexander Hamilton were Federalists, though the latter's efforts to create a fiscal-military elite propelled by a powerful national bank and an expanding army aroused the former's concern. Alarmed by the French Revolution's presumably radical impact in America, High Federalists, favoring aristocratic Britain and following Hamilton's lead, voted into law the Sedition Act, which in practice restricted the freedom of speech of Federalism's domestic critics, the Jeffersonians. To justify this assault on the Constitution and maintain their hold on power, the Hamiltonians needed a crisis and better yet a war and this Adams, elected in 1796 as George Washington's presidential successor, refused to give them. Largely as a result, Federalism fractured internally in 1800, was routed in that year's elections, and never regained its old relevancy. Despite himself being swept away in the Jeffersonian deluge, Adams always considered his opposition to "ultra" Federalism a kind of national service. Although he maintained a spirited correspondence with Jefferson in their final years, he never ceased to condemn what he called Hamilton's "villainy."

The nation's second moderate coalition, the Clinton-Democratic Republicans (1812), brought together the New York–New England wing of the Jeffersonian Party along with some Federalist support. Having grown resentful of slaveholder political dominance, it sought to defeat the planters at the polls. Its chief grievance was with Jefferson's unpopular embargo (1807–9), which, in the name of protecting American neutrality in the ongoing wars of the French Revolution, forbade U.S. export trade with any nation. To his mainly northern opposition, Jefferson, the southern agrarian, seemed intent on wrecking the North's free-labor economy. As if to pour salt in its wounds, Jefferson subsequently signed the "supplementary acts" to enforce the embargo, and these empowered federal agents to confiscate shipments without a warrant *merely on the suspicion* that a transporter had considered evading the restriction. Frustrated with the Lake Champlain region's continued illicit trade with Canada, Jefferson declared it to be in a state of insurrection and sent regular army units to deter exchanges. Looking to stop this executive overreach, critics within the Jeffersonian camp would within a few years ally with the remnants of Federalism to run the New Yorker DeWitt Clinton against James Madison—Jefferson's handpicked heir—in the 1812 presidential election. In a tight race, Madison won by claiming Pennsylvania, without which he would have been bested. In both 1812 and 1800, in other words, largely internal oppositions had challenged the ruling parties over their claims to unconstitutional power.

The country's third moderate coalition, made up of a number of antislavery groups that began to congeal under the Republican Party banner in 1854, shared a common aversion to the expansion of the peculiar institution into the western territories. For a generation these future Republicans had watched as southern irreconcilables sought to bend the Constitution to fend off their greatest fears—democracy and free labor. In all, their attack on popular government was remarkable. The 1836 Gag Rule prevented abolitionist petitions from being read or discussed in the House; the protracted struggle over the fate of Kansas (1850s) included outright voter fraud that resulted in the sitting of pro-slavery legislatures in a territory with a clear anti-slavery majority; and the notorious Dred Scott decision (1857) held that African-Americans, free or otherwise, could not be U.S. citizens. In the face of such extremism many critics of the Slave Power sought in 1860 a moderate solution, the recognition of slavery where it currently resided, but no future extension into the nation's territories.

Though abolitionists denounced this course, its ultimate goal was in fact the end of black bondage. The historian Richard Sewall has justly observed that "more moderate Republicans—men like William Pitt Fessenden, Samuel Bowles, Edwin D. Morgan, John Sherman, Caleb Smith, and Abraham Lincoln—exhibited greater patience, greater reverence for the Union and the Republican party as ends in themselves, and less crusading zeal than did their radical colleagues. Yet on the whole they shared the radicals' hatred of slavery as well as the Slave Power and viewed the destruction of both as the prime task of their party." In the end, Lincoln's practical leadership proved decisive. By spurning ideological labels and candidly facing the political realities of his time, Lincoln belonged to what historian David Herbert Donald called "the American Pragmatic Tradition."[7]

The nation's fourth moderate coalition spanned several decades (1870s–1910s) and consisted of no fewer than three distinct parties or movements (Liberal Republicans, Mugwumps, and the Progressive Party). What links them together is a patrician-led rejection of the political corruption that had become so prominent in Gilded Age America. The most notable of their number, Theodore Roosevelt, inherited as president a nation struggling under the multiple pressures of industrialization, urbanization, and large-scale immigration. Concerned that anti-progressive Old Guard Republicans had given too many advantages to big business, he advanced a series of reforms known collectively as the Square Deal. It broke up "bad" trusts, condemned "predatory wealth," and more generally recognized the growing influence of an increasingly consumer-oriented middle class. Broadly interpreted, the Square Deal sought to create a fairer balance of power in America and gave the GOP its first major reform agenda since Reconstruction. After Roosevelt left office, however, Old Guardism returned in force and rejected the regulatory state idea, which would not be seen again until New Deal Democrats employed it to both reshape and dominate the electoral landscape.

It is easy to forget today that from 1936 to 1976, moderate Republicans controlled the GOP, and thus constituted the country's fifth moderate coalition. They engineered the presidential candidacies of the one-time Democrat Wendell Willkie (1940), the pro–New Deal governor of New York, Thomas Dewey (1944 and 1948), and Dwight Eisenhower (1952 and 1956), the symbol-in-chief of, as Ike put it, "Modern Republicanism." Reasserting themselves after Barry Goldwater's "ultra" conservative 1964 campaign, moderates capped an era of relative dominance within the party by supporting Gerald Ford's 1976 nomination over Ronald Reagan.

Conservative Republicans have since argued that because the GOP won few national elections during this period—four to be precise—it should have broken with the social welfare model and given voters a "real" choice between right and left. It is implied in this analysis that if offered such an option, most would have gone right. But that seems, particularly in light of the Goldwater debacle and the genuine if transitory appeal of postwar liberalism, a rather dubious premise. In fact, by maneuvering their party to the middle, moderate Republicans helped to sustain its relevancy, perhaps even its existence. The GOP, after all, was a fast failing concern in the 1930s and we sometimes forget that not all major parties, one thinks of the Federalists, Whigs, and Populists, live to fight another day.[8] Certainly some conservative reaction to the social welfare model was bound to set in. Untethered to GOP moderates, however, it might well have alienated those many undecided voters eager to prune back but by no means uproot the New Deal State.

The nation's sixth and, at this writing, latest moderate coalition is the contemporary (post 1990) Democratic Party. It arose only after an extended internal struggle between party progressives (supporters of 1972 presidential candidate George McGovern) and party pragmatists (supporters of Bill Clinton). Unable any longer to win national elections as tax-and-spend liberals and effectively smeared by their opponents as the party of "amnesty, abortion, and acid," a string of Democratic candidates—Humphrey, McGovern, Carter, Mondale, and Dukakis—dropped five of six presidential campaigns between 1968 and 1988.

Clinton, the first Baby Boomer elected to the White House, made common cause in the late eighties with an emerging group of "New Democrats" to redefine their party by making it more responsive to the suburbs, the middle-class, and critics of the "entitlement state." Successful in the 1990s, the Democrats' march to the middle had in fact begun a generation earlier during the Carter presidency. A moderate in a party still very much tied to its Rooseveltian roots, Jimmy Carter struggled to master a fracturing New Deal coalition. Many of his in-house critics believed him a "typical" southern conservative and, in the 1980 Democratic primaries, rallied around the "typical" northeastern liberal Ted Kennedy in protest. Their support gave Kennedy an impressive 37 percent of the vote in what was something of an opening phase in a hard fought contest for the party's future. By the early 1990s, after liberal Democratic candidates suffered consecutive lopsided losses in the 1984 and 1988 presidential elections, the New Democrats broke through. Trending toward the center on such hot button issues as tax cuts, welfare reform, and the trimming of federal entitlements, they have captured more popular votes than their GOP opponents in every national election save one since 1988.[9]

The most recent winner of those elections, Barack Obama, has proven an adept New Democrat. As former *Washington Post* columnist Ezra Klein argued in 2011, "If you put aside the emergency measures required by the 2007–9 global financial crisis, three major policy ideas have dominated American politics in recent years: a plan that uses an individual mandate and tax subsidies to achieve near-universal health care; a cap-and-trade plan that attempts to raise the prices of environmental pollutants to better account for their costs; and bringing tax rates up from their Bush-era lows as part of a bid to reduce the deficit. In each case, the position that Obama and the Democrats have staked out is the very position that moderate Republicans have staked out before."[10] Klein's article may have turned a few heads (Obama a moderate?!), but not Obama's. In a 2012 interview with a Miami-based television station, the president responded to critics who called him a socialist by saying, "the truth of the matter is that my policies are so mainstream that if I had set the same policies that I had back in the 1980s, I would be considered a moderate Republican." Public intellectual Noam Chomsky (ruefully) agreed, observing recently that the president is "kind of a mainstream centrist with some concerns for liberal ideas and conceptions, but not much in the way of principle or commitment." With the moderate GOP "more or less disappeared," he continued, today's Democratic Party has become the moderate party.[11]

Chomsky's epitaph for GOP centrism, like that of the major media outlets, may be a bit premature. In fact the right believes just the opposite, arguing that an unwillingness to nominate "true" conservatives dooms its candidates in general elections. As Texas senator Ted Cruz caustically put the matter before a 2015 Tea Party gathering, "you know what 'electability' is? Nominate the candidate who is closest to the Democrats."[12] Far from reaching the kind of consensus assumed by Chomsky, the GOP is engaged, rather, in a prolonged internal battle to define itself before the electorate—the same kind of ideological skirmishing its opponents went through in the 1970s and 1980s. The question of whether it will be as successful as the New Democrats is at this point unclear. What we know is that its hard right wing is incapable of making a majority within the party, let alone around the country. Whether the GOP can find enough common ground to advance compelling ideas and candidates in coast-to-coast campaigns remains to be seen and is, in any case, beyond the scope of this study. My interest, rather, is in recovering the history of a moderate persuasion that has on occasion proven to be a saving grace of sorts in American politics. Older than the liberal-conservative consensus, the nation's centrist tradition has influenced every important public debate from early republic concerns over executive overreach to more contemporary questions regarding organized conservatism's future. Put another way, by reviewing the role of the middle we may come to recognize the important and still vital pragmatic lines of leadership that connect the partisan past with the partisan present.

Part I   **Patriot Kings**

· ·

The greatest dangers to American democracy once came from
within. Before the Civil War, the country's early radical right—
New England's ultra-Federalist elite and the secession-making
southern plantocracy—questioned the constitutional
arrangement negotiated in 1787. Each sought solace in the past.
Wedded to traditional hierarchical worldviews, they hoped to
stem the quickening pace of popular government. This proved
impossible. Under the pressure of westward expansion, the first
stirrings of industrial development, and the decline of an older
deferential political culture, the character of the United States
changed dramatically from the Age of Washington to the Age of
Lincoln. The pivot of history had turned. A quasi-colonialism
gave way to social mobility, gentry rule fell before a broadening
electorate, and states' rights gave way to the notion of a
perpetual and powerful Union.

1 Between Aristocracy and Democracy

John Adams

· ·

Aristocracy will continue to envy all above it, and despise and oppress all below it; Democracy will envy all, contend with all, endeavor to pull down all.

—John Adams, 1814

The moderate persuasion in American politics begins with John Adams. A man of the liberal right, he viewed with suspicion the nation's emerging rule of the strong right, the dominant wing of the Federalist Party loyal to Alexander Hamilton. He condemned its vision of a small civil service elite holding both private wealth and state power as contrary to the self-governing spirit of the Revolution. Neither, however, could he follow the philosophy of Thomas Jefferson, the other dominant ideologue of the day. The Virginian's buoyant brand of Enlightenment egalitarianism struck Adams as too populistic, too reliant upon the good will of "the people" to be practical. In an era of iconic personalities touched by the volatility of the French Revolution and prone to factionalism at home, Adams's search for the center found few allies. Indeed, then and for several generations thereafter, Americans seemed at a loss to reconcile with the nation's second president, the only one of the country's first five chief executives not to be reelected. Hamilton and Jefferson, by contrast, conveniently ascended from men to myths. They came quickly to personify the poles of American politics, symbols of aristocracy and democracy clashing in a timeless struggle over the centuries.

There were, to be sure, dissenters from this tidied-up political drama. In the late 1920s the distinguished Progressive literary historian Vernon Parrington drew a suggestive portrait of early republic politics that strayed beyond the traditional Jeffersonian-Hamiltonian dualism. Though recognizing the "liberal" and "conservative" strains in American life, he veered off the prescribed path, perceptively writing that "midway between" these two points "stands John Adams." Independent of mind, intellectually aggressive, and blessed with astonishing energy that often exceeded the patience of his peers, Adams appeared always to be in a state of doing, acting, making, and moving, much to the bounce of his own drummer's beat. Striking the proper chord, Parrington notes that "he was an uncompromising realist" and "refused to be duped by [either the] fine dreams of humanitarian panaceas" that so delighted Jefferson or the push for centralized power that drove Hamilton.[1] He feared, rather, top and bottom alike. As his colleagues quickly grouped into rival factions, Adams resisted their lead as a false choice between "democracy" and "aristocracy." A stubborn republican, he found himself ideologically alienated from the sharp partisanship that dominated post-Revolutionary politics.

An avid observer of human limitations, Adams wore an impulsive skepticism like a second skin. Unlike Jefferson, he approached the Enlightenment's promise of perfectibility as an intelligent carnivore might accost a porcupine—curious and with a certain instinctive hunger, but exceedingly wary. This guarded cast of mind colored Adams's opinions on both representative rule ("There was never a democracy yet that did not commit suicide," he once avowed) and the heaven-on-earth hopes inspired by the French Revolution. Accordingly, he foreswore the colossal optimism that underlined the Jeffersonian faith in virtue as the blessed product of vice. It is impossible to imagine Adams ever repeating anything remotely close to Jefferson's remarkable claim that "the liberty of the whole earth was depending on the [French Revolution], and . . . rather than it should have failed, I would have seen half the earth desolated."[2]

True, Hamilton too questioned America's French connection and, more broadly, the philosophical underpinnings that shaped the Age of Reason. Yet he presumed that an abiding social stability might be cobbled by combining the stock jockeying of nascent capitalists with the martial prowess of a standing army. As the country's first treasury secretary, Hamilton sought to centralize financial power in such a way as to strike at states' rights and turn local loyalties to national allegiances. His controversial proposal for the creation of the First Bank of the United States (chartered by Congress in 1791) provided a uniform currency and monetary engine for elites to acquire loans. It also spurred a speculative boom that threatened to launch a money monopoly among the very rich. This ersatz aristocracy offended Adams, who broke early from Hamiltonianism, concerned that it promised the rise of a new tyranny.

More broadly, Federalism and Republicanism emphasized conflicting visions of development. The great question facing Americans from the

1787 drafting of the Constitution to the 1861 dissolution of the Union involved the tense relationship between localism and nationalism. In various permutations, the confusion of critical issues challenging the new nation during these decades—slavery, internal improvements, and expansion across the frontier—intersected with this fundamental problem. By their very natures, localism and nationalism were incompatible. One would have to give way, peacefully or otherwise. In ruminating on the ideological world formed by the Jeffersonian-Hamiltonian contest, Adams insisted that the nation suffered for its association with extremism. He believed this to be the natural if injurious outcome of political parties that held contrasting views on where power resided. Most Americans at this time abhorred the concept of party spirit, but in the end most drifted into the party system. Adams never did. This independence proved to be the ultimate source both of his proud self-sovereignty and of his inevitable failure as president to offer a viable third way of governing.

· · · · ·

A fourth-generation New Englander, John Adams never strayed far from the Puritan persuasion that had brought his great-great grandfather, Henry Adams, to the Massachusetts Bay Colony. From this auspicious landfall succeeding Adamses settled in Braintree, a small village some dozen miles south of Boston. Here they made their living, heir after heir, chiefly off the land. John Adams's father, also named John, ventured a bit beyond a plow-and-cow existence. Settled near North Precinct Church, he served both community and congregation as tax collector, militia officer, deacon, and selectman. In this last office, the elder Adams ensured that the district's indigent received adequate care, typically a meal and a bed. When no placement proved possible he welcomed the poor into his own home, apparently absorbing the cost out of pocket. Known for his generosity, intelligence, and good character, the deacon was once warmly recalled by a proud John as "the honestest Man I ever knew. In Wisdom, Piety, Benevolence and Charity In proportion to his Education and Sphere of Life, I have never seen his Superior."[3]

The easy sociability of the senior Adams, a popular figure at the meetinghouse, does little to suggest let alone explain the temperamental volatility that shook his son. Gripped by strong passions, the younger John gave every indication of living his life more slave than master to the potent combination of engagement, ambition, and insecurity that pressed his political career forward. Reared in a Puritan tradition that questioned cravings for personal distinction, he twitched constantly between pride and a punishing self-denigration, oppressively, confessionally aware of both his real and imagined shortcomings. In need of the occasional brimstone, Adams found that a chilly deism offered him nothing. Reflecting in late age upon the special and wholly unanticipated success enjoyed by his simple kin, he concluded that a humble faith had spared more than their souls. "What has preserved this race of Adamses in all their ramifications, in such numbers, health, peace, comfort and mediocrity? I believe it is religion, without which they would have been rakes, fops, sots, gamblers, starved with hunger, frozen with cold, scalped by Indians, &c., &c., &c., been melted away and disappeared."[4]

If the religion observed by Adams resembled in faint outline the once exacting Calvinism of the Bay Colony's earliest elect, it also contained more liberal qualities. Adams believed, as he once put it, in a "Being existing from Eternity" with supreme power over His creation, and while he considered it an absolute certainty that in this world of wonder "there . . . never was but one being who can Understand the Universe," he reasoned by analogies from nature and society that his Maker refrained, as he explained to Jefferson, from condemning "innumerable millions to . . . miser[y], forever." To the partisans of predestination, Adams cribbed a stark reply: "I believe no such Things." His faith found strength, rather, in the following simple, affirming metaphysics: "The Love of God and his Creation; delight, Joy, Tryumph, Exultation in my own existence . . . are my religion."[5] Devoted to a personal and sympathetic divinity, Adams was no more abstract spiritualist than condemning Calvinist. He appears to have occupied an ecclesiastical middle ground that we might designate as harmonious, just, and Whiggish—God loved His cosmos and offered His children a rewarding life if they lived in a condition of moral accord. This search for a meaningful saintly center proved also to be the temperamental path on which Adams pursued his public career. Though teased by strong emotions, he considered extremes, whether in worship or in politics, to be symptomatic of indiscreet impulses.

Of course the question of what constituted a state of moral accord proved, in the vicissitudes of daily life, elusive and complex. Seeking structure, Adams circled back on the path that led to the old Puritanism. Shaped by Calvinism's penchant for introspection and haunted by the blurred line separating sin and salvation, he disclosed in his letters and diaries a practiced attachment to self-analysis. Collapsing society with self, he sought to subject his country to the same kind of restless internal dialogue in a language more Jeremiad than Enlightenment. Certainly he never lingered so long or so lovingly on the latent possibilities of the republic as did Jefferson in his eloquent *Notes on the State of Virginia* (1781), a document tying the presumed environmental superiority of the New World to its rising political prospects.

In this study, Jefferson read Virginia's agrarian vision across the continent as a case of a wishful Edenic innocence sustained in a republic mercifully absent, as he put it, "the mobs of great cities." Nor could Adams embrace the "penny saved is a penny earned" homilies that underlie Benjamin Franklin's famous *Autobiography*, which has long served as shorthand for the nation's worship of self-help strategies and self-made men. The memoir opens with a boastful oration touting its author's worldly success: "Having emerg'd from the Poverty and Obscurity in which I was born and bred, to a State of Affluence and some Degree of Reputation in the World, and having gone so far thro' life with a considerable Share of Felicity . . . my Posterity [may find my situation] fit to be imitated."[6] Adams too could assume a pedantic attitude, though his sermons typically arrived in the clipped cadence of the cold scold. For an earthy art of living, the fruits, that is, of Parisian cuisine, London theater, and Philadelphia's secular-minded modernity, interested him far less than Franklin. He felt compelled, rather, to apprise his countrymen of their assorted shortcomings, this but a preface to a pedagogy heavy on the special sacrifices born by the sons and daughters of 1776 in their moment of nerve and mettle.

Practiced in the psychology of self-effacement, Adams projected a host of private insecurities across America's ideological landscape. In *A Defence of the Constitutions of the United States of America*, a survey of republicanism ancient and new that he completed in the late 1780s, Adams emphasized the various forms of failure known to have crippled past governments, aristocratic and democratic alike. Here, he needed no prompting to read the seventeenth-century Puritan concern for moral decline onto the next century's political world. Accordingly, he held more conventional and less confident views of human nature than a rising chorus of thinkers and philosophes claiming a progressive personality type. Self-interest, greed, and corruption, he little doubted, retained their traditional influence. Reason alone would never trump misplaced power; the "people" comprised both the promise and the problem of respectable government.

Responding to the strong stirrings of Western liberalism, the *Defence* counseled a callow American democracy to dismiss the uneven model of European republics from the ancient to the modern world. They had, so Adams insisted, underestimated humanity's prideful quest for autonomy, overestimated religion's capacity to provide a binding moral social core, and turned an ignorant eye to the confused impact of commercial forces on the body politic. At heart, he believed in a dispersal of mastery to check both ruler and ruled. In contrast to many of his contemporaries, Adams appeared, if not precisely hostile to, then certainly suspicious of the Enlightenment's new trinity of reason, liberty, and equality. He preferred a more mundane set of principles and clear constitutional guidelines that spelled out both the prerogatives and limitations of government. "The predominant passion of all men in power," he wrote, "whether kings, nobles, or plebeians, is the same; that tyranny will be the effect, whoever are the governors, whether the one, the few, or the many, if uncontrolled by equal laws, made by common consent, and supported, protected, and enforced by three different orders of men *in equilibrio*."[7]

Unwilling to privilege the confident claims of humanity, Adams's *Defence* recalled the religious compact produced nearly a century earlier in Cotton Mather's *Magnalia Christi Americana* (1702). Pastor of Boston's original North Church, controversial defender of the Salem witch trials, and a voluminous writer, Mather won recognition as a learned and influential spiritual leader. Addressing second- and third-generation Puritans, his literary output helped establish the philosophical foundations for Calvinism in the New World. Notably, both Mather's *Magnalia* and Adams's *Defence* bore the impress of authors influenced by the anticipation of civilizational decline. Mather's study offered a historical perspective of New England's presumed descent from the august days of the Puritan ministerial elite to the rise of the Yankee shopkeeper. The recent and tragic witchcraft panic, sporadic conflicts with neighboring Indians, and the omnipresent fear of Catholic New France to the North darkened the divine's vision and discolored his narrative.

Working through the *Defence*, Adams faced in his own day an equally unsettling assortment of issues. In 1786 a debtor party won control of the Rhode Island legislature and passed a paper money law that radically inflated the state's currency. Although this extraordinary bill eased the financial burden of debtors, it concurrently drove some creditors from Rhode Island lest they be forced to accept essentially worthless script. In the eyes of more than a few wary observers, democracy had run riot and class warfare now threatened all of New England. In the *Anarchiad*, a satiric-heroic verse sequence published anonymously in 1786–87, Rhode Island's troubles were laid bare:

> Hail! realm of rogues, renown'd for fraud and guile.
> All hail, ye knav'ries of yon little isle.
> There prowls the rascal, cloth'd with legal pow'r.
> To snare the orphan, and the poor devour;
> The crafty knave his creditor besets,
> And advertising paper pays his debts;
> Bankrupts their creditors with rage pursue
> No stop, no mercy from the debtor crew.
> Arm'd with new test, the licens'd villain bold,
> Presents his bills, and robs them of their gold.[8]

Tensions escalated the following year as debtors in western Massachusetts's Pioneer Valley, threatened with foreclosures and bereft of tax relief from an unsympathetic statehouse, concentrated in August under the leadership of Daniel Shays, a veteran at the battles of Lexington, Bunker Hill, and Saratoga. Wounded during the War for Independence, Shays had received no pay for his services excepting, in a sense, an ornamental sword given to him by General Lafayette. Faced with dire financial obligations, he later sold the prize. Under his leadership, the populist Shaysite army threatened to march on the state capital. Many of the men in its ranks were poor farmers calling for the issuance of paper currency as a means of relieving their financial distress. These 1,500 or so "rebels" were scattered at a battle near the federal armory in Springfield by a smaller but well-provisioned force marshaled by the state government and under the command of former Continental Army officer General William Shepard. Sporadic arrests followed.

These striking examples of post-Revolutionary class unrest in New England served to confirm Adams's mounting doubts about human nature. Criticized by Jeffersonians as a closet monarchist, he more interestingly adopted a set of prickly views anticipating in some respects those of the popular twentieth-century theologian Reinhold Niebuhr. Both men believed in the reality of sin, in the destructive capabilities of an amoral capitalism, and in the unfortunate tendency of Americans to mark themselves a transcendent people. Niebuhr's classic caution on humanity's capitulation to Enlightenment thought in *Moral Man and Immoral Society* (1932)—"moralists, sociologists and educators . . . [offer incomplete social analyses by] failing to recognize those elements in man's collective behavior which belong to the order of nature and can never be brought completely under the dominion of reason or conscience"—reprised Adams's hesitancy to embrace the lynchpin of America's civic faith: assurance in the inevitability of progress.[9]

Adams's quasi-Hobbesian worldview cut against the main lines of popular early republican thought. His confidence in a constitutional structure promoting measured liberty may have reinforced the Whig doctrines of the day, yet a more powerful skepticism steered his views on human nature and individual rights. Thus while popular opinion made a civic religion of social mobility, Adams reserved grave doubts about the coming of commercial capitalism, the sanctification of personal liberty, and the sacrifice of community interest to self-interest. Melding the language of Enlightenment naturalism with the cautionary points of Protestant pessimism, he insisted that individuals were incapable of commanding their own contentment. The atmospheric chaos unleashed by lightening, earthquakes, and floods, he wrote, was analogous to the temperamental passions that provoked the human spirit. "God has told us, by the general Constitution of the World, by the Nature of all terrestrial Enjoyments, and by the Constitution of our own Bodies, that this World was not designed for a lasting and happy State, but rather for a State of Moral Discipline."[10]

Naturally Adams worried about his own state of moral restraint and in doing so demanded much of himself and inevitably much of others. Although he coveted the trappings of material success including a fine house, expensive clothing, and one of the largest private libraries in the country, he concurrently craved the grace of self-control to live a simple republican life. In this struggle he embodied a surfacing Yankee personality type that wrestled futilely with the ancient religious injunctions against worldly gain even as its Boston bank account inevitably swelled. In reply, Adams reverted to a tried and true Puritan practice, balancing private desire with public abnegation. Accordingly, his correspondence sings with qualifications and recantations. A strongly sensual man, Adams once counseled his then fiancée, Abigail Smith, to make mastery over physical intimacy: "Patience my Dear! Learn to conquer your Appetites and Passions!" while his *Autobiography* chastely swears to a satisfied celibacy: "No Virgin or Matron ever had cause to blush at the sight of me, or to regret her Acquaintance with me."[11] More than a priggish affectation, Adams practiced the art of self-denial in a range of relationships to guard against the temptations of pride and secular ambition. In due time, the bartering cycle of success and sacrifice became a permanent constellation in his emotional makeup.

Rather than rest easy with material advancement ("Am I grasping at money, or scheming for power?" he habitually raised the specter of selfishness), Adams channeled his energies into civic engagement. This too presented temptations, for as he grimly observed in the early years of the Revolution, "the Love of Power is insatiable and uncontroulable."[12] Of course, crafting a kind of interior code to control the remote workings of the human heart proved a problem beyond any statesman's ken. And so Adams looked to the creation of a republic of countervailing constituencies to police one another. In this dialectical relationship politics again resembled Protestantism. Both statesman and clergy hued closely to the public's expectations of moral accountability, and each emphasized the importance of personal piety within the broader canopy of communal virtue. In this blending of secularism and spiritualism, Adams imagined a checks-and-balances political culture more deeply rooted in the soil of Mather's quasi-feudal New England than in Franklin's metropolitan-pointing Philadelphia.

Complementing Puritanism's impact, the modern English politics of sovereign versus commons shaped the ideological universe that produced Adams. And in contextualizing his thought, it might be helpful at this point to discuss briefly the "Country" ideology that emerged from the seventeenth-century bloodletting between King (Court) and Parliament (Country). Among the most prominent theorists in this school stands James Harrington, author of *The Commonwealth of Oceana* (1656), a work of political philosophy that advanced what became the classic argument for a republic of mixed powers in England. The 1649 execution of Charles I made Parliament preeminent and radically discounted the idea of divine-right kingships. By arguing for a model of politics that fused monarchy, aristocracy, and democracy, Harrington helped to establish a way of arranging government and classes that conveniently converged with the Enlightenment's assault on oligarchy. The Glorious Revolution of 1688—Parliament replaced yet another king, James II— only reinforced *Oceana*'s reputation in both England and its colonies. As one perceptive student of Country thought has written, "Shortly after the Restoration, ideas about mixed government were seriously discussed in the circle of influential men concerned with the colonization of America. The Fundamental Constitutions of Carolina, drafted by

John Locke, may well have been the earliest effort . . . to incorporate the thought of Harrington."[13] Though unpopular with Carolina's early settlers and never ratified by its assembly, that document anticipated a varied legislature of hereditary nobles and freeholders; as a "mixing" forum for contending classes, it prefaced the popular direction of politics in British North America.

In the eighteenth century, Country ideology, which had appeared triumphant with the Whig conquest of 1688, faced a revived Court consensus that prized centralized direction, complex commercial relationships, and a risk-laden speculative market. Robert Walpole's ministry aroused a particular loathing among Country leaders who saw in the fiscal-military revolution of the 1720s—the combining of imperial and mercantile dreams sustained by a powerful credit nexus—a perversion of the mixed commonwealth constitutional ideal. Walpole's critics complained that his power extended so deep into the pulse of British politics that the delicate balance of the parliamentary system neared collapse. This Anglo ideological debate had important repercussions for England's North American colonies. By the 1760s, in the aftermath, that is, of the victorious but financially crippling French and Indian War, patriots like Adams were beginning to interpret British attempts to directly tax and police its dominions as evidence of a corrupting governing culture steeped in Court philosophy. These "intrusions" included the Sugar and Stamp Acts, which sought to generate revenue to pay for British courts and soldiers to monitor American colonial trade. They further comprised the Currency and Quartering Acts, which respectively prohibited colonials from issuing legal-tender paper money and required the same to house and feed British troops if no other accommodations—barracks, inns, barns—were available. Shortly after the March 1766 repeal of the Stamp Act, a Deacon Webb took tea with Adams, asking his opinion of Massachusetts's Tory lieutenant governor. "I told him, what I once thought of him," Adams recounted, "and that I now hoped I was mistaken in my judgment. I told him I once thought, that his Death in a natural Way would have been a Smile of Providence upon the Public, and would have been the most joyful News to me that I could have heard."[14]

Adams's sardonic thoughts on "joyful" deaths for designing public officials survived the Revolution. In the 1790s, Hamilton, the American Walpole, seemed determined to bring the Country-Court conflict to the United States. Intent that the new government strike a lasting blow against localism, Hamilton pursued, under Washington's presidential aegis, a policy of financial planning that closely resembled the English system, complete with a stock market, public debt, and a national bank. In full, speculation fueled investments, made fortunes for the well placed, and bound a new moneyed aristocracy to the federal departments that facilitated its rise. Along the way, ancient attachments to states' rights weakened while a profitable mercantilism and fledgling industrial growth challenged the traditional agricultural rhythms and relationships once central to colonial development.

For Adams, the Walpolean cum Hamiltonian vision threatened to pit private vice against public virtue. Court, after all, advanced individual goals, aspirations, and advantages; Country struck a more paternal pose. As an expression of civic well-being, Adams found the Country ideology pleasing in no little measure as a validation of the Christian cosmology he had come to rely upon. It implied a peaceable kingdom of checks and balances by imperfect interests over equally imperfect interests while synchronously countering Court claims for worldly gain with one of thrift and renunciation. The deistic Jefferson is quite rightly associated with the Enlightenment wing of this Country ideology; Adams's Protestant sensibilities underwrote a similar skepticism of Court principles from the moderate right.

Indeed, what impresses the contemporary observer is the divergence in conservative visions posited by Hamilton and Adams. Though both are remembered ideologically as architects of a common Federalist persuasion, their differences easily overshadowed their similarities. Hamilton anticipated a speculative economy sustaining a deferential republic backboned by the wellborn, or at least the well heeled. Adams trended as well toward a grandee's republic, though one marked by clear distinctions in talent and integrity rather than merely class and cash. The contrast in political philosophies between the two impressed Jefferson to the extent that he made notes of an April 1791 dinner at which they exchanged clashing views on good government. At that gathering Adams had argued that the British body of laws "would be the most perfect constitution ever devised by the wit of man" if only their authors saw fit to "purge that constitution of its corruption and give to its popular branch equality of representation." Hamilton dissented. "Purge it of its corruption," he corrected Adams, "and give to its popular branch equality of representation, and it would become an *impracticable* government: as it stands at present, with all its supposed defects, it is the most perfect government which ever existed."[15]

Hamilton's neomercantilism held center stage in the 1790s until a more powerful and pervasive Lockean liberalism became, under the stewardship of the Jeffersonians, the defining ideology of its era. Following the tribulations of slavery and race, this struggle between classes developed into the great public issue of the nineteenth century. Country politics evolved over the next few generations from its distinct Jefferson and Adams wings into a post–Civil War front uniting southern and midwestern populists against the encroachments of industrial society. Historians have long recognized the liberal-Jeffersonian roots of Gilded Age reform, though they have been largely silent on the contributions of the moderate line connected to Adams. The ties are selective, of course, for more than simply a handful of decades distanced the patrician Adams (and the patrician Jefferson, for that matter) from the political evangelicalism of, say, William Jennings Bryan. Yet on two vital issues, sympathy for agrarianism and suspicion of fiscal malfeasance, they shared considerable common ground. Adams's belief, for example, that "commerce, luxury, and avarice have destroyed every republican government" and his arguments against what he called "the mercenary spirit of commerce" anticipated the quasi-Country rhetoric of both the two-term Democratic president Andrew Jackson and the thrice-nominated Democratic presidential candidate Bryan.

In his 1832 veto of the Second National Bank, heir to Hamilton's earlier creation, Jackson had singled out for criticism "the rich and powerful" who sought "too often [to] bend the acts of government to their selfish purposes." And in his famous 1896 Cross of Gold speech delivered before the Democratic National Convention, Bryan tore into the corporations for abusing labor: "It is the issue of 1776 over again. . . . We shall fight them to the uttermost, having behind us the producing masses of the nation and the world." To be sure, Adams lacked the democratic bona fides of these two popular politicians and never presumed plebeian power to be any nobler or any less corruptible than patrician power. Yet his instinctive defense of farmers and laborers, coupled with an equally inborn suspicion of bankers and speculators, was reprised in the radical producer politics of the nineteenth century. Adams's "populism," though laced with a patronizing paternalism, retains a great rhetorical power often overlooked by those who see him firmly and only as a figure on the right.[16]

Of course Adams's financial thinking appears woefully anachronistic to us today. He considered depository institutions acceptable in theory but then denounced them in practice when they performed usury. "Every bank by which interest is to be paid or profit of any kind made by the deponent is downright corruption," he wrote Benjamin Rush. "It is taxing the public for the benefit and profit of individuals." In response to the dangers of inflated stock and market bubbles, he envisioned a more limited bimetallic system of finance that, again, anticipated the "moral" economies later advanced by Jackson and Bryan. All three preferred a check, what Old Hickory called an independent treasury, on making the public's money available to private profiteers. "My opinion," Adams said, clarifying his position, "is that a circularity medium of gold and silver only ought to be introduced and established," and he cannily drew out for Jefferson his disagreement, as a moderate, with those with whom he shared uneasily the affiliation "Federalist": "This System of Banks begotten, hatched and brooded by [leading men of the right, William] Duer, Robert and Gouverneur Morris, Hamilton and Washington, I have always considered as a System of national Injustice. A sacrifice of public and private Interest to a few Aristocratical Friends and Favorites."[17]

The banking question touched upon Adams's fears that speculation, or "landjobbing" as he sometimes called it, threatened the delicate mixed government equilibrium by favoring one class at the expense of others. Human nature, he wrote in one essay, had set man upon man in a lifelong contest fired by "avarice and ambition, vanity and pride, jealousy and envy."[18] No doubt the combative, pugnacious Adams recognized himself in this abrasive profile. As a matter of course he deemed it the central state's obligation to mesh clashing temperaments and conflicting ambitions into a cohesive, stable society. To permit the rise of an erratic financial engine fueled by a congeries of loans, credits, and congressional favors struck Adams as an abdication of the golden-mean ideal to be discovered in the framework of balanced government.

Not that Adams reserved much hope of driving the moneychangers from the republican temple. Like his Puritan forebears who lamented the backsliders in their midst, Adams glumly supposed that America's rapid material advancement compromised the Christian ascetics and homespun Yankee values presumably the mother's milk of earlier generations. For even without the lure of investment banking, stocks, and bounties, temptations abounded. "Will you tell me," he knowingly queried Jefferson, "how to prevent riches from becoming the effects of temperance and industry? Will you tell me how to prevent riches from producing luxury? Will you tell me how to prevent luxury from producing effeminacy intoxication extravagance Vice and folly?"[19]

As for preventing luxury from clouding his own judgments, Adams adopted the role of a simple Massachusetts farmer. If slightly affected, his calling "my dear blue Hills . . . the most sublime object in my Imagination" nevertheless rings truer than not. As an investor he spent freely, even foolishly, to extend his land holdings. His 1787 purchase of Peacefield, also known as the Old House and currently the jewel of the Adams National Historical Park, situated the family on some seventy acres of orchards and farmlands about two miles north of the saltbox home of his birth. That and subsequent acquisitions, including the nearby Mount Wollaston farm, left him, as the New England saying goes, "penny poor and property rich."[20] Although Adams bemoaned his precarious financial circumstances as a case of penury prompted by years of service to a tight-fisted government, he never launched himself or his sons into the rising American commercial orbit. Not until his grandson, Charles Francis, married into the wealthy, Boston-based Brooks family in 1829 did the Adams family secure what we might call a fortune.

· · · · ·

Considering Adams's doubtful opinion of mankind's prospects for perfectibility, he stands out as a qualified Enlightenment figure. His sober, Burke-like reaction to the French Revolution is a case in point. The Jacobin embrace of liberty, fraternity, and democracy as a budding universal faith struck Adams as antithetical to the mixed republican politics earned in the Anglo-Saxon blood of earlier English and American revolutions. He routinely disparaged the men of his generation who imbibed freely from the font of French radicalism. Such was the case when he caustically reported that the British political theorist and natural philosopher "Dr. [Joseph] Priestly . . . told me soberly, cooly and deliberately that though he knew of Nothing in human Nature or in the history of Mankind to justify the Opinion, Yet he fully believed upon the Authority of Prophecy that the French Nation would establish a free Government and that the King of France who had been executed, was the first of the Ten Horns of the great Beast, and that all the other Nine Monarks were soon to fall off after him." As the years went by and the revolution passed through various permutations leading up to the Caesardom of Napoleon, Adams felt increasingly assured that his skepticism had earned an honorable acquittal. In truth, he never doubted the eventual outcome. A Catholic civilization fresh from the moorings of monarchy and priest-craft could no more secure his confidence than could a Whiggish Anglo-Protestantism's promise to turn out a godly heaven on earth. The potent residue of peasantry, superstition, and aristocracy—in a phrase, the weight of history—worked, Adams insisted, against the kind of culturally rooted constitutional liberalism Americans hoped to see emerge in western Europe. Sure of his ground, he nettled Jefferson late in their lives for tying his hopes to a flickering French comet: "You was well persuaded in your own mind that the Nation would succeed in establishing a free Republican Government. I was as well persuaded, in mine, that a project of such a Government, over five and twenty millions people, when four and twenty millions and five hundred thousands of them could neither write nor read . . . was as unnatural irrational and impracticable . . . as it would be over the Elephants Lions Tigers Panthers Wolves and Bears in the Royal Menagerie, at Versailles."[21]

Adams considered this Gallic circus wholly undeserving of the honorable designation "republic." He observed, rather, that by embracing regicide and a post-Christian pantheism, Jacobinism had stunted liberalism's advance. "The French Revolution," he candidly declared from the distance of 1813, "I dreaded; because I was sure it would, not only arrest the progress of Improvement, but give it a retrograde course, for at least a Century."[22] As for the revolution's greatest advocate in America, the transatlantic radical Thomas Paine, Adams reserved a particular contempt. "A Star of Disaster," he dismissed the celebrated author of *Common Sense*, seeing in his opponent's ultrademocratic pamphlets a polemical rebuke to reality. Paine put his faith in the power of the people and rejected the idea of mixed government in favor of a commanding unicameral house with a judiciary accountable to, rather than independent of, the public. He also grandly, if somewhat obliquely, proposed the abolition of social distinctions.

As a defender of bicameralism and the efficacy of class accountability, Adams dismissed Paine as a serious political theorist. In what was for him a truly wounding comparison, he put the English-born revolutionary on par with the hated Hamilton, in the process slyly denouncing both right and left. "I could," he sarcastically wrote Jefferson, "have enumerated Alexander Hamilton, and Thomas Paine, The two most extraordinary Men that this Country, this Age or this World, ever produced. 'Rinendo dicere verum quid vetat?' [What forbids me to speak the truth by joking?]"[23] In carving out an ideological middle ground between what he regarded as an ultra Federalist right and a Jacobin-Jeffersonian left, Adams believed that he had fallen upon a pragmatic politics consistent with the best rather than the worst of human nature. Thus his moderate leanings were part of the Revolutionary-era settlement as assuredly as were Hamilton's and Paine's. The former summoned, in Adams's opinion, too little regard for the "people," and the latter too much. In assuming a centrist position on this vital question, his views on governance, republicanism, and representation ran naturally to a certain realism not clearly recognized in the oversimplified "left" and "right" ideological salad of the late eighteenth century. Adams rejected the presumption that one must be either Jeffersonian or Hamiltonian or that an American must commit without question either to the French Revolution or to its English antagonist. In this way he began to carve out a third path in American politics fated to be little understood and thus little appreciated.

While Adams's distance from the Republican-Federalist system freed him from certain prejudices, it unfortunately reinforced others. He rigidly adhered to the Harringtonian view that only by holding property could a citizen achieve independence and thereby earn the right to participate in elections. He was thus slow to absorb the recasting of "equality" that took root in Revolutionary America. Politics in the new nation pointed to an expanding suffrage increasingly at odds with barriers to balloting. Adams exhibited remarkably little sympathy for this trend, and his 1776 insistence that "men in general, in every society, who are wholly destitute of property, are also too little acquainted with public affairs to form a right judgement" accurately conveyed his jaundiced view on the subject. Still, while he assailed Paine's theories—"His plan was so democratical, without any restraint or even an Attempt at any Equilibrium or Counterpoise, that it must produce confusion and every Evil Work"—he nevertheless recognized the power and historical "voice" behind the pamphleteer's rhetoric. "I know not," he wrote in 1805, "whether any Man in the World has had more influence on its inhabitants or affairs for the last thirty years than Thomas Paine."[24]

If Adams condemned the French experiment and its "Age of Paine" permutation, he nevertheless avoided a consummate rejection of the developing complex of liberal thought, attitudes, and values then remaking the West. He accepted, after all, "reason" as an instrument to assess the full range of human capabilities *and limitations*; he further joined the philosophes in discarding Christian mysticism while concurrently cherishing the emerging beliefs in rule of law and a bill of rights that had begun to march firmly against divine-right kingships. Even so, Adams remains a qualified Enlightenment figure, and he knew this worked against him. Convinced that the first historians of the American Revolution were slighting his contributions and distorting his views, Adams promised correspondents that history would in fact bear his opinions out. "Let me now ask you, very seriously my Friend," he wrote Jefferson, "Where are now in 1813, the Perfection and perfectibility of human Nature? Where is now, the progress of the human Mind? Where is the Amelioration of Society? . . . When? Where? And how? is the present Chaos to be arranged into Order?"[25] The year 1813 was a trying one for an Atlantic world exhausted by the wars of the French Revolution. Napoleon's European armies were still a factor in the field, while the United States and Great Britain clashed in North America. Peace on earth seemed a far and fantastic dream in the Age of Reason's end days.

More fruitfully, the Enlightenment provided Adams a welcome intellectual challenge, provoking his most original and searching social criticism. In a series of essays appearing first in the *New York Gazette of the United States* and then collectively as *Discourses on Davila* (1790), he insightfully and counterintuitively argued that the diffusion of education had failed to dim the public's unfortunate passions for wealth and notoriety. By encouraging, rather, a one-against-all individualism at the expense of certain age-old communal restraints, postfeudal civilization had "multipl[ied] rivalries . . . among men." Reason, logic, intelligence, and instruction were supposed to yield a superior citizenry, but, Adams countered, the opposite had occurred. "On the contrary," he wrote, "the more knowledge is diffused, the more the passions are extended, and the more furious they grow." Competition rather than equality proved to be the real legacy of the Revolution. The American mania for social mobility coaxed fierce rivalries among a rising professional class fighting over a limited pie of public honors.[26]

Adams's critical reading on this subject found little traction until taken up much later by a fine stable of Progressive-era (1900–20) thinkers. The Harvard philosopher William James warned that a cult of higher-education accreditation had spawned what he ominously called a "Ph.D. Octopus." Amid the scramble for money and titles, the professoriate plumed itself with self-important signage. This, James insisted, had nothing to do with real education. He recalled the sad story of a brilliant Harvard philosophy student struggling to keep his appointment teaching English literature at a nearby school. Why the struggle? Because, as James wryly wrote, "the quality per se of the man signified nothing. . . . [Rather,] three magical letters were the thing seriously required. The College had always gloried in a list of faculty members who bore the doctor's title, and to make a gap in the galaxy, and admit a common fox without a tail, would be a degradation impossible to be thought of." After special pleading from James and his colleagues, their protégée won a reprieve of sorts. He could keep his job "on condition that one year later at the farthest his miserably naked name should be prolonged by the sacred appendage the lack of which had given so much trouble to all concerned."[27]

James's contemporary, the radical sociologist Thorstein Veblen, approached the problem of status from a strikingly original anthropological angle. In his classic *The Theory of the Leisure Class* (1899), Veblen detailed the tendency of the "upper sort" to parade its rank through extraordinarily lavish and highly visible spending habits that had little to do with utility. Where Adams argued that "the more the passions are extended . . . the more furious they grow," Veblen insisted that in a culture marked by conspicuous consumption, "the gifts of good-nature, equity, and indiscriminate sympathy do not appreciably further the life of the individual. . . . The individual fares better under the régime of competition in proportion as he has less of these gifts. Freedom from scruple, from sympathy, honesty and regard for life, may, within fairly wide limits, be said to further the success of the individual in the pecuniary culture."[28] Put plainly, Veblen observed a class against class dynamic that argued against optimistic assumptions of postfeudal "all men are created equal" progress. As a critic of Court principles, Adams had made a similar diagnosis a full century earlier.

Closer to our own time, postwar postmodernists have advanced lines of cultural argument that bear resemblance to Adams's cutting reaction to the Enlightenment. These intellectuals, including the Frankfurt School critical theorists Theodor Adorno and Jurgen Habermas and the French historian of ideas Michele Foucault, wrote in the wake of two world wars, the Holocaust, and the Western psyche's postcolonial decentering. Adams's historical orientation responded to different stimuli, of course, for he matured in an era of egalitarianism and expansion, the inspirited early hours of Western liberalism. Yet both Adams and the critical theorists share a common resistance to the worship of rationality, objectivity, and progress as secular replacements to an earlier Christian worldview. Postmodernists pointed out that "reason" privileged class-specific attitudes, assumptions, and chauvinisms, which were then neatly transcribed as transcendent universal norms. They argued further that rationality's crucial contributions to advanced manufacturing, technology, and mass communications played a role in the production of a plastic, "inauthentic" culture that alienated the individual from certain dissenting emotions which, when aimed at the new system, were dismissed clinically as "irrational" or "mad." "The age of reason confined," Foucault wrote. "It confined the debauched, spendthrift fathers, prodigal sons, blasphemers, men who 'seek to undo themselves,' libertines. And through these parallels, these strange complicities, the age sketched the profile of its own experience of unreason."[29] As a matter of course, the architects of Enlightenment expediently advanced a constricting mentality that negated an entire range of "anti-rational," "anti-liberal" opinions and reactions that might have called their hegemony into question.

Adams too believed that "the age of reason confined." But more so than the postmodernists, he held out hope for "irrationality's" prospects. "Has the progress of science, arts, and letters yet discovered that there are no passions in human nature?" he queried. "Are these passions," he doubtfully asked, "cooled, diminished, or extinguished?" Anticipating the critical theorists, he pointed out the moral neutrality of knowledge. True, it may, as the philosophes noted, provide immense assistance to society, though it could also be employed by a host of wreckers, despots, and tyrants to further their own private interests. "Bad men increase in knowledge as fast as good men," Adams reminded the optimists, "and science, arts, taste, sense, and letters, are employed for the purposes of injustice and tyranny, as well as those of law and liberty; for corruption as well as for virtue."[30]

Such sentiments accurately convey Adams's doubts about democracy. Yet rather than making him a man of the right, they made him more a man of his times. His mild declamation that "few men will deny that there is a natural aristocracy of virtues and talents in every nation and in every party, in every city and village" won over even his most important political opponent. "I agree with you that there is a natural aristocracy among men," Jefferson wrote Adams in their retirement. "The natural aristocracy I consider as the most precious gift of nature, for the instruction, the trusts, and government of society." Jefferson's opposition to Hamiltonianism softened the edges of his antipopulism; Adams, by contrast, never sought a filter. If anything, his "disinterested" position and intellectually hawkish temperament produced sharp and unsympathetic statements on democracy meant, perhaps, to shock as much as instruct. In 1814 the Virginia political philosopher John Taylor of Caroline penned a refutation of Adams's quarter-century-old *Defence*, which he regarded as scandalously proaristocracy. Adams fired back to Taylor, "What can I say of the democracy of France? I dare not write what I think and what I know. Were Brissot, Condorcet, Danton, Robespierre, and Monseigneur Egalité less ambitious than Cæsar, Alexander, or Napoleon?" And on the long train of violence that trailed the French Revolution, he overlooked a decrepit, backward-looking monarchical system and a war-happy Corsican dictator to announce in a shattering epigram that "Democracy is chargeable with all the blood that has been spilled for five-and-twenty-years."[31]

These tendentious remarks do Adams, nearly eighty at the time he made them, no credit, though neither do they make him a Hamiltonian. His commitment to a "natural aristocracy" collided with Hamilton's contrived efforts to create a high caste based on patronage, speculation, and financial self-interest. Adams mustered, after all, no more faith in an erratic capitalism than an erratic democracy. Furthermore, the naked favoritism that propelled Hamilton's programs troubled Adams. As one presumably situated among the "natural aristocracy," he noted not a little peevishly that some of his more distinguished contemporaries availed upon advantageous marriages to further their careers. "Would Washington have ever been commander of the revolutionary army or president of the United States, if he had not married the rich widow of Mr. Custis? Would Jefferson ever have been president of the United States, if he had not married the daughter of Mr. Wales?"[32] To his great discomfort, Adams found himself negotiating an Atlantic world in flux, one that accommodated both the quasi-aristocracies favored by Hamilton and the new democratic temperament championed by the Jeffersonians. Having no distinct liking for either, it seems something of an unkind joke that he became president of a nation soon to be known for its speculative boom cycles, its imperfect aping of European culture, and its persistent if uneven commitment to political and spiritual equalitarianism. Adams and "the modern" made for an ill fit.

· · · · ·

The kind of Anglo antipartyism practiced by Adams came out of the sharp seventeenth-century divisions that dominated Civil War–era England. Injury, exile, and executions distinguished the conflict between Royalists and Roundheads while succeeding Tory versus Whig confrontations continued to incite a citizenry that regarded factions as the pernicious authors of social upheaval. "By 1688," the British historian J. H. Plumb has observed, "violence in politics was an Englishman's birthright. . . . Conspiracy and rebellion, treason and plot, were a part of the history and experience of at least three generations of Englishmen."[33] Consequently, an oppressive irony hung above Parliament and populace alike. The English believed parties to be suspect if not seditious, yet still they stewed in an all-pervasive party system.

In the 1730s, the political theorist Viscount Bolingbroke emerged as the chief opponent of parties. He wrote as a firm critic of the clever maneuvering managed by Walpole's Whig regime. In place of competing interests, Bolingbroke introduced the idea of a Patriot King, a leader embodying the concerns of all his countrymen and thus able to harmonize individual agendas with the broader needs of state. The great Patriot, Bolingbroke wrote, fulfilled his role by "defeat[ing] the designs, and break[ing] the spirit of faction, instead of partaking in one and assuming the other."[34] Although he understood that parties were not soon, if ever, to be uprooted, Bolingbroke's views on the perils of partisanship greatly influenced American political thought during the administration of George Washington. Perhaps inevitably so, many looked hopefully to the venerable general as the embodiment of the Patriot ideal; "First in war, first in peace, and first in the hearts of his countrymen," is the elegant way in which Henry Lee articulated this holy pact, yet both Washington's cabinet and his country quickly divided into rival Jeffersonian and Hamiltonian camps. It was this impossible situation that Adams, as Washington's certain-to-pale-by-comparison presidential successor, inherited in 1797. As an object of analysis, that presidency, along with its combative relationship to Federalism, is treated lightly in this chapter and somewhat more extensively, if from the vantage of George Cabot's contributions, in the next.

Superficially, Adams's commitment to a strong executive office and his rejection of Jacobinism in its French and American permutations suggest a clear affiliation with the Hamiltonians. But just days after assuming the presidency, Adams wrote of his alienation from the men ostensibly sharing his ideological convictions. He obviously craved a nonpartisan politics for himself and the nation. "All the Federalists seem to be afraid to approve anybody but Washington. . . . If the Federalists go to playing pranks, I will resign the office, and let Jefferson lead them to peace, wealth, and power if he will. From the situation where I now am, I see a scene of ambition beyond all my former suspicions or imaginations; an emulation which will turn our government topsy-turvy. . . . I see how the thing is going. At the next election, England will set up Jay or Hamilton, and France, Jefferson, and all the corruption of Poland will be introduced; unless the American spirit should rise and say, we will have neither John Bull nor Louis Baboon. Silence."[35]

Adams believed that Hamilton had already played one "prank." It was an open secret that the former treasury secretary had preferred the South Carolinian Thomas Pinckney to succeed Washington. The son of a prominent colonial official, beneficiary of a European education, officer in the Continental Army, and United States Minister to the United Kingdom, Pinckney made a credible candidate. But his credentials next to Adams's were thin. So why did Hamilton press his case? In his study of the Federalist era, historian John C. Miller writes, "Unwilling to elevate Adams—whom he could not hope to control—to the Presidency, . . . Hamilton attempted by stratagem to seat . . . Pinckney, a far more pliable man, in the President's chair. Hamilton's plan called for the Federalist electors in the North to cast their ballots for Adams and Pinckney, while the South Carolina electors voted unanimously for Pinckney but withheld a few votes from Adams. Thus Pinckney would stand first in the poll and John Adams would be relegated to the Vice-Presidency." But something else happened. "Hamilton's political intrigues always turned out badly," Miller explains; "He was too indiscreet and impulsive to make a successful Machiavellian—but this one almost ended in disaster. In effect, he risked the breakup of the Federalist party in the face of mounting evidence that Jefferson . . . might steal the prize. Getting wind of Hamilton's 'plot,' the New England electors deliberately scratched Pinckney in order to ensure that he would not nose out Adams."[36]

In a tight election Adams came in first with seventy-one votes, while Jefferson's sixty-eight earned him the vice presidency; the errancy in Hamilton's strategy can be noted in Pinckney's distant third-place finish with fifty-nine votes. Viewed ideologically, a Federalist had finished third, a Republican had come in second, and the country, whether it realized it or not, had elected a moderate inclined to steer a consensual course. That this ultimately proved impossible says less about Adams than about the fierce partisanship of the 1790s. That he so obviously had no instinct for the kind of sectarian leadership then coming to dominate American politics only made his presidency more difficult. Of his relations with the Hamiltonians, the noted Hamilton biographer Forrest McDonald has rightly observed, Adams "was his own man, the Federalist party was its own party."[37]

McDonald's point is particularly relevant regarding Adams's rejection of military adventuring. More than any other single principle or program, Adams devoted his presidency to remaining neutral in the wars of the French Revolution. France insisted that its 1778 Treaty of Alliance with the United States obligated that nation to now aid the Republic in its struggle with the British. But the Bourbon signatory to that accord had been toppled and executed. In America, High Federalism, seeking closer commercial ties with Britain, pushed Adams to lead the country into a French war in the hopes of crushing Jacobinism. But Adams held back. He did, however, defer to the Hamiltonians in other respects. On July 14, 1798, the ninth anniversary of the storming of the Bastille, he signed into law the Alien and Sedition Acts, the latter of which made it a criminal offense to publish "false, scandalous and malicious writing" against government officials. In short, Federalism tried to inoculate itself from public criticism.

According to its proponents, the acts were designed to prevent internal clashes in a time of national crisis. The Federalist broadsheet *Columbian Centinel* argued somewhat dubiously that freedom of speech was not on trial. "It never was intended," the paper claimed, "that the right to side with the enemies of one's country in slandering and vilifying the government, and dividing the people should be protected under the name of the Liberty of the Press." Republicans reasoned differently. American freedoms were endangered, they agreed, though not by French armies or fellow-traveling American Jacobins, but rather by Federalism itself. The *New Jersey Journal* called the acts "the most diabolical laws that were ever attempted to be imposed on a free and enlightened people."[38]

A few weeks before the measures passed through Congress, Adams signed an equally controversial bill authorizing a new provisional army of 20,000; Hamilton accepted the prized commission of commanding officer in the field. These unpopular Federalist initiatives of 1798, however, received only minimal support from Adams. He neither instigated the "war measure" acts nor spoke in their favor as they came before Congress. Hamilton won his elevated position in the restructured military only after Washington made this a condition of his service as senior officer of the United States Army. Adams seethed but did as Washington asked. Years later, he offered to Jefferson a careful interpretation of what had transpired during this fractious period. He defended his actions, putting the onus on a congress operating under the pressure of foreign intrigue: "As your name is subscribed to that [Alien and Sedition] law, as Vice President, and mine as President, I know not why you are not as responsible for it as I am. Neither of Us were concerned in the formation of it. We were then at War with France: French Spies then swarmed in our Cities and in the Country. Some of them were, intollerably, turbulent, impudent and seditious. To check these was the design of this law. Was there ever a Government, which had not Authority to defend itself against Spies in its own Bosom? Spies of an Enemy at War? This Law was never executed by me, in any instance."[39] The veracity of Adams's statement is open to debate. More obvious is that the Hamiltonian program of 1798 failed to corroborate Republicanism's worst fears. Quite the opposite: within two years Federalists were swept from office.

Combined, the Alien and Sedition Acts, expanding military establishment, and an uptick in taxes catalyzed a crisis-like mood in America. As a result, when popular opinion inevitably grew skeptical of the war scare, Jeffersonian complaints about Federalist tyranny began to win support. The anti-Hamiltonian *America Aurora* captured the prevailing sentiment: "It is well known that the *Republican* party are attached to . . . a constitution of equal rights; free from all hereditary honours and exclusive privileges; where the officials of Government are responsible for their conduct." Federalists, the paper continued, "think the government should have *more* and the people *less* power. To this party . . . we are indebted for all our late taxes . . . for a Standing Army [and] an extensive Navy."[40] Clearly if the Hamiltonians hoped to retain power they would have to make good the French threat. This meant a declaration of war. And this Adams refused.

In 1798 the president sent three American peace emissaries, John Marshall, Charles Pinckney, and Elbridge Gerry, to Paris. There they remained largely inactive for several weeks having incurred the displeasure of the governing directorate and Charles-Maurice de Talleyrand, the minister of foreign affairs. During the American Revolution the United States received great and perhaps decisive aid from France, whose troop strength at the siege of Yorktown rivaled its own. Now, the First Republic expected the United States to join its opposition to monarchy, imperial power, and British rule of the seas. It was under such circumstances that the American envoys were finally approached. Negotiations, they were informed, hinged on a few conditions, including a $250,000 bribe to be distributed among Talleyrand and various officials and a $12 million loan advanced to the French government. The asking price seemed excessive. Marshall and Pinckney returned home, Gerry followed later. Adams's report to Congress revealed the ill treatment of the three envoys, and Federalists pushed anew for a declaration of war. Again, Adams disappointed them.

Instead, in February 1799 he sent a new commission to France headed by the U.S. minister to the Netherlands, William Vans Murray. High Federalists were livid, but the mission ultimately bore fruit; the signing of the Treaty of Mortefontaine in September 1800 set in motion the end of the naval conflict between the two countries. Self-interest carried the day. France, then at war with Great Britain, saw the virtue of a neutral America servicing its empire; the United States came to the peace table with the same motivation in mind. The loser at Mortefontaine was Federalism. Peace knocked all of its war-footing pillars out of place and put the party on the road to extinction. For his part, Adams almost certainly would have won reelection had he stoked the war sentiment that captivated the nation in 1798–99. Instead, he pursued peace and lost a close contest to Jefferson by eight electoral votes.

In power, Republicanism faced many of the same foreign policy threats as its predecessor. Its returns were ironic to say the least. Jefferson wrestled less successfully than Adams with the pressures of maintaining neutral America's right to trade in a global market enflamed by the British-French standoff. In frustration, he levied an embargo on U.S. exports that shut down New England trade and used government power to enforce the ban in draconian ways never imagined by his predecessors, excepting, perhaps, the hated Hamilton. Writing in the 1880s, Henry Adams, great grandson to John and an eminent scholar of the early republic, concluded of Jefferson's troubled reign that "not even in 1798 had factiousness been so violent as in the last month of President Jefferson's power; in 1800 the country in comparison had been contented. . . . So complete was his overthrow that his popular influence declined even in the South. Twenty years elapsed before his political authority recovered power over the Northern people; for not until the embargo and its memories faded from men's mind did the mighty shadow of Jefferson's Revolutionary name efface the ruin of his Presidency." By that time, a generation on, Jefferson's putative republican heir Andrew Jackson had advanced presidential power even further. Jackson had implemented a spoils system that strengthened the Democracy's hold on patronage, oversaw the removal of tens of thousands of Native Americans from the

Southeast, and brushed aside congressional support for the renewal of the Second Bank of the United States with a pocket veto. Supreme Court justice Joseph Story had no doubt of Jackson's "despotic" designs: "Though we live under the form of a republic, we are in fact under the absolute rule of a single man."[41]

Adams's record, by contrast, even with the stain of the Alien and Sedition Acts, bears little resemblance to the bogeyman conjured by his opposition. In fact, Adams's dissent from the Hamiltonian right and his moderate response to the vexing question of war or peace situated him in the center between more extreme politics. When attacked for belonging to a war party, he brought peace; when accused of championing a speculative economy, he invested his own shaky finances in farmland. His postpresidential remarks to a cousin on the Hamiltonian structure—"The Funding system and Banking systems which are the work of the Federalists, have introduced more corruption and injustice . . . than any other cause"—accurately convey his outlook and ring of the old Country republicanism that breathed life into the Revolution.[42]

Naturally Adams's agrarian sympathies and suspicion of Hamiltonianism made little headway with the Jeffersonians. They had their own iconic presidential candidate, a firm commitment to the French Republic, and a strong suspicion of New England leadership—only once in the decades bookended by the Constitution and the firing on Fort Sumter did the Democratic Party nominate a New Englander (Franklin Pierce) for the presidency. Adams lived a full quarter century in retirement, and posterity's negative judgment weighed heavily on his heart. "It is my opinion," he wrote the pro-Republican historian Mercy Otis Warren, "that your history [of the Revolution] has been written to the taste of the nineteenth century, and accommodated to gratify the passions, prejudices, and feelings of the party who are now predominant." In such "political" works, Adams could see his reputation receding. Most disappointing, the honorable designation of Patriot King continued to elude him. "Washington and Franklin could never do anything but what was imputed to pure, disinterested patriotism," he once protested. "I never could do anything but what was ascribed to sinister motives."[43]

If the vagaries of public life teased Adams, however, at least his private life proved more secure and affirming. Worried about his treatment at the hands of Mercy Otis Warren, he could be sure of a more favorable portrait emerging in his wife's many letters, peppered as they were with her—their—politics and points of view. Certainly Abigail Adams's disdain for Hamilton approached her husband's. Observing the former treasury secretary's efforts to vault Pinckney into the presidency, she scored him a coward for not daring "to come out openly in opposition" of John—"I despise a Janus"—and closed the door on High Federalism.[44]

Abigail's feelings for Jefferson were more mixed. In the summer of 1787 Jefferson's then eight-year-old daughter Mary (called Polly) was in transit to meet her father in Europe. She first stopped off in London where Abigail cared for Polly until the child could make for the continent. They grew close in their brief time together, which only encouraged Abigail and Jefferson's letter-writing relationship; the two exchanged more than three dozen letters between 1785 and 1788. Then came a loud silence that extended until 1804. Like her husband, Abigail believed that factions harmed the republic, and she made little distinction between the machinations of Federalists and those of Republicans, or the men who led them. In one letter she pointedly reserved for her and John the high ground: "The S. of the Treasury [Hamilton] has suffered as much as the Secretary of State [Jefferson]. Ambition is imputed to both, and the Moral Character of both has Suffered."[45]

There is no doubt that Abigail's friendship with Jefferson was a casualty of partisan politics. Not until the sad occasion of Polly's death in April 1804 did their correspondence revive, and then only briefly as the burden of the past ensnared them both. Moved by Polly's passing, Abigail wrote to Jefferson, then in the final full year of his first term as president, offering condolence. Jefferson mistook the letter as a sign of Abigail's eagerness to renew their friendship and sought to explain away their previous differences: "[I] am thankful for the occasion furnished me of expressing my regret that circumstances should have arisen which have seemed to draw a line of separation between us. . . . Altho' events have been passing which might be trying to some minds, I never believed yours to be of that kind, nor felt that my own was." In other words, Jefferson maintained that despite their differences, both he and Abigail, and by extension John, had been above politics. Well, almost above politics. He less than tactfully pointed out that Adams's appointment of judicial positions in his final days as president, rather than allowing Jefferson, the incoming executive, to make the appointments, was an act "personally unkind," but quickly noted with all the agreeableness of a southern gentleman, "I forgave it cordially."[46]

Abigail refused to allow Jefferson's interpretation of the 1790s to pass unchallenged. "You have been pleased to enter upon some subjects which call for a reply," she coolly answered his note, "and as you observe that you have wished for an opportunity to express your sentiments, I have given to them every weight they claim." And then she told him just how light she found them. She noted that at the time her husband had made the judicial appointments it was unclear who would be the next president as both Jefferson and Aaron Burr were then tied in the Electoral College. How, she asked, could John's act have been personal? She then took the offensive: "And now Sir, I will freely disclose to you what has severed the bonds of former Friendship, and placed you in a light very different from what I once viewd you in"—and this was Jefferson's treatment of James Callender. A Scottish immigrant and political writer, Callender had fallen afoul of the Sedition Act for criticizing the Adams administration; he was sentenced to nine months in prison and fined $200. Abigail reminded Jefferson that as president he had released Callender and remitted his fine; more injurious still, she continued, he had praised the pamphleteer's attacks on Adams and even given him money. She closed the letter quoting Proverbs, "Faithful are the wounds of a Friend."[47]

In two subsequent posts, Jefferson defended his actions on the points raised by Abigail. Callender, he argued, was released from prison because he had been "unjustly persecuted," and there was nothing personal about the matter: "I discharged every person under punishment or prosecution under the Sedition law." And yes, Jefferson acknowledged, he had given Callender money, as any one might give alms to a destitute man: "My charities to him were no more meant as encouragements to his scurrilities than those I give to the beggar at my door are meant as rewards for the vices of his life." Abigail found Jefferson's line of argument self-serving and pursued it doggedly in her own follow-up letters. In one she accused him of overstepping his powers as chief executive by releasing prisoners convicted in a court of law. Knowing full well the sting of her words, she wrote, "If a Chief Majestrate can by his will annul a Law, where is the difference between a republican, and a despotic Government?" And in a second she negatively contrasted his administration with her husband's: "May I be permitted to pause, and ask whether in your ardent zeal, and desire to rectify the mistakes and abuses as you may consider them, of the former administrations, you are not led into measures still more fatal to the constitution, and more derogatory to your honour, and independence of Character? Pardon me Sir if I say, that I fear you are." Then, wishing to end this tense negotiation of seven letters extending over six months, she signed off, "I will not Sir any further intrude upon your time, but close this correspondence."[48]

Viewed from a contemporary perspective, Abigail and John's concerns about posterity seem quaint. Picking up scholarly steam in the 1970s, the Adamses have in recent years been the subject of numerous biographies as well as an award-winning 2008 HBO miniseries. Without them, the booming Founding Fathers cottage industry would lose much of its buzz. This popular turn in the historiography, however, has only scratched the surface of John Adams's significance. Outside of the Jeffersonian-Hamiltonian framework that has long served as shorthand for students of the early republic, Adams pioneered a moderate persuasion that has become a basic feature in American politics—the tendency of centrists to break from those factions they regard as radical, even when said factions occupy the seats of power, as Federalism did in the 1790s. Adams interpreted his criticism of the Hamiltonians as an act of individual conscience, though it in fact owed much to the line of Country and Patriot King thought that had shaped modern English politics. That line did not end with Adams. The Federalist far right survived his presidency and, beyond it, there would be other far rights to come.

2 Up from Federalism

George Cabot

· ·

Easily the intellectual leader of his party since the death of
Hamilton, George Cabot in his study at Brookline saw what no
other Federalist had the wisdom to see, that a page of democratic
evolution had been turned, and the days of Federalist ascendancy
had passed never to return.

—Samuel Eliot Morison, 1912

After canonizing the lives and legacies of George Washington and Alexander Hamilton, Federalism ultimately turned to Salem statesman George Cabot for leadership. On no fewer than three occasions did he challenge the secessionary exchanges that circulated among a small but influential number of disenchanted New Englanders looking to leave the Union. These men resented the remarkable popular success of the Jeffersonian Republicans, the party's plantocracy power base, and its sympathy for French Jacobinism. Heirs apparent of colonial America's storied Puritan fathers and patriot stalwarts, they watched nervously as post Revolutionary New England lagged behind a dynamic artisan-agrarian mid-Atlantic and a burgeoning cotton South just beginning its inexorable sweep through the Gulf region. The imminent ascent of a new West in the democratic Ohio and Tennessee Valleys promised to further erode the old Northeast's influence. Facing an uncertain future, High Federalism attended in its final years to a self-defeating vision that sought regional redemption in the promise of a divided Union. Formerly the party of nationalism, it now circled the wagons.

Cold to Federalism's schismatic turn, the moderate Cabot became the de facto chieftain of American conservatism in the Age of Jefferson. Much like John Adams before him, he moved against the men who occupied Federalism's radical right, but he moved against a somewhat different party. Once filled with Founders, Federalism's leading lions were quickly passing from the scene. In December 1799 Washington died of pneumonia compounded by the then-common medical practice of bleeding; fifteen months later Adams surrendered the presidency to Jefferson, and some three years after that Aaron Burr, vice president at the time, killed Hamilton in the country's most famous duel. This string of setbacks consumed the self-confidence of a party that had once been the beneficiary rather than the casualty of crises. The 1780s failure of the national government, then operating under the weak Articles of Confederation, to meet its financial obligations created momentum for a more powerful constitution and soon thereafter opened the door to Hamiltonianism. Concurrently, the radical incline of Jacobinism abroad encouraged the nation to adopt a pro-British foreign policy much favored in New England and culminating in an undeclared naval war with the French Republic.

Yet when these troubles tapered off, so did Federalist hegemony. In the Sixth Congress (1799–1801), conservatives held majorities of 60 to 46 in the House and 22 to 10 in the Senate; in the Seventh Congress (1801–3) they were sharply reduced to minorities in each, 38 to 68 and 15 to 18. Even at this early stage in its disintegration, Federalism's days as a viable opposition were plainly numbered. Its more radical brethren displayed little desire to remain in a Union dominated by southern potentates propped up by slave labor. The Massachusetts statesman Timothy Pickering, for one, envisioned a different destiny for New England, and his ruminations on the subject chime with an eerie clairvoyance. "Although the end of all our Revolutionary labors and expectations is disappointment, and our fond hopes of republican happiness are vanity, and the real patriots of '76 are overwhelmed by the modern pretenders to that character," he wrote a Philadelphia judge in 1803, "I will not yet despair: I will rather anticipate a new confederacy, exempt from the corrupt and corrupting influence and oppression of the aristocratic Democrats of the South. There will be—and our children at farthest will see it—a separation."[1]

No doubt some unreconstructed conservatives believed that Republicanism sought, if not exactly Federalism's "separation," then certainly its exile. Bereft of executive power, Federalists were turned out of office en masse as the Jeffersonians built a potent patronage machine. Jefferson himself excused this behavior by dryly inquiring, "If a due participation of office is a matter of right, how are vacancies to be obtained? Those by death are few; by resignation, none. Can any other mode than that of removal be proposed?" Pleading no alternative, he offered an actor's regret and brought out the ax: "This is a painful office, but it is made my duty, and I meet it as such."

More troubling, Republicans seemed intent to introduce a kind of judicial spoils system by impeaching Federalist magistrates from their posts. In his annual message of 1801, Jefferson appeared to sanction this effort when he cryptically observed, "The nation declared its will by dismissing functionaries of one principle [Federalism] and electing those of another in the two branches, executive and legislative, submitted to their election. Over the judiciary department the Constitution had deprived them of their control. That, therefore, has continued the reprobated system." In regard to his private views, Jefferson left no doubt that he looked forward to his political rivals' extinction. "Our majority in the House of Representatives," he wrote in 1802, "has been about two to one; in the Senate, eighteen to fifteen. After another election it will be of two to one in the Senate. . . . A respectable minority is useful as censors; the present one is not respectable, being the bitterest remains of the cup of Federalism rendered desperate and furious by despair."[2]

In response to the president's naked partisanship, a number of northern men once firmly committed to the Union now believed that only separation could save their region from ruin. This insurrectionary sentiment became an important component of High Federalist conversations through the War of 1812. By opposing these men, several of whom were close political friends, Cabot emerged as the most consequential moderate in America between the presidencies of John Adams and John Quincy Adams. His influence overshadowed by larger personalities, he remains unjustly obscure. Before Lincoln, only Kentucky senator Henry Clay stood as a greater figure than Cabot in the long struggle to preserve the Union. Father of the 1820 Missouri Compromise, champion of the 1833 tariff that kept South Carolinian loyalty for another generation, and early advocate of the Compromise of 1850, Clay is well known to students of history. Cabot remains something of an enigma. Less understood as well is the Patriot King nature of his nationalism. While Clay, a western Whig, battled distant southern Democrats, Cabot absorbed the additional burden of taking on secessionists in his own section and party. A man of the right nudged by circumstances to the center, he regarded the ultraright's determination to create a northern confederacy as dangerously wrong headed; like the elder Adams, he scorned Jeffersonianism but thought its enemy extreme.

· · · · ·

The son of a middling North Shore merchant, Cabot hailed from Salem, Massachusetts, where he was born in 1752. Owing to a paucity of family papers, little is known of his early years. Withdrawal from Harvard College at sixteen—a "great neglect of . . . exercises" stands as the official explanation—offers one of the few glimpses we have of Cabot in youth. From that point on, however, the record becomes far more discernable. Taking to the Atlantic, Cabot demonstrated an instinctive facility for nautical training and within a single apprenticeship year became master of a trade schooner. Soon thereafter the American Revolution broke out over the colonies and with it the economic and ideological upheavals that changed the course of Cabot's life. Through a thrifty combination of privateering, commercial trade, and government contracts he accrued a substantial fortune soon to be translated into political power. Although more than a few Founders sprinkled their letters with references to the war's injurious impact on their pocketbooks, Cabot and his kin nursed no such complaints. As one observer remarked in 1780, with perhaps only a trace of exaggeration, the family was presumed to be "by far the most wealthy in New England."[3]

A Bay State nabob, Cabot maintained cordial relations with Essex County neighbors Pickering and jurist Theophilus Parsons and Dedham congressman Fisher Ames, the major figures making up Massachusetts Federalism's far right. Deeply suspicious of Jeffersonian democracy and critical of Adams's unwillingness as executive to wage war on France, they operated in the late 1790s as an opposition party within a ruling party. In regard to national affairs, Pickering left the biggest impress. The son of a Salem farmer, he too rode the Revolution to prominence. Author of *An Easy Plan for a Militia* (1775), briefly the drill book for the Continental Army, he rose to an adjutant generalship in 1777 and three years later was elected quartermaster general by Congress. Pickering later served for nine years in the Washington and Adams administrations as postmaster general and as secretaries of war and state. He subsequently sat in both the Senate (1803–11) and House (1813–17) as a champion of New England localism in the formative years of Republican supremacy. On more than one occasion he hoped to create a northeastern confederation freed of the planter kingdom to the South.[4]

Aside from Salem's bustling commercial harbor and Gloucester's steady fishing and shipbuilding economy, eighteenth-century Essex lagged behind New England's more prosperous counties. A rugged upland area "of hills, swamps, and plains," it was already at this early date watching nervously as its population trickled down to the Boston basin in search of better opportunities.[5] Farther to the south was Quincy, where, in contrast to the Pickering circle, a more liberal patrician strain under the Adams family held court. In both distance and socioeconomic connections, Quincy proved to be a closer companion to the budding Boston metropole than to Essex. The latter nurtured an almost perverse pride in its direct descent from the original Puritan plantationeers who arrived under the escort of John Endicott and John Winthrop. Tales of provincial honor and obligation wound down through the Essex generations, proving to be important sources of regional identification as well as barriers to embracing broader national initiatives.

Writing in 1878, Cabot's great-grandson, Henry Cabot Lodge, neatly sized up his forefathers' conflicting legacy: "The inhabitants of Essex, at the close of the last century, more fully perhaps than those of almost any other New England county, represented the Puritan character both in its strength and its limitations. Strong, honest, in many cases of an almost reckless courage, they were sagacious in civil, and bold in military life. But their intellectual vigor and clear perceptions were in many instances combined with great mental narrowness and rigidity."[6] In the midst of this mixed mental universe George Cabot made his name.

As a catalyst for social unsettling, the 1776 break with Britain proved to be a transcendent moment in American, New England, and Essex County history. As many as 20 percent of the estimated half a million loyalists in the former colonies left the United States. The Bay State's defections included former royal governor Thomas Hutchinson, *Massachusetts Gazette* publisher John Howe, and John Gray, deputy collector of customs in Boston. Their departures opened a raft opportunities for a rising class of powerbrokers that included the likes of the wealthy mercantilist-turned-revolutionary, John Hancock, Continental Congressman Samuel Adams, and James Bowdoin, who served Massachusetts as president of its constitutional convention and later as its governor. Cabot and his Essex colleagues were doubly blessed by the conflict. Seafaring men, they fought a war for independence that, in their cases, conveniently combined patriotism with profits; they were merchant princes of a county they regarded as a quasi-country.

Even before the Revolution's conclusion, Cabot's circle had drawn the tart attention of its downstate neighbors. Around 1780 the Boston-based Hancock reputedly christened this ambitious clique the Essex Junto. Intended or not, the catchphrase quickly jelled into an insult. It conveyed a number of unflattering impressions—idiosyncratic, ill tempered, vainglorious, and, later, secessionary. It signified further a patriotism warped by insularity and eager, during the early republic ascendency of Virginia, to abandon the old Revolutionary continentalism for a strictly northeastern conception of nationhood. As both a cultural expression and an ideological force, the Junto rapidly emerged as a reckoning voice in postindependence Massachusetts politics.

Like all good Essex men, Cabot adopted the fiscal philosophy advanced by Alexander Hamilton. As formerly noted, Hamilton sought to repair the new nation's dismal financial record through various government-sponsored speculative programs designed to quicken the pace of northern commercial interests, strike against states' rights, and cultivate a gentry of wealth and talent to replace the old colonial deference class. The leviathanesque impulse implicit in the Federalist political economy shocked the South. Consequently, a vigorous opposition gathered around the leadership of James Madison and Thomas Jefferson. The latter wrote, with obvious concern to then-president Washington, that Hamilton's "system flowed from principles adverse to liberty, & was calculated to undermine and demolish the republic."

More assertively, Jefferson challenged the treasury secretary and his supporters by heading their opposition. For his part, Cabot, like most public men, regretted the rise of a party system; he had presumed that the constitution makers were one and all Federalists, even the Virginians. "I am at a loss to account for the conduct of some . . . men . . . I have been accustomed to think well of," he wrote as the two sides began to square off. "I can't reconcile Madison's present conduct [as a censor of Hamiltonianism] with his former principles."[7] He had in mind Madison's important contributions to the Constitutional Convention and his partnering with Hamilton and John Jay on *The Federalist Papers*. No doubt sectionalism goes some way in accounting for this fissure among federalist slaveholders and federalist merchants, though another and equally pressing issue pitting the patrons of democracy against the proponents of deference widened the divide.

When, in 1794, the Whiskey Rebellion revolutionized parts of western Pennsylvania, Cabot regarded the popular uprising as depressing proof of the polity's folly. Rejecting Hamilton's excise tax, a revenue generating impost to aid in the funding of government bonds, many of them held by eastern speculators, the Monongahela Valley erupted in protest. The duties fell disproportionately hard upon Pittsburgh-area spirits distillers, and those who could not pay lost their property. The cosmopolitan-colonial struggle of 1776 seemed to have rekindled in the coastal-backwoods conflict now moving through the Appalachians. The protestors, taken to intimidating government officials in the region and disrupting property foreclosure courts, believed that Federalism had declared economic war on the West, and the old riposte of "no taxation without representation" became again a critical rallying cry. One opponent of the government's whiskey revenue program damned the excise as the plan of "a dangerous aristocracy which, if not crushed in the bud, will destroy our liberties forever." The rhetorical sleight of hand practiced by "ambitious and designing men," he continued, lulled a simple agrarian class into presuming that "whilst [it] enjoys the freedom of electing [its] legislators there is no danger of [its] rights being violated. This is a dangerous and false doctrine."[8]

To Cabot, by contrast, extralegal opposition to the impost strikingly illustrated the perils of a peoples' republic. He predicted anarchy if it were not quickly and firmly quelled. "The public good has always been the victim of private vices," he wrote at the time. "We witness the ready sacrifice which personal ambition makes of equal rights. We see the facility with which a wicked faction has triumphed over public liberty by assuming popular names. We have seen . . . a band of relentless murderers ruling . . . with rods of iron. Will not this, or something like it, be the wretched fate of our country, if the people can be excited to resist the laws of their own making, and to consider as tyrants those who are appointed to execute them?"[9]

The "tyrants" certainly thought so, and acted accordingly. In the small Pennsylvania town of Carlisle, Washington and Hamilton drilled an army of nearly 13,000, intimidated the would-be insurrectionists into acquiescence, and scattered the irreconcilables. If one challenge to Federalism had been rebuffed, however, another and more potent threat came hard on its heels. The French Revolution, as noted, rattled Federalist America to its foundations. During its early years, distinguished by the ruling National Assembly's abolition of ancient feudal privileges and the promulgation of a representative constitution, the old regime's critics won the support of most Americans. But as the Revolution radicalized, leading to regicide, mass executions, and a general European war, Hamiltonians sided with the conservative continental forces arrayed against it. Jeffersonians, by contrast, tended to remain wedded to the French cause as a welcome Gallic adjunct of American republicanism. Writing in 1793 to William Short, the U.S. minister at The Hague, Jefferson equated "the Jacobins of France . . . with the Republican patriots" who would later bring about his presidency. But from the vantage of Essex, Cabot observed a far darker connection between the two republics. "I cannot forbear to express to you my apprehensions," he informed Pickering. "Our country is destined to act over the same follies, to practice the same vices, and of consequence to suffer the same miseries which compose the history of revolutionary France."[10]

The French Revolution inevitably encouraged a poisonous partisanship in American foreign policy, with Federalists backing industrial-Protestant Britain and Republicans supporting agrarian-deistic France. The question of remaining at peace with both sides soon became impossible. Locked in a desperate war, neither Britain nor France respected the United States' right as a neutral to trade with the enemies of the other. Those ships doing so risked confiscation. Recognizing the necessity of coming to terms with America's greatest trading partner and largest creditor, the Washington administration struck a deal with Britain in 1794, the Jay Treaty. One of the most divisive and debated concords in the country's history, the Treaty of Amity, Commerce, and Navigation addressed a number of cankerous issues left over from the American Revolution—including British occupancy of forts in U.S. territory and the closing of the British West Indies trade to American ships—while dealing with new questions arising from the Anglo-French conflict. In sum, the treaty codified the United States' consent to Britain's abusive maritime policies. James Monroe captured Republican hostility to the entente when he complained, "The opinion which is gone forth to the world . . . is that we are reduced by it to the condition of British colonies." Federalists countered that the treaty promised to increase trade and avert war. Giving the New England perspective, Cabot explained to New York senator Rufus King that these two considerations were connected: "Our commercial and maritime people feel themselves deeply interested to prevent any *act* that may put our peace at hazard."[11]

Less then two years after Jay's Treaty was enacted into law, Washington retired from the presidency, leaving Adams a problematic foreign policy further encumbered by a divided country. As noted earlier, he countered Federalist war cries by sending two separate peace missions to France. The first collapsed under the weight of the XYZ affair, and Adams had promised at that time not to send another minister to negotiate "without assurances that he will be received, respected and honored, as the representative of a great, free, powerful and independent nation." Several months later he believed these criteria met. In an about-face, the

French Directory, now looking to American trade to break British shipping dominance, clamped down on its West Indian raiders and released embargoed American ships. John Quincy Adams thought the French concessions aimed toward "a mongrel condition between peace and war," but his father took the higher road: "The end of war is peace," he proclaimed, "and peace was offered me."[12]

The Hamiltonians were livid. Accommodation with France threatened to undercut the crisis they counted on to sweep the 1800 elections. Damning the Adams Federalists' support of the president's peace plan, ultra Federalists sought instead a British alliance, a war on the First Republic, and a permanent standing army. For months they debated and delayed the proposed mission. Cabot accurately conveyed the rupture within American conservatism when he wrote to Pickering in October 1799, "Thus from the moment the nomination of Minister to France was made known to me I saw an unavoidable division of the Federalists and apprehended the triumph of Jacobinism in the United States." Blaming the president for "break[ing] all terms with his best friends his only real friends who are in fact the genuine friends of the government of the country," Cabot, at this point critical of the moderate politics he would soon adopt in reaction to ultra Federalism's growing sympathy with secession, hoped that Adams might refuse to seek a second term. This, he concluded, "would indeed be the most effectual reparation and atonement that could be made."[13]

But Adams had every intention of running for reelection and used the French emergency as an opportunity to cleanse his cabinet. Showing little loyalty, Secretary of War James McHenry and Secretary of State Pickering had repeatedly obstructed the president's peace initiatives and freely shared administration information with Hamilton. At Adams's insistence McHenry resigned; Pickering refused to do the same and was duly sacked. This exile of the ultras, combined with the president's decision to reconcile with France, convinced Cabot that Adams courted public approval in order to win a fresh term. "It is impossible . . . that Mr. Adams should govern *as a federal man* and this must be seen presently by all sagacious men who attend to public affairs," he wrote to Oliver Wolcott. "It is evident Mr. Adams calculates upon engaging the force of the passions and prejudices of the populace on his side and with this reinforcement to overcome or beat down his federal opponents."[14]

Cabot reserved his private criticisms of the president to a small circle of intimates; Hamilton sought to acquaint a wider audience. In the summer of 1800 he prepared a document enumerating Adams's shortcomings, the *Letter from Alexander Hamilton, Concerning the Public Conduct and Character of John Adams, Esq. President of the United States*—fifty-four octavo pages of political suicide. Apprising Wolcott in July of his unusual plan to publish for a small audience the president's sins, Hamilton insisted that it was "essential to inform the most discreet [Federalists] of the facts which denote unfitness in Mr. Adams."[15] Undoubtedly expecting a far milder and more judiciously circulated statement from Hamilton than what emerged, Cabot encouraged the endeavor. He would be sorry.

After reading a preprinted copy of the *Letter* in late summer, Cabot wrote to Hamilton, encouraging him to kill the document. A great admirer of the former treasury secretary, he nevertheless thought his friend had gone too far. The *Letter* opened with acid: "I should be deficient in candor, were I to conceal the conviction that [Mr. Adams] does not possess the talents adapted to the *Administration* of Government, and that there are great and intrinsic defects in his character, which unfit him for the office of Chief Magistrate." From there followed an indelicate airing of Federalist dirty laundry. As Cabot knew, the *Letter* came perilously close to emulating the attack on executive power associated with both the Jacobins and Whiskey rebels. "All agree that the execution is masterly," he bowed to Hamilton, "but I am *bound* to tell you that you are accused by respectable men of egotism; and some very worthy and sensible men say you have exhibited the same *vanity* in your book which you charge as a dangerous quality and great weakness in Mr. Adams."[16] Soon after, the Republican *New-York Gazette and General Advertiser* obtained a copy of the *Letter* and serialized it for all to see. The gambit had clearly blown up in Hamilton's face, further handicapping Federalist chances in the fall campaign.

But Hamilton hardly paused. As the election of 1800 drew nearer he planned to deny Adams the presidency by a sub rosa backing of South Carolina's Pinckney, the Federalist candidate for vice president, in effect reprising his failed 1796 plan. Accordingly, he urged New England electors to cast their two ballots for Adams and Pinckney yet intrigued with South Carolinians to hold back votes from Adams. Catching wind of the plot, Cabot pushed his differences with the president aside and tactfully revealed his knowledge of the stratagem to Hamilton. "It is perceived by Mr. Adams's personal friends that while the party profess a zealous desire to unite *all* the federal votes for Adams and Pinckney, there are many or at least some individuals among those who compose it whose *wishes* are known to be that the election may issue in favor of Mr. Pinckney and therefore it is inferred such persons will not act and do not aim as they profess." By attacking Adams and engaging in intrigues designed to deny him Federalist support, Hamilton, Cabot believed, both compromised his personal integrity and that of the party he had done so much to build. He conceded, nevertheless, the dilemma that ultra Federalists now faced— "It is true there is an apparent absurdity in supporting a man whom we know to be unworthy of trust"—and yet the dictates of personal honor called upon conservatives to support the president's reelection.[17] In the end it did not matter. Adams edged Pinckney by a single electoral vote to finish third as Jefferson, following a contingent House election in which he defeated Aaron Burr with whom he had tied in the Electoral College, claimed the coveted prize.

The repercussions of the 1800 election were felt nowhere more forcefully than in Cabot's Massachusetts. During the 1790s only about 20 percent of the Bay State's white males typically voted in gubernatorial elections. By 1804 the percentage had doubled to some 40 percent and reached nearly 70 percent in 1812. Amid this blooming democratic backdrop, Cabot retired from politics. A director of the Bank of the United States since 1793, he subsequently presided over its Boston branch. Out of government, his detestation of Jeffersonian democracy matured rather than mellowed. In power for the first time, the Virginians and their allies seemed intent to overturn any sign of Federalist influence. They attacked the "aristocratic" federal court system by withholding writs of mandamus—signed judicial commissions—to conservative appointees and installed instead their own partisans to the posts. More troubling, two Federalist judges, one a Supreme Court justice, endured impeachment trails in a crude attempt by Republicans to incriminate their opposition. Jefferson's purchase of the Louisiana Territory in 1803 caused more concern for Cabot, who thought the acquisition constitutionally dubious (a suspicion that troubled Jefferson as well) and one that assuredly prefaced the political eclipse of the Northeast. "*We are democratic altogether*," he lamented to Pickering in 1804, "and I hold democracy in its natural operation to be *the government of the worst*."[18]

Following three years of Republican rule, some Federalists looked to make a clean break from their political masters. Pickering, now a U.S. senator, observed from up close the opposition's successes, and with Jefferson's reelection all but assured he began to think seriously of rending the Union. "Without a separation," he reasoned, "can those [northern]

States ever rid themselves of negro Presidents and negro Congresses, and regain their just weight in the political balance?"[19] Pickering's unflattering reference alluded to the constitutional compromise between North and South allowing three-fifths of the enumerated population of slaves to be counted for purposes of taxation and representation. This article gave slaveholding states a disproportionate share of power in both the House and the Electoral College and thus, by their connections, the Speakership of the House and the presidency. Southern power, Pickering had come to believe, posed a direct threat to the nation's moral well-being.

Anticipating a subset of abolitionists who later pleaded for northern severance from a "sinful" South, Pickering sought honor in disunion. The nation's glorious origins, after all, revealed the obvious solution to Federalism's troubles: "The principles of our Revolution point to the remedy—a separation." Writing to Cabot on the eve of New England's 1804 spring elections, he boldly proposed the creation of a northern confederacy. "It must begin in Massachusetts," he declared and presumed the ready compliance of Connecticut and New Hampshire. If New York could then be coaxed in, Pickering continued, "Vermont and New Jersey would follow of course, and Rhode Island of necessity." Incredibly, he believed that Nova Scotia and Newfoundland might, "at no remote period," be permitted by Britain to enter the league. The old mother country would still retain Atlantic Canada's trade, he reasoned, while relinquishing the cost of its upkeep and striking a blow against both Jeffersonianism and Jacobinism. "A liberal treaty of amity and commerce," he very questionably concluded, "will form a bond of union between Great Britain and the Northern confederacy highly useful to both."[20]

But wouldn't the U.S. government employ force to oppose such plans? Pickering thought not. Southern transatlantic commerce, after all, traveled in Boston, New London, and New York ships. Faced with a destructive civil war or cutting a deal with their neighbors to the north, the planters who shaped southern opinion, Pickering argued, would almost certainly opt to keep their trade intact. Besides, he further conjectured, division need not harm either section: "We wish no ill to the Southern States and those naturally connected with them. . . . A friendly and commercial intercourse would be maintained with the States in the Southern confederacy, as at present. Thus all the advantages which have been for a few years depending on the general Union would be continued to its respective portions, without the jealousies and enmities which now afflict both, and which peculiarly embitter the condition of that of the

North." More broadly, Pickering held out hope that the threat of seces-sion might induce "our Southern brethren . . . [to] abandon their virulent measures." He conceded, however, that the odds were much against that. Laying out this grand plan, which promised to forever alter the course of American history, he wanted to know Cabot's views. Had he deduced correctly, could such a plot be pulled off? "Are these ideas visionary or impracticable?" he wrote. "Do they not merit consideration? If they do, let me know."[21]

Two weeks later, Cabot let him know. He opened on a conciliatory note, "All the evils you describe and many more are to be apprehended," and he acknowledged further that "a separation at some period not very re-mote may probably take place." Yet he advised Pickering to drop the idea. True, he agreed, the kind of democracy advanced by the Jeffersonians defied the old values, morals, and social codes, but what could be done? For human nature itself, he argued, conspired against the Federalist vi-sion of a deferential community. Voters sought instinctively, after all, to enlarge their individual freedoms, and they cast their ballots accordingly. "Even in New England, where there is among the body of the people more wisdom and virtue than in any other part of the United States," he sighed, "we are full of errors, which no reasoning could eradicate."[22]

Addressing Pickering's implied invitation to join the would-be seces-sionists, Cabot demurred: "I do not desire [disunion] at this moment, [and] I add that *it is not practicable* without the intervention of some cause which should be very generally felt and distinctly understood as chargeable to the misconduct of our Southern masters: such, for example, as a war with Great Britain, manifestly provoked by our rulers. But they will not haz-ard a war."[23] Of course in 1812 the Republicans did "hazard a war" with Britain and that forced Cabot to once again face down the trend of a New England bolt. But that gets us ahead of our story. To Pickering, in the late winter of 1804, Cabot offered a sympathetic ear, a knowing agreement on the Union's deficiencies, but no aid to end that Union. He offered fur-ther an indication of his subtle political evolution. Once a firm Hamilto-nian, Cabot began to move away from his old political partners. While never relinquishing his disdain for Jeffersonianism, he quietly adopted a more circumspect tone with colleagues on the right, even as they began to look increasingly to his counsel.

Undeterred by Cabot's letter, Pickering moved ahead with his plans, which included supporting Vice President Aaron Burr's bid for New York's gubernatorial chair. Installed in Albany, Burr, Pickering presumed, would likely join a northern league. Jefferson, after all, had slashed away at his New York power base by appointing supporters of the competing Clinton and Livingston clans to office; now, close observers whispered, the president meant to sacrifice Burr in order that secretary of state and fellow Virginian James Madison might ascend in due time to the presidency. Clearly Burr had no future in the Jeffersonian party; in late February a Republican caucus met and not a single attendee voted for his renomination to the vice presidency. Tellingly, his in-state nemesis George Clinton captured the prize.

Around that time, and again, on 4 April, a group of ultra Federalists met with Burr, purportedly offering him a leadership role in a new confederacy should he capture the governor's race. As the outline of Pickering's plans came into focus, Cabot grew increasingly restive. Avoiding the poisonous words "secession," "disunion," and "separation," he wrote to New York senator Rufus King, "The thing proposed is obvious and natural, but it would now be thought too bold, and would be fatal to its advocates as public men; yet the time *may* soon come when it will be demanded by the people of the North and East, and then it will unavoidably take place. I am not satisfied that the thing itself is to be desired. My habitual opinions have been always strongly against it; and I do not see, in the present mismanagement, motives for changing my opinion." He then carefully concluded his letter: "I should rejoice to see, Burr win the race in your State, but I cannot approve of aid being given him by any of the *leading* Federalists."[24]

In a Republican year, in a Republican state, the ideologically limber Burr never had a chance. On 26 April his opponent, Morgan Lewis, a Clintonian endorsed by Hamilton, swept to victory with nearly 60 percent of the vote. For ultras, however, the worst was yet to come. Two days before the election, the *Albany (N.Y.) Register* published a gossipy letter written by a Dr. Charles D. Cooper, detailing various insults levied by Hamilton upon Burr. This included one particularly cutting characterization of the vice president as a "dangerous man" and culminated with Cooper's teaser conclusion: "I could detail to you a still more despicable opinion which General HAMILTON has expressed of Mr. Burr." Shortly thereafter, the publicly abused Burr sent a note to Hamilton seeking an explanation. Hamilton's reply, sporting with the term "despicable"—"'Tis evident, that the phrase 'still more despicable' admits of infinite shades, from very light to very dark. How am I to judge of the degree intended?"— seemed calculated to antagonize Burr further, and his conclusion,

"I trust, on more reflection, you will see the matter in the same light as me. If not, I can only regret the circumstance, and must abide the consequence," could only have aroused his reader's indignation.[25] Another round of fruitless exchanges followed. On 27 June, Burr challenged Hamilton to a duel. Two weeks later, they met in the early morning at the Heights of Weehawken in New Jersey. There, Hamilton suffered a lethal wound through the lower abdomen and died the following day in a friend's Jane Street home in Greenwich Village. His fatality, Burr's defeat, and Jefferson's autumn reelection mocked Federalism's secessionary fantasies but did not end them.

· · · · ·

During Jefferson's difficult second term, the Napoleonic wars once again called into question neutral America's right to trade with combatant nations. From 1800 to 1807, Napoleon's navy seized over two hundred American ships in Caribbean waters alone. Because of its superiority on the seas, the British fleet inflicted even more damage on U.S. ocean trade. Responding to British impressment and French marauding, Jefferson signed into law the extraordinary Embargo Act of 1807, which forbade U.S. exports to all nations. Shortly thereafter, the president wrote to John Taylor of Caroline explaining his stunning decision as a case of time buying. "The embargo keeping at home our vessels, cargoes & seamen, save us the necessity of making their capture the cause of immediate war: for if going to England, France had determined to take them; if to any other place, England was to take them. Till they return to some sense of moral duty therefore, we keep within ourselves. This gives time, time may produce peace in Europe: peace in Europe removes all causes of difference, till another European war: and by that time our debt may be paid, our revenues clear, & our strength increased."[26] Federalists, of course, saw the situation very differently. They claimed that the plantocracy threatened to destroy New England's economy. In a region where free trade constituted the very lifeblood of commercial existence, the embargo proved devastating—and strangely familiar. In the spring of 1774, following the previous December's Boston Tea Party, the British Parliament had shut down the city's port until the East India Company, owner of the destroyed leaves, received reimbursement. The policy, known variously in the colonies as the Port Bill, the Intolerable Acts, and the Coercive Acts, proved to be the catalyst for a long train of events that led, within a year's time, to the battles of Lexington and Concord, and one year beyond that to the adoption by the Continental Congress of the Declaration of Independence, a secession movement sustained by both North and South.

As a member of the Virginia House of Burgesses in 1774, Jefferson had helped orchestrate the Old Dominion's protest against the British acts. "Three or four other members . . . and myself," he later wrote, "agree[d] that we must boldly take an unequivocal stand in the line with Massachusetts." Accordingly, the group "rummaged over . . . the revolutionary precedents and forms of the Puritans" for guidance and inspiration. "We cooked up a resolution," Jefferson continued, "for appointing the 1st day of June, on which the Port Bill was to commence, for a day of fasting, humiliation, and prayer to implore Heaven to avert from us the evils of civil war, to inspire us with firmness in support of our rights, and to turn the hearts of the King and Parliament to moderation and justice." Soon thereafter, Jefferson supplied a detailed critique of Britain's behavior in *A Summary View of the Rights of British America*, his first important public paper. "Shall these governments be dissolved," he asked of Massachusetts and its peers, "their property annihilated, and their people reduced to a state of nature, at the imperious breath of a body of men . . . over whom they have no powers of punishment or removal?"[27]

Interestingly, *Summary View* anticipated the conspiratorial projection on events that later tormented Federalist minds. In 1774 Jefferson had insisted that the Port Bill stood alongside earlier Stamp, Declaratory, and Townshend Acts as allied parts of a parliamentary plot to curb colonial independence: "Single acts of tyranny may be ascribed to the accidental opinion of the day; but a series of oppressions, begun at a distinguished period, and pursued unalterably thro' every change of ministers, too plainly prove a deliberate, systematical plan of reducing us to slavery."[28] Now, change the British provocations to the removal of Federalist appointments (1801), the impeachment trials of Federalist judges (1803–05), and the long train of embargos and nonintercourse acts (1807–12), and the quotation could easily have come from Timothy Pickering. After all, Boston Port again sat shuttered, this time by order of a Virginia president.

From that point on, Federalism's dissatisfaction with Jefferson only grew. In the early spring of 1808 the president passed recommendations on to Congress designed to strengthen the embargo. One in particular proved wholly offensive to New Englanders. It asserted, as one historian has written, "that collectors should be empowered to seize cargoes, without a warrant or the prospect of a trial, upon the mere formation of a suspicion that a shipper or merchant *contemplated* a violation of the embargo. This was in direct opposition to the Fourth and Fifth amendments of the Bill of Rights; it was also a more sweeping power than had been given to the king's agents by the hated writs of assistance, one of the principal forms of 'tyranny' that had provoked the American colonists to revolution." As Congress discussed the measures, Jefferson issued a proclamation declaring the Lake Champlain region of New York, open to a bourgeoning if illicit raft trade with Canada, to be in a state of insurrection. The president ordered civil and military officials in the region "by all means in their power, by force of arms or otherwise," to halt the commerce. Accordingly, the New York and Vermont militias were turned loose on their citizens. Six days later Jefferson's recommendations, now known as the Enforcement Act, became law.[29]

Aside from the economic violence the embargo inflicted upon New England, Cabot condemned the Jefferson administration for failing to join Britain in alliance against Napoleonic France. On one side, he claimed, resided tradition, order, Christianity, and constitutional monarchy; on the other idled anarchy, upheaval, atheism, and dictatorship. In essence Cabot called for an Anglo-American imperium, anticipating the "special relationship" that later bound the two powers together in a common liberal internationalist vision. Thus, the Western containment of twentieth-century communism that once struck so many Americans as a departure from their country's isolationist roots actually adhered to an earlier foreign policy formula. In Federalist Boston, New York, and Philadelphia, and late-Georgian London, Bristol, and Portsmouth, defenders of a Lockean Atlantic world sought to stem French expansion as a preface to annihilating Jacobinism, the eighteenth century's Marxism. Cabot stood among them. "In the tremendous contest in which Great Britain is engaged," he wrote Pickering, "she has the strongest motives for rescuing or preserving from the grasp of France every state that can be saved. Thus her policy is as obviously wise as it is invariable. Our country, ill organized as it appears, with all its ports, peoples and resources, would be a powerful auxiliary to France, but to England as an ally, it might be inestimable. Great Britain and the United States united in a common cause of defense, would be an over-match for all the powers on the globe."[30]

By the summer of 1808, a number of Bay State Federalists began to organize against both the embargo and Jefferson's transparent passing of the presidential crown to James Madison. In June a twenty-man council named by the Massachusetts legislature appointed a smaller committee to begin correspondence with Federalists in neighboring states with the intent to identify a presidential candidate capable of defeating Madison. They settled on George Clinton, a Founding Father, a longtime New York governor, and Jefferson's vice president. They looked, in other words, to exploit a fissure in Republican solidarity. Though Jefferson's vision of states' rights democracy and agrarian economy captured the party's southern base, Republicanism could never have won national elections without support in the North, and particularly New York. Its dozen electoral votes in 1800 gave Jefferson a margin of eight over the incumbent Adams. By 1808 there were clear signs that New York Republicans thought their state was owed the presidential chair. More, they had watched their shipping economy suffer appreciably under the lash of the Jeffersonian embargo. Without markets abroad, Albany wheat prices quickly dropped from two dollars a bushel to only 75 cents; the decline in agricultural income created a debt crisis among farmers that clogged county courts and challenged the yeoman ideal of earning a living off the land. "Jefferson's embargo and the War of 1812," Sean Wilentz has written, "marked a calamitous interlude in New York's rise to supremacy among America's mercantile cities."[31]

Federalists hoped to play upon this discontent. As James Banner Jr. has observed, a small group of moderates, including Cabot, were intrigued by the prospect of a Clinton candidacy.

> Five high-placed party activists—[Harrison Gray] Otis, George Cabot, Christopher Gore, James Lloyd, and Timothy Bigelow— made up this special committee. Within a few days of its appointment, the group met and decided to propose a general meeting of Federalists from the states—in effect, the first presidential nominating convention at the national level—in order to agree upon a national party policy for the election and to fix on a party standard-bearer. Then, for the next two months, it bent its every effort to secure a full representation of the states at the convention and labored to commit the convention beforehand to the anti administration candidacy of Republican George Clinton. The Clinton scheme recommended itself for two reasons: it might in the first place most effectively raise the political heat on the Jeffersonian Republicans, and in the second it would allow the Federalists either to assume credit for an unlikely Clinton victory or to blame the Republicans for his defeat.[32]

The possibility of a Clinton candidacy backed by moderates evoked the earlier ultraconservative flirtation with Burr's gubernatorial run. In both cases, New York vice presidents, with virtually no chance of displacing a Virginian for the coveted presidential nomination, held for New Englanders the faint hope of rebuking, through secession or electoral success, Republicanism. In fact, they together were the longest of long shots, suggesting the desperate state to which a once-mighty Federalism had fallen.

In his pro-Clinton capacity, Cabot maintained a brisk correspondence throughout the summer. To the Massachusetts lawyer, businessman, and politician Harrison Gray Otis, he listed with measured enthusiasm the benefits to be won by New Englanders if the vice president carried the autumn campaign. "There are some circumstances peculiarly favorable to our expectations of advantage from Clinton's election—his partisans in general & especially in New York are hostile to the Virginian system of destroying commerce, and they are keen in their resentments against the Madisonians whom they fear as men trying to supplant them in the popular favor; they will be likely to coalesce with the Democrats of the neighboring states against the Demos of the South." But to Cabot's disappointment, many Federalists across New England were cold to the idea of supporting any Republican. He lamented to Otis that former congressman and *Hartford (Conn.) Mirror* publisher Theodore Dwight "has strongly expressed his belief that no Electors could be chosen in Connecticut who would vote . . . for Clinton, & in our own State I find there is a great reluctance to the same thing." Cabot, like John Adams before him, began to realize that his relationship with Federalism was far more complex than he had once imagined. He noticed in 1808, if not before, its rigid cast of mind, episodic political paranoia, and a perverse focus on the New England condition that contradicted its pretensions to national leadership. "Some individuals," he fumed in one reference to Federalism's hard-liners, "have incidentally discovered an aversion from what they call compromise."[33]

But to Cabot, conservatives were in no position to do anything else. If Federalists could not produce an electable man among their own, he insisted, they should support a candidate capable of ending the hated embargo, pursuing a friendlier line toward Britain and overturning the Jeffersonian philosophy of spoils appointments. Emphasizing the need for conciliation with elements of the opposition, he alerted Otis that "in my judgment it is of more importance to put Mr. Jefferson & Mr. Madison out of the presidential chair, than it would be (if they were out there) to put in their places the most wise & virtuous men our country contains. . . . It is under this kind of impression that I apprehend a Federalist could render us but little service." He further pointed to an inconvenient political fact that many conservatives seemed unwilling to acknowledge: combined, the Jeffersonians and Clintonians could not lose; "they are a majority in the United States." Only a Republican could defeat a Republican. And with the Hamiltonians in abeyance and thus no longer able to "frighten" their opposition into observing strict party discipline, Cabot believed that the unholy marriage between free labor and slave labor must soon collapse. Referring to Jeffersonianism's all-important Virginian and New York wings, he wrote, "If you give to a portion of them a great interest & influence which must disappoint the other portion you create a division which must break their force."[34]

Of course a lingering question for those Federalists willing to consider supporting a Republican loomed large: Was Clinton safe? Would he offer New England an olive branch? Cabot approached the issue pragmatically. "I think," he wrote to one correspondent, "much reliance may be placed on the force of circumstances and local causes to dissuade him from the support of those destructive projects which are now executed by his Rivals & which they are much more strongly attached to than he can be—& indeed if his disposition should be the same as theirs I should imagine his power to injure us would be less than theirs—to me this view of our affairs is so obvious that I cannot doubt the result of any conference to be in favor of supporting the election of Clinton."[35] In the end, Cabot's appeals came to naught. In August, a small gathering met in New York and nominated the perfectly conventional and thus eminently defeatable Federalist ticket of Pinckney and Rufus King. The ultras had won out.

As the autumn wore on, a Madison victory looked increasingly likely. From the perch of his Senate seat, Pickering composed a series of caustic letters. In one he warned that simply shuffling Virginia executives would have no impact on national policy. He regarded Madison as a mere cipher, Jefferson's once and always "monkey on a leash." Against such a funereal backdrop New England's secessionist wing again became active. Seeking to register his objection, Cabot forwarded to Pickering a judicious if pointed note. "I have seen from several quarters letters expressing apprehensions that a disunion of the States is meditated by the Federalists," his opening line rang. True or not, he continued, the weight of such rumors burdened the party with the taint of treason. And Cabot, whether to slay a false rumor or to quash a rebellion in waiting, offered Pickering the following frank advice: "I think . . . it will be well to pass some very decided resolution on the importance of maintaining the Union inviolate under every trial, &c."[36]

Come November, the Jeffersonian surge continued. Madison scored 122 electoral votes to Pinckney's 47, nearly half of which came from a politically neutralized New England; Clinton, Madison's running mate and the would-be wildcard for moderates like Cabot, captured six ballots, all from his native New York. Beyond question Federalism had become a permanent minority party. With the hated Jeffersonians entering a third term, the voices of New England opposition grew less patient and more radical. Under such trying circumstances fewer Federalists sought to reconcile their section's grievances through the chain of national government command. Outvoted and out-peopled with no relief in sight, the more distraught among their number now invested almost wholly in state and section as the sole means to redress their grievances and defend their liberties.[37]

· · · · ·

In a winter meeting of the Massachusetts General Court held shortly after the 1808 elections, a group of aggrieved Federalists tendered a series of resolutions that challenged both the embargo and its offensive policing apparatus. The first resolve struck a condemnatory note, declaring the Enforcement Act "unjust, oppressive, and unconstitutional, and not legally binding on the citizens of this state." Those that followed were vigorously assertive of the Bay State's rights but steered clear of secessionary rhetoric. Even so, they collectively conveyed a firm determination to alter the current constitutional framework that, in the General Court's opinion, so transparently favored southern and western interests. One clause emphasized the tribunal's preference to "co-operate with any of the other states, in all legal and constitutional measures, for procuring such amendments to the constitution of the United States, as shall be judged necessary . . . to give the commercial states their fair and just consideration in the government of the union."[38] The General Court's penultimate provision called upon Massachusetts's senators and congressmen to seek a consensus with their New England equals in opposition to the commerce quarantine.

In response, northern Republicans, sensitive to the brewing opposition in the East as well as to the unpopularity of the embargo among their own constituencies, pushed for a continuation of trade that resolved many of New England's economic, if not constitutional, complaints. A lame-duck Jefferson was resigned to complying and planned to see the embargo lifted on 1 June. But a surprisingly effective Republican opposition beat down the president's proposal 73 to 40 and substituted 4 March, the day after Madison took office, as the repeal date. Unaccustomed to being bested by factions within his own party, Jefferson testily denounced "this sudden and unaccountable revolution of opinion." One Republican congressman, Joseph Story of Massachusetts, recalled that a meeting with administration leaders designed to shore up his commitment to the president had much the opposite effect. Story's account could have been written by any number of Federalists: "In the course of these consultations I learned the whole policy of Mr. Jefferson; and was surprised as well as grieved to find, that in the face of the clearest proofs of the failure of his plan, he continued to hope against facts. . . . The very eagerness with which the repeal was supported by a majority of the Republican party ought to have taught Mr. Jefferson that it was already considered by them as a miserable and mischievous failure."[39] Previous illusions put aside, the president now understood where northern Republicans stood. In his final days in office Jefferson signed the Non Intercourse Act, a replacement for the hated interdiction. It declared U.S. ships free to trade with all nations excepting England and France.

There the situation simmered for four difficult years under the new administration, with Republicans unable to effectively defend either the country's neutrality or its shipping. With the embargo over, Jeffersonians made up in the 1810 elections many of the seats they had lost to Federalists in the previous campaign. This Twelfth Congress included an influential core of Republicans from southern and western states eager to avenge American honor in light of Britain's interference with U.S. shipping and presumed instigation of American Indian attacks on frontier settlements. In June 1812, with his reelection in jeopardy, Madison asked this congress for a declaration of war. "Such is the spectacle of injuries and indignities which have been heaped on our country," he gave the Republican position, "and such the crisis which its unexampled forbearance and conciliatory efforts have not been able to avert."[40] Predictably, the country divided. The House approved the war measure 79 to 49, with Ohio, Kentucky, Tennessee, North Carolina, South Carolina, and Georgia recording 25 to 2 in favor, and Massachusetts, Rhode Island, Connecticut, New York, and New Jersey voting 29 to 8 in the negative. On 12 June the Senate deadlocked on the bill; following five days of intense and at times bitter negotiation, the bill passed 19 to 13.

The war brought additional hardships upon New England, now exposed to British naval power, and provoked resistance throughout the region. Massachusetts governor Caleb Strong emulated his Puritan predecessors by asking Bay Staters to fast in contrition for a sinful government. The blasphemous war, he claimed, aimed to excite America "against the nation . . . which for many generations has been the bulwark of the religion we profess." In Essex County, Byfield divine Elijah Parish encouraged his parishioners to "break those chains, under which you have sullenly murmured, during the long, long reign of democracy . . . and once more breathe that free, commercial air of New England which your fathers always enjoyed. . . . Protest did I say, protest? *Forbid this war to proceed in New-England*." For his part, Cabot vowed to sit the conflict out. If his moderation had prevented his joining an "extreme" secession party, no more would it allow him to support a "radical" war party. "Since our nation is so wicked and unjust as to enter upon this war, if it suffers, its sufferings will be salutary," he informed Pickering. "I, therefore, shall obey the laws constitutionally made, but shall conscientiously refrain from every voluntary aid to the war, in thought, word, and deed."[41]

In Massachusetts, the men of Cabot's circle looked to the fall presidential election to overthrow southern rule without resorting to the secessionary threats previously employed by ultra Federalism. Madison was clearly vulnerable even as the war declaration briefly revived his fortunes outside of New England. Two invasions of Canada, one in July and the other in October, ended in defeat; the United States had surrendered much of the Michigan Territory. Amid these setbacks the 1808 plot to run George Clinton as a Republican congenial to Federalists resurfaced with a new Clinton, DeWitt, taking on the Patriot King-in-waiting role. Later remembered as the father of the Erie Canal for his gubernatorial efforts to get "Clinton's Ditch" dug, DeWitt Clinton, nephew to George, served as mayor of New York City in 1812 and detested the long monopoly of executive power claimed by the Virginians. Assured of Clinton's willingness to challenge Madison as a Peace Republican, dissident Jeffersonians joined with Federalists in lining up behind the New Yorker and with 89 ballots to Madison's 128 came within a single state (Pennsylvania) of claiming the election.

Some years later, in his history of the United States during the Madison administrations, Henry Adams ranked Clinton as a mere opportunist looking to ride a mongrel coalition of disaffected factions to power: "No canvass for the Presidency was ever less creditable than that of DeWitt Clinton in 1812. Seeking war votes for the reason that he favored more vigorous prosecution of the war; asking support from peace Republicans because Madison had plunged the country into war without preparation; bargaining for Federalist votes as the price of bringing about a peace; or coquetting with all parties in the atmosphere of bribery in bank charters— Clinton strove to make up a majority which had no element of union but himself and money."[42] Viewed more charitably, the anti-Madison coalition effectively challenged a war party that had thus far failed to meet its war aims. Madison's 50 percent of the popular vote in 1812 represented both the lowest percentage of all his presidential predecessors and a comedown from the 64 percent he had captured in 1808.

Leaner numbers aside, the Jeffersonians nevertheless retained control of the government in 1812, causing Federalists to more boldly oppose what they saw as the "Republican war." Its northeastern economy in tatters, its coastlines unprotected, and its national political opportunities handicapped by a slaveholder-friendly Three Fifths Compromise, the usual rounds of prayers, fasts, and petitions, would no longer do. Momentum began to build in the autumn of 1814 for a convention of New England states to discuss their common grievances. On 5 October the Massachusetts General Court convened. Eight days later it passed a resolution authorizing Governor Strong to raise an army of 10,000 to defend the Commonwealth. Three days after that it approved another resolution calling for a convention to assemble at Hartford, nearly 20 percent of the yeas coming from Essex County. Most of the New England states responded positively to the summons, and in all twelve representatives from Massachusetts, seven from Connecticut, and four from Rhode Island were appointed by their legislatures; county conventions elected New Hampshire's two attendees, while citizens of Windham County, Vermont, chose one deputy.

This was not a secession movement, though it did have the slight potential to move in that direction. Madison entertained such concerns and ordered the Virginian Colonel Thomas Sidney Jesup to Hartford to watch over the assemblage. If a rupture occurred, Jesup planned to march north and safeguard the federal armory at Springfield, Massachusetts. In fact, moderates dominated the gathering. As a statement of invitation put it, delegates were to meet "for the purpose of devising and recommending such measures for the safety and welfare of these States as may be consistent with our obligations as members of the National Union."[43] More specifically, the representatives sought to register their opposition to the war in a formal and recognizable forum, a legislature-like setting suggesting the Continental Congresses and Constitutional Convention of 1787, while preparing a statement on revisions to that Constitution designed to secure minority rights.

Cabot served as president over the three weeks of meetings and, with his power to designate committee appointments, kept any latent revolutionaries in line. He was an impressive figure, with unpowdered hair pulled back and tied in a queue; adorned in black, he sported knee breeches and silk stockings, even at that time out of fashion. Explaining his reason for going to Hartford, he said simply that he hoped "to keep young hot-heads from getting into mischief." But small chance existed of an ultraconservative insurrection. More than a few delegates had major financial, shipping, and mercantile interests with the several states of the Union, New England's vast classes of pensioners and investors were reliant on government securities, and it was by no means certain that the people of the Northeast would sustain a separation movement carried out in their name.[44]

Still, it did no harm to have the caucus under the command of a firm nationalist and one who conjured comparison to George Washington, the great American Patriot King of the recent past. Samuel Goodrich, nephew of Hartford mayor Chauncey Goodrich, recalled in an 1857 memoir meeting the delegates. One in particular stood out.

The most imposing man among them, in personal appearance, was George Cabot, the president. He was over six feet in height, broad-shouldered, and of manly step. His hair was white—for he was past sixty—his eye blue, his complexion slightly florid. He seemed to me like Washington—as if the great man . . . had walked out of the canvas, and lived and breathed among us. He was, in fact, Washingtonian in his whole air and bearing, as was proper for one who was Washington's friend, and who had drunk deep at the same fountain—that of the Revolution—of the spirit of truth, honor, and patriotism. In aspect and general appearance, he was strikingly dignified, and such was the effect of his presence, that in a crowded room, and amid other men of mark—when you once became conscious that he was there, you could hardly forget it. You seemed always to see him—as the traveler in Switzerland sees

Mont Blanc towering above other mountains around him, wherever he may be.[45]

Under Cabot's leadership, the convention put together a long indictment of Republican sins that must have served a cathartic end for men used to operating outside the Jeffersonian orbit. They loathed, as the convention's report put it, "the political intolerance displayed and avowed in excluding from office [individuals] of unexceptionable merit, for want of adherence to the executive creed."[46] More broadly, the document emphasized New England's regional and legal concerns, offering several ways to amend the Constitution in order to recreate the old balance between free and slave states. Other recommendations revealed a defensive inflection including proposals that naturalized citizens be banned from sitting in Congress and that presidents serve no more than a single term (the two suggestions aimed at Federalism's biggest bugaboos, Republican-voting immigrants and Virginia presidents).

Yet under Cabot's leadership the Hartford delegates advanced other constructive if elusive articles including recommendations to end the "unjust and unequal" Three Fifths Compromise and restricting the power of making offensive war to two-thirds support in both houses of Congress. Although these propositions stood absolutely no chance of adoption by the national government, the convention had intelligently brought to light lethal flaws in the current constitutional arrangement. It was, after all, the later "offensive" Mexican War (1846–48) that raised the specter of slavery's advance in the western territories and played a critical role in bringing about the destruction of the old Union. In sum, northern Federalism sought to protect New England by pressuring the Madison administration to sign an honorable peace with Britain. The dire war situation in the autumn of 1814 seemed in their eyes to dictate such a response. The nation's lightly defended capital kindled to the torch in August while Hampden, Bangor, and Machias, Maine—then parts of Massachusetts— were raided and looted; Castine endured enemy occupation for months. In the old Puritan quarters, confidence in the central government had dipped dramatically and many looked reflexively to their state governments for redress.

Events far from New England all but destroyed the delegates' work. The Sixth Coalition's defeat of Napoleon earlier that spring had reoriented the entire European situation, resulting in a British-American peace signed in the Belgium city of Ghent on 24 December. At that point events moved quickly and conclusively against Madison's critics. On 30 December the final report of the Hartford Convention appeared; one week later the *Hartford Courant* published the proceedings. The transcript emphasized localism and limitations. In the name of preserving sectional autonomy, Cabot and his colleagues sought to undermine the super-state edifice they had once supported under Hamilton. This convention's "object," they explained, "is to strengthen, and if possible to perpetuate, the union of the states, by removing the grounds of existing jealousies, and providing for a fair and equal representation, and a limitation of powers."[47] On 8 January, two days after the report's publication, a small multiracial force composed of regular U.S. troops, militia, civilian volunteers, Choctaws, free blacks, and slaves under the command of Major General Andrew Jackson, turned back a larger invading British army at the Battle of New Orleans. Jackson's casualties for the entire Louisiana operation amounted to fewer than 350, whereas the British lost a staggering 2,400; it was the greatest American land campaign of the war, if not the greatest in the young republic's history. Cassandras were decidedly out of fashion.

Obviously the egalitarian drift of national life overtook Federalism, yet the party succumbed as much to self-inflicted wounds as to the popular appeal of its opponents. Excessively consolidationist, perversely Anglophilic, and surprisingly receptive to the politics of paranoia, Federalism suffered considerably under the whip of its own anxieties. Still, given different circumstances, it might have survived. We may recall that the dominant southern wing of the Republican Party too pursued a localist (Virginia) vision, advanced a controversial foreign policy (Francophile), and betrayed through the spoils system and judicial impeachment trials ample evidence of its own insecurity. Why did the one thrive as the other died? Above all, the Jeffersonians fielded a strong populist element that Federalism nearly completely lacked. This "middling-sort," a conglomeration of farmers, artisans, mechanics, and day laborers, resented conservative insistence on rule by the rich and the wise. The Pickerings and, despite their moderate position on the secession question, the Cabots of early American politics never grasped this basic principle and paid the price. "They have attempted to resist the force of current public opinion, instead of falling into the current with a view to direct it," lexicographer Noah Webster reflected of late Federalism. "In this they have manifested more integrity than address."[48]

Ironically, the fate of Federalism anticipated the breakdown of southern Jeffersonianism. The post–War of 1812 wave of capitalist economics, egalitarian politics, and coastal populations pulling west established a far different "common man" ideological dynamic than the slavocracy could command. In 1860 the system fell apart and now southern voices— distrustful of Lincoln, shaken by their loss of mastery in the U.S. Congress, and anxious of free labor's growing political power—cried for secession.

Interestingly, history has dealt more kindly with the "lost cause" of southern nationhood than with the "lost cause" of New England nationhood. The romance of the Confederacy rang with cries of liberty and localism, a far remove from the decidedly unromantic corporatist, consolidation state envisioned by the Hamiltonians. For many Americans, the post-Appomattox thrust toward centralization gave Dixie a nostalgic glow against the uncertain backdrop of urbanization, industrialization, and imperialism then remaking the country. Matched against this moonlight-and-magnolias mythology, the Hartford conventioneers long ago lost any chance to claim the historiographical high ground.

Circling back to Essex, it seems appropriate to include Cabot on any short list of, if not great democrats, then certainly great unionists. In all, he proved a more constructive and substantial statesman than any post-1800 Federalist. Along with John Adams he offered the early American right a moderate alternative to the increasingly extreme politics practiced by first Hamilton and then Pickering. In forswearing these friends he showed a higher allegiance to country and to compromise.

3 Reckoning with the Original Sunbelt Right

John Quincy Adams

• •

> Finally, after all is said, our good grandpapa must always be in a
> historical point of view, the most important public figure of the half
> century, 1800–1850.
>
> —Henry Adams to Brooks Adams, 1909

Henry Adams's generous summation of his "good grandpapa['s]" contributions to American political life is all the more striking considering John
Quincy's poor historical timing. A northerner and a nationalist, the elder
Adams forged his career in the long shadow of a contentious southern,
states' rights ascendancy. For a generation he made peace enough with
the plantocracy to secure a seat in its diplomatic missions and presidential cabinets. He even managed to serve a single term in the executive
office after a trio of slaveholding Virginians had taken their turns. It was
in this capacity, and still later and more emphatically as a lowly congressman, that Adams broke with his former patrons, recognizing the
radicalism implicit in pushing slavery from coast to coast, deep into the
nineteenth century.

Comparatively, he can be linked with Theodore Roosevelt, another
moderate of a kind, who is examined in a later chapter. Both men were
recognized by contemporaries as fierce political competitors, militants in
their own way who challenged, in Adams's case, the extreme agrarian
wing of Jeffersonianism and then, in Roosevelt's, the mounting power of
the industrial elite. As such, their centrism reflected pragmatic responses
to "radical" opponents rather than inborn predispositions to compromise.
In this sense they make a special pairing in these pages as statesmen who,
though not temperamentally inclined to moderation, worked for results—
the end of slavery, the reduction of corporate authority—deemed reasonable and urgent by a growing number of Americans. Taken together, they
were combative personalities, fighting for the center.

In place of the slavocracy's backward glance, Adams sought to shake
the nation from its premodern past. His vision of what the Kentucky

statesman Henry Clay coined the "American System," shorthand for centralized economic growth under the pilot of government paternalism, promised a path to national development both more inclusive than the old Hamiltonianism and more committed to free labor than the reigning Jacksonianism (1828–54). Looking forward, the American System envisioned a country filled with industry and internal improvements, commerce and canals. It prefaced further the coming day of the social welfare state. Philosophically, the American System believed in government's responsibility to oversee an economy responsive to the needs of all citizens, foreshadowing the big idea behind Theodore Roosevelt's Square Deal and Franklin Roosevelt's New Deal.

To place Quincy Adams in a line of liberal Republican (Theodore Roosevelt) and liberal Democratic (Franklin Delano Roosevelt) presidents is to weigh in on an old historical debate. Arthur Schlesinger Jr.'s classic Pulitzer Prize–winning study, *The Age of Jackson* (1945), dismisses the American System as "rebaptized Federalism" designed to keep property and power in the hands of the few. A New Deal Democrat who wrote campaign speeches for Adlai Stevenson in the 1950s and later served in the Kennedy administration as a special assistant, Schlesinger understood American politics as a cyclical struggle between liberal and conservative interests. He regarded the populistic Andrew Jackson, enemy of the "aristocratic" Second National Bank of the United States and champion of the "common man," as FDR's (and Stevenson's and Kennedy's) true predecessor. The attack on plutocracy in the 1830s, in other words, anticipated the New Deal of the 1930s. Straining to make political personalities fit a pattern, Schlesinger portrays Quincy Adams, Jackson's opponent in two national elections, as the uncaring capitalist forerunner of Herbert Hoover. "Adams," he too neatly argues, "gave the business community its last chance."[1]

Since the 1960s, Jackson's stock has fluctuated within the historical community. Although the General has not longed for defenders, many scholars now argue that his economic programs aggressively promoted the interests of southern slavery. The Civil War has become a thorny legatee of his statecraft. Naturally the rethinking of Jackson has meant the rethinking of his opponents, too. In 1979 Daniel Walker Howe's stimulating book, *The Political Culture of the American Whigs*, inaugurated a fresh reappraisal of Quincy Adams and the partisan struggles of his times. Taking together Whiggery's influence on religious, economic, and political questions, Howe places the party at the forefront of American development. "While the Jacksonians won more presidential elections," he persuasively writes, "the Whigs probably contributed more to shaping the new industrial society of Victorian America."[2]

Despite a new awareness of Adams's ties to economic modernization, his major achievements are still generally presumed to reside in the field of foreign affairs. As secretary of state, he negotiated the acquisition of Florida, extended American power to the Pacific Northwest, and masterminded the Monroe Doctrine. His domestic record, however, deserves an equally respectful reading. Adams's concern for the treatment of African Americans and Indians, support for government investment in the nation's economy and infrastructure, and dedication to a mobile, multiethnic, free-laboring workforce staked out advanced positions familiar to us today. Unable to command either party or popular will, his presidential plans never got off the ground. Rather, the Jacksonian mania for small government, hard money, and chattel servitude limped along until the election of Lincoln. At that time southern fire-eaters nearly engineered the permanent division of the Union, the deadly fulfillment of the secessionist dreams that had once tempted the old Essex Junto.

Adams's break with the Slave Power, along with Cabot's earlier efforts to oust Madison from the presidential chair, are touchstones in the moderate tradition. Their resistance to southern rule prefaced efforts by succeeding generations of centrists to put down the Confederacy, challenge Jim Crow, and take on the post–Second World War Sunbelt right. From the southern perspective, John Quincy, long dependent upon slaveholder patronage to secure government appointments, thanklessly bit the hand that had once fed him. Adams, in turn, blamed southern radicalism for driving him away. When the Slave Power moved in the 1830s and 1840s to silence abolitionist petitions to Congress, to extend black bondage into Texas, and to war on Mexico as a prelude to a Pacific cotton kingdom, he rebelled and discovered late in life a second career as a free-labor crusader. He absolutely delighted in the task. "I was born for a controversial world and cannot escape my destiny," he once wrote. "My life must be militant to its close."[3]

The pretense of noble public struggles served to deflect the sting from painful private ones. John Quincy's brother, Charles, succumbed to alcoholism in 1800; his eldest son disappeared from the *Benjamin Franklin* in 1829, almost certainly a suicide born of insobriety; and in 1834 his middle son died at thirty-one; again, alcohol precipitated the early exit. This devastating pattern suggests, beyond the possibilities of hereditary predisposition, the colossal pressures of being an Adams. As one historian of the family writes, the exacting parental standards of John and Abigail "had the youngsters struggling with apprehension, compulsive behavior, rebelliousness, withdrawal, and depression." Unhappily, the children were made to carry the weight of history on their slender shoulders. In April 1776, as British forces invaded Boston, John Adams informed his offspring of the great duty now before them: "I hope that you will all remember, how many Losses, Dangers, and Inconveniences, have been borne by your Parents, and the Inhabitants of Boston in general for the Sake of preserving Freedom for you, and yours—and I hope you will all follow the virtuous Example if, in any future Time, your Countrys Liberties should be in Danger, and suffer every human Evil, rather than Give them up."[4]

Shortly thereafter John Quincy, all of nine but clearly going on thirty, guiltily reported to his father the nursery-day temptations that pulled him from "respectable" pursuits: "My thoughts are running after birds eggs, play and trifles, till I get vexed with myself. Mamma has a troublesome task to keep me steady, and I own I am ashamed of myself."[5] Failure to complete an impossibly rigorous study schedule occasioned this particular self-censure. Young Adams had hoped to polish off Tobias Smollett's sixteen-volume *A Complete History of England* by his tenth birthday but found himself inconveniently sidetracked by childhood. With a famous if demanding father to pave his path and a host of Smolletts on the reading docket, his options seemed limited: crack-up or prodigy. Perhaps in the name of self-preservation, he threw in his lot with the family "business." In 1794 George Washington appointed a twenty-something John Quincy American minister to the Netherlands, a post once held by his father. Thus began a pattern of nepotistic père-fils overlaps. After his Amsterdam days, John Adams went on to negotiate a peace treaty with Britain, serve as U.S. ambassador to the Court of Saint James's, and claim the presidency. His son duplicated each of these accomplishments.

Alike in occupation, the two men varied in their emotional makeup. John Quincy's exacting standards of statesmanship combined with, as his grandson Henry Adams put it, "a nasty temper" to create a mental world more rigid and less forgiving than his father's. Late in life, the senior Adams had (largely) forgotten his ancient animus with Thomas Jefferson and famously renewed their correspondence. Yet the son could never forgive a man, even *this* man, for the sin of partisanship—above all if it had brought pain to a loved one. More than a decade after the Virginian's death, John Quincy had yet to unpack his annoyance, recording a peevish postmortem aimed to reset the historical scales. "Between my father and Jefferson the final decision of that same justice was reserved for a higher state of being. The double-dealer succeeded in this world; yet his death-bed was less tranquil and composed than that of him whom he had wronged." Perhaps the American electorate had preferred Jefferson, but, if John Quincy read the Almighty right, the angels favored the company of old man Adams.[6]

John Quincy may have shared his father's hostility to political factions, but that hardly kept him from partnering with nearly every major political party in America. Federalists secured his appointment to the Netherlands, Jeffersonians made him secretary of state, National Republicans ran him for the presidency, Anti-Masons for the governor's seat of Massachusetts, and Conscience Whigs embraced his persistent rhetorical assault on the South. A self-professed "non politician," John Quincy had an artful talent for fostering a perpetual eligibility that, in fact, revealed remarkable political instincts. For the balance of his career he owed far more to party machinery than to popular mandate. After he lost a congressional campaign in 1802, the Bay State legislature coolly elevated him to the Senate, and in the contentious 1824 presidential race Adams's popular and electoral vote totals trailed Andrew Jackson's by considerable margins (113,000 to 151,000 and 84 to 99); nonetheless, in a contingent ballot prescribed by the Constitution when no candidate receives a majority of the Electoral College's votes, the House of Representatives awarded Adams the office. Jacksonians claimed that a "corrupt bargain" had deprived the people of their preferred candidate, and Adams could not forget that he served as a minority president in a democracy or that nearly 70 percent of the electorate had opposed him. John Quincy's one conspicuous success among voters, a surprising second career as a congressman (1831–48), commenced at the advanced age of sixty-four.

As a young man, Adams professed interest in a quiet, scholarly situation, but a literary life satisfied neither his driving personality nor his sense of public service. In truth, the partisanship he so passionately attacked played a vital role in sharpening his self-identity. "The country is so totally given up to the spirit of party," he fumed in 1803, "that not to follow blindfold the one or the other is an inexpiable offence. The worst of these parties [the Jeffersonian Republicans] has the popular torrent in its favor, and uses its triumph with all the unprincipled fury of a faction;

while the other [Federalism] gnashes its teeth, and is waiting with all the impatience of revenge for the time when its turn may come to oppress and punish by the people's favor." In such a dogmatic ideological climate, Adams feared for his political soul. The twin extremes of Jeffersonian democracy and Hamiltonian aristocracy demanded partisanship rather than principle and challenged his naive dreams of independence. "Between both," he laid out the dangers, "I see the impossibility of pursuing the dictates of my own conscience without sacrificing every prospect, not merely of advancement, but even of retaining that character and reputation I have enjoyed."[7] For Adams, in other words, the political center represented a kind of nondoctrinal ideal.

Inevitably, enticements came along to tempt John Quincy and sometimes got the better of the self-proclaimed nonpolitician. In 1803 he made a pledge to Massachusetts powerbrokers to support Timothy Pickering for the state's second open Senate seat, presuming he received the first. Aside from violating a personal resolution against backroom deals, his promotion of Pickering rewarded a politician who, as secretary of state, had opposed to the point of insubordination the elder Adams's French peace policy. As if to cleanse himself of this unholy pact with New England Federalism, Adams seemed positively eager to antagonize his patrons. Arriving in Washington just a few hours after the Senate voted to affirm the Louisiana Purchase, he might have respected Massachusetts's aversion to the land grab with a judicious silence. The acquisition, after all, triggered a general reversal in early republic dominance from the commercial coastal states to the agrarian interior and naturally antagonized a number of important eastern constituencies.

The bill passed twenty-four to seven with every Federalist in attendance, including Pickering, dissenting. Needlessly rubbing salt in their wounds, Adams declared his support for the purchase. He regarded the transaction as a providential opportunity to remove Napoleonic power from the New World while expanding the fledgling republic's frontier. "The alternative," he wrote years later, "was Louisiana and the mouths of the Mississippi in the possession of France, under Napoleon Bonaparte. The loss of sectional influence, [I] hoped and believed, would be more than compensated by the extension of national power and security. A fearful cause of war with France was removed. From a formidable and ambitious neighbor, she would be turned, by her altered and steadily operating interest, into a natural ally."[8] These are noble and defendable sentiments for sure, though Adams's critics occupied sound ground, too. The purchase, after all, played a role in promoting nearly sixty years of sectional divisiveness that culminated in a devastating civil war.

From the vantage of 1803 this was all very far away. Factionalism rather than sectionalism earned Adams's enmity at this time, and in the aftermath of the contentious Louisiana debates he knew his days as a Federalist were coming to a close. The *Worcester (Mass.) Aegis* agreed, predicting, "The Hon. John Quincy Adams will certainly be denounced and excommunicated by his own party." Some believed Adams wanted nothing less. Federalism's future appeared already a narrowing proposition, and serving on the national stage meant making peace with the Republicans. Boston banker Stephen Higginson, knowing something of the private demons that drove Adams, shrewdly scored the new senator for shielding, during the purchase debate, a fierce ambition behind the pretense of patriotism: "Like a kite without a Tail, he will be violent and constant in his attempts to rise . . . and will pitch to one side and the other, as the popular Currents may happen to strike."[9]

Soon thereafter, international affairs provided Adams an excuse to pitch Federalism altogether. The 1803 renewal of European warfare had initially benefited American shipping, which reaped handsome profits servicing the British, French, and Spanish empires. But in 1806 Britain threw up a "paper blockade" of Europe, insisting that vessels planning to make for the continent first submit to British inspections and obtain British trade licenses. In retaliation, Napoleon issued the Berlin and Milan decrees, which called for the seizure of neutral ships complying with the British barricade. In the summer of 1807 matters heated up considerably. Searching for deserters, the British warship *Leopard* confronted the American frigate *Chesapeake* off the coast of Norfolk, Virginia. The *Leopard's* commander, Salisbury Pryce Humphreys, requested permission to board and, when Commodore James Barron refused, he ordered several broadsides fired into the *Chesapeake*. Three of its crewmen were killed; eighteen were wounded, including Barron, while four were identified as deserters of the Royal Navy and taken to Halifax for trial. Only one, Jenkin Ratford, was a British citizen. In a special session of Congress, Jefferson declared the security of the country threatened by British actions.

Not everyone in attendance shared the president's indignation. Federalists, as we have seen, tended to regard Britain as a bulwark against the radicalism of the French Revolution and hoped to protect their commercial and cultural relations with the former mother country. "I . . . know that, in the present unexampled state of the world," wrote Timothy Pickering during this troubled period, "our own best citizens consider the interests of the United States to be interwoven with those of Great Britain, and that our safety depends on hers." Adams took a different and characteristically provocative tack. After failing to convince Boston's Hamiltonians to call a *Chesapeake* summit, he showed up at a public gathering organized by local Jeffersonians hostile to Britain. "I attended without preconcert with any one individual," he said, playing the innocent. "I was very unexpectedly to myself appointed a member of the committee, and assented to the resolutions drawn up and reported to the meeting by them." Maybe. But it does require a certain suspension of judgment to accept Adams's claim that as a sitting U.S. senator and past-president's son he expected to slip quietly into a public conference unnoticed, or that the opposition party, espying his presence, would not take advantage of it. In any case, the anti-British resolutions adopted that day in Boston were published in the local papers. "This was my unpardonable offense to Federalism," John Quincy proudly observed, "and from that day forth I was treated as an outcast from the party and marked for vengeance."[10]

Yes, but might Adams be received by the *other* party? Josiah Quincy, a congressman and prominent Massachusetts Federalist, thought not and warned Adams that, despite his timely Anglophobia, he should expect no favors from Republicans. "He said," Adams reported, "my principles were too pure for those [Jeffersonians] with whom I was acting, and *they would not thank me for them*. I told him I did not want their thanks. He said they would not *value me* the more for them. I told him I cared not whether they valued me for them or not. My character, such as it was, must stand on its own ground, and not upon the bolstering of any man or party."[11] Bold words to be sure, but Adams had already learned of high-placed Republican interest in his future. Several months before his exchange with Quincy, Adams had received from Jefferson's friend, Dr. Benjamin Rush, assurances of the president's respect for his talents. More, Jefferson had hinted of certain gifts. Would Mr. Adams consider accepting a future diplomatic post from the hand of a Virginia Republican? Might he abandon Federalism?

Adams's delicate reply to Rush amounted to an unequivocal affirmation. "I told him," John Quincy replayed the conversation, "that I . . . was obliged to Mr. Jefferson and Mr. Madison for their good opinion; that I never had, and I hoped I never should ask for any office of any man, and certainly never should solicit Mr. Jefferson for any place whatsoever; that all I could say to him was, that if Mr. Jefferson should nominate me for any office abroad to which he thought me competent, I would not refuse it merely because the nomination should come from him. He said this assurance was entirely satisfactory."[12] To be fair, more than personal ambition informed Adams's remarks to Rush. He believed Federalism selfish and slavishly beholden to its British creditors. While the Jeffersonians appeared to embrace a broad vision of expansion and national greatness, New England seemed stuck in a negating, self-centered parochialism.

The question of U.S. neutrality came to a head in December 1807, the *Chesapeake* affair being merely the most egregious example of Britain's abusive tactics. Jefferson called for an embargo of goods coming in and out of America. As observed in the previous chapter, the restraint of trade promised to wreck New England's commercial economy. Accordingly, every Federalist senator voted against the proposal, excepting Adams. "On most of the great national questions now under discussion," he recorded nine days after the passage of the Embargo Act, "my sense of duty leads me to support the administration, and I find myself of course in opposition to the federalists in general."[13] Spurned, scorned, and outmaneuvered, they repaid his defiance in full. Shortly after the embargo ballot, the Massachusetts legislature elected Boston merchant and state senator James Lloyd to replace Adams upon the expiration of his term. The vote ran solidly against the incumbent, 240 to 169; his chief support came from Bay State Republicans. The legislature further and explicitly instructed Adams to oppose Jefferson's British policy. Citing his unwillingness to do so, John Quincy used the order as a pretext to tender his resignation.

Leaving the Senate, Adams figured prominently in the thinking of Republicans eager to enlist his talents. Massachusetts's anti-Federalist governor, James Sullivan, informed Jefferson of Adams's sudden availability and eminent suitability for diplomatic work. "The federal party in this State have obtained the government. Their principal object, at present, appears to be the political and even the personal destruction of John Quincy Adams. They have yesterday come to the choice of a senator in Congress to succeed him next year. . . . It is of great consequence to the interest of Mr. Adams, and to that of your administration, to rescue him from their triumphs. I know not how this can be done otherwise than by finding him a foreign appointment of respectability."[14] A few months later, incoming president James Madison offered Adams the post of minister plenipotentiary to Russia. John Quincy accepted and, over Federalist opposition, won confirmation.

Protestations to the contrary, Adams delighted in feuding with Federalism. These battles complemented his well-petted ideological independence while connecting him rather closely to another great critic of the Hamiltonian circle, his father. Tellingly, the two Adamses rose to the presidency in periods of political flux when factions were not so powerful as to command absolute obedience. John Adams tried to adopt the Patriot King legacy left by Washington and imagined himself occupying a stable ideological center between Jeffersonianism and Hamiltonianism. Years later, the so-called Era of Good Feelings (1817–25) cleared the way for John Quincy's presidency. Following Federalism's post–War of 1812 implosion, nearly everyone assumed a generic Jeffersonianism. Monroe, a veteran of the great partisan feuds of the past, pursued a policy of "amalgamation" or "fusion," an antiparty creed in which New England's holdouts were encouraged to adopt the Virginia model. "My impression is that the Administration should rest strongly on the Republican party," he wrote shortly before his inauguration, "indulging toward [Federalism] a spirit of moderation, and evincing a desire to discriminate between its members, and to bring the whole into the republican fold as quick as possible."[15]

As Monroe's secretary of state, Adams witnessed firsthand the final destruction of Federalism as a governing force. In its wake arose a unitary political culture—"a spirit of moderation"—that briefly held out the promise of eradicating forever party distinctions in a reconfigured Jeffersonian consensus. Adams thrived during these years, taking advantage of the country's partisan-free Indian summer. His diplomatic efforts affirmed U.S. territory in the Northeast from British efforts at "rectifications," shaped the Monroe Doctrine into a defense of Western Hemispheric republics hostile to European colonialism, and produced the Adams-Onis (Transcontinental) Treaty with Spain in 1819. This last achievement was described by John Quincy's major biographer as "the greatest diplomatic victory won by any single individual in the history of the United States."[16]

If Adams shared Monroe's antiparty preference, however, he failed to emulate his success in presidential politics. The last of the Virginia Founders, Monroe ran unopposed for reelection in 1820, taking every electoral vote cast save one. Adams, by contrast, faced a balkanized politics of regions. Without viable party distinctions in 1824 he ran as a New Englander, while former Speaker of the House Henry Clay of Kentucky represented the West and Treasury Secretary William Crawford of Georgia the South. Tennessee's Andrew Jackson, though principally a creation of the Southwest, came closest of any candidate to assuming a national constituency. Although Adams claimed to respect men who transcended sectional prejudices, he regarded the General's popularity as a case of demagoguery connecting with the public's "unnatural passions" for a military man.[17] More to the point, without a dominant Virginia candidate, the short season in which a spirit of moderation might predominate had come to an end.

If Monroe valued John Quincy's studied independence as a form of fusion politics, Adams's grandson, Henry, doubted its authenticity. More than a half century after the old man's death, Henry's brother Brooks attempted to write John Quincy's biography, giving for criticism a completed draft to Henry. Though appreciative of his brother's efforts, Henry believed the manuscript blind to the opportunistic impulse that drove their grandfather; on balance, he thought it best to drop the life story altogether. In an unsparing letter to Brooks, he called John Quincy "a robber" for craftily extracting Florida from a vulnerable Spanish empire. "In my History I had to tell a part of the . . . story, and it gave me the vomit." He concluded that Adams had "deliberately acted as the tool of the slave oligarchy . . . and never rebelled until the slave oligarchy contemptuously cut his throat. . . . The sum of it . . . is . . . that he had no business to serve Jefferson or Jackson; that he knew better, that he did it for personal ambition quite as much as for patriotism."[18] The manuscript never made it to the printers.

Henry was, however, greatly attracted to his grandfather's congressional career as a slavery-baiting Cicero. After years of sustaining the South—defending the Louisiana Purchase and the War of 1812, the acquisition of Florida, and the Missouri Compromise—John Quincy felt personally aggrieved by its presidential preference for Tennessee's Jackson. Following the General's decisive 1828 victory over Adams, "life," Henry wrote, "took to him the character of tragedy. With the same old self-mortification which he and we all, more or less, inherited from Calvinism." Cut free from the South in a humiliating defeat, John Quincy sought, Henry argued, to diminish Dixie's influence on the Union, reassert the universal principles celebrated in the Declaration of Independence, and serve his Maker all in one fell swoop. Accordingly, he devoted his final public years to battling the Slave Power. Henry could not have been happier. "No man in our political history," he informed Brooks, "except [the erratic Virginia congressman] John Randolph has approached him in the rough and tumble fight of savage pure fighting. He hit and bit without scruple, and gouged, too, when he could. This was a field where his temper stood him in good service. . . . I take keen pleasure in every outburst of his malignant tongue, and wish only that it had been more malignant still. Nothing can do justice to that cotton-planting gang of brutes, with their vile crew of northern hangers on."[19] For John Quincy, the struggle against the slaveholding South proved to be the logical course of his "amalgamation" politics. After taking on a parochial Federalism, he now faced a far more powerful plantocracy.

• • • • •

A critic of slavery, John Quincy never lost his suspicion that a speculative market also undercut free labor. Though he steered clear of the genteel farmer persona adopted by his father, he remained a Country statesman at heart. "Even [as] he strongly supported economic development," notes Howe, "he despised sordid motives and remained essentially unsympathetic with the businessman's outlook." During the Panic of 1837 Adams's antipathy to the nation's financial community boiled over. The circumstances were thus: A badly inflated investment market burst, and specie-hoarding banks in New York City refused to dole out silver coinage in the course of meeting their obligations. A general slide commenced, catalyzing several years of unemployment as small-scale wildcat banks around the country collapsed. An irate Adams recommended jailing bankers who sat on their stocks.

More generally, he had long recognized that for all its dynamism, a privatized economy inevitably failed to meet a moral society's each and every need. According to his writings, he appeared quite prepared to use centralized power to oversee large public works programs, practice city planning, aid university education, and regulate a chaotic economy that lapsed into periodic "panics." In his inaugural address Adams defended the constitutionality of federally subsidized internal improvements, touting their efficacy in a rising republic. "To how many thousands of our countrymen has it proved a benefit? To what single individual has it ever proved an injury? Repeated, liberal and candid discussions in the Legislature have conciliated the sentiments and approximated the opinions of enlightened minds upon the question of constitutional power. I can not but hope that, by the same process of friendly, patient, and persevering deliberation, all constitutional objections will ultimately be removed."[20] In calling for an antebellum activist state as a pragmatic means of national development, Adams anticipated some of the more vital lines of liberalism that shaped twentieth-century political debate.

Jackson's constitutional objections to the American System and more broadly the activist state idea, by contrast, provoked his most controversial presidential action—vetoing a bill to recharter the Second National Bank of the United States. Popular sentiment solidly backed his decision, seeing the bank, with its deep pockets and presumed influence over Congress, as a threat to republican government. As one Jacksonian newspaper in Pittsburgh observed, the bank "maintains its political party, cherishes its political favorites, bribes and corrupts the public press, and unfeelingly crushes all within its reach who may be so honest and fearless to express disapprobation at its course and character." There is some truth in this critique, though it failed to reckon with the bank's more positive possibilities both as a sponsor of public works and as a brake against excessive speculation. With the bank in abeyance, unsecured lending proliferated and played a major role in creating the economic bubble that burst in 1837. This crisis only confirmed Adams's faith in the virtue of practical government intervention. "The great effort of my administration," he wrote,

> was to mature into a permanent and regular system the application of all the superfluous revenue of the Union to internal improvement—improvement which, at this day, would have afforded high wages and constant employment to hundred of thousands of laborers, and in which every dollar expended would have repaid itself fourfold in the enhanced value of the public lands. With this system, in ten years from this day, the surface of the whole Union would have been checkered over with railroads and canals.

The Jacksonian reliance on state governments and private capitalism to forge a national economy, by comparison, availed Adams as quaint, crude, and wrong. "It may still be done," he said of the localist Democratic vision, but "half a century later, and with the limping gait of State legislation and private adventure. I would have done it in the administration of the affairs of the nation." At another time he conjoined his presidential defeat with the public's resistance to centralized planning: "I fell and with me fell . . . the system of internal improvement by national energies."[21]

· · · · ·

Denied reelection, Adams returned to Quincy in the late winter of 1829 unreconciled to his forced retirement. "I go into it," he wrote, "with a combination of parties and of public men against my character and my reputation such as I believe never before was exhibited against any man since this Union existed."[22] After his own single-term presidency, John Adams seldom left home, but John Quincy was far more constitutionally inclined to the stimulation of public debate than a farm and family life allotted. His energy and drive were remarkable. He daily walked several miles, took half-mile swims in the Potomac River and Quincy Bay till nearly the age of eighty, and, apart from writing poetry, reading history, and studying the Bible, kept a diary that ran from beginning to end some several thousand pages. It wasn't enough. When the Boston *Daily Courier* advanced his name as a candidate for Congress in September 1830, he signaled distinct interest.

Adams's five presidential predecessors had all retired to their plantations and homesteads. Only Washington could be cajoled into an official capacity, commissioned in 1798 as lieutenant general and commander-in-chief of the armies expected to be raised in case the country warred with France. Though he planned for a provisional army, Washington never took the field. Then, as now, the country puzzled over what to do with its former presidents. None before—or after—Quincy Adams ever stood for a modest House seat. His family preferred its patriarch remain retired.

But when National Republicans from the Twelfth Congressional (Plymouth) District proceeded to court Adams, he met them more than halfway. Hewing to the political code of the day, he wished to simultaneously express his "availability" for the seat and reticence to claim it. Power corrupted, after all. In careful communiqués to would-be backers, he struck just the right note. "No person can be degraded by serving the people as a Representative of Congress. Nor, in my opinion, would an ex-President of the United States be degraded by serving as a Selectman of his town, if elected thereto by the people." In October he accepted the National Republican nomination with characteristic morbidity: "And so I am launched again upon the faithless wave of politics." A few weeks later Adams decisively defeated his "Old Federalist" and Jacksonian opponents to complete his political resurrection. "This call upon me by the people of the district in which I reside, to represent them in Congress, has been spontaneous," he rejoiced, "and, although counteracted by a double opposition . . . I have received nearly three votes in four throughout the district. My election as President of the United States was not half so gratifying to my inmost soul."[23]

As a congressman, John Quincy witnessed firsthand the intensification of northern abolitionism and free-soil activity on the political process. The Liberty Party, the American Missionary Association, and the American Anti-Slavery Society were just a few of the hundreds of organizations that arose in the 1830s and 1840s to condemn chattel servitude. Abolitionist literature flooded the country's mails, and proemancipation petitions swamped Congress; some 400,000 appeals arrived in the capital between the springs of 1837 and 1838 alone. Adams cultivated critical views on the peculiar institution, believing, as he once flatly put it, that "slavery is the great and foul stain upon the North American Union."[24] Yet as a moderate he had little sympathy for radical remedies, including abolitionist William Lloyd Garrison's fitful suggestion that the sections go their separate ways. Disunion, Adams believed, would compromise America's experiment in republican government, weaken the United States' ability to act as a moral force in the world, and literally destroy the country created by a generation of sacred holies that included his father. Rather than tackle slavery head-on, Adams clipped and cut. He fought a running rhetorical battle in Congress with its defenders designed to awaken northern public opinion to the coming crisis.

Remembered by some today as an eloquent emancipationist, Adams in fact offered precious little public support for abolitionism. His 1844 abuse of, as he put it, "the Colonization Society, the Anti-Slavery and Abolition Societies, the no-government, non-resisting, and women-membered societies" accurately conveyed his jaundiced view of New England's perfectionist crowd. He eyed its missionary zeal with the same skepticism his father had reserved for the Enlightenment. Concern that a radical reformism now threatened to upend Yankee civilization no doubt conditioned Adams's tart assessment, though the passing of generational dominance by the men of his set may also have played a role. His moral principles began and ended with a flinty Calvinism, and he resisted the advent of fresh spiritual expressions as faddish and dangerous. His description of Transcendentalism as the Concord magnet that attracted religious failures and political freaks is a case in point: "A young man, named Ralph Waldo Emerson, a son of my once-loved friend William Emerson, and a class-mate of my lamented son George, after failing in the every-day avocations of a Unitarian preacher and school-master, starts a new doctrine of transcendentalism, declares all of the old revelations superannuated and worn out, and announces the approach of new revelations and prophecies. Garrison and the non-resistant abolitionists, Brownson and the Marat Democrats, phrenology and animal magnetism, all come in, furnishing each some plausible rascality as an ingredient for the bubbling cauldron of religion and politics."[25] But if Adams hoped to quiet the "cauldron" of reform, the reformers themselves prized John Quincy's congressional defiance of the planters and never ceased initiating overtures to cultivate a closer connection. Their quarry held back. He no more wanted to belong to the "party" of abolition than those of Federalism, Jeffersonianism, Jacksonianism, or Whiggery.

In due time, however, circumstances tipped Adams's hand. The Texas War for Independence (1835–36) brought American settlers to power, and they soon sought annexation into the United States, a move that threatened to balloon the Cotton Belt. One might have expected John Quincy to side with those mainly southern interests advocating incorporation. As secretary of state, after all, he had orchestrated a remarkable expansionist policy that brought into the Union territories from the Gulf to the Pacific. A case can be made that Texas statehood, achieved in December 1845, was the logical outcome of these efforts. Adams, however, saw the situation very differently. He presumed that the purchase of Spanish lands a generation earlier had strengthened the nation, but that seizing Mexican lands beyond the Sabine River, where slavery would surely be introduced, threatened free labor, the American System, and indeed the Union. In 1836, a decade before the Mexican War, Adams accurately predicted the violent outcome of America's Texas fever. "You," he goaded his congressional colleagues, "are now rushing into war— into a war of conquest, commenced by aggression on your part, and for the re-establishment of slavery, where it had been abolished, throughout the Mexican Republic. . . . In that war, sir, the banners of *freedom* will be the banners of Mexico, and your banners, I blush to speak the word, will be the banners of slavery."[26]

Over a fractious decade, the years bookended by Texas's independence and statehood, the divide between North and South widened. In the late winter of 1837, in his final days as president, Jackson, upon a contested twenty-three to nineteen recommendation from the Senate, recognized the Lone Star republic as an independent nation; in the late winter of 1845, in *his* last days as president, John Tyler, upon an equally contested twenty-seven to twenty-five joint resolution by the Senate, oversaw the controversial annexation of Texas. Ten months later, under Tyler's successor, James Polk, Texas became the twenty-eighth state.

Once a believer in manifest destiny, Adams saw in the Texas outcome the old Revolutionary-era promise of equal rights giving way to a slaveholder's republic. Accordingly, he ceaselessly hectored the South from his House seat. He once brought to the floor a petition from a Massachusetts constituent calling for the break-up of the United States as it "does not present prospects of reciprocal benefits . . . because a vast proportion of the resources of one section of the Union is annually drained to sustain the views and course of another section without any adequate return." Southern Whigs met that same evening and drafted a censure resolution condemning their colleague for advocating "the destruction of our country and the crime of high treason." Savoring the opportunity to defend himself, Adams geared up for a lengthy debate. Abusing his accusers while attacking slaveholders and their congressional retainers, he put into sharp relief the welter of painful issues that faced a fast-dividing nation. "He spares no one," reported a House clerk. "He has exhibited more temper, more obstinacy, & more desire to attack everybody, friend & foe indiscriminately, than I ever saw either him or any other mortal exhibit before." A thin House majority, wanting to end the spectacle, quickly proposed a motion to set aside the censure resolution. Out of nearly 200 votes cast, it passed by a meager 13.[27]

Convinced that the South meant to export its economy west by right or by revolution, John Quincy commenced a counterrebellion. In a series of prodding public actions he confronted both sections, hoping to arouse northern opinion while embarrassing southern. In 1838 he wrote a laudatory introduction to a biography of the martyred Massachusetts minister-journalist Elijah Lovejoy, murdered by a mob in Alton, Illinois, for publishing abolitionist material. "Led by his destiny, in the pursuit of happiness, and in the fulfillment of his religious and moral duties, to the western region of his country," Adams wrote, "he there fell a victim to the fury of a band of ruffians, stung to madness, and driven to despair, for the fate of their darling Slavery, by the terrors of a printing press. That an American citizen, in a state whose Constitution repudiates all Slavery, should die a martyr in defence of the freedom of the press, is a phenomenon in the history of this Union. It forms an era, in the progress of mankind towards universal emancipation."[28]

Three years later Adams defended before the Supreme Court Sengbe Pieh and dozens of other Mende peoples kidnapped by slave traders in Sierra Leone. While being transported in Cuban waters aboard *La Amistad,* a two-masted schooner owned by a Spaniard living in Cuba, the Africans overpowered the crew and took control of the ship. Not long afterward it turned up in U.S. waters near Long Island, New York. The Spanish government demanded that the schooner and its cargo be restored to the Kingdom of Spain. The U.S. District Court for Connecticut ruled, however, that an 1817 treaty between Britain and Spain recognized the illegality of the Atlantic slave trade. It found in favor of the Africans. On the order of President Van Buren, then facing a difficult reelection campaign and hoping to shore up southern support, the U.S. Attorney for the District of Connecticut appealed to the U.S. Circuit Court. In April 1840 it sustained the lower court's ruling. Consequently, the U.S. Attorney's office appealed to the Supreme Court. There, Adams addressed the justices twice, over some eight hours. "Little did I imagine," he later recalled, "that I should ever again be required to claim the right of appearing in the capacity of an officer of this Court; yet such has been the dictate of my destiny—and I appear again to plead the cause of justice."[29] Eight days after Adams concluded his oral argument the court ruled seven to one to uphold the earlier decisions—the Mende captives were freed.

During these contentious years John Quincy successfully rallied northern congressional support to overturn the infamous gag rule, which prohibited the discussion of abolitionist appeals in Congress. Noting the First Amendment's guarantee "to petition the Government for a redress of grievances," abolitionists had routinely sent to their congressional representatives appeals condemning slavery. In response, proslavery men began in 1835 to marshal through Congress a spate of rules that worked to automatically table such communications, thus preventing their being read. The committee that put this legal machinery into motion maintained that because "it is extremely important and desirable, that the agitation of this subject should be finally arrested, for the purpose of restoring tranquility to the public mind . . . all petitions, memorials, resolutions, propositions, or papers, relating in any way, or to any extent whatsoever, to the subject of slavery or the abolition of slavery, shall, without being either printed or referred, be laid on the table and that no such further action whatever shall be had thereon." Adams responded by denouncing the gag decree and aimed toward its end. "I hold the resolution," he asserted, "to be a direct violation of the Constitution of the United States, the rules of this House, and the rights of my constituents." By bringing a notorious attention to the issue, Adams helped to popularize public fear above the Mason-Dixon line that slavery represented a grave danger to the civil liberties of free citizens. In December 1844, the rule was finally rescinded, 108–80.[30]

Such battles gave John Quincy the reputation of a secret abolitionist. His pragmatic nationalism, however, preceded his moral impulse. Adams's dread of slavery's expansion dated to the Missouri debates of the early 1820s and to his conversations at that time with cabinet colleague John C. Calhoun of South Carolina. Recalled today as a fierce antebellum defender of slavery and states' rights, Calhoun had won a reputation before the Missouri crisis as a nationalist; indeed, in 1816 he favored the creation of the Second Bank of the United States, federally financed internal improvements, and a protective tariff to aid industry—three pillars of post–War of 1812 centralization. "When our manufactures are grown to a certain perfection as they soon will under the fostering care of government," Calhoun stated at the time in a declaration that could just as easily have come from Adams, "the farmer will find a ready market for his surplus produce; and what is almost of equal consequence, a certain and cheap supply of all his wants. His prosperity will diffuse itself to every class in the community."[31]

Like Calhoun, Adams had supported the admission of Missouri into the United States. Yet their exchanges, carried out against the broader backdrop of a sectionally divided Congress, caused him to doubt both his longstanding views and the long-term health of the country. On one of their evening walks, Calhoun had observed to Adams that slavery was the surest guarantee of white equality. It was at that point, Adams later recorded, that he began to understand that to the southern mind liberty was inconceivable without black bondage, and that the South would never voluntarily relinquish slavery. This realization produced a great turn in Adams's thinking. "I have favored this Missouri Compromise, believing it to be all that could be effected under the present Constitution, and from extreme unwillingness to put the Union at hazard," he wrote in the late winter of 1820. "But perhaps it would have been a wiser as well as a bolder course to have persisted in the restriction upon Missouri, till it should have terminated in a convention of the States to revise and amend the Constitution." And what did Adams believe the likely outcome of such a convention to be? The splintering of the nation. "This would have produced a new Union of thirteen or fourteen states unpolluted with slavery, with a great and glorious object to effect, namely, that of rallying to their standard the other States by the universal emancipation of their slaves. If the Union must be dissolved slavery is precisely the question upon which it ought to break."[32]

The Union endured, of course, but only for another generation. During much of this time a pessimistic Adams, his conception of a progressive free-labor republic compromised, his anxieties over eventual disunion yearly heightened, and his own private political aspirations reduced to a house seat, repeatedly predicted the nation's death. In the midst of the Texas debates, in the privacy of his notes, he clarified his personal views on slavery and the Union as never before: "If the most ardent desire, and a most vivid hope of the total extinction of Slavery on Earth, and especially at no distant day throughout this North American Union, constitutes an abolitionist, I am one, to the extent of readiness to lay down my life in the cause."[33]

While a combination of principled concerns drove Adams to take on the Slave Power, he nevertheless delighted in one last great fight. Surveying his southern congressional opposition, he wrote with a scarcely concealed pride that "one hundred members of the House represent slaves; four-fifths of whom would crucify me if their votes could erect the cross." The underdog role suited him until the end. "What can I . . . with a shaking hand, a darkening eye, a drowsy brain, and with all my faculties dropping from me one by one, as the teeth are dropping from my head," he brooded late in life, "what can I do for the cause of God and man, for the progress of human emancipation? . . . Yet my conscience presses me on; let me but die upon the breach." He didn't have long to wait. On 21 February 1848, shortly after voting nay on a measure to acclaim veterans of recent battles in Mexico, John Quincy collapsed, suffering from a cerebral hemorrhage. Two days later, in the Speaker's Room of the Capital Building, he died. His solemn ode to Lovejoy—"Such men are often fated to be martyrs"— might well have been carved upon his own exposed headstone, lying in the family's Quincy crypt, feet away from his father.[34]

· · · · ·

The martyrdom of John Quincy has long passed. His mind is more recognizable to us than that of his great antagonist, Jackson. Although the

Tennessean's efforts to extend slavery, remove Native Americans from their southeastern lands, and promote a banking system based on hard money made him a popular if controversial figure of his times, Americans today are far less willing to embrace the General. In Jackson we see the forerunner to the problematic imperial presidency complex and a literal and symbolic racism that continues to haunt our country.

Adams, by contrast, strikes a more modern note on a number of critical issues. If we still contest the *degree* of federal aid to the economy, we no longer debate that it has *some* role; and John Quincy's insistence on humane treatment for Native peoples and denouncement of the Indian Removal Act of 1830 ("we have talked of benevolence and humanity . . . but none of this benevolence is felt where the right of the Indian comes in collision with the interest of the white man"), align closely with contemporary cultural sensibilities.[35] Finally, the vast public works projects that have spilled across the American landscape are philosophically akin to Adams's elaborate vision of centralized support for transportation, finance, and manufacturing. In many and important ways, our America is more John Quincy's than Andrew Jackson's.

If Old Hickory and his heirs dominated antebellum politics it is largely because their opponents, be they National Republicans, Anti-Masons, or Whigs, were unable to develop a compelling response to the Jacksonian embrace of frontier democracy. Undoubtedly the patrician Adams offered little help on this score—Jacksonians successfully portrayed him as a blue blood fundamentally tone deaf to the laboring class's perspective. To be relevant in the age of the "common man," the moderate persuasion would have to venture beyond the province of a few dynastic New England families. Within a few years, this is precisely what happened. Not long after John Quincy's death a new Republican Party, conceived as a brake to the ultraconservatism coming from the South, adopted the basic tenets of the American System. Sensitive to the free-labor politics practiced by more liberal northern Whigs, Abraham Lincoln led that coalition to a great victory over the aristocratic principles long the source of southern power.

4 The Jeffersonian Origins of the GOP

Abraham Lincoln

. . . .

> Bearing in mind that about seventy years ago, two great political parties were first formed in this country, that Thomas Jefferson was the head of one of them, and Boston the head-quarters of the other, it is both curious and interesting that those [in the Republican Party who are] supposed to descend politically from [Federalism] should now be celebrating [Jefferson's] birthday . . . while those claiming political descent from him, have nearly ceased to breathe his name everywhere.
>
> —Abraham Lincoln, 1859

John Quincy's resistance to southern rule constituted an important if transitory phase in the antislavery crusade. As a Patriot King, as an Adams, he raised hell from on high, a cut above the crisis below. But no more could New England's patrician class expect to collect upon the public's fidelity to the "better sort"; the democratization of northern life, after all, demanded of its leaders a different style of politics. With an electorate increasingly informed by small-scale farmers, merchants, and mechanics, the post-Revolutionary experiment in American freedom moved decisively toward a populistic tone of partisanship. "No doubt the cost that America paid for this democracy was high," historian Gordon S. Wood has written, "with its vulgarity, its materialism, its rootlessness, its anti-intellectualism. But there is no denying the wonder of it and the real earthly benefits it brought to the hitherto neglected and despised masses of common laboring people."[1] The nation's evolving political culture, in other words, would never make room for another Adams.

What this rising middle class meant for American conservatism in the late antebellum period has caused no little confusion. In the popular mind the modern Republican Party, born in 1854, stands as ideological heir to Federalism. But this is a selective and incomplete connection that focuses on perceptions of what the GOP became *after* the Civil War, rather than on what it was *before*. Thus the postbellum decades, a Gilded Age of corporate collusions and political corruptions, comes to stand for Republicanism writ large, the robber baron beneficiaries of Hamilton's industrial dream. In fact, the party's less-studied Jeffersonian origins suggest a more complex makeup. The Enlightenment's promise of natural-law liberalism and its bold rights-of-man rhetoric touched the GOP deeply in its formative years. That is to say, the designation "Republican" in Lincoln's day signified a clear and conspicuous intent to connect with the Jeffersonian Republicans of the past.

But more than a name linked new Republicanism with old. The ripening free-soil movement of the 1850s embraced Jefferson's epigrammatic avowal that "all men are created equal" as the rallying cry of common-man democracy. And thus, as the aegis of petty artisans and agrarians, it claimed a more direct descent from Jeffersonian principles than the caste-ridden clash of slave, cracker, and master lodged below the Mason-Dixon line. Among the GOP's first generation, this liberal lineage looked perfectly clear. Eliding over Jefferson's conflicted reaction to the peculiar institution, one Republican newspaper in Pennsylvania asserted on the eve of the Civil War that "no person ever denounced American slavery in plainer English than did Thomas Jefferson."[2] In truth, however, the natural-rights character of 1790s Republicanism coexisted uneasily with another and no less formidable impulse deeply embedded in that persuasion's makeup: slavery's protection as *the* vital right in southern life. Accordingly, the nation's 1861 implosion exposed not so much one section's misreading of the Jeffersonian tradition as the impossibility of conflicting Jeffersonian traditions to serve both sections.

The battle for Jefferson's legacy commenced not long after Federalism's collapse. Especially in the infrastructure-starved West did Jeffersonianism grow beyond a negating—read southern—conception of states' rights to accommodate an emerging system of internal improvements. In an 1818 congressional speech touting the efficacy of domestic manufacturing, the Kentucky nationalist Henry Clay professed it "the opinion of Mr. Jefferson, that, although there was no general power vested, by the constitution in Congress to construct roads and canals, without the consent of the states, yet such a power might be exercised with their assent." Quincy Adams subsequently concurred with Clay's observation, calling in his 1825 inaugural address for the promotion of internal improvements "within the limits of the constitutional power of the Union."[3] He had no doubt that during the previous quarter century of Republican rule these "limits" had been sensibly enlarged by the Virginia dynasty. To future Whigs Clay and

Adams, that is, Jeffersonianism at its best embraced a grand continental vision eager to engage the potential of government paternalism.

If not altogether correct, neither were they altogether wrong. As an out-of-power opponent of Federalism in the 1790s, Jefferson distrusted government's encroachment on private liberties, but as president, his fear of foreign intervention aroused a latent nationalism. During the Napoleonic Wars, as noted, Jefferson watched the British and French navies abuse American neutrality in their lawless confiscation of U.S. commerce. In response, he backed a stunningly comprehensive approach to internal improvements later to be claimed by Whigs as the genesis of Clay and Quincy Adams's American System. Jefferson's program called for canals around the falls of the Susquehanna, Potomac, and James Rivers, a host of accesses leading from the Allegheny, Monongahela, and Tennessee Rivers, and, in the name of locating western farmers within the orbit of eastern markets, a National Road connecting Cumberland, Maryland, with (ultimately) Vandalia, Illinois. Jefferson further proposed a constitutional amendment empowering Congress to appropriate funds for public education and internal transportation, all of which would have effectually expanded federal authority.

Jeffersonian nationalism, later to be embraced by Lincoln Republicanism, flourished during the Madison presidency as well. Continued fear of American dependence on European markets prompted the progressives of this 1810–20 generation to aggressively support domestic industry. In his first inaugural address Madison urged Congress "to promote by authorized means, improvements friendly to agriculture, to manufactures, and to external as well as internal commerce." As historian Jack Rakove has observed, "To arch-Republicans of the old school, Madison seemed to be flirting with Hamiltonian Federalism." But outside of this "old school" cadre Madison's proposals and their implementation caused little dissent within his party. Jeffersonians understood in 1816, the year Congress instituted the first protective tariff and chartered the Second National Bank of the United States, that the country, repeatedly raided and invaded in the War of 1812, needed a diversified economy, dependable home markets, and military security. Broadly speaking, this meant a significant amplification of the country's manufacturing base complemented by a nationwide network of improvements. Backing Madison's postwar program, Jefferson anticipated Whig and Republican aspirations toward commercial prosperity. Or, as he put the matter to one correspondent in 1816, "He . . . who is now against domestic manufacture, must be for reducing us either to dependence on [a] foreign nation, or to be clothed in skins, and to live like wild beasts in dens and caverns. I am not one of these; experience has taught me that manufactures are now as necessary to our independence as to our comfort."[4]

· · · · ·

Many second-generation Jeffersonians claimed Andrew Jackson as rightful heir to the Republicanism of the 1790s, but Jefferson's leading lieutenants, indeed Jefferson himself, had disparaged the comparison. Jackson's steep expansion of executive power, strictures against internal improvements, and veto of a bill to extend the life of Madison's Second Bank of the United States cut against various Virginia dynasty initiatives. Unlike Quincy Adams, who thrived under Republican patronage, the old Republican powerbrokers had little use for Jackson, whom they regarded as an intemperate, even volatile personality. To an 1807 request that the Tennessean be appointed to the Russian mission, Jefferson flatly refused, offering in the withholdance an acid complaint: "Why, good God! he would breed you a quarrel before he had been there a month!" Jefferson later opposed Jackson's 1824 presidential bid, confiding to Massachusetts congressman Daniel Webster that the General was "one of the most unfit men I know of for such a place. He has had very little respect for laws or constitutions,—& is in fact merely an able military chief." John Quincy's victory in that contest, Jefferson subsequently attested, settled the question of "whether we are at last to end our days under a civil or a military government," mercifully in favor of the former.[5]

Jackson fared little better with Madison and Albert Gallatin, Jefferson's treasury secretary. Both men supported Henry Clay's 1832 presidential bid to unseat the General, whose impatient nature and martial predisposition drew their concern. Gallatin warned that "whatever gratitude we owe [Jackson] for his eminent military services, he is not fitted for the office of first magistrate of a free people and to administer a government of laws." Once in office, Jackson accentuated the divide between old and new Republicans, the latter now known as Democrats, by rotating many of his predecessor's appointments out of office. James Monroe, offended by the presumption that he had presided over anything less than a "clean" administration, complained to former naval secretary Samuel Southard of "the removal of my many friends from office."[6] In Monroe's mind, Jackson's shabby treatment of Republican officeholders resembled the earlier and presumably necessary exclusion of Federalists from government posts a generation earlier.

The defining struggle of Jackson's presidency proved to be the 1832 Bank War. And here again the new Democrats, defenders of an increasingly southern, conservative, and states' rights vision, seemed out of tune with the old Enlightenment-tinctured Republicanism. Briefly, Jacksonians feared the power of centralized banking and sought to end the government's employment of public funds housed in the Second National Bank. So concerned were they of the corrupting properties of credit and speculation that they promoted a hard-money alternative designed to, in effect, take the country's finances back to bullion. Jackson's supporters repeated Jefferson's dated criticisms of Hamiltonianism while ignoring more germane evidence that both during and after his presidency Jefferson had made peace with the nation's banking system. Though Jackson's fellow Tennessean, James Polk, claimed that "the political principles of Thomas Jefferson . . . can never be overturned or destroyed by the corrupt power of an irresponsible corporation which seeks by its money to controul public affairs," the political principles of Jefferson had in fact rather easily accommodated the country's national banks. Wary of *Federalism*'s bank in the 1790s, he later accepted it as a *Republican* bank. He subsequently voiced no constitutional objections to a bill creating its successor in 1816, and he turned to its Richmond branch in 1817 for a personal loan of $3,000.[7]

Now, less then a generation later, having vetoed a bill to extend the life of the Second National Bank, Jackson looked to bypass its offices in its final years of operation by ordering federal monies to be deposited in state banks. Secretary of the Treasury Louis McLane refused to go along with this constitutionally dubious command and was shuffled off to the State Department; his successor, William Duane, also resisted and was sacked. Jackson then nominated Attorney General Roger Taney to the post, and though the Senate never confirmed his appointment, Taney carried out the president's orders as acting secretary. For his controversial crusade against the bank, Jackson received a senatorial censure, the only president to receive such a reprimand. While this debate brewed, Clay denounced Jackson's entire White House record as a sharp and perilous break from his Republican predecessors. "The Indians and Indian policy, internal improvements, . . . the Supreme Court, Congress, the banks, have successively experienced the attacks of his haughty and imperious spirit," he argued. "And if he tramples the bank in the dust, my word for it, we shall see him quickly in chase of some new subject of his vengeance. This is the genuine spirit of conquerors and of conquest."[8]

Circumstances proved Clay more or less correct. From Polk's projection of American power into Mexico, to the disastrous Dred Scott denial of Congress's authority to keep slaves out of the nation's territories, to James Buchanan's ill-conceived presidential push to bring Kansas into the union with slavery, a host of Jacksonians sought to ensure the future of unfree labor in the United States by circumventing popular opinion. Amid this assault Clay argued accurately enough in a Norfolk, Virginia, address, "The democratic party of the present day profess to be of the Jefferson School, and yet they are carrying out the principles against which he warned them many years ago:—They are upholding the extension of Executive power."[9]

Clay's admonition underscored the underlying dissonance among Jeffersonianism's multiple wings. Its chaotic mix of yeoman farmers, urban immigrants, and southern slaveholders produced a coalition of contradictions. Once the Hamiltonian threat had passed, conflicts of policy, aspiration, and interest were bound to bloom. The party's New York wing, in particular, thought its vision of a free-labor future now due. The Virginia–New York "axis" had, after all, agreed in 1791 to jointly oppose Federalism and Burr's bringing the Empire State into the Republican fold ensured its initial national success in the 1800 elections. Later, George Clinton, eager to break Virginia's hold on the presidency, had to make do serving two terms as vice president, while his nephew De Witt captured the majority of northern states from Madison in the 1812 campaign. Long before the rise of Lincoln, in other words, supporters of the quasi-aristocratic Clintons had demonstrated a brewing disenchantment with the southern ascendancy.

Despite its anti-Hamiltonian origins, much of southern Republicanism shared Federalism's suspicion of government by the people. These elite enclaves favored a politics of deference and were intensely skeptical of the Enlightenment's "all men are created equal" assurances. In a speech written in the early 1840s, John C. Calhoun had argued, "It is a great and dangerous error to suppose that all people are equally entitled to liberty. It is a reward to be earned, not a blessing to be gratuitously lavished on all alike;—a reward reserved for the intelligent, the patriotic, the virtuous and deserving." In his 1854 study, *Sociology for the South*, Virginia social theorist George Fitzhugh maintained that slavery produced a superior civilization precisely because of its antidemocratic tendencies, and he denounced the populistic struggle for status in the North. "In free society," he wrote, "none but the selfish virtues are in repute, because none other help a man in the race of competition. In such society virtue loses all her loveliness, because of her selfish aims. Good men and bad men have the same end in view: self-promotion, self-elevation."[10]

Agreeing with the argument for inequality, important segments of southern Republicanism quietly quit their northern collaborators, and though Jefferson continued to be held up as something of a patron saint of the section, its more conservative elements drifted toward the philosophical principles espoused by Calhoun, Fitzhugh, and Virginia's John Randolph. The latter fancied himself an "Old Republican," ever true to the anti-Hamiltonianism of the 1790s. Once a Jeffersonian, he broke with Jefferson after the president and his party gained power and set about, with the controversial embargo of American shipping, entry into the War of 1812 and the levying of a federal tariff, expanding the sphere of centralized authority. As early as 1806 he had complained, "The old Republican party is already ruined, past redemption. New men and new maxims are the order of the day." And when war with Britain loomed, Randolph condemned the Jeffersonians in a congressional address for being Federalists in disguise. "I know not how gentlemen, calling themselves republicans, can advocate such a war. . . . Republicans were . . . [once] unwilling to trust a standing army even to his hands [Washington's] who had given proof that he was above all human temptation."[11]

As cultural critics, Randolph, Calhoun, and Fitzhugh believed that the United States suffered under the influence of twin evils, the French and Industrial Revolutions. These powerful challenges to traditional agrarian life, they argued, provoked political radicalism, encouraged spiritual agnosticism, and trended toward a corrupting materialism. Many southern churches shared these suspicions, treating the first movements of American modernism as heresies exported from the North. In 1862 the Reverend Joel Tucker observed from his Fayetteville, North Carolina, pulpit, "a conflict of truth with error—of the Bible with Northern infidelity—of a pure Christianity with Northern fanaticism—of liberty with despotism—of right with might." Also during the war, the Reverend W. A. Cave, rector of St. John's Episcopal Church in Tallahassee, Florida, informed his congregation that "we have failed to lay the stress of the argument on the right and duty of society to care for all its members, placing all in the positions for which God fitted them, partly because our minds have to some degree been infected by the virus of Red Republican theory which has made the social system at the North rotten to the core." In criticizing the progressive religions of the North, the liberal theologies of Unitarianism and Universalism as well as the more exotic strains of spiritualism, mesmerism, and Swedenborgianism, conservative southern clergy stressed the reality of sin, the inescapability of human depravity, and the virtue of tradition. Accordingly, in both the southern ecclesiastical and political worlds, a mounting rebellion against the direct democracy rhetoric of the 1790s had long shaped the region.[12]

The enveloping traditionalism of southern church and state found a receptive audience among the section's folk. Whereas northern opinion grew anxious over the machinations of the Slave Power, many southerners detected a different kind of conspiracy—the American System. In the thickening network of banks, speculative markets, and paper money stood a vigorous challenge to the older agricultural cosmology. Polk observed in the American System an ambitious scheme to unfairly aid elites all the while expanding central state suzerainty. Its supporters, he argued, sought "to encourage large and extravagant expenditures, and thereby to increase the public patronage, and maintain a rich and splendid government at the expense of a taxed and impoverished people." Government's current composition as the "plain, cheap, and simple confederation of States" envisioned by the Founders, he continued, would devolve, if the nationalists had their way, into "a consolidated empire, depriving the States of their reserved rights and the people of their just power and control in the administration of their Government."[13]

Polk's doomsaying conformed to southern Jacksonian fears that neither states' rights nor slavery could survive in an American System–dominated economy. The region's Republicans reacted with a sharp ideological shift, becoming a more conspicuously proplanter party increasingly interested in pushing the peculiar institution deeper into the nation's territories. As long as the American System and accompanying disputes about banks and credit comprised the principal points of debate, Jeffersonians on either side of the Mason-Dixon line had more or less occupied common ground. But the insertion of the slavery question into the center of American life poisoned their relations. As the Texas debates of the 1830s and 1840s began to hypersectionalize politics, the southern republicanism of Calhoun, Fitzhugh, and Randolph came to the fore, encouraging free-labor Jeffersonians to rethink their partnership with the Slave Power.

· · · · ·

Ratifications of the Treaty of Guadalupe Hidalgo were exchanged by the United States and Mexico on 26 May 1848. Four days earlier, Democrats had opened their presidential nominating convention in Baltimore. It proved to be a raucous affair. Former president Martin Van Buren and his New York allies sought to suppress the slave question in national politics. Instead, they were exasperated by their southern colleagues' eagerness to make slavery's exodus west the sine qua non of party loyalty. Hoping to recapture the nomination that he had first won in 1836 as Jackson's successor and then as an incumbent in 1840, Van Buren was instead shelved by a faction of his party favorable to Michigan senator Lewis Cass. An advocate of popular sovereignty, that is, permitting slavery into a territory if supported by its population, Cass won the crucial assent of southern conventioneers.

Their decision proved costly. Van Buren's Empire State supporters refused to back Cass. Instead, they moved toward an all-out rebellion. As one pro–Van Buren newspaper put it, the irreconcilables' remedy "consists in deserting a party, rending asunder all its ties, and planting [itself] upon those just and true principles upon which all republics must be based."[14] For their apostasy, regular Democrats denounced the bolters as "Barnburners," a reference to an old Dutch tale about the farmer who foolishly set fire to his barn in order to run off a few rats. Whereas Democrats saw this renegade faction as practicing an extreme politics, the short-lived Free Soil Party embraced the Barnburners by giving its nomination to a willing Van Buren. Though he captured no electors in the fall race, Van Buren siphoned off enough popular votes in New York (26 percent) to perhaps throw it and the presidency to the Whig Zachary Taylor. More telling, his candidacy offered a template for northern Democrats to abandon their old party allegiances if southerners rode the slave issue too hard.

These Jacksonians, found throughout the North but particularly thick in New York and Ohio, shared the northern Whig reading of Jeffersonianism. They too abhorred inherited privilege and emphasized the virtue of the producing class. As one northern Democratic congressman put it, with a disdainful swipe at his southern colleagues, a white laboring man in America "feel[s] a sense of humiliation when he looks up to the vast distances between himself and the lordly planter, in the shadow of whose aristocratic possessions he lives as an inferior, if not a dependent." Jacksonian antislavery picked up steam in the 1840s, though its central argument against "aristocratic" privilege began a decade earlier in the contest over the National Bank. If northern Whigs and Democrats had fought fiercely against each other on that line, however, they now found common ground on the question of slavery's extension west. Whiggery injected an evangelical and self-consciously moralistic style of debate into the antislavery crusade while, as historian Jonathan H. Earle has noted, their colleagues from across the aisle advanced "arguments, rooted in Jacksonian notions of egalitarian democracy."[15] Combined, they built a growing front against the plantocracy founded on the principle of free soil.

Perhaps the most significant northern Democratic contribution to the antislavery cause was the Wilmot Proviso, a rider to a bill appropriating money for peace negotiations with Mexico proposed by Pennsylvania congressman David Wilmot. The proviso called for slavery's exclusion from any territories that might be gained from the Mexican War and shaped the terms of sectional debate that held until the Civil War. Hardly the work of one man, the amendment emerged from discussions among several antislavery Jacksonians. As Wilmot later remembered, the controversial speech that he read before Congress was "the result of our united labors." With a nod to northern Whiggery, the address stressed the Enlightenment principles that shaped the nation and included language fashioned from Jefferson's Northwest Ordinance.[16] Against southern opposition, both the amendment and the broader bill passed the House but the former died in the Senate.

Nearly four years later, with the proviso debate still troubling the southern psyche, representatives from nine Dixie states convened in Nashville and recommended that the old Missouri Compromise line permitting slavery below the parallel 36 degrees 30 minutes north be extended to the Pacific, thus ensuring the planters a cotton kingdom that reached across California. A symbol of southern nationalism, the Nashville Convention led to a spate of congressional bills designed to ease sectional tensions. But this so-called Compromise of 1850, in fact an armistice, as historian David Potter noted some years ago, merely delayed rather than prevented war.[17] Southerners were dismayed to see in the legislation California's free-soil statehood; northerners detested the Fugitive Slave Act, a provision that compelled law enforcement officials to aid in the arrest and rendition of runaway slaves. Voting on the several bills generally followed along sectional rather than party lines.

This precarious peace held a scant three years. In 1854 the usually adroit Illinois senator, Stephen Douglas, made a colossal political miscalculation. Envisioning a transcontinental railroad cutting across newly opened prairie lands, he introduced a bill to organize the Nebraska Territory. But Nebraska sat north of the old Missouri Compromise line and was thus closed to slavery, and Douglas needed southern support to pass the bill. He thus imbedded in the legislation an implicit annulment of the 1820 act by calling for resident settlers to determine the fate of slavery in their territories. His logic? The principle of 1850—popular sovereignty— had replaced the principle of 1820—exclusion. This concession failed, however, to appease southern senators. They held out for, and eventually secured, an explicit repeal of the 1820 bill. In other words, land once closed to slavery might now be opened.

In the following election cycle, incumbent northern Democrats paid for this "betrayal" with their political blood, losing dozens of house seats. Across the free states, fears that a Solid South endeavored to impose slavery throughout the frontier began to reach a critical consensus. Abraham Lincoln, a one-term Whig congressman now some five years out of office, credited the Nebraska firestorm with pulling him back into politics. "I look upon that enactment not as a *law*," he insisted, "but as *violence* from the beginning. It was conceived in violence, passed in violence, is maintained in violence, and is being executed in violence."[18] If Lincoln hoped to formally oppose the new politics, he would have to find a new party. The repeal of the Missouri Compromise severed Whiggery along sectional lines, and from its northerly remains emerged a number of Anti-Nebraska, nativist, and abolitionist coalitions, their ranks augmented by perhaps a quarter of former Democrats. These forces would soon fuse into a revived Republicanism.

Those free-state Democrats who left Jacksonianism did so for numerous reasons. Some, as we have noted, resented the plantocracy's aristocratic pretensions, others were profoundly disturbed by the immorality of slavery while still others, holding the more generally racist views of the day, wanted to preserve the western territories for white free labor. Perhaps most were offended by the blatant attempt of southern Democrats to circumvent both law and logic by exporting the peculiar institution through extra legal means. "Border Ruffians" in Missouri tried through violence and voter fraud to foist a territorial constitution supportive of slavery upon neighboring Kansas; a prosouthern Supreme Court engineered the Dred Scott decision; and, more broadly, northern Jacksonians had wearied of their southern associates' increasing influence in territorial affairs. Wilmot undoubtedly spoke for a good many of them when he complained to Franklin Pierce in 1852, "I am jealous of the *power* of the South. . . . The South holds no prerogative under the Constitution, which entitles her to wield forever the Scepter of Power in this Republic, to fix by her own arbitrary edict, the principles & policy of this government, and to build up and tear down at pleasure. . . . Yet so dangerous do I believe to be the spirit and demands of the *Slave Power,* so insufferable its arrogance, if I saw the way open to strike an effectual & decisive blow against its domination at this time, I would do so, even at the temporary loss of other principles."[19]

True to his word, Wilmot struck "an effectual and decisive blow" against the planter complex by leaving the Democratic Party. He was joined by fellow Jeffersonians of various political persuasions, the Jefferson who hoped to bar slavery from the territories, who popularized the Enlightenment ideal of human equality, and who helped to eliminate Virginia's antiquated institutions of primogeniture and entail. Among their ranks stood Lincoln. His story is well sketched and traffics in the venerable themes of self-education and self-reliance so elemental to the mythology of American individualism. Certainly true to a point, this profile is incomplete without adding that Lincoln's Whiggish views served as a moderate alterative to southern Jacksonianism's extreme states' rights stand.

In his first political speech, Lincoln, only twenty-three at the time and a candidate for state office, sang the praises of government paternalism. Its power to contract canals and turnpikes, open up isolated communities, and promote public schooling promised a bigger boon to the nation's moral and material infrastructure than Jacksonianism's hard-money vision. "Time and experience have verified to a demonstration," Lincoln maintained, "the public utility of internal improvements. That the poorest and most thinly populated countries would be greatly benefitted by the opening of good roads, and in the clearing of navigable streams within their limits, is what no person will deny. . . . For my part, I desire to see the time when education and by its means, morality, sobriety, enterprise and industry, shall become much more general than at present, and should be gratified to have it in my power to contribute something to the advancement of any measure which might have a tendency to accelerate the happy period."[20]

In Whiggery, Lincoln recognized a politics of improvement popular among commercial farmers, manufacturers, budding professionals, and nascent industrialists. Until its definitive sectional split in the 1850s, even many substantial planters, attuned to the possibilities of an enlarged agrarian market, had made their home in this party of modernization. As to spiritual matters, Whiggery responded alertly to postmillennialism, the belief that a golden age would preface Christ's second coming. To prepare for that day, evangelical Protestants looked to reform society. This moralistic impulse made a deep impact on antebellum life; its crusades included the promotion of prohibition, foreign missions, children's aid societies, women's rights, almshouses, mental hospitals, and, increasingly, abolition.

If evangelicalism's otherworldly aspects made little impact on the freethinking Lincoln, its convergence with a Whiggish faith in social mobility struck a truer chord. Casting off his father's primitive premarket views, Lincoln aspired to station, status, and personal improvement. Honored in American lore for his nimble rise from penury to presidency, Lincoln was in fact embarrassed by his plebian roots. Responding to a compiler's 1858 request for biographical information, he offered a terse forty-nine-word reply meant to conceal rather than reveal. Shorthanding a spotty school record as "Education defective" hinted at his discomfort. In Whiggery's modernizing economy he envisioned a far different future, a kind of politicization of the Protestant work ethic.

Lincoln's faith in the diligent and industrious is altogether evident in a preachy 1851 communication to his stepbrother, John D. Johnston, who, in financial straits, hoped to sell the family farm and move to Missouri. Lincoln advised Johnston to stay put and farm his fields. "You have raised no crop this year, and what you really want is to sell the land, get the money and spend it—part with the land you have, and my life upon it, you will never after, own a spot big enough to bury you in. . . . Now do not misunderstand this letter. I do not write it in any unkindness. I write it in order, if possible, to get you to *face* the truth—which truth is, you are destitute because you have *idled* away your time. Your thousand pretenses for not getting along better, are all non-sense—they deceived nobody but yourself. *Go to work* is the only cure for your case."[21] Lincoln's counsel to Johnston is the homiletic he reserved for himself. Through applied effort he had ambled up the social scale, from farmhand to postmaster, to surveyor and finally lawyer. Is it any wonder he spoke so knowingly and passionately about the possibilities of free labor?

In Lincoln's day Henry Clay was the great figure associated with the "self-made" idea. The *Oxford English Dictionary* credited the Whig senator with coining the phrase in a 1832 speech in which Clay observed, "In Kentucky, almost every manufactory known to me, is in the hands of enterprising and self-made men, who have acquired whatever wealth they possess by patient and diligent labor."[22] Ironically, Clay himself was something of a frontier aristocrat. His Baptist clergyman father enjoyed a secure income while his mother owned nearly 500 acres and eighteen slaves in her own right. Clay's educational opportunities were modest, though they did include some training in the classics with George Wythe, a prominent Virginia lawyer, judge, and gentleman who had once tutored Thomas Jefferson.

As a border state modernizer concerned that his adopted Kentucky lagged behind thriving free-labor Ohio, Clay championed the American System. And as the proprietor of Ashland, a Lexington plantation primarily engaged in hemp production, he understood well the economic challenges men of his class and region faced. In principle Clay abhorred the system of slavery, though in practice he owned, bought, and sold slaves. He believed in phased manumission and, while in his early twenties, unsuccessfully urged its inclusion in the new Kentucky constitution. In his will, Clay provided for the liberation of Ashland's slaves (at the not-so-tender ages of twenty-five for females and twenty-eight for males) followed by their subsequent removal to Liberia, a West African "repatriation" colony established in the 1820s by the American Colonization Society. In many respects his views of slavery—morally, economically, and socially—anticipated Lincoln's own. Clay condemned the institution but also denounced immediate emancipation; he believed chattel ought to own their labor but could not be "amalgamated" into a free-labor society; and he held that abolition under any condition should be followed by the deportation of the former slaves from the United States, a point pressed by Lincoln late into the Civil War.

Similarities aside, substantial differences distanced Clay's Whiggery from Lincoln's. The former's conservative unionism made him something of an appeaser to southern power. Lincoln's pragmatic unionism, on the other hand, made him responsive to the political and economic realities of a steadily rising northern power. Clay further favored the quasi-aristocratic side of the Whig Party—not unusual for Whigs of his generation—that reminded some of Federalism. And for this both he and it paid a high price. Between 1828 and 1852 Whiggery and its National

Republican antecedent largely failed to connect with a rapidly democratizing culture, capturing only two of seven presidential elections; candidate Clay was outpolled on three attempts. Old Whiggery further retained a self-defeating interest in property qualifications for balloting, evinced a patrician's taste for paternalism, and recommended a snail's paced migration to the western territories that struck a sour note with would-be settlers. Younger Whigs, by contrast, those soon to make up the first GOP generation, had come of age amid a fresh set of state-building circumstances. Transportation and market revolutions upended traditional economic relationships; expansion pushed the nation's borders to the Pacific; and a dynamic egalitarian populism had taken hold in the North. While, as historian Michael Holt has written, the balance of Whig opinion in some of the older states "wanted no part of the [third-party] Free Soil movement," midwestern Whigs did.[23] In Ohio, Michigan, Iowa, and Wisconsin, keeping slavery out of the territories became the paramount issue, and upon it they would link with Conscience Whigs in New England.

Conventional lines of conservative leadership had changed during this period as well. In contrast to Whiggery, the emerging Republican Party elevated a different kind of man. Lincoln's modest background is well known, though it hardly stands alone. Ulysses Grant farmed near St. Louis, took a turn as a bill collector, and worked in a tannery before the Civil War; Michigan's first Republican senator, Zachariah Chandler, managed his father's farm before establishing a general merchandise store in Detroit; Ohio's first Republican senator, Benjamin Wade, migrated with his several brothers to Cleveland's Western Reserve, whose forests they helped clear with ax and oxen. Wade later toiled on the Eric Canal "with," as one early biographer put it, "pick and shovel and barrow . . . for means to carry himself forward, receiving, probably, not exceeding forty-five or fifty cents per day."[24] The Old Northwest was filled with such meanly situated figures, ambitious men, typically in search of opportunity.

If Whiggery retained a fundamentally patrician outlook, Republicanism met the culture more than halfway. Its endorsement of frontier homesteads enlarged the party's draw to include what we might call "Jackson Republicans," northern Democrats annoyed equally by the shared aristocratic sensibilities of old Whiggery and the southern plantocracy. To these voters, many of them urban workingmen or rural farmers, Republicanism offered an aggressive and inclusive voice for free labor absent the often irritating entreaty for social reform so embedded in Whig ideology. Its first national platform (1856) concluded with a plea for a Jeffersonian unanimity among the North's politically discontent. Stressing that "the maintenance of the principles promulgated in the Declaration of Independence . . . are essential to the preservation of our Republican institutions," the plank invited "the affiliation and cooperation of the men of all parties, however differing from us in other respects, in support of the principles herein declared."[25]

If Whiggery's lingering affection for a politics of deference jarred northern democratic sensibilities, its yielding response to southern powerbrokers proved equally unsatisfying. True, as a national coalition Whiggery could survive only by finding a point of accommodation on the slave question amenable to both sections. But this rather large caveat diluted its capacity for growth and sowed the seeds for its eventual extinction. Republicanism, on the other hand, flourished *because of* the free-soil crisis; its very subsistence and success were predicated on abandoning Whiggish compromises. Accordingly, it scanned the American past for more suitable ideological ancestors than Clay and his generational cohort. Jeffersonianism had once offered Whiggery a language and politics to oppose the imperial presidency of Andrew Jackson. It would now endow Republicans with the vitality of a Revolutionary-era natural-rights philosophy from which to contest the Slave Power.

In all, the parallels between the Republicans of the 1790s and the Republicans of the 1850s are striking. Both originated in opposition to ruling parties that advanced hierarchical visions, the deferential state preferred by Hamilton and the Cavalier culture posited by southern apologists. Their commercial outlooks also shared important congruencies. Where Federalism and Whiggery accentuated the importance of an Atlantic economy firmly indebted to British markets and credit, Jeffersonians and Lincolnians looked to the rapid development of the American frontier as the chief source of the country's economic independence. Accordingly, both brands of Republicanism found strong support in the nation's interior. Without claiming the electoral votes of the country's two westernmost states, Kentucky and Tennessee, Jefferson would have lost the election of 1800. Lincoln came to power in 1860 because he swept every midwestern state (free territory as prescribed by Jefferson's Land Ordinance of 1784, the basis of the Northwest Ordinance) along with the two Pacific appendages, California and Oregon.

Western constituencies in both contests cast ballots against privilege. For laborers, artisans, and small agrarians circa 1790, Jeffersonianism promised social equality in a rising agricultural economy contra the older Atlantic commercial aristocracy. Much the same can be said of Republicanism circa 1860. An army of tradesmen and mechanics, merchants and middling farmers looked to spill into the nation's territories in search of fresh opportunities. The Jeffersonian impetus to westward migration resulted in ten new states entering the Union between 1803 and 1840; under the homesteading stimulus of the Civil War and its aftermath, eleven new states joined the Union between 1861 and 1890. Alike, both brands of Republicanism promoted an ideology of aspiration pledged to a politics of self-liberation for anyone willing to uproot.

Finally, a shared rights-of-man vision united Jeffersonians of both generations, serving as the ideological pillar from which they built nearly unbeatable coalitions. As Gordon S. Wood has recently observed in regard to the 1790 cohort, "the Northern Republicans were . . . supported by a variety of social interests, ranging from fairly wealthy manufacturers and entrepreneurs to journeymen-employees and common laborers. . . . These mostly middling sorts increasingly came together in angry reaction to the contempt in which they were held by the Federalist gentry. . . . These rising Northern workers and entrepreneurs were in fact the principal contributors to the capitalist world that the Southern Republicans were coming to fear."[26] Much the same could be said of northern Republicanism on the eve of the Civil War. It too found a wide range of support among various "middling" occupations and constituencies, it also rejected a gentry class's claim that poor white farmers were mere mudsills, and it similarly promoted a capitalist logic inimical to the slave states.

Given the complexity of the Jeffersonian legacy, the preceding paragraphs obviously hold truer for the party's northern wing than for the party as a whole. No doubt many southern Jeffersonians were less concerned with Federalism's vision of a deferential social order than its commitment to a speculative economy. But above the Mason-Dixon line, old and new Republicans shared a more egalitarian worldview consistent with the natural rights principles put forward in 1776.

Lincoln himself believed strongly in the Jeffersonian origins of Republicanism. He explained, before his presidency, in a letter to a group of prominent New Englanders how the roles of the country's great parties had been reversed, that liberal had gone conservative and conservative had gone liberal. Appropriate to his Illinois background, he turned the nation's political history into a frontier fable: "I remember once being much amused at seeing two partially intoxicated men engage in a fight with their great-coats on, which fight, after a long, and rather harmless contest, ended in each having fought himself *out* of his own coat, and *into* that of the other. If the two leading parties of this day are really identical with the two in the days of Jefferson and Adams, they have performed the same feat as the two drunken men."[27]

But claiming that southern Democrats were the true heirs of Federalism would not be enough. Crucially, Lincoln Republicanism had to demonstrate that the Jeffersonians, and more generally that the Founders, intended to put slavery on the road to extinction. Briefly summarized, the argument runs as follows: the Constitution permitted the closing of the Atlantic slave trade as early as 1808; several of the Fathers manumitted their own slaves; and most important, the Ordinance of 1787 barred slavery from entering the Northwest Territory ceded by Britain. Republicans, many of whom were midwesterners living in the former territory, pointed to this legislation as a template for westward settlement, offering proof of the Founders' faith in free labor, and to the democratic sentiments contained in the Declaration of Independence. The Missouri Compromise of 1820 had largely affirmed this territorial policy by barring slavery in most of the Louisiana Purchase lands before the Texas debates, the Mexican War, the Kansas-Nebraska Act, and the Dred Scott decision threatened to "nationalize" black servitude. Cumulatively, these southern legislative and judicial victories overthrew Republican claims that the Declaration's "all men are created equal" foundation was the critical idea behind nationhood.

Lincoln cannily addressed this concern, and contextualized Republicanism's place in American history, in an 1858 speech at Edwardsville, Illinois. "The Republican party," he promised, "will, if possible, restore the government to the policy of the fathers—the policy of preserving the new territories from the baneful influence of human bondage, as the Northwestern territories were sought to be preserved by the ordinance of 1787 and the Compromise act of 1820. They will oppose, in all its length and breadth, the modern Democratic idea that slavery is as good as freedom, and ought to have room for expansion all over the continent, if people can be found to carry it."[28]

Lincoln's cutting reference to "the modern Democratic idea" is revealing. For Democrats had taken to portraying their party as the stable foundation upon which the nation's politics rested while tarring Republicanism as a dangerous abolitionist upstart. Lincoln turned this argument on its head, insisting instead that under the influence of radical slaveholders the "formerly" Jeffersonian Party had overturned the Founders' efforts to create a free-labor republic. Thus only in Republicanism redux did the Age of Reason continue to inform the American party system. In contesting the influence of southern swayed congresses, courts, and presidents, Lincoln and his supporters presumed to have stayed true to the liberal, moderate, and altogether enlightened laws present at the nation's creation.

Bearing in mind that the post–Civil War GOP evolved into a great champion of property rights at the expense of individual rights, its egalitarian origins are somewhat ironic. It was the slavocracy, after all, that had once carried the cross of property ownership. Most notably, it demanded the privilege to take slave property into territories, to keep slave property in the nation's capital, and to compel northern law-enforcement officials to pursue and if possible capture runaway slave property. Young Republicanism condemned all of this as a blatant abuse of property-rights theory as practiced by the Jeffersonians. In an 1859 communication to Boston's free soilers Lincoln wrote, "The Jefferson party were formed upon their . . . superior devotion to the *personal* rights of men, holding the rights of *property* to be secondary only. . . . [And thus it is] interesting to note how completely [liberals and conservatives] have changed hands as to the principle upon which they were originally supposed to be divided."[29]

Lincoln had first embraced the personal-rights "principle," as a liberal Whig, and the sentiment remained strong in certain—but not all—pockets of the party. In some New England mill towns, for example, conservative industrialists and their "Cotton Whig" congressional adjuncts appeared eager to keep their textile trade with the South open under any circumstances. And southern Whigs adopted views on slavery's place in the territories essentially indistinguishable from their southern Democratic "opposition." Lincoln's pilgrimage to Republicanism, on the other hand, commenced from a more expansive and searching social criticism. His 1846 contention that suffrage restrictions for white men should be lessened and that white women deserved the vote are cases in point. So too is the spirited attack he aimed upon the shortsighted nativism that seduced some Whigs into the Know-Nothing Party. "They are mostly my old political and personal friends," Lincoln complained to one correspondent, "and I have hoped their organization would die out without the painful necessity of my taking an open stand against them. Of their principles I think little better than I do of those of the slavery extensionists. Indeed I do not perceive how any one professing to be sensitive to the wrongs of the negroes, can join in a league to degrade a class of white men."[30]

Lincoln's liberal approach to the immigration question emphasized a commitment to equal rights that extended to the slavery question. On both accounts he was accused in some quarters of zealotry. In reply, he pled firm ties to tradition, accentuating what he insisted to be the "conservative" qualities in the new Republican Party, principally its reverence for the Founders' pragmatic natural rights worldview. He did so foremost because he believed it to be the case but further as a strategy to fend off Democratic attacks that "radical Republicanism" threatened the Union. Indeed, even in his old party, Lincoln was suspect. As Sean Wilentz has noted, "Lincoln's conversion to the Republicans . . . marked him as a certain kind of Whig, an inveterate foe of the Slave Power, at odds with the minority of northern Whigs and the majority of southern Whigs who chose a very different political course in the 1850s."[31]

This splintering of Whiggery Lincoln blamed for authoring his greatest political defeat, the loss of a prized U.S. senate seat belonging to Stephen Douglas. Shortly after that setback he confided to the physician Anson G. Henry, "Of course I *wished*, but I did not *expect* a better result. . . . As a general rule . . . much of the plain old democracy is with us, while nearly all the old exclusive silk-stocking whiggery is against us. I do not mean nearly all the old whig party; but nearly all of the nice exclusive sort." To Lincoln, the election typified a democratic shift in American politics. In defeat he foresaw victory. Republicanism's rejection of the more elitist, the more socially and culturally conventional pillars of its predecessor could only enlarge its ranks. And with the eventual merging of liberal Whigs with former nativists and Free Soilers, Independent Democrats, and abolitionists, that is precisely what happened. "The party is newly formed," Lincoln observed of the GOP genesis, "and in forming, old party ties had to be broken, and the attractions of party pride, and influential leaders were wholly wanting. In spite of old differences, prejudices, and animosities, its members were drawn together by a paramount common danger. . . . That [party] is to-day, the best hope of the nation, and of the world."[32]

· · · · ·

Any assessment of the "Age of Lincoln" must wrestle with the brevity of its tenure. This has less to do with the president's April 1865 assassination than with the freakishly rapid rise of the modern corporate state. Lincoln, it seems fair to say, envisioned a far different future. It is difficult to believe that Lincoln, propelled back into politics following the Kansas-Nebraska Act, resisted the prewar slavocracy simply to hand the country over to a postwar industrial oligarchy. And yet if we confine our notions of an Age of Lincoln to the years 1848–65, then we arrive at a decidedly different outcome. In fact we might more effectively divide this period into two parts, the era of moderate Republicanism and the more famous era of radical Republicanism. The first is known for its successful appeal to free labor in sweeping the 1860 House, Senate, and presidential elections, by its refusal to bargain those results away by extending slavery to the Pacific under a proposed Crittenden Compromise, and, of course, by its willingness to go to war rather than allow southern fire-eaters to sever the Union.

Without this foundation, radical Republicanism, the emancipation party that began to take hold in 1863, might never have come into existence. When it did tensions between the two wings existed but, as the moderate Ohio congressman John Sherman wrote to the abolitionist Lydia Maria Child in February 1860, ultimately they were on the same side. "A chronic disease, which has been the growth of centuries, cannot be cured in a day or a generation," he argued. But the Republican policy of keeping slavery out of the territories, he continued, would ultimately yield "the gradual . . . but eventually certain eradication of this great social and political evil."[33] In other words, all Republicans, be they moderates or radicals, were abolitionists of a kind.

It was Lincoln's great gift to keep the two strains of his party together. A pragmatist, he responded alertly to rapidly changing circumstances, demonstrating in the direst of conditions a truly remarkable ability to move with the times. When southern radicalism forced his hand, this former Whig adopted the mien of a warrior president on his way to becoming the "Great Emancipator." More than a Republican, he belonged to a line of nationalists who combined in the period 1790–1865 to resist the encroachments of "aristocratic" power by either plutocracy or plantocracy. All were in a precise sense centrists. John Adams stood between Hamiltonianism and Jeffersonianism, Cabot between Jeffersonianism and High Federalism, Quincy Adams between Jacksonianism and Cotton Whiggery, and Lincoln between radical abolitionism and radical states' rights. Only with his nation engulfed in civil war did Lincoln himself embrace radical measures, and this a radicalism founded in the same Jeffersonian principles formerly the source of his moderation.

Part II **Progressives**

. . . .

Following the Civil War, a new mass society emerged in America, energized by corporations, unions, and a slowly expanding national government. Of these large-scale organizations, the great industrial-financial nexus proved to be the most powerful. And under its direction the weight of atomization, urbanization, and immigration remade the old republic. The new circumstances produced a legion of discontents resulting in bloody battles between capital and labor, fears of political corruption, and concerns of cultural coarsening in a material age. Into this breach stepped the era's liberal Victorians. Disdainful alike of the tycoons and the city bosses, the new moneyed and the old "spoils" systems, they pushed for civil service reforms to leaven the power of patronage and open the political process to more qualified candidates— presumably themselves. Boxed in by politics-as-usual, they led (in 1872, 1884, and 1912) a series of rebellions against the dominant Republican Party, demonstrating their independence from the Big Business right. Ascendant during the presidency of Theodore Roosevelt, these GOP "insurgents" advanced a spate of Square Deal initiatives that sought to tame the trusts, protect consumers, and conserve public lands from commercial exploitation.

5 The Last Patrician

Henry Adams

. . . .

My scheme is to organise a party of the centre and to support
the party which accepts our influence most completely.

—Henry Adams, 1875

Following the collapse of the southern Confederacy, the rise of industrial
capitalism remade America. Once the warm commercial center of artisans, planters, and merchants, the country now moved toward a far more
complex economic identity built on manufacturing and machinery. Along
the way, an opportunistic knot of moneymen rose to prominence and captured the cultural imagination. Taking a long view, the deferential governing philosophy still resonant in the days of Washington and Jefferson
was now and forever gone. The patrician gave way to the "robber baron,"
the wielder of unprecedented powers largely uncompromised by constitutional restraints, enlightened labor law, or popular control. Untethered
by old traditions, the new politics renounced the antediluvian dynasties
present at the republic's founding. Where Adamses once reigned, Rocke-
fellers now ruled.

No one understood this altered cultural climate better than the historian Henry Adams, who looked upon his patrimony as a gilded prison.
While forebears John and John Quincy made history, Henry's generation
of Adamses could only watch history in the making. Born in 1838 and educated in the cramped classical curriculum once the punched ticket for
public office, Adams discovered in Wall Street's confidence men, Chicago's meat-packing princes, and Washington's senators for sale new corporate and political types feasting on the choicest cuts of what a caustic
if observant Vernon Parrington had tartly proclaimed the "Great Barbe-
cue." Caesardom seemed imminent.

Like his distinguished ancestors, Adams was pushed to the center by
the volatility of his times. Temperamentally he was arch, aloof, and con-
descending, a patrician who felt a proprietary call on the republic his
family did so much to serve. He identified industrial capitalism, with its

ability to dwarf mere politics, as the greatest danger the nation had faced since the Civil War. Without its pressures he might well have withdrawn from public life, opting for the seclusion of a gentleman scholar. Instead, he carried out a largely literary assault on what he coined the "Dynamo," the focus of force that now threatened to pit rural versus urban, farmer versus financier, Anglo versus ethnic. Believing this process of interior "breakdown" to be inevitable, he nevertheless attacked its congressional and corporate wings in a number of his writings. Conspicuously intellectual, effortlessly idiosyncratic, and darkly fatalistic, he could not hope to fulfill his celebrated family's presidential ambitions. Too removed from the practical affairs of his day, his print resistance to modernism's pressures on the American republic could only accomplish so much. But there were compensations. Aside from winning a reputation as a distinguished historian, he proved to be a surprisingly compelling proponent of a new profession, the scholar-in-politics. Under the subsequent presidencies of Theodore Roosevelt and Woodrow Wilson, this persuasion, situating itself between capital and labor, proved crucial in taking on the new industrial order.

As a critic of post–Civil War Republicanism, Adams conformed to an old family pattern, offering a from-the-center censure of American conservatism. The pressing issues that framed this era, chiefly the growth of industry and empire, moved the country far from its republican roots. Deeply troubled by big business's expanding role in national affairs, Adams regarded the industrialists as agents of irresponsible change blindly committed to a coarse, self-serving social morality. In these dawning days of prosperity theology, even the angels sang in the choir of the new rich. "The good Lord," John D. Rockefeller piously swore, "gave me the money."[1] This emphasis on the material and the immediate, what Adams dismissively called the *Nunc Age*, undermined older and to his mind more satisfying models of economy, society, and spirituality. Steel and steam on the instant now drove history; a menacing machine and cash culture prefaced this latest Fall of Man.

Adams's sense of possession flowered naturally enough from equal parts pecuniary privilege and ancestral instinct. Descendant of Quincys, Boylstons, Brookses, and Adamses, grandson and great grandson of presidents, Harvard historian, and gentleman scholar, Henry counted American history as household history. True, he tried to empty the immense emotional burdens of familial expectations—alcoholism and suicide touched the charter generations—with a play-acting appeal to irrelevancy.

"What could become of such a child of the seventeenth and eighteen centuries," he shrugged, "when he should wake up to find himself required to play the game of the twentieth?"[2] But this pose did little to conceal his real and positive engagement with society. For rather than slide into a lazy dilettantism, Adams crafted a career of unceremonious statesmanship, education, and advising in the capital's more exclusive dining and drawing rooms. Qualms to the contrary, he wanted very much to leave his mark, even as the door to national office had quietly but firmly closed on Adamses. Consequently, Henry forged ahead as a patrician critic of that great hope and great scourge of modern Western civilization, the industrial process. In this venture he followed a household tradition, setting out for the center. As John Adams had once navigated between Jeffersonianism and Hamiltonianism, Henry proposed to steer clear of both robber baronism and the radical mélange of Populists, socialists, and communists arrayed against it.

Weaned on the deadly serious secessionist debates that prefaced the Civil War, Adams observed in the assorted corruption, petty thievery, and raw greed that rippled through the Ulysses Grant–era the specter of an altogether fresh menace. In his eyes the promise of American life had broken down in the 1870s, never to be fully recovered nor, he guessed, fully reconciled with the passage of power from the statesman to the speculator. Counting himself among the casualties, Adams took it all quite personally: "I have always considered that Grant wrecked my own life, and the last hope or chance of lifting society back to a reasonably high plane. Grant's administration is to me the dividing line between what we hoped, and what we have got." Hope had stood on the side of public interest and private sacrifice; its heroes included Washington, Lincoln, and a small galaxy of Adamses. While the history books cheerfully declared these men incarnates of a national character norm, Henry Adams just as firmly dissented. Scoring Grant as the half-brained embodiment of an action-oriented society, he argued that in the new America "the intellect counted for nothing; only the energy counted. The type was pre-intellectual, archaic, and would have seemed so even to the cave-dwellers."[3]

Abandoning Republicanism, Adams joined a coalition of genteel reformers that sought to serve as the balance wheel between the major parties. It may have been the most hopeful political action of his life. His venture into postwar partisanship reminds us that the celebrated "age of reform" (1890–1940) combining the populist, progressive, and New Deal campaigns cannot be adequately understood without reckoning with the moderate republicanism of the 1870s. A generation of patricians trained for political careers had watched politics lose its luster as wealth and status increasingly gravitated to the industrialists. Even before the war's conclusion, Adams anticipated the imminent need among the bluer bloods to justify their social standing through public service. "What we want . . . is a *school*," he wrote his brother, Charles, in 1862. "We want a national set of young men like ourselves or better, to start new influences not only in politics, but in literature, in law, in society, and throughout the whole social organism of the country. A national school of our own generation. And that is what America has no power to create."[4]

Adams's sojourns in Britain and the Continent revealed the salutary combination of university preparation and urban amenities. The flower of English youth, he observed, grew morally and intellectually in Oxbridge before concentrating its abilities in London's sprawling cultural topography. His native country, Adams knew, offered no comparable experiences. The universities were mere social clubs, he sighed, while insular Boston and commercial New York lacked modern metropolitan imaginations. As a capital city, Washington paled in comparison to its European sisters. Built in a southern swamp and burned out by British invaders just a half century earlier, the green American seat of government could point to no distinguished university, library, symphony, or social class.

Adams countered the naiveté of his native land by looking to a critical mass of highborn Best Men to raise the country's moral tone. No doubt a presumptive snobbery underlined this genteel vision, though it should be remembered that to Adams's circle the lack of a compelling, disinterested, and patriotic peerage had culminated disastrously in the horror of civil war. During the 1850s, this argument ran, irreconcilables from both sections pushed a politics of extremism. Talk of nullifying federal laws, emancipating slaves through violence, and the constant chatter of secession weakened the bonds of union long before the firing of Fort Sumter.[5] Now, in the war's aftermath, arrived a host of fresh dangers delivered by a looming industrial crisis. Again, a number of the Best Men, believing themselves above divisive "left" and "right" distinctions, sought to neutralize the two poles and center an unstable society.

With Adamses no longer electable, Henry sought to make his impact on national affairs as an intellectual. In his essays, histories, and reminiscences, he shaped a formidable critique against the industrial state. Generally, these efforts were designed to make his countrymen aware that without the reassertion of independent congressional and presidential power, republican government in America could no longer survive. He stressed this perspective in an important 1870 article, "The New York Gold Conspiracy." Briefly, spoilsmen Jay Gould and James Fisk attempted to corner the gold market by bidding up a bullion spike likely to inflate crop prices, thus raising transport rates on the Erie Railroad, which they controlled. The speculation resulted in a grand "Black Friday" panic before the Grant administration intervened and released government gold reserves to stabilize the market. The speed and magnitude of the adventure stunned Adams. Suddenly, frighteningly, money seemed to have burst beyond all closures and controls. "For the first time since the creation of these enormous corporate bodies," he wrote, "one of them has shown its power for mischief, and has proved itself able to override and trample on law, custom, decency, and every restraint known to society, without scruple, and as yet without check." This, he ominously warned, was but the beginning. "The belief is common in America that the day is at hand when corporations far greater than the Erie—swaying power such as has never in the world's history been trusted in the hands of private citizens . . . will ultimately succeed in directing government itself."[6]

Holding capital stock of some $35,000,000 and employing 15,000 workers, the Erie Company, Adams argued, had set itself up as "an empire within a republic." Who enjoyed more influence than the executives of this line? What European king could claim the cash resources sitting in the company's kitty? With the national legislature and judiciary willing to abet the great financers and railroad men, "Gould and Fisk," Adams insisted, had "created a combination more powerful than any that has been controlled by mere private citizens in America or in Europe since society for self-protection established the supreme authority of the judicial name." Such unprecedented command in private hands, he continued, was "far too great for public safety either in a democracy or in any other form of society." It further pained this displaced patrician to see the hands in which power now rested. "Both these men," he sniffed, "belonged to a low moral *and social type*."[7]

A few months after the "New York Gold Conspiracy" appeared, Adams began a seven-year stint teaching medieval and U.S. history at Harvard. Along with the post he took over the editorial reigns of the *North American Review*, perhaps the nation's most distinguished literary magazine. In this journalistic capacity, he advanced reform politics through the power of the press. His first efforts included an entreaty to the Republican Missouri senator Carl Schurz, a sharp critic of Grantism: "I would like to support your course, and make known to the eastern people the true nature of the contest you are engaged in. . . . I want the public to know, if possible, how far you and your party represent principles which are of national interest."[8] Schurz's "party" housed a sprinkling of important politicians and journalists, academics and men of letters. Its membership included Samuel J. Tilden, later to capture the most popular votes in the 1876 presidential election, E. L. Godkin, editor of *The Nation*, and a young Samuel Clemens.

The moment to make a putsch within Republican ranks presented itself in 1872. Grant handily won the party's nomination and stood poised to ride his martial reputation to a second presidential term. No doubt the yet-to-be-named Democratic contender, his base an occupied South, stood little chance, and those men opposed to the spoils system, including the Schurz circle, rebelled and launched a new party, the Liberal Republicans. The split reflected fundamental philosophical differences within the GOP. The party's patrician-tinged wing sought, in the wake of the Civil War and the passage of constitutional amendments securing freedom, citizenship, and suffrage for the former slaves, to advance beyond Grantism. Many of these men looked to Henry's father, sixty-five-year-old Charles Francis, to lead their internal opposition, and though he refused to make assurances as to his willingness to serve as the new party's presidential nominee, his magic name suggested a kind of residual availability. But Charles Francis, who served his country capably as a diplomat, had little appetite for electoral politics. Accordingly, he spurned his sons' (Henry, Charles, and Brooks) requests to make pledges on his behalf at the splinter group's Cincinnati convention. There, the spirit of antebellum reform permeated the halls. Indiana congressman George W. Julian recalled that he was "delighted to meet troops of the old Free Soilers of 1848 and 1852" at the convention.[9] Other prominent progressives in the Queen City included the Kentucky abolitionist Cassius Clay, former Liberty Party member and future associate justice of the U.S. Supreme Court Stanley Matthews, and the noted New York legal theorist David Dudley Field II.

For those attending the Liberal Republican convention of 1872, a strong sense of déjà vu set in—it looked like 1860 all over again. "The leading delegates from several Midwestern states had been prominent Lincoln men a dozen years before," writes historian Matthew T. Downey.

The New York *Tribune* reported that the "Men who were at Chicago when Lincoln was nominated, comment on the wonderful resemblance in men. . . . Indeed many of the men that named the great Abolitionist, are here, seeking a successor of the same sort." The list of names appended to the call issued by the Illinois Liberal Republicans contained several of the Lincoln electors of 1860 and many of the Republican state officials whom Lincoln had carried into office with him. One of the leading contenders for the Cincinnati nomination was Justice David Davis, who had been Lincoln's campaign manager in 1860. Lincoln's law partner, William H. Herndon, went to the convention to work for Davis' nomination. Other well-known Lincoln men at Cincinnati from the Midwest were John D. Defrees of Indiana, Jacob D. Cox and Roeliff Brinkerhoff of Ohio, and Josiah B. Grinnell of Iowa. Although many of the Lincoln Republicans had not held office for several years, they were far from naive about party politics and convention maneuvering.[10]

The three-day convention proved to be a peculiarly disharmonious affair for a group of insurgents supposedly connected by the common goal of toppling Grant. In fact, beyond a shared hostility to the machine politics favored by "regular" Republicans they shared very little. The gathering included free traders and protectionists, defenders of black rights and southern Redeemers, eastern patricians and western agrarians. A party platform calling for reform in the civil service, and an end to Reconstruction was all they could agree on.

Schurz supported Charles Francis's candidacy and called on his fellow conventioneers to do the same. The reluctant nominee's Anglophilia, however, alienated Irish voters in the East, while midwesterners were suspicious of his patrician background. And still he nearly won the Liberal Republican nomination. Needing 358 votes to claim the prize, Adams led early and plateaued at 309 on the fifth ballot before giving way to the crusading editor of the *New-York Tribune*, Horace Greeley. Here was but another reminder that the political times had passed the Adams family by. Charles Francis and his sons, one Liberal Republican complained, "[represent] too much the anti-popular element—the sneering, and sniffling element." Adams's sons were reduced, on his behalf, to employing coyness rather than candor. Some two months before the convention met, Jacob Cox wrote to one correspondent that Henry had "inferred" to him that Charles Francis "was cordially with us." While Henry noted with familial generosity after Greeley walked off with the prize that his father had "come out of the fight very strong and sound," the same could not be said of Liberal Republicanism. Its nomination proved disastrous. Democrats too claimed Greeley as their candidate, thus dashing any possibility of a third-party impact. Together, they limped to a lopsided defeat in the November election.[11]

Deficient in practical political skills, Henry had clearly overestimated the influence of the reformers. Still, a reflexive ancestral absorption in presidential politics held him tightly—1876, after all, offered a new opportunity to build a coalition that might serve as a balance between the urban-ethnic Democratic machine politics and the Wall Street—sensitive GOP. The death of Senator Charles Sumner two years earlier had made Charles Francis the major Massachusetts statesman, and the subsequent publication of Brooks Adams's *North American Review* article, "The Platform of the New Party" (imitating Henry's pox on Grantism), announced the family's intent to recover its old political relevancy. Throughout this period Henry and his allies sought to purchase a newspaper to advance their views. Their efforts to acquire Boston's *Daily Advertiser* and *Post* came to naught, but their fledgling movement continued.

The reformers were motivated by both good intentions and self-interest. They considered that "true" patriots such as themselves had been pushed out of government service by party managers eager to offer favors to the emerging industrial state. Failing to register the lengths southern whites would go to deny black rights, Henry came to see Reconstruction above all as a vast storehouse of sinecures that kept real Republicans at bay. Looking toward 1876, he realized that those loyal to good government would have to find influence in a new coalition. With this in mind, he apprised an English friend of his plans to "organise a party of the centre" and force the two major parties to bid for its support. A few months later, with the independents moving forward, he dubiously claimed, "Our organisation has . . . unquestionably the power to say that any given man shall not be President." As for who should be president, Adams had no doubt—"Our first scheme," he wrote, "[is] to force my father on the parties."[12] When that intrigue inevitably fell through, he signaled a general call to arms among the patrician discontented. In a circular letter to colleagues mailed in March, he described the dominant Republican-Democratic arrangement as a danger to the moral man's soul: "The present condition of political affairs is such as to create grave concern in the minds of all reflecting men. The great party conventions are soon to meet. As yet there is no indication that the choice of these conventions will fall upon persons in whom independent voters can place confidence. All the indications of the time point to the possibility that, in the conflict between personal interests, the interests of the nation may be overlooked, and either a combination of corrupt influences may control the result, or, as has so often happened, the difficulty of harmonising personal claims may lead to the nomination of candidates whom you cannot support with self-respect."[13]

Calling for a "conference of gentleman independent of party ties," Adams played a weak hand out to a predictable end. In May some 200 "Independent Movement" men convened at the Fifth Avenue Hotel in New York. As historian Michael Holt has written, "This was not a convention but a private, invitation-only gathering of leading academics and professional men."[14] The attendees included the past and present presidents of Williams College, the Yale professor of political economics William Graham Sumner, and Adams's doctoral student Henry Cabot Lodge. As a whole, the assembly seemed to know less what it wanted than what it didn't want. After announcing a general disdain for politics as usual the reformers could come to no consensus on who to support for the presidency. Some favored Secretary of the Treasury Benjamin Bristow (scourge of the Whiskey Ring) while others preferred New York governor Samuel J. Tilden. This split all but ensured the independents' irrelevancy, for the great hope of the "convention" was to put the major parties, their own conventions looming, on alert that by not choosing a progressive they risked alienating a potentially powerful constituency. As matters turned out, both Republicans and Democrats made gestures toward reform, and that proved to be enough to bring the majority of independents back into the fold. In the end, many of them, including Henry, went for Tilden as the lesser evil. In November they watched him lose one of the closest and most contested national elections in American history.

As something of political adieu, Henry and his brother Charles Francis Jr. published "The 'Independents' in the Canvas." A vigorous attack on regular Republicanism, the essay proved to be Henry's last edition with the *Review,* whose regular Republican editors were unamused. Calling Tilden "the most distinguished reformer" in the race, Henry and Charles were eager to see government power reduced by trimming northern oversight in the South which, they insisted, "overstepped the bounds of moderation." Tone deaf to the emerging segregationist system in the former slave states, they wrongly presumed that, in regard to the "old" issues of race and rebellion, "little remains over which to struggle." The same might be said of Henry's waning interest in organized politics. Checked by the failure of the independents and disappointed in the *Review*'s modest reach, he marked 1876 as a year of leavings. "I must content myself," he wrote to one reformer in August, "by remaining outside any healthy political organisation."[15]

If the patrician party failed to provide the difference in the election, as Henry had hoped, it nevertheless affected Republican Party strategy. Its call for reform resonated as various scandals within the government came to light. This, combined with an economic downturn in 1873, cost the Republicans dearly in the 1874 elections in which Democrats captured a majority in the House, effectively ending a generation of GOP congressional supremacy. Chastened, Republicans now promised to be more progressive. "Virtually every northern Republican state platform in 1875," Holt notes, "explicitly praised Grant's administration . . . for prosecuting the Whiskey Ring and seeking the collection of tax revenues of which the government had been defrauded."[16]

Adams, of course, refused to see this GOP posturing as any kind of victory, and his consequent retreat from popular politics is unsurprising. Subdued, the new mood colored his work. In 1880 he anonymously published *Democracy: An American Novel*, a political satire whose heroine, Mrs. Lightfoot Lee, a widowed philanthropist newly arrived in Washington, is in sympathies and sensibilities a female Henry. The book topically ruminates on political corruption in a capital dominated by GOP powerbrokers. A woman of independent means and the daughter of a distinguished clergyman, Lee is pursued romantically by Silas P. Ratcliffe, an ethically challenged senator whose political prospects would be decidedly furthered by their marriage. Revolted by the decadent Washington scene, Lee decamps and medicates her disillusionment on a journey to the Near East. When Adams wrote "She honestly acknowledged herself to be tortured by *ennui*. . . . She had felt no interest in the price of stocks, and very little in the men who dealt in them; she had become serious. . . . The more she read, the more she was disheartened that so much culture should lead to nothing—nothing," he opened a small corner of his heart. A competent if undistinguished dark comedy of political manners, *Democracy* savaged the graft culture that gripped Washington and baited the independent men of his circle. "The idea of my purifying politics is absurd," his protagonist discovers, and through a literary ventriloquy she is made to mouth the ancient Adams oath: "I will not share the profits of vice; I am not willing to be made a receiver of stolen goods, or to be put in a position where I am perpetually obliged to maintain that immorality is a virtue!"[17]

If *Democracy*'s power-versus-principle morality play is Adams's *Faust*, his largest work, *The History of the United States of America during the Administrations of Thomas Jefferson and James Madison*, is a New World rewrite of Gibbon's majestic *The History of the Decline and Fall of the Roman Empire*. Published in nine volumes between 1889 and 1891, it offered a rare model of an elite yet popular form of democratic rule; Jefferson the planter aristocrat captured the public's imagination, won its allegiance, and directed its energies—only to have it all turn to ashes. The Louisiana Purchase, commercial conflict with England and France, and the War of 1812 quickened the pace of historical circumstances beyond the control of gentlemen statesmen. Herein lay the seeds of the urban, industrial, and political crises that confronted Adams's own generation. Frustrated with the patrician's fall from grace, he performed in the *History*'s two thousand-plus pages an elegant autopsy on his kin, his caste, and their failure to provide the Best Men of his own day with a living, usable past.

It would be easy if untrue to read Adams's imposing *History* as a case of score settling. While great grandfather John's political career may have been cut short by the Republican "Revolution of 1800," grandfather John Quincy's prospects, as observed earlier, moved steadily upward under the Jeffersonians. The generous patronage of Virginia presidents argued against a family vendetta. Moreover, Henry understood history less as a case of great men shaping great events than as a mass of impersonal forces combining to produce irresistible change. All men, even the Best Men, were prisoners to processes beyond their control. Thus Adams saw nothing inherently tragic in Federalism's decline. That it represented a spent force of the cosmos he had little doubt. Its tribalistic perspective and stale regionalism naturally succumbed to the might of a growing people. "Even Boston," Adams wrote, "the most cosmopolitan part of New England, showed no tendency in its educated classes to become American in thought or feeling."[18] The Jeffersonians, by contrast, successfully tapped into the era's egalitarian zeitgeist, embodying for a short season the historical incline toward popular politics, frontier democracy, and a burgeoning cotton capitalism that propelled the new nation forward. In time their reign, too, ended abruptly. By the 1830s, if not earlier, the power of free labor had begun to pass the planters by.

As an exercise in self-awareness, the *History* offered its author the opportunity to understand his own past. What had been behind the Adamses' ebbing political fortunes? And why was Henry, educated to serve in the highest public offices, reduced to spectatorial status? The answers, he felt certain, could be discovered in "the new epoch of American history" that followed the War of 1812. Only by the reduction of New England, he argued, might the expansive instincts of the country find suitable outlets, opportunities, and encouragements. "The sudden decline of Massachusetts to the lowest point of relative prosperity and influence she had ever known," Adams wrote, was accompanied "by an equally sudden stimulus to the South and West."[19] The interior now possessed steamboats to counter the ocean schooners favored by the old coastal shipping elite and population flowed from the Atlantic regions into and beyond the Alleghenies, while corn and cotton frontiers began generating immense wealth in the Ohio and Mississippi Valleys. In simple terms, the West waxed while the East waned.

As a work of "scientific" inquiry, Adams's *History* recorded the development of early nineteenth-century life with one overarching end in mind: to trace the velocity of change from a quaint seaboard republic to a continental leviathan. In effect he performed an exercise in last rites. For the death of one America anticipated the birth of a larger, stronger, and wealthier unit. Trailing in the turbulence of this process, personal mastery proved impossible, even for an Adams or a Jefferson. The celebrated Virginia dynasty, Henry wrote, was "carried along on a stream which floated them, after a fashion, without much regard for themselves."[20] In the end, Adams observed, it scarcely mattered who occupied the seats of power once held by his ancestors. For history had no heroes, only types, and no class ruled a day beyond its destiny.

In place of an erratic American republic, Adams fell hard for a Francophone model that to his eyes offered a more humane, "gradual," and giving culture—a revisitation of sorts of patrician privilege. Racing to the past, the twelfth century became Henry's sentimental sanctum sanctorum. Eager to capture the mood and spirit of late medievalism, his minor masterpiece, *Mont Saint Michel and Chartres* (1904), avoided the sundry affairs of courts, diplomacy, and religious conflicts for mentality, imagination, and cultural consciousness. Accordingly, he wrote on architecture, myths, mystics, sensibilities, and songs. One finds enormously informative reflections on cobalt blue stained-glass windows, a philosophical discursion into the conceptualist ideas of Abelard, and a brief, moralistic seminar on *La Chanson de Roland*—"Our age has lost much of its ear for poetry, as it has its eye for color and line." If, as Adams repeatedly argued, industrial America provided no coherency, no mystery, and no marvels, a sensitive mind had to take flight for its nourishment. Accordingly, he adopted a romantic feudal fetish meant to evoke a renewed world of wonder. "The twelfth century had the child's love of sweets and spices and preserved fruits," he wrote, "and drinks sweetened or spiced, whether they were taken for supper or for poetry; the true knight's palate was fresh and his appetite excellent either for sweets or verses or love; the world was young then; Robin Hoods lived in every forest, and Richard Cœur-de-Lion was not yet twenty years old."[21] With newly imperial America aging quickly, Adams looked to a "young" Europe for inspiration, beauty, and balance.

Given his medievalism of the heart, perhaps it is not surprising that a strong anticapitalist undercurrent sharpened Adams's critique of the modern world. His looking-back allegiances came straight from the crib. "Quincy had always been right," he wrote late in life, "for Quincy represented a moral principle—the principle of resistance to Boston." The dignity of labor, open transactions, and small-scale exchanges defined the quasi-colonial economy of Adams's imagination, yet the new industrial order and its positivistic underpinnings beat to a quicker rhythm. In the end, something greater than Quincy expired in its commotion. His country had shattered in the Civil War, his inherited god fell before the Darwinian revolution, and the promise of a new progressive order struck him as absurd in an age of profitable imperialism and Bismarckian realpolitik. The immense scale of energy expended to create the modern West both impressed and startled Adams, and he wondered what it all meant. "There is only one thing in life that I must and will have before I die," *Democracy*'s Dowager Lee vowed, "I must know whether America is right or wrong."[22]

As the years passed, Adams's dreaded Dynamo increased its rate of revolutions, with the industrial crisis giving way to the temptations of colonialism. The Spanish-American War and annexation of Hawaii and the Philippines brought the United States a parcel of Pacific possessions and forced the country to wrestle with the paradox of entering the twentieth century as an imperial republic. Adams threw up his hands in disgust: "The octopus is stretching its tentacles everywhere, quite blindly, like octopuses or octopodes elsewhere, but with an accurate sense of touch. As for traditions, constitution, principles, past professions, and all that, the devil has put them back into his pocket for another thousand years. By common agreement, we all admit that the old slate must be washed off clean. We all admit that we cant help it if the world does tip over. We are only glad we are on top."[23]

Here, in sentiment, one is evocatively reminded of Vladimir Lenin, another and more famous anti-imperialist. Adams shared the future Soviet leader's conviction that a globalized industrial system sustained Western imperialism. They parted, however, in their respective views of the future. A more optimistic Lenin believed that the increasing sophistication of capitalism could pave the way for humane socialist and communist economies. He hoped, in other words, to master the Dynamo. Adams supposed, however, that the industrial process moved at its own unpredictable rate, created its own culture, and followed its own inscrutable outline. Still, the din and drama of "history's" unfolding drew him on. "For the historian's business," he explained, "was to follow the track of the energy; to find where it came from and where it went to; its complex source and shifting channels; its values, equivalents, conversions." Consequently, Adams adopted elaborate statistical models of global development to decipher the scramble for colonies in Africa and Asia. After dividing the world into a have and have-not balance sheet, he wrote that "America, England and France . . . contain, according to my figures, six-sevenths of the energy of the world; and the other seventh is much divided and scattered. These three countries now make an Atlantic system, which will swing any possible Asiatic system for two generations more. Add the Rhine countries and northern Germany and Scandinavia, which must always belong to the Atlantic system, and it is clear that we embrace practically the whole motive power of the actual world." This Western dominance Adams refused to celebrate. He fumed in December 1898, the month the Paris Peace Treaty officially ended the war with Spain, of "the tyranny of money" and condemned "our present state of Washington. We are disgustingly fat, oily, greasy and contented."[24]

In all, a series of violent events had conspired to narrow Adams's affection for America. The concurrent crises of imperialism and war suggested a moral decay beyond redemption. Still scholarly productive, he nevertheless ceased writing for a popular audience. His late efforts, the aforementioned *Mont Saint Michele and Chartres* and *The Education of Henry Adams* (1907) were published privately by their author and distributed to select friends and colleagues. The latter in particular remains a poignant statement on the struggle between New World Faustians—the mind of culture and imagination—and New World Caesars—the mind of corruption and conquest. A book of lamentations, it told the story of an American tragedy.

In *The Education*, Adams again played the role of consummate ironist. Instruction for his generation had rested upon a patrician pedagogy of orations, recitations, and dead languages. The indolent swing through Harvard by the Best Men's boys was meant to perpetuate social advantage, not promote a particular artistic awareness or vocational competency. His training conformed to an Enlightenment worldview that recognized structure and symmetry, hierarchy and balance as the intrinsic anchors of a universal order. But life, and America, had turned out very differently. Democracy and capitalism met a stormy ascent, and formal schooling proved a mocking exercise in misdirection. After attending his last Hasty Pudding production, Adams recalled that he "knew nothing. Education had not begun."[25]

His formal training in tatters, Adams presumed through travel and friendships, scholarship and reflection, to master a certain genteel perspective in a world whose tempo pulsed to the cadence of gold bugs, socialists, and the "whole mechanical consolidation of force." From Berlin to Rome and from London to Chicago he observed, puzzled, and meditated. Then one day in 1900, while perusing the Great Paris Exhibition, the awful answer arrived at last. Education and unity were right before his eyes. The Virgin was dead, but the Dynamo, in the guise of the forty-foot electrical contraption dominating the Expo's gallery of machines, had just been christened. Adams noticed a solitary figure standing reverently before its base as peasants, priests, and kings had once lingered before the cross. The seeker paused to offer an unconscious prayer—the "inherited instinct . . . of man before silent and infinite force."[26] Now Adams understood. For all his advantages of birth and name, station and instruction, history had other plans, had elevated other men. John Adams and John Quincy Adams once made their educations pay in the old agrarian republic; in an age of industry and empire, however, Henry's options were considerably condensed. Providence had played him for a fool.

· · · · ·

Not long out of college, Charles Francis Adams Jr. issued a friendly brotherly admonition to the younger Henry: "I DO wish you took a little more healthy view of life. . . . My advice to you is to . . . do anything singularly foolish and exposing you to uncalled for hardship. . . . All a man's life is not meant for books, or for travel in Europe."[27] No doubt a practiced dilettantism tapered Henry's horizons, yet between the pangs of self-pity the shrewd counsel of a savvy social critic emerged. Adams's untiring opposition to speculative capitalism, political corruption, and the general coarsening of culture before the altar of industry retains, even today, a provocative and elegiac sort of higher criticism. Unfortunately his blank response to the lower classes, in their own way equally alienated from the new sources of power, diminished the impact of his efforts.

Perhaps the fundamental difference between Adams and the masses had to do with the latter's largely optimistic response to the machine age, which promised to advance their own standards of living. They were not willing, in other words, to place a brake upon the capitalist system but sought instead through labor organizations, farmers' alliances, cooperative movements, and tax and utility reforms, to redirect the fruits of the factory along more equitable lines.[28] That this embrace of a heightened commercial nexus might compromise their morals or lead them into hellish mill towns far away in time and place from Adams's twelfth-century Chartres seemed beyond their ken, or self-interest.

On balance, Adams's efforts to situate American politics and culture on a plane somewhere to the left of capitalism and to the right of socialism must receive mixed reviews. His youthful efforts to enter the great public debates of the period—taking his "share"—are particularly worthy of praise. With an independent income, Adams might have passed his days much differently. A quiet academic life in Cambridge, an early retirement in Washington, or an aesthete existence in Paris were all and easily within his reach. Yet bowing to instinct or perhaps an inherited sense of family duty, he emerged in the age of industry as something of a modern-day Cotton Mather, recording in his acidulous, penetrating jeremiads the moral crises of the modern condition. Few of his contemporaries understood better the volatile nature of corporate power in the United States.

Ironic, then, that Adams, in a symbolic sense, backed away from America, preferring to lose himself in the medieval past. As the years passed he grew increasingly conservative, discouraged that his efforts to find a middle ground among Grantism and populism had come to naught. To say, then, that he fits into a line of American moderates is to invoke both qualification and context. Adams's brand of centrism, after all, cut in a different direction from, say, Lincoln's. Much of what Adams had to say about democracy he said in *Democracy*, and he did not say it kindly. His doubts characterized a broader generational suspicion of popular government among patricians, who believed themselves inhabitants of a critical political center torn between capital and labor. But their day, if it had ever come, had now gone. Leaving behind the deferential salon for the democratic saloon required a temperament and common touch wholly lacking in the makeup of men like Henry Adams. Still, if they had failed to "cleanse" American politics, they did contribute to a broader criticism of the era that gave way, with the turning of a new century, to a new age of reform. They helped to prepare, in other words, the grounds for one of their own—Theodore Roosevelt—to claim both power and a progressive pedigree. A product of the patrician backdrop that informed Adams, Roosevelt shared Lincoln's appetite for popular political activity and the courage to embark upon a great crusade.

6 Between Privilege and Poverty

Theodore Roosevelt

. . . .

I fight against privilege . . . I fight against mob rule.

—Theodore Roosevelt, 1908

In an age defined by industrial development, Theodore Roosevelt embraced a romantic conception of life that briefly abetted his mastery of American politics. The nation's first significant political leader since Lincoln, he ushered in the modern presidency by piloting the twentieth-century social welfare state. Disdainful of plutocracy, Roosevelt sought a "Square Deal" for the middle class based on conservation, consumer protection, and controls over corporations—important if somewhat milder variations of German and English efforts to reconcile the struggle between capital and labor. Ever since their passage the GOP has wavered between the politics of Rooseveltism and Old Guardism. The former, evident in the Me-Too Republicanism of the 1930s and 1940s, the Rockefeller Republicanism of the 1960s and 1970s, and the Republican in Name Only (RINO) of the 1990s, aligns philosophically with the progressive underpinnings of the Square Deal. The latter, dominant in the Harding-Coolidge-Hoover 1920s, the Reagan 1980s, and the second Bush presidency, espouses the virtues of a privatized economy while flatly repudiating Roosevelt's faith in a shared "strenuous life." For this reason, small government conservatism's claim to TR's mantle is more wrong than right.

Roosevelt's most direct descendants have, in fact, resided on the opposite side of the political divide, with Franklin Roosevelt and John F. Kennedy coming closest to identifying with TR's belief that the greatness of the nation—its destiny—lies in its commitment to mutual sacrifice and equal justice. At the 1932 Democratic convention, the second Roosevelt accepted the presidential nomination of his party in language that promised an all-points crusade: "I pledge you, I pledge myself to a new deal for the American people. . . . This is more than a political campaign, it is a call to arms." Over the next dozen years FDR marshaled the nation's resources to combat the Depression, regulate the business state, and fight fascism. His presidential speeches often referenced Theodore Roosevelt as a model for the kind of government activism he pursued. In one, delivered at the 1938 Jackson Day dinner, he emphasized particularly their common convictions: "In the last campaign, in 1936, a very charming lady wrote me a letter. She said: 'I believe in you and in what you are trying to do for the Nation, I do wish I could vote for you—but you see my parents were Republicans and I was brought up as a Republican and so I have to vote for your opponent.' My reply to her ran as follows: 'My father and grandfather were Democrats and I was born and brought up as a Democrat, but in 1904, when I cast my first vote for a President, I voted for the Republican candidate, Theodore Roosevelt, because I thought he was a better Democrat than the Democratic candidate.' "[1]

Kennedy also conceived of his presidency as one of shoulder-to-shoulder sacrifice, famously imploring his "fellow Americans," "Ask not what your country can do for you—ask what you can do for your country." His brief tenure in the White House attended to a set of programs known collectively as the New Frontier. Domestically this included a war on poverty, extensive job training programs, and support (if belated) for the growing civil rights movement. Abroad it translated into a jingoistic call to curb communism in Cuba and Southeast Asia that, less productively, evoked TR's "big stick" bullying. Declaring that "the complacent, the self-indulgent, the soft societies are about to be swept away with the debris of history," Kennedy revived a favorite Roosevelt theme in a 1961 speech that urged the West to get serious about the Cold War. "Only the strong, only the industrious, only the determined, only the courageous, only the visionary who determine the real nature of our struggle can survive."[2] Kennedy and both Roosevelts all reigned in reaction to their predecessors: TR broke from Old Guardism, FDR from Hooverism, and JFK from the prewar "appeasers" who had condoned Hitler's rise to power. All, moreover, looked to national leadership in the areas of economy, race, and war, where localized and privatized direction could not or would not act. This governing philosophy dominated much of the American Century, and though understandably associated with the "big-government" Democratic Party, its origins in fact resided in the reform Republicanism advanced under the original Roosevelt.

As a presidential pragmatist, TR must be understood within the context of the Progressive era. Revisiting the Patriot King theme in a new century, he sought to steer the nation away from the sharp class conflicts that accompanied the transition from agrarianism to industrialism. He hoped, rather, to reach a governing consensus that, within the parameters of ongoing economic growth and a robustly contested multiparty system, would promote a kind of collective political life in which the national good won out over special interests. As historian Joshua Hawley has written, Roosevelt "was forging an argument and, by extension, a politics, that would appeal beyond narrow segments of the economically affected to an entire nation disconcerted by the modern market, if not modern life."[3] A measure of TR's centrism can be gleaned by his opponents' reaction to both his policies and his rhetoric. Conservatives, worried about his arraignment of the "wealthy criminal class," thought him too far left, while radicals knew that his reforms were designed to stem socialism and thought him too far right. The public, in contrast, tended to regard the presidential Roosevelt as a pragmatic leader deserving of their backing. His legislation during these years largely diluted what remained of Populist support, won over many Democrats, and convinced nearly 57 percent of the electorate to return him to office in 1904.

Considering Roosevelt's outsized, even cartoonish personality, it is easy to lose sight of his practical executive actions. Shamelessly self-promoting and boyishly larger-than-life, this war hero, president, big-game hunter, and bully-pulpit moralist seemed the antithesis of a moderate in either mood or deed. It was said with some justice that he wanted nothing so much as to be the bride at every wedding and the corpse at every funeral. And yet the secret of TR's presidential success was his reputation as an "honest broker," a man in the metaphorical middle able to discern the needs of capital, labor, and consumers alike. During these years, in other words, he was regarded as pragmatic and constructive rather than obstinately ideological. For this reason, and before his notorious postpresidential break with the GOP's Old Guard in 1912, an action that negatively recast his reputation, Roosevelt briefly dominated the American party system. In a time of some upheaval he played a vital role in helping to bring progressivism to the center of the nation's politics.

· · · · ·

In the early nineteenth century Roosevelt's grandfather, Cornelius Van Schaack Roosevelt, a sixth-generation Knickerbocker, opened a hardware and plate-glass firm that flourished amid Manhattan's Jackson-era building boom. Having shrewdly invested his money in real estate, Cornelius amassed a fortune. His son, Theodore Roosevelt Sr., could have led a life of leisure yet instead discovered a passion for public service, the consequence of what he called a "troublesome conscience." Aware of wealth's responsibilities, he raised funds for New York hospitals, cofounded the city's Children's Aid Society, and, as an allotment commissioner, encouraged Civil War sailors to set aside for their families a portion of each paycheck. To the manor born, Roosevelt Sr. cultivated a then-novel occupation among Americans, the professional philanthropist. He practiced the role but briefly. Dead from stomach cancer at a youthful forty-six, he both ensured his children's security (to the tune of $8,000 annually, roughly $190,000 in current dollars) and modeled an ethic of obligation. "My brother's great love for his humankind," TR's sister Corinne remembered, "was a direct inheritance from the man who was one of the founders in his city of nearly every patriotic, humanitarian, and educational endeavor." Roosevelt fils described his debt in more concise terms: "My father . . . was the best man I ever knew."[4]

Roosevelt's references drew beyond the typical patrician pathways linking the American Northeast and the European tourist cities. He inherited from the maternal side, rather, a distinctive southern heritage that begged a broader continental vision. In 1853 Martha (Mittie) Bulloch wed Theodore Roosevelt Sr. The descendent of Scottish and French Huguenot ancestry, Bulloch was raised in a white-columned plantation house in Roswell, just north of Atlanta. The saga of the old South gripped her children completely. "The . . . slaves were treated as friends of the family," said Corinne Roosevelt, summarizing her siblings' perspective, "and they became to us . . . figures of great interest." Adding to the intrigue, several Bullochs served the Confederacy, including TR's Uncle Irvine, the youngest officer on board the Atlantic raider CSS *Alabama*, nemesis of some sixty captured or sunk Yankee vessels before it went down off the coast of France. Mittie herself remained "entirely unreconstructed," her son wrote, "until the day of her death." Taken altogether, the Bullochs suggested the warrior romance of a Cavalier culture and offered TR a visceral example of the martial life that he would come to tout as antidote to the material life. The Roosevelts, by contrast, yielded no heroes. Young Theodore's father avoided military service by hiring a substitute soldier, perhaps as much a domestic necessity, in consideration of his wife's fragile health and southern sympathies, as a rich man's privilege. The child "had to explain it always, about the father he admired so hugely," remembered one relative.[5] From his paternal branch, rather, TR acquired the financial independence and civic-spiritedness once the province of the old Patriot Kings.

Complementing his southern ancestry, Roosevelt adopted in young manhood the persona of a western dude. Embracing the legend of the fading frontier, he purchased a cattle ranch in the Dakota Territory, remembering fondly of his time there—"Ours was the glory of work and the joy of living."[6] An expensive hobby—the ranch extracted from its proprietor's deep pockets some $80,000 over the years—"cowboy land" offered TR something larger than the incestuous Boston, New York, and London social circles that invariably informed men of his class. It further enhanced his sense of American-ness by providing an expanded regional exposure closed to congressional types familiar with their local districts, Washington politics, and, TR thought, little else. Roosevelt's Dakota exodus, combined with a turn officering in a mostly western contingent of cavalry volunteers in the Spanish-American War, made him a popular figure in the trans-Mississippi and prefaced his pending importance in national politics.

Born in the East, weaned on tales of the South's lost cause, and attracted to the West's cattle culture, Roosevelt claimed an unusual range of continental experiences. Conversely, he believed himself surrounded by men lacking both his appetite and his appreciation for national greatness. Referring to William McKinley and more broadly to the larger power structure steering 1890s Republicanism, he once wrote with a mixture of pride and frustration, "The President in a cold-blooded way has rather always liked me, or at least has admired certain qualities in me. There are certain bits of work he would be delighted to have me do. But at bottom neither he nor [party boss Marcus] Hanna . . . sympathize with my feelings or feel comfortable about me, because they cannot understand what it is that makes me act in certain ways at certain times, and therefore think me indiscreet and overimpulsive."[7] In just a few deft strokes, Roosevelt had sketched out the source of his problematic relationship with Old Guard Republicanism: in his view its ranking members were deficient in the heroic qualities necessary to challenge the nation's new money men and resented the frank and few visionaries among them. They hoped to maintain, rather, the prevailing post–Civil War practice of running the GOP as a kind of joint stock company amenable to the entreaties of an industrial elite that sustained its coffers and its candidates.

This standpattism troubled TR but had to be abided. For much like John Quincy Adams, a driving ambition made him less independent of party priorities than he imagined. "My whole career in politics," he once wrote, "is due to the simple fact that when I came out of Harvard I was firmly resolved to belong to the governing class, not to be governed." And this meant making peace enough with the bosses, the bankers, and the politicians. Even so, as a fledgling pol he questioned Old Guardism's wisdom, the first stirrings of a pragmatic strain that led him to the Square Deal. In 1884 Roosevelt joined a group of progressive Republicans at the party's Chicago nominating convention that backed the presidential prospects of Vermont's reform-minded senator George Edmunds. "It included all the men of the broadest culture and highest character that were in the [Exhibition Hall]," TR immodestly reported; "all those . . . who were above average, who were possessed of a keen sense of personal and official honesty, and who were accustomed to think for themselves." By contrast, he counted among the boosters of the front-running senator from Maine, James G. Blaine, a healthy number of "scoundrels" leading a mass of "ordinary men, who do not do very much thinking."[8]

Blaine, a seemingly perpetual candidate for the GOP crown, was dogged by rumors of misconduct. The heart of this charge stemmed from an 1876 allegation that he had used worthless railroad stock as collateral for a $64,000 loan. The accusation caused him to lose that year's GOP nomination to Rutherford B. Hayes. But in 1884 Blaine won the coveted prize, and many aggrieved reformers bolted, threatening to either sit out the election or support the Democratic candidate, Grover Cleveland. Dubbed "Mugwumps" by their critics, these men were educated business leaders and professionals largely from New York and New England; they pursued a classical liberal kind of reform advocating lower tariffs, sound currency, and civil service exams to counter political corruption. Though sorely tempted to join their ranks, an ill-at-ease Roosevelt stayed put in the GOP, alienated a host of bygone allies, and campaigned that fall for his party and against his conscience. Blaine's November defeat to Grover Cleveland—Mugwump votes may have tipped New York and thus the election to the Democrat—marked the candidate as one of only three Republicans to lose a national contest between 1860 and 1912. In defending his actions, TR offered his critics a bland rebuttal: "Mr. Blaine was clearly the choice of the rank and file of the party; his nomination was won in fair and aboveboard fashion, because the rank and file of the party stood back of him."[9]

But Roosevelt's former friends were in no mood to forget his "treachery." As one embittered Mugwump complained to the novelist Owen Wister, "You can tell that young whipper-snapper in New York from me that his independence was the only thing in him we cared for, and if he has gone back on that, we don't care to hear any more about him." Accused of abandoning principles for power, Roosevelt would later argue that the battle of 1884 (a losing struggle for incremental reform) had paved the way for the triumphant progressive presidential years 1901–9. Till then, Roosevelt gave as good as he got. He scored his critics for lacking practical experience, trafficking in absolutes, and mistaking principle for opportunism. "They . . . suffer[ed]," he inelegantly insisted, "from a species of moral myopia, complicated by intellectual strabismus." In a patently masculine political culture where facial hair and military pedigrees were prized, TR accused the Mugwumps of effeminacy. Dismissing the likes of Carl Schurz and the *Nation* circle, he declared, "They were not robust or powerful men; they felt ill at ease in the company of rough, strong men."[10]

Impressed by martial prowess and the cult of Lincoln, Roosevelt repeatedly read contemporary problems through the lens of America's Civil War. Accordingly, he cast Mugwumpery, with its holier-than-thou refusal to back Blaine, as the heir of abolitionism, one of his favorite bêtes noires. Too "pure" to bend on principle, the Mugwumps, so Roosevelt believed, threatened in the 1880s to divide the country over the capital-versus-labor issue, just as the radical antislavery men had cursed the antebellum compromises patched together by previous political generations. "I am endeavoring," Roosevelt once said in explaining his centrist inclinations, "to work in the spirit in which Abraham Lincoln worked. I believe his success was due to the fact that he refused to be swerved out of the path of cautious and moderate advance by the denunciations of the fiery and sincere enthusiasts like [the Boston abolitionist] Wendell Phillips. . . . I do not think that these extremists were purer and better men than Lincoln. . . . I think they were merely more foolish men, and that if they had had their way, instead of bringing about a better condition of affairs, they would have wrecked the Union and destroyed the antislavery cause."[11]

In Roosevelt's view, the true patriot refused to be seduced by the rhetoric of irreconcilables. On this score, he rejected both left and right. "In social and economic, as in political reforms," he observed, "the violent revolutionary extremist is the worst friend of liberty, just as the arrogant and intense reactionary is the worst friend of order." Thinking back to the country's foundations, he fell upon a variation of the Best Men theme, contending that George Washington, the original Best Man, had transcended his times by making a group of disparate colonies prone to follow demagogic leadership abide the benevolent force of his wise will. While the history books flattered the "liberty men" for sustaining the patriot cause, Roosevelt abused them in correspondence as "liberty mobs."[12] One wonders if he saw the specter of radical Tom Paine whispering in the ear of union leader Eugene Debs, or if he imagined circa-1770 Redcoat-baiting Bostonians as the knee-breeched forebears of the Industrial Workers of the World.

Enamored of the cult of iconic leadership, Roosevelt believed that just as Lincoln's measured tactics had freed the slaves, Washington's surmounting of both the British army and large pockets of unruly locals led to the framing of America's constitutional government. "Washington," he argued, "did the real work in securing us national independence and then the national unity and order without which that independence would have been a curse and not a blessing." In this and in other such statements TR's abridged and elitist review of the country's past is obvious though in need of some qualification, for Roosevelt disdained philosopher kings as much as "mobs." His heroes were cowboys and hunters, explorers and military officers. He embraced especially Washington's unusual mix of patrician authority and pragmatic resolve. Before rendezvousing with immortality, the General had cut his teeth in the Pennsylvania backwoods contesting the Appalachians and the elements along with the French and the Indians. Here stood a sterling example of the strenuous life that Roosevelt paid unconscious tribute to when, following the 1884 Valentine's Day deaths of both his wife and his mother, he lit out for the Dakota Territory in a tripartite exercise of numbing, forgetting, and overcoming.[13]

In the aftermath of Blaine's candidacy, the reform impulse took on a new urgency. A string of violent industrial strikes in Chicago, Pittsburgh, and elsewhere sharpened class divisions, while plains-states farmers sought to crack the eastern grip on crop prices through a third-party Populism. The ailing nation appeared to Roosevelt ripe for revolution. The rapid transition from early-republic agrarianism to post-Lincoln industrialism imposed few restraints upon those making the greatest fortunes. On these grounds Roosevelt arraigned the new rich, rather than the arm of labor, for disturbing the peace. And as such he may have given voice to a concern as much personal as public. For TR observed the status (Henry Adams had used the word "education") of his caste in eclipse.

But where Adams engaged in a kind of detached print criticism, Roosevelt was determined to enter the arena and raise a host of critical questions facing his class: Did the Brahmin type have a constructive role to play in modern politics? Might it do more than collect in a pious Mugwum-pery? Could it come to power in partnership with the people? The violent times, Roosevelt argued, called for nothing less. The industrialists may have surpassed the patricians in sheer wealth, but their moral failure to put public interest ahead of private profit demonstrated their unfitness to lead a great democratic nation. "In the reaction after the colossal struggle of the Civil War," TR wrote, "our strongest and most capable men had thrown their whole energy into business, into money-making, into the development, and above all the exploitation and exhaustion at the most rapid rate possible, of our natural resources—mines, forests, soil, and rivers. These men were not weak men, but they permitted themselves to grow shortsighted and selfish; and while many of them down at the bottom possessed the fundamental virtues, including the fighting virtues, others were purely of the glorified huckster or glorified pawnbroker type—which when developed to the exclusion of anything else makes about as poor a national type as the world has seen."[14]

One might deduce from this critical and certainly simplistic sketch that the business-oriented GOP housed more than its fair share of confidence men. If so then Roosevelt faced an unpleasant paradox, for how could he offer allegiance to such an "unheroic" outfit? A simple historical sleight-of-hand did the trick. There were, he concluded, really two Republican parties. The original reflected the concerns of urban mechanics, prairie farmers, and small-town artisans—the men and women, that is, honorably bound to Lincoln's free-labor vision. Its successor, by contrast, aided the plutocrats while turning a deaf ear to the demands of working-class Americans.

Following the debacle of 1884, Roosevelt had questioned Republicanism's future as well as his own. Insulted by the Mugwumps, he turned his back on reform-minded intellectuals, writing in 1896, "If we ever come to nothing as a nation it will be because the teaching of Carl Schurz, [Harvard] President Eliot . . . and the futile sentimentalists of the international arbitration type, bears its legitimate fruit in producing a flabby, timid type of character, which eats away the great fighting features of our race."[15] Again, he referenced the past to make sense of the present. Schurz and his kind were safely and variously dismissed as the kindred spirits of the antislavery "zealots" or as the heirs of the peace-at-any-price Copperhead Democrats who had hoped to derail Lincoln's reelection. Mugwump hostility to the 1898 war with Spain, the conquest of the Philippines, and the general course of the fledgling American empire unsurprisingly aroused his irritation.

Yet Roosevelt, as noted, could no more embrace the nation's rising business elite. He likened it to the Cotton Whig gentry of the 1850s, a privileged quarter of a dying party eager to partner with the slave power if it meant that New England's textile factories continued to enjoy the bounty of southern surplus. They were selfish men, Roosevelt believed, whose wealth had been saved in the 1860s by fighting men. They now again, in Wall Street's flush financial mines and in Carnegie's company towns, jeopardized the Union through greed. Roosevelt often explained his presidency as an exercise in restoration, and Lincoln as his predecessor. Destiny's children, both men experienced rapid and unexpected rises to power during times of national crises. Lincoln prosecuted the Civil War in the face of stiff resistance while suffering the slings of evangelicals and abolitionists unimpressed by his slow march to emancipation. Roosevelt battled the robber barons in the name of economic opportunity while weathering the censor of reformers upset by his concentration of presidential power, martial disposition, and overseas ambitions. Brushing these abuses aside, TR professed his fealty to Lincoln's vision—in his mind the free-labor issue had suddenly resurfaced in the age of industry, and GOP progressives looked now to return the party to its roots.

But if Roosevelt hoped to lead Republicanism he would have to reconcile with its soldierly traditions. During the nearly thirty years spanning from the Grant to the McKinley administrations, every Republican elected to the presidency laid claim to a Civil War résumé. A mere boy when the guns fell silent at Appomattox, Roosevelt must have wondered if he would ever earn his spurs. He was nearly forty years old in February 1898 when the U.S. battleship *Maine* exploded and sank in Havana Harbor; he had a wife, six children, and a comfortable government sinecure, and the Spanish-American War might have quietly passed him by. Instead, it became the defining experience of his life. A studied Dakota dude, he resigned his post as assistant secretary of the navy to become a lieutenant colonel in the First United States Volunteer Cavalry—the Rough Riders.

Fought against a fading European power, the war came to an altogether quick and victorious end for the Americans. A mere 115 days separated the April congressional mandate authorizing the president to use military force to expel Spain from Cuba and the end of hostilities in August. Suddenly, unexpectedly, the former Spanish possessions of Puerto Rico,

Guam, and the Philippines fell to the United States. For his part, Roosevelt lived his crowded hour of glory to the fullest. In a charge against a provisioned blockhouse and trenches occupying the San Juan Heights just outside of Santiago, his Rough Riders stormed the hill and captured the American imagination. It is easy to forget today, when the "splendid little war," as John Hay put it, is but a dim memory, that Roosevelt and his men engaged in spurts of deadly combat. One-third of the First Volunteer Cavalry's officers and 20 percent of its soldiers sustained casualties. Roosevelt eagerly threw his lot in with destiny, coolly calculating the prospects of death. "We had a bully fight at Santiago," he wrote his brother-in-law shortly after taking the Heights, "and though there was an immense amount that I did not exactly enjoy, the charge itself was great fun. Frankly, it did not enter my head that I could get through without being hit, but I judged that even if hit, the chances would be about 3 to 1 against my being killed."[16]

Surviving, Roosevelt returned home in August a national hero. And power suddenly took notice. The cagey old New York senator Thomas Platt, like most of the great bosses, immune to TR's magic, bowed to political pragmatism and, following a careful interview, supported Roosevelt's bid for governor. He backed a winner, but just barely. Roosevelt claimed the November contest against former New York state supreme court justice Augustus Van Wyck by fewer than 18,000 ballots out of more than a million cast. Mindful of the war's importance in catapulting his star into the center heaven of American politics, Roosevelt frequently and fondly recalled the charmed events of 1898 with a mixture of wonder and appreciation—the antithesis of the dark year 1884. "San Juan," he smiled a few months before his death, "was the great day of my life."[17]

A little more than three years after the charge, at the age of forty-two, Roosevelt became the youngest man ever to serve as president. The nation's fifth "accidental" chief executive, TR took power following the September 1901 assassination of McKinley by the anarchist Leon Czolgosz. If, during his White House years, Roosevelt kept a close eye on his Democratic opposition, he showed even greater concern for the Old Guard right and Mugwump left wings of republicanism. This is perfectly understandable. For in presidential politics Gilded Age Democrats mattered hardly at all. Until the age of fifty-four Roosevelt had watched only one, Grover Cleveland, take the oath of office. Derisively tagged as the party of "Rum, Romanism, and Rebellion," Democrats, though capable of holding their own in congressional contests, struggled to mold a coalition backboned by southern whites and urban immigrants into a formidable organization able to elect chief executives. This advantage gave TR the necessary political space to reform the industrial state by reforming the Republican Party.

Roosevelt liked to think of his progressivism as a kind of "enlightened conservatism" which he contrasted favorably to the "sham" conservatism he believed common among so many of his peers. Allowed a free hand, corporations had, in his opinion, eroded patriotism, sharpened class divisions, and mocked the dream of social mobility. "I have always maintained," Roosevelt wrote in retirement, "that our worst revolutionaries to-day are those reactionaries who do not see and will not admit that there is any need for 'change.' . . . It is these reactionaries . . . who . . . incite inevitably to industrial revolt." Having proved himself a maverick on the U.S. Civil Service Commission, as president of the New York Police Board, and as governor of New York, Roosevelt threatened certain Republican powerbrokers eager to keep him judiciously distant from the executive office. Their fears were about to come true. As the emotionally charged Philadelphia conventioneers prepared in the summer of 1900 to give the Rough Riders their second slot, Marcus Hanna, the party's present kingmaker, was incredulous. "Why everybody's gone crazy!" he thundered to a colleague as the delegates cast their ballots. "What is the matter with all of you? Here is the convention going headlong for Roosevelt for Vice President. Don't any of you realize that there's only one life between that madman and the Presidency?"[18]

That one life erased by an assassin's bullet, Roosevelt commenced the Square Deal, progenitor to the cycle of twentieth-century "deals"—New, Fair, Frontier, and Great Society—that long sustained the Democratic Party's hold on American politics. The consensus-seeking philosophy driving TR's presidency is outlined easily enough. As Roosevelt himself broadly put it, "Somehow or other we shall have to work out methods of controlling the big corporations without paralyzing the energies of the business community and of preventing any tyranny on the part of the labor unions while cordially assisting in every proper effort made by the wageworkers to better themselves by combinations."[19] Specifically, the Square Deal sought to limit the influence of the great trusts, promote a fairer government response to strikes and strikers, and, perhaps most important, use the law as a protective presence for both producers and consumers concerned with industry's growing clout.

In both theory and practice it constituted a moderate response to the industrial "crisis." The government sought to serve as an "honest broker" between powerful interests, and TR, in acting as its head, believed himself to be beyond partisanship. Accordingly, he tended to dismiss his critics on both the left and the right for selfishly trying to impede the work of a bigger man: "I . . . retain a feeling of profound anger and contempt alike for the malicious impracticable visionaries of the N.Y. Nation type on the one hand, and for the vicious and cynical professional politicians . . . on the other." Roosevelt's genuine appeal among the people, accompanied by an independent streak that was the bane of party higher-ups, added to his presumption that, while a Republican, he above all identified with the dominant progressive spirit of the time. Fate smoothed his path to power; he owed nothing to man or political machine. "I have no Hanna," he stressed, "there is no person who could take hold of my canvass and put money in it and organize it, and the big corporations who supply most of the money vary in their feeling toward me from fear to tepid dislike. I have never won any office by working for it by the ordinary political methods. . . . I don't think I can play the game that way."[20]

· · · · ·

Roosevelt became the first president since Jackson to serve two consecutive terms and choose his successor. Neither of these next-in-lines, Martin Van Buren and William Howard Taft, escaped the long shadows cast by their predecessors; neither won a second term. In Van Buren's case the 1837 Panic and resulting economic downturn proved insurmountable. Taft, by contrast, lost control when he lost Roosevelt's confidence. Wishing to honor the informal convention limiting presidents to no more than eight years, Roosevelt worked diligently to ensure that Taft, his loyal governor-general of the Philippines and later secretary of war, captured the Republican nomination. "I would have felt very differently, and very much more doubtful about what to do," he explained, "if my leaving the Presidency had meant that there was no chance to continue the work in which I am engaged and which I deem vital to the welfare of the people. But in Taft there was ready to hand a man whose theory of public and private duty is my own, and whose practice of this theory is what I hope mine is; and if we can elect him President we achieve all that could be achieved by continuing me in the office, and yet we avoid all the objections, all the risk of creating a bad precedent."[21]

Bad precedent avoided, Roosevelt safaried in British East Africa, the Belgian Congo, and Sudan for a year—expenses paid by the specimen-seeking Smithsonian Institution, Charles Scribner's Sons publishing house, and the retired industrialist Andrew Carnegie. The San Juan Hill side of Roosevelt luxuriated in the violent adventure: "We are sending back the skins of three elephants five rhinos, four hippos, four buffalos, seven giraffe, seventeen lion &c, in addition to skeletons, headskins, &c ad libitum."[22] From "the bush," he proceeded to a hero's welcome in Europe. Cheering crowds, impromptu speeches, and a belated Nobel Address brought TR before an audience of kings and emperors amid a blur of palaces and parties. The only bad news came from home.

In the last days of his African withdrawal, while sailing on the Upper White Nile, Roosevelt received a disturbing letter from Gifford Pinchot. Appointed chief of the United States Forest Service by TR, Pinchot was fired by Taft in January 1910 for accusing Interior Secretary Richard Ballinger of corruption; more broadly, Pinchot criticized the secretary for abandoning the previous administration's conservationism. Taft, Pinchot now informed TR, had fallen under the spell of the powerful conservative Republican bosses that Roosevelt had once kept at bay. In place of the progressive politics advanced in the Square Deal, the new president, he complained, had "established . . . a vicious political atmosphere in his Administration" and "yielded to political expediency of the lowest type." Pinchot assured Roosevelt that "the hold of your policies on the plain people is stronger than ever" yet warned that "the line between the friends of special privilege and the friends of an equal chance is daily growing sharper." A letter from Indiana civil service reformer Lucius B. Swift put the matter still more succinctly: "My dear Roosevelt, Taft is a damn, pig-headed blunderer. Affectionately yours."[23]

At this point Roosevelt smelled blood—and opportunity. "It is a very ungracious thing for an ex-President to criticize his successor," he wrote Pinchot, "and yet I cannot as an honest man cease to battle for the principles for which you and I . . . and the rest of our close associates stood. I shall of course say nothing at present." Within a couple of months, he was saying quite a lot. Returning to America, he agreed with Pinchot's sour assessment of Taft, insisting that his heir had bent before GOP ultraconservatives. Making the case for a will-to-power presidency as a means to achieve progressive ends, Roosevelt informed Massachusetts senator Henry Cabot Lodge, "Our own party leaders did not realize that I was able to hold the Republican party in power only because I insisted on a steady advance and dragged them along with me."[24]

Looking to do more dragging, Roosevelt worked himself into a fighter's lather for the political break that he longed to make. To be sure, Taft's peace with party conservatives stalled the progressive agenda, but it seems unlikely that any successor could have satisfied TR. Rather, Roosevelt cast Taft as a suitable caretaker executive to avoid the stigma of running for what amounted to three consecutive terms. Put another way, had either Washington or Jefferson, Jackson or Grant established a three-term precedent, would Roosevelt have made way for Taft? The dominant political figure of his day and only fifty-one when he returned from Africa, TR had no more worlds to conquer, excepting the Republican Party.

The situation in 1912 must have looked familiar to Roosevelt. Following McKinley's death he had moved to wean the GOP from its reactionary wing only to discover that the party bosses had planned all the while to wait him out. Now he was determined to have his say. "For me to go into a wholehearted campaign [on behalf of Republican congressional candidates], battling for the Administration through thick and thin, upholding Congress, making such appeals as I did in 1906 and 1908, would be, as far as I can now see, out of the question," he explained to Lodge. "The party leaders have shown with the utmost possible distinctness that while they welcome and are anxious for my help in carrying an election, they are cynically indifferent, or rather cynically and contemptuously hostile to doing themselves anything after election which shall show the slightest regard to what I have promised."[25]

Challenging Taft for the Republican presidential nomination, Roosevelt fell shy in the delegate count at the party's national convention. Abandoning the GOP, he and several allies, including Pinchot, California governor Hiram Johnson, and former Indiana senator Albert Beveridge, created the Progressive Party. Its platform called for the establishment of a national health insurance agency, social insurance for the elderly, unemployed, and disabled, and an inheritance tax. It further, and to the minds of many conservatives more ominously, advocated a "direct democracy" program of initiative, referendum, and recall, designed to allow citizens the right to propose new laws, void existing ones by popular vote, and remove elected officials before the ends of their terms. The Old Guard was aghast. "If I should fight him personally," wrote Lodge during the campaign, "I should be guilty of a disloyalty in friendship." Yet there was never any question what the Massachusetts senator planned to do on Election Day. "Taft stands for representative government and the maintenance of the independence of the courts. . . . I am going to support him for that reason which is a sufficient one for me. I am also going to support him because I still believe that with all its shortcomings the Republican party is the best instrument we have for intelligent government and I do not want to see it destroyed." The "new" Roosevelt, predictably, earned a less polished reaction from Henry Adams: "Never did I see such maniac doings out of an asylum, and the most maniacal part of it is that I think him unconscious of what he is about."[26]

If a bit over the top, Adams's denunciation of Roosevelt contains more than a little truth. Angered over the resurgence of Old Guardism and disappointed in the public's failure to sustain the political principles that undergirded the Square Deal, TR lost perspective. The president who once ruled by placing the government in the center of competing interests now ran for the presidency promising unprecedented change. At that point, much of his old support vanished. As Hawley argues, "Roosevelt's consolidation of political power in the executive, his direct appeals to the public for the purposes of affecting congressional deliberation, and his attempt to achieve social regeneration though a national welfare state" were too far ahead of public thinking.[27] Moving forward, TR ceased to be regarded by the electorate as a pragmatic, "get things done" politician and took on the mien, rather, of an angry preacher no longer able to catch the imagination of his congregation. The moderate Roosevelt of 1904, in other words, gave way to the Bull Moose moralist of 1912.

A more positive assessment, however, might see in TR's support of "direct democracy" a principled and public-spirited campaign to make the GOP and indeed American politics responsive to the concerns of American citizens in an age of unprecedented industrial growth. As Beveridge put matters in his keynote address at the Progressives' Chicago convention, "The Progressive party believes that the constitution is a living thing, growing with the peoples' growth, strengthening with the peoples' strength, aiding the people in their struggle for life, liberty and the pursuit of happiness, permitting the people to meet all their needs as conditions change. The opposition believes that the constitution is a dead form, holding back the peoples' growth, shackling the peoples' strength, but giving a free hand to malign powers that prey upon the people." In seconding Roosevelt's 1912 nomination at the convention, Hull House founder Jane Addams praised TR's fitness for the presidency on the grounds that "he is one of the few men in our public life who has responded to the social appeal and who has caught the significance of the modern movement." Wisconsin progressive Charles McCarthy concurred that Taft Republicanism had turned a blind eye to what he also called the "modern movement": "The people are jealous of losing control of the situation. They had four years of Mr. Taft, have seen him constantly thwart their will, and they wish to have greater control over the presidency."[28]

Though still an object of public adulation, Roosevelt failed to grasp that his moment had passed and with it the golden age of reform Republicanism. At the insurgents' Chicago convention he called for a national campaign to overcome the trusts, the bosses, and the standpatters, and then promptly lost himself in the effort to meld the Patriot King into the Christian soldier. The militant evangelism that permeated the gathering tugged at the deep strain of sentimentalism never far below Roosevelt's emotional surface. Itching for a nomination, a platform, and a crusade, the candidate was more than willing to give his new loyalists the political theater they craved. Standing before a clamoring assembly of true believers, Roosevelt laid bare his political testimony. In a "confession of faith," he assured both God and man that "our cause is based on the eternal principles of righteousness. . . . We stand at Armageddon, and we battle for the Lord!"[29]

The Lord lost in 1912, but it was an honorable defeat. Carrying six states to Taft's two, and earning 27.4 percent of the vote to the president's 23.2 percent, Roosevelt remains the only third-party candidate in the nation's history to finish ahead of a nominee from one of the two major parties. He knew the race to be unwinnable ("I expect to lose," he conceded three months before the election) yet hoped to take down Old Guard Republicanism. "I believe that we are founding what is really a new movement," he wrote in the thick of campaigning, "and that we may be able to give the right trend to our democracy, a trend which will take it away from mere short sighted greedy materialism."[30] In time several of the major planks of the progressive portfolio—unemployment insurance, Social Security, and women's suffrage—came to pass, though Roosevelt played no direct role in any of it.

All told, TR left a complex legacy. Many of Roosevelt's supporters credit him with laying the foundations for the social welfare programs that made America a more economically just nation, yet they shy away from his big-stick diplomacy and strangely ebullient faith in cultural renewal through violence. More favorably, Roosevelt shattered the paralysis of Gilded Age politics and rejuvenated the presidency. By situating the government between capital and labor, he turned the bully pulpit into a powerful agent of change. Envisioning a dynamic Republicanism capable of facilitating economic growth while easing class tensions, TR sought to enlarge the "mission" of the GOP. But this was not to be. For when this governing philosophy did come to pass, it took on the name "liberalism." Under Woodrow Wilson, FDR, and their successors, a revived Democratic Party crafted a vast welfare-warfare state of unprecedented reach and power. It occupied the ideological high ground for two generations and engineered one of the more significant realignments in American political history.

7 Losing the Square Deal Center

William Howard Taft

• •

> I believe Roosevelt to be the most dangerous man that we have had
> in this country since its origins, and that by preventing his election
> to a third term we [Old Guard Republicans] are entitled to the
> gratitude of all patriots.
>
> —William Howard Taft, 1912

In 1948 the distinguished Harvard historian Arthur Schlesinger Sr. asked fifty-five colleagues from around the country to rate the nation's presidents according to a five-sort sliding scale running from "great" to "failure." Since then, some dozen polls of U.S. presidents have followed. Although a consensus has gelled on a handful of heroes (Washington, Lincoln, and FDR quickly come to mind) and villains (Buchanan, Harding, and Nixon are the usual suspects), a certain murkiness underscores the selections. John F. Kennedy's youth, charisma, and capacity to inspire typically land him high marks despite a truncated tenure clouded by Cold War overreach in Cuba and Vietnam. George W. Bush, author of an unpopular Iraqi invasion and occupation, scored a relatively healthy nineteen in a 2005 *Wall Street Journal* poll; presumably his actions were deemed more significant than successful. One could say much the same of William Howard Taft, twentieth in the *Wall Street* ranking. His difficult reign, after all, is remembered less for what it achieved than for what it lost. Faced with the opportunity to solidify the first Roosevelt's Square Deal style of Republicanism, he backed away; hindsight tells us that the price proved to be steeper than either he or his supporters could have imagined. For with the 1929 collapse of the bull market came a concurrent eclipse of Old Guardism—the babbittry branch of the party. And over the next two political generations the nation's ideological center shifted toward a progressive persuasion closer to TR than to Taft.

During these decades the meaning of political moderation in America shifted as well. The late nineteenth-century Wasp consensus, referred to by the philosopher George Santayana as the "genteel tradition," could no longer contend with the realities of a rapidly industrializing nation. Shaken, a vast consumer class looked increasingly to the central government for price and quality protection in a hitherto largely laissez-faire economy. In this way did the growth of federal oversight strike many Americans less as "socialistic" than as a pragmatic response to the unprecedented power of big business. As evident in the Bull Moose break with Republicanism, the country's party system had yet to assimilate this transition into its platforms, procedures, and philosophical outlook.

Aside from reflecting certain social and economic schisms, Taft's unwanted war with GOP insurgents prefaced a seismic shift in presidential politics. Between 1860 and 1912 Republicans carried eleven of thirteen national elections, the most successful stretch of such campaigns by one party in our nation's history. But beginning with Taft's 1912 thrashing and extending through Barry Goldwater's landslide loss to Lyndon Johnson in 1964, they limped along to a meager five victories while sustaining nine defeats. Clearly, the times had passed the old GOP by. While placidly advancing a de rigueur probusiness platform fundamental to Gilded Age Republicanism, Taft and a tight congressional circle of anti-insurgents led by Rhode Island senator Nelson W. Aldrich and Speaker of the House Joseph Cannon badly misread the public's eagerness to experiment with a regulatory state model. The subsequent splintering of conservatism in the 1912 contest, brewing since the emergence of Liberal Republicanism in the 1870s and Mugwumpery in the 1880s, constituted the latest and by far the greatest challenge to ideological unity in a party claiming a common Lincolnian legacy.

Taft's presidency closed a period of GOP dominance and inaugurated a fresh phase in the philosophical struggle that divided twentieth-century Republicanism. An Ohioan, Taft, along with Herbert Hoover (Iowa), Barry Goldwater (Arizona), Ronald Reagan (California), and George W. Bush (Texas), subscribed to middle and southwestern styles of Rotarian Republicanism in tension with GOP progressives. Reform-minded midwesterners, most conspicuous in the region's upper tier extending from Grand Rapids, Michigan, to St. Paul, Minnesota, remained an important constituency in the party but no longer—since Lincoln—offered national leadership. Rather, the GOP's northeastern wing, ancestral home of Adamses and Cabots, once again met their stand-pat cousins in ideological battle. This cohort's brighter constellations included the New Yorkers Theodore Roosevelt, Thomas Dewey, and Nelson Rockefeller, while senators Henry Cabot Lodge Jr. and Prescott Bush represented New England.

Their careers as critics of robber-baron Republicanism bore witness to the Old Guard's failure in 1912 to either convert or evict its liberal wing.

But this became apparent only later and in a period of great crisis for the party. For its success in the 1920s—three lopsided national electoral victories in which Republican candidates defeated Democratic candidates by an average of 410 electoral votes to 116—inured the Old Guard from the complaints of its in-house critics. Consequently, when the Great Depression swept across America, the GOP had little reform experience outside of its distant, reticent abolitionism and its more recent if also reticent Square Deal days. Unable to address the crippled economy, the party stood paralyzed. But matters, and history, might have been different. By rewarding TR's faith with a progressive presidency, a third Roosevelt term as it were, Taft might have helped wean Republicanism from its aversion to the future—the coming role of the central state as the champion of the American middle class.

A distinguished jurist, a loyal cabinet member, and a seeker of consensus in his personal and professional relations, Taft lacked the temperamental latitude for an informed alienation that had once animated GOP reform politics. This proved to be a great opportunity lost. At its inception, Republicanism carried the concerns of northern workers to victory in 1860. With greater vision and a more capacious historical imagination, Taft might have appealed to the past, substituted the aristocratic plutocrat for the aristocratic planter, and placed his presidency on the side of free labor. He might, in other words, have altered the course of modern American conservatism.

• • • • •

William Howard Taft's father, Alphonso (1810–91), began the Taft dynasty.[1] New England bred, Alphonso, the only child of a Vermont judge, attended Amherst Academy and Yale (class of 1833), where he cofounded the secret society Skull and Bones with four classmates. Following graduation Taft taught high school, tutored college students, and earned a law degree. Returning to rural New England held no interest for the ambitious young man—"I should like right well to live in Vermont," he politely wrote his parents, "but I can't at any rate for the present." In search of more appealing opportunities, Alphonso briefly considered hanging out his shingle in bustling Manhattan before piously condemning its legal culture. "I dislike the character of the New York bar exceedingly," he reported; "the notorious selfishness and dishonesty of the great mass of the men you find in New York is in my mind a serious objection to settling there." Instead, Alphonso migrated to Ohio in 1839, apprenticed in a Cincinnati law firm, and shrewdly sized up the primitive professional climate in the Queen City as much to his advantage—a clear case of eastern education meeting western expansion: "I believe, they have but very few men at this Bar of much talent . . . while there is an immense amount of business." He thought it easily within his reach "to earn from $3,000 to $5,000 a year."[2]

Alphonso's star rose quickly in Cincinnati. A railroad enthusiast, he served on the directors' boards of two Ohio lines and argued at every opportunity the case for internal improvements. "If we would be that shining center to which shall converge, and from which shall radiate, the untold commerce of the West," he reasoned in an 1850 address, "we must present attractions and facilities for traffic and for travel." He preached to a congregation of the converted. The enterprising spirit made and remade antebellum Cincinnati, whose population grew from less than 10,000 in 1820 to 160,000 by 1860. Considering the dramatic growth of midwestern economic power in the post–Civil War decades, Taft's eastern exodus proved fortuitous. Five of the last six presidential elections of his life went to candidates from Ohio and Indiana. He grew in reputation apace with his new state and laid the requisite local foundations for a national political career. Still, there were certain New England chauvinisms he never shook. In 1841 Taft returned to Vermont to marry Fanny Phelps, the daughter of a respected jurist; their union produced five children. Never robust, she died at the age of twenty-nine of "congestion of the lungs and of the brain" in 1852.[3] The following year Taft returned East to take a second New England bride, Louise Torrey. Their son, William Howard, was born in 1857.

Sometime in his early Ohio years Alfonso Taft had joined the Whig Party, cultivating Washington contacts on capital-city sojourns to argue cases before the Supreme Court. A coming western man, he served as a delegate in the last Whig convention and in 1856 ran unsuccessfully for Congress under the Republican banner. All the while the nation spiraled toward civil war. In the secessionist winter of 1860 Taft met president-elect Lincoln, whom he considered ill-suited to meet the southern challenge. As late as December 1862, Taft complained to one relative, "You see I am not satisfied yet with Lincoln's performance. He must come up to the work and do his duty before this great war rendered threefold greater by his 'vacillations and inefficiency' can be brought to a successful conclusion. . . . You know I am a radical and find a good deal of fault with the administration."[4]

With far more warmth did Taft regard Lincoln's 1864 appointment of Salmon Chase, like him a New England émigré advantageously situated in Cincinnati, to lead the nation's Supreme Court. "To be Chief Justice of the United States is more than to be President, in my estimation," he congratulated Chase. "I rejoice beyond what I can express, in the confidence that now the momentous interests of Liberty will be protected in that High Court."[5] Two years later, Taft won a seat on the Superior Court of Cincinnati and soon thereafter he assumed the presidency of the Cincinnati Bar Association. More than anything he wished to join the Chase court; a dissenting opinion in a bitterly contested Bible-reading case doomed this dream.

The undoing of Taft's national ambitions began locally. Since the 1829 founding of the Cincinnati public school system, daily recitations of the King James Bible, accompanied by the singing of Protestant hymns, complemented the city's curriculum. But in the late 1860s protests by John Baptist Purcell, the first Roman Catholic archbishop of Cincinnati, and Rabbis Isaac Wise and Max Lilienthal called for the practice's end. In 1869 the adjudicating Board of Education, which included two Unitarian ministers, voted to cease Bible readings in the city's public schools. Shortly thereafter a Protestant group, which included a number of prominent citizens, won a temporary injunction to table the board's decision until a three-judge panel of the Cincinnati Superior Court reviewed the case.

Several weeks later, the panel met. Two of the judges were conservative Protestants; Taft was the other. Brought up Baptist in Vermont, Alphonso had moved on in his new surroundings to Unitarianism and later Congregationalism, liberal churches established in New England that were deeply at odds with the conservative Protestantism that shaped much of the Midwest. The Superior Court's closely observed two-to-one decision permitted Bible reading in the schools; Taft cast the dissenting vote. "I can not doubt that the use of the Bible with the appropriate singing . . . is sectarian," his minority opinion read. "It is Protestant worship. And its use is a symbol of Protestant supremacy in the schools, and as such offensive to Catholics and Jews." Neither anti-Protestant nor anti-Bible, the Board of Education's position, Taft argued, adhered closely and consistently to the establishment clause of the First Amendment, which states in part, "Congress shall make no law respecting an establishment of religion, or prohibiting the free exercise thereof." The board, he concluded, had "simply aimed to free the common schools from any just conscientious objections, by confining them to secular instruction, and moral and intellectual training."[6] Pockets of the Ohio press denounced Taft as a godless man.

Five years later the state Supreme Court reversed the Superior Court's decision, in effect siding with Taft, but his reputation never recovered. Hoping to cap his career in high office he began, after two fruitless attempts to garner Republican gubernatorial nominations, to look beyond Ohio. He perhaps too obviously pined for a seat on the U.S. Supreme Court, even writing in 1874 to Chief Justice Morrison Waite (a fellow Ohioan and Skull and Bones brother, class of '37) advertising his availability for the next open position. Finally, in 1876 President Grant, sensitive to complaints that he presided over a scandal-ridden administration, appointed Taft secretary of war. Honest but ill-suited for the assignment, Taft served only seventy-five unhappy days before the resignation of Attorney General Edwards Pierrepont (another Yalie) opened up a new cabinet slot. In it, Taft made a dubious kind of history.[7]

In the tumultuous 1876 campaign Republican Rutherford B. Hayes defeated Democrat Samuel J. Tilden by the slimmest possible margin, 185 electoral votes to 184. But charges of corruption questioned the election's legitimacy. The initial returns from Florida (four electoral votes), South Carolina (seven), and Louisiana (eight)—the final three "unreconstructed" southern states and thus still occupied by federal troops—produced Tilden majorities, while one of Oregon's three electoral votes also went to Tilden. Any one of the twenty would have defeated Hayes. There is no doubt that fair elections were compromised in each of these states. The suppression of black voters, stuffing of ballot boxes, and handing out of Democratic ballots with Abraham Lincoln's image to confuse illiterate Republican voters were tactics liberally employed in the South. In Oregon, Hayes had plainly carried the state, but its Democratic governor, La Fayette Grover, declared one elector ineligible and substituted a Democrat in his place. Accordingly, GOP-dominated electoral commissions awarded every elector in the disputed states to Hayes; it was now time for Democrats to cry fraud. Facing a constitutional crisis, President Grant signed in January the Electoral Commission Act, which established a fifteen-member board to settle the dispute. It was composed of five members from each house of Congress along with five Supreme Court justices; the party affiliation of the commission broke eight-to-seven in favor of the Republicans. Unsurprisingly, every single disputed electoral ballot went to Hayes by eight-to-seven margins, and the GOP held on to the presidency. Looking over the blunt math of the matter, one Democrat swore, "We have been cheated, shamefully cheated."[8]

As attorney general, Taft had set up the Electoral Commission, taking care of his party and, as things turned out, his adopted state. In effect, a president from Ohio appointed an attorney general from Ohio who oversaw the post-election process by which yet another Ohioan became president. With Grant leaving office and no Supreme Court seat coming up, Taft returned to the practice of law before securing an appointment from the incoming administration as U.S. ambassador to Austria-Hungary, a largely ceremonial position considered an attractive sinecure. Three years later he briefly headed the American embassy in Russia. Chasing better health along the Pacific, he and his wife took a cottage in San Diego, where he died in 1891.

In many respects, Alphonso was the most important Taft. While the historical scales have privileged his son, to a remarkable degree William Howard followed the path cut carefully by his father. It was Alphonso who left rural New England and began a family dynasty in the Midwest, and it was Alphonso's Yale turn, Supreme Court aspirations, and diplomatic-cabinet careers that were each and all emulated by his son. So closely did their professional interests intertwine that William interpreted his father's death as an ill omen to his own prospects. Bereft of paternal guidance, he never felt so alone. "I am not superstitious as you know," he wrote his wife, "but I have a kind of presentiment that Father has been a kind of guardian angel to me in that his wishes for my success have been so strong and intense as to bring it and that as his life ebbs away and ends, I shall cease to have the luck which has followed me thus far."[9]

• • • • •

Despite his difficult presidency and failure to win reelection, William Howard Taft ranks among the more notable public officials in American history. The only man to serve as both president and chief justice, he held no fewer than nine government appointed posts, including solicitor general of the United States, president of the Second Philippine Commission, and secretary of war. On two occasions he declined a much-coveted seat on the Supreme Court, citing competing duties but also holding out for the plum placement of chief justice, which he received from fellow Ohioan Warren G. Harding in 1921. In a legal and political career that spanned nearly a half century, Taft brought his name before voters on only two occasions, both times for the presidency. The results, as noted, were decidedly mixed. A diligent administrator but a poor politician, Taft moved hesitantly through the halls of government, pushed by stronger and more assertive personalities. "I got my political pull, first, through father's prominence," he candidly admitted, "then through the fact that I was hail-fellow-well-met." After Alphonso's death, Taft's wife, Helen, tended to his professional advancement. "Nellie" Taft, the daughter of a distinguished Cincinnati lawyer and state senator, provided all the ambition for office that her husband so clearly lacked. "I wonder, Nellie dear," he wrote shortly before their 1886 marriage, poking at their differences with a genial but pointed humor, "if you and I will ever be [in Washington] in any official capacity. Oh yes, I forgot, of course we shall when you become Secretary of the Treasury."[10]

Nellie's contributions to her husband's career were considerable, though they did have obvious limits, for only Roosevelt's wire pulling could make Taft president. Days after capturing the 1908 contest, Taft generously acknowledged his debt to TR: "I have just reached Hot Springs, and have only now taken up correspondence. The first letter I wish to write is to you, because you have always been the chief agent in working out the present status of affairs, and my selection and election are chiefly your work." Nellie's distrust of Roosevelt, whom she suspected of angling for a third term while using her husband as a stalking horse, placed Taft uncomfortably between a suspicious spouse and a powerful patron. Their tense trio, along with the accumulated pressures of an appointment-filled public life compromised Taft's health. A naturally large man, he ballooned to 355 pounds while serving four fitful years in the presidency; far more happily situated as chief justice he slimmed down to a comparatively svelte 260.[11]

Accustomed to appeasing stronger personalities, Taft appeared to amble easily enough up the ladder of political success, but his accomplishments came with a cost. As president, his native conservatism—obscured and irrelevant in the brilliant shine of TR's star—pushed to the fore, nurtured by an Old Guard freed from the political purgatory imposed upon it in the Square Deal and bully-pulpit days. Those who knew Taft well quietly questioned his commitment to reform, and this included his skeptical predecessor. When asked by the journalist Mark Sullivan shortly before leaving office, "How do you really think Taft will make out?" Roosevelt replied with some resignation, "He's all right, he means well, and he'll do his best. But he's weak. They'll get around him." Roosevelt then suddenly buried his shoulder into Sullivan's—"They'll lean against him."[12]

No doubt differences in temperament and personality distanced Taft from Roosevelt, though other factors must be considered when assessing their complex relationship. To the manor born, TR never knew the necessity of economizing; Taft, by turns, struggled on government salaries to make ends meet. His half-brother Charles, married to a pig-iron heiress, generously supplemented his income for years. "The truth is," Taft acknowledged to Charles shortly before winning the presidency, "that we could not live [in Washington] at all, we couldn't have come into the cabinet, if it had not been for you."[13] And if Taft lacked the luxury of financial independence he missed as much the comfortable sense of historical place and possession that shadowed many of his East Coast colleagues. Whereas greater Boston and New York aligned with the cosmopolitan sensibilities of the country's first families and added depth to their European travels, Taft's orientation remained intrinsically tied to the Midwest; the three years he served in the provincial colonial city of Manila as the first civilian governor-general of the Philippines (1901–3) constituted his most indelible overseas experience.

Taft's comparatively limited range of references accompanied a narrowly legalistic mind-set. He revered the law in an orthodox and fundamental way that imparted precious little compassion for the kind of democratic constitutional upheavals the United States sustained in the Progressive and New Deal eras. While one can certainly find much to admire in his veneration for the nation's body of laws, Taft's high-court colleague Oliver Wendell Holmes Jr. more nearly captured the pragmatic legal climate of the times with his aphoristic insistence that "the life of the law has not been logic; it has been experience."

Taft's reflexive respect for property and contracts converged with a simple social Darwinism at odds with the rising current of reform. Neither his Civil War–era Cincinnati background nor his circa-1875 Yale education prepared him to view with sympathy government intervention in the activities of business. A generous and personally kind man, Taft could be remarkably cold in his antilabor attitude. During Chicago's 1894 Pullman strike, President Grover Cleveland sent 12,000 army troops to quell the unrest; Taft, at that time a U.S. circuit court judge, calmly sized up the crisis in detached terms. "The situation in Chicago is very alarming and distressing and until they have had much bloodletting, it will not be better," he wrote to one correspondent. "Word comes tonight that thirty men have been killed by federal troops. Though it is bloody business, everybody hopes that it is true."[14]

How ironic that just as his public career began to advance, the conservative Taft should find himself in the middle of great and far-reaching progressive change. Much at odds with the public will, he could neither master the times nor defer to them. Recalling John Adams and John Quincy Adams, fellow one-term presidents, Taft proved incapable of reconciling his reign with a moving democracy. Tacking in TR's wake, he rode to a ready-made victory in 1908 by defeating William Jennings Bryan, a spent candidate running in his third national election in twelve years. Despite a host of advantages, Taft's plurality of more than 1.2 million was less than half that of Roosevelt's four years earlier. He lacked his predecessor's charisma, energy, and destiny "complex"; TR had wanted the presidency badly and enjoyed it immensely. Taft, by contrast, exhibited a remarkable diffidence that gave way to doubt. "The truth is," he fretted, "he [New York governor Charles Evans Hughes] ought to be president and then I would not have to be."[15] Lacking a solid center with no real Republican base to call his own, Taft proved impressionable, as Roosevelt had predicted, to the persuasions of the party's Old Guard. Having suffered through seven years of post-McKinley progressivism, it was delighted to discover Taft's disinclination to make reform, or indeed to make history. Passive by nature, Taft pursued a presidency much in line with those of his late nineteenth-century predecessors, men who largely deferred to Congress and genuflected before the great fortunes amassed by the industrialists. Though he adopted Roosevelt's trust-busting strategy, he did so in the name of preserving competition rather than pursuing a greater degree of economic equality.

It is generally conceded that a lack of political acumen rather than a lack of achievement doomed Taft. Like any president, he could point to a thick packet of signed bills and policy initiatives. A favorable reading gives his record a near shiny gloss. Taft supported the consumer-friendly Payne-Aldrich Tariff, his administration drew up more than seventy antitrust suits (eclipsing TR's total), and he praised the Sixteenth and Seventeenth Amendments, which provided for a federal income tax and the direct election of U.S. senators. Yet whatever he touched in the White House had a morbid way of biting him. The tariff controversy is a case in point. The first alteration in duties since the 1897 Dingley Act, the

Payne-Aldrich tariff lowered 650 tax schedules but raised more than 200 while leaving some 1,000 unchanged. To party progressives, precious little reform survived in this package and, following its April 1909 House passage, they demanded that Taft kill the bill. "Unless the rates are very greatly reduced," Wisconsin senator Robert La Follette argued, "the [act] should be vetoed." Instead, following senate approval of the measure, Taft not only signed it but then thoughtlessly angered GOP insurgents by insisting that Payne-Aldrich was the "best tariff bill that the Republican Party has ever passed, and therefore the best tariff bill that has been passed at all." In fact, as Taft scholar Lewis L. Gould has recently noted, the battle over the Payne-Aldrich tariff "turned out to be a self-inflicted wound that shaped the rest of the presidency."[16]

Much of the damage endured by Taft during the tariff fight might have been avoided had he been able to maintain a cordial relationship with Roosevelt. Yet he could do little that pleased his predecessor, even when he tried to follow his policies. As noted, Taft proved to be a surprisingly effective antimonopolist; his Justice Department mechanically pressed suit after antimonopoly suit in the nation's courts. But this troubled TR, a cagey trustbuster who nevertheless knew that the nation's growth and power relied upon industrial development. Certainly government regulation policed this process, he conceded, but it had to operate skillfully, selectively, Solomon-like. Accordingly, when U.S. Steel incorporated in 1901 to become the nation's largest, and the world's first billion-dollar, firm, it had received TR's blessing. And why not? U.S. Steel's chairman, Elbert H. Gary, had grandly promised the president that his company's books would always be open to the government. And should TR "find anything in them that you think is wrong, we will convince you that we are right or will correct the wrong." An impressed Roosevelt called the proposal "the fair thing."[17]

But in October 1911 Taft's Justice Department declared that U.S. Steel had violated the Sherman Antitrust Act with its 1907 purchase of stock in the Tennessee Coal and Iron Company. It now moved to break up the trust. The Roosevelt administration had approved the purchase in the middle of a financial panic, hoping it might stem the downturn, and TR personally promised J. P. Morgan at the time that the government would not pursue an antitrust suit. The consensus is that he struck a poor deal. In the words of one scholar, "Roosevelt had been deceived in 1907" by the bankers, and in approving the transaction, he "had served their financial interests far more than the interests of the public."[18] Hindsight aside, as the Justice Department built a case against U.S. Steel, a number of important constituencies were angry with Taft. The corporations felt abused by the president, progressives were confused by his seemingly inconsistent support of both the tariff (old Republicanism) and the targeting of trusts (reform Republicanism), and TR fumed over his protégé's legal assault on a vast and profitable enterprise that had won his imprimatur. As president, Roosevelt shrewdly employed provocative rhetoric but understood well the power of his popular appeal and knew how to read the mood of Congress and of the American people. Taft, by contrast, proved to be politically tone deaf. In both the tariff and antitrust cases he unwittingly courted disaster, underestimating the importance of interparty politics and taking too lightly a former and still potent patron's feelings.

· · · · ·

Thinking today about Republicanism's 1912 insurgents–Old Guard feud, what stands out is how common such ruptures in party regularity are. The Jeffersonians weathered a bout of internal dissent when the mercurial Virginia congressman John Randolph of Roanoke, upset at his party's creeping nationalism, led a group of "Old Republicans" in opposition. This faction, known also as the tertium quid (third thing) for its independence from both Federalism and Jeffersonianism, preferred a strict states' rights constitutionalism. Accusing his more orthodox colleagues of augmenting the powers of the central government, Randolph reasoned that "I might co-operate or be an honest man—I have therefore opposed, and will oppose them."[19] A far greater threat to Jeffersonianism arose in the aftermath of the War of 1812. Given Federalism's demise, nearly all claimed allegiance to the Republicans. But this proved problematic. The party, after all, took root in the 1790s mainly as a slaveholders' response to the centralizing impulse behind Hamiltonianism. It now fell victim to its own success. How, after all, could the country's only major political coalition defend the peculiar institution if most of its members resided above the Mason-Dixon line? During the Missouri Crisis (1819–21), this contradiction became obvious when northern Jeffersonians overrode the opposition of southern Jeffersonians to bar slavery from the bulk of the Louisiana Territory. Accordingly, the planter wing of the party reconstituted under the banner of the Tennessean Andrew Jackson; its adversaries, a largely northern menagerie of parties, went through a number of permutations—National Republicans, Anti-Masons, Whigs, Free Soilers, Know Nothings—before congealing in the late 1850s under the Republican banner. Both Taft and Roosevelt, in other words, made their political homes within a partisan system possessed of a vigorous dissenting tradition.

Of course the modern Democracy experienced its own bouts of doubt. With much of its strength in the South, the party split during the Civil War, while later in the century the Populist movement seemed to be on the cusp of creating a "producer" coalition made up largely of discontented Democrats. It was by no means clear that the parent party would long survive their secession. Its strength diluted, its ranks thinned by electoral defeat, and its philosophy of Jeffersonian individualism outdated in an age of incorporation, it would have to either change or die.

It changed. In 1896 the Democratic Party made Bryan its standard bearer. His nomination signaled a fundamental shift in American reform politics; out went states' rights, in came the regulatory state. Though unsuccessful in 1896, and in 1900 and 1908, Bryan's candidacies moved the Democrats closer than their opponents to the progressive mood then beginning to influence the country. While it is customary to think of the New Deal 1930s as the founding era of the modern Democratic Party, one could argue that its origins reached deeper into the past, back to the desperate days of the 1890s.

In 1912 Republican insurgents were making a similar effort to ideologically recenter their party. It proved a difficult case to make. Unlike the Democrats, losers of every national election between James Buchanan and Woodrow Wilson save two, the GOP had long ruled the political roost. Why change? And yet careful observers were quick to note that a looming demographic revolution threatened to shake up the status quo. Republicanism attracted a sturdy contingent of rural Wasp voters who identified strongly with the Union victory in the Civil War. But that Victorian electoral universe was waning. The great and recent migration of eastern and southern Europeans—some 15 million had entered the country between 1890 and 1914—had begun to alter the complexion of American politics.

Democrats struggled to reconcile with the new realities as well. The turn to Bryanism may have struck at the heart of the laissez-faire state, but culturally Bryan embodied the values of an older, Protestant, Anglo America. In the famously fractious 1924 Democratic nominating convention at Madison Square Garden, Bryan's constituency, headed now by former treasury secretary William Gibbs McAdoo, squared off for sixteen long days against the party's urban wing led by New York governor and

Catholic of primarily Irish descent, Al Smith. Battle lines were drawn between "pagans" and Christians, ethnics and natives, and perhaps most conspicuously, wets and drys. As historian David Burner has noted, "The major political battleground for prohibition during the twenties was the Democratic party. There the opposing forces were personified in the party leaders Bryan and Smith: the one totally committed to the crusade that looked forward to a 'millennial Kansas afloat on a nirvana of pure water'; the other a child of the saloon, offspring and faithful representative of a social milieu in which that institution held an honored place."

Amid the bunting and banners decorating the convention hall, the two sides went to war. After considerable sound and fury, no one won. Unable to agree on a candidate after 102 contentious ballots, the deadlocked Democrats turned to—were resigned to—former West Virginia congressman and securities lawyer John W. Davis. Nebraska governor Charles W. Bryan, brother of William Jennings, was given the vice presidential nomination to mollify the party's cultural conservative wing. In Burner's words, "The incongruous teaming of the distinguished Wall Street lawyer and the radical from a prairie state provided not a balanced but a schizoid ticket." As the official tally confirmed Davis's nomination and the convention chairman's gavel fell, one disoriented partisan spoke for many dazed delegates when he asked, "Is it true, or is it a dream?"[20] Come November, it proved to be a nightmare. Davis and Bryan received less than 30 percent of the popular vote and lost badly in the Electoral College to Calvin Coolidge; the Progressive candidate, La Follette, captured nearly 17 percent.

No one could have guessed in 1924 that the Democrats were approaching a golden age of governance. Bryanism may have resonated in certain farm and fundamentalist regions, but FDR's appeal would break more broadly. A generation of struggle had placed a strengthened Democratic Party in position to ride to power the economic chaos of the 1930s and the global crisis of the 1940s. Republicans, by comparison, lost the American electorate during these troubled decades, their wounds largely self-inflicted, their deference to Old Guard dogma a ticking time bomb.

• • • • •

On 21 January 1911 Taft took a train north from the capital, arrived in Manhattan, and proceeded to the Hotel Astor as the honored guest of the Pennsylvania Society. Amid hundreds of celebrants, the president entered the banquet room promptly at 7:00 P.M., escorted by a carnival-like procession complete with flags and banners, fifes and drums. Addressing the crowd, Taft urged the fortification of the Panama Canal before a friendly audience. "The great throng that filled the floor of the grand ball room," the *New York Times* reported, "and the hundreds of women who filled both balconies, cheered again and again in the course of Mr. Taft's address."[21] Dined, applauded, and petted, the president could be excused for dismissing, at least for a few hours, his troubles with a snowballing group of GOP dissidents.

Back in Washington, however, the unraveling of Taft's presidency had begun in earnest. Earlier that day Senator La Follette had convened a meeting of insurgents dismayed at the recent midterm election results. Under TR the GOP had fared well in the 1902 and 1906 off-year contests, claiming respectively 54 and 57 percent of the House. The 1910 results were a disaster. Knocked down to only 41 percent in the House, Republicans lost 57 seats and control of Congress. Here seemed solid proof that party standpatters misread the public's passion for reform. Among those attending La Follette's affair were nine senators, more than a dozen representatives, and half a dozen governors. Calling themselves the National Progressive Republican League, they demanded a thorough revision of the Payne-Aldrich tariff, direct primaries, and the democratic inducements of initiative, referendum, and recall. More broadly, they took aim at what they considered to be a crisis in GOP leadership. "Popular government in America," they announced in their Declaration of Principles, "has been thwarted and progressive legislation strangled by the special interests, which control caucuses, delegates, conventions, and party organizations; and, through this control of the machinery of government, dictate nominations and platforms, elect administrations, legislatures, representatives in Congress, United States Senators, and control cabinet officers." Accordingly, they called for a complete overhaul of the nominating-electioneering apparatus. The following year, under the aegis of Roosevelt, who had edged La Follette aside and made himself the instrument of insurgency, the league and its progressive appendages proved to be the catalysts of Taft's destruction.[22]

The president saw it coming. As well as anyone he understood Roosevelt's compulsion for action, influence, and the spontaneous thrill of a good fight. Caesar would return, as soon as he could squelch the third-term stigma. Archibald Butt served as chief military aide to both Roosevelt and Taft, a post that allowed him to observe closely the complex nature of their relationship. He wrote in late 1911, "Just now the trouble with the Colonel [Roosevelt] hangs over [Taft] like a big, black cloud and seems to be his nemesis. He frets under it, I can see. Yet I do not think he would have it otherwise. I have studied him pretty carefully in this matter, and I am convinced that he would rather be at odds with the Colonel and suffer what he does suffer from it, than be on terms of intimacy and be subject to the charge of being dominated by the ex-President. I think he has felt from the first that this separation was inevitable, and, while he would have liked to be on outwardly good terms, he would prefer to have it as it is than to have been forced to consult the Colonel or defer to him in matters of policy or State." Weeks later, with presidential primaries looming, Taft confirmed Butt's premonition of a coming conflict when he ruefully apprised his sister, Frances Taft Edwards, "Politics are very absorbing. I don't know how it is coming out, but I do know that Mr. Roosevelt's coming out as a candidate, and that the fight will be on." Four days after that, TR officially entered the ring.[23]

If Roosevelt broke with Taft, Taft also broke with Roosevelt. He revered the Constitution and complained that TR sought nothing less than to overthrow the nation's established legal code. Roosevelt had alarmed conservatives by championing the power of referendum—popular vote—to review judicial decisions. The great trusts and their legions of lobbyists, he argued, bought sanctuary in the country's courts and rigged the game of justice in their favor. "I contend," he stated in a March 1912 address that raised Republican eyebrows, "that the people, in the nature of things, must be better judges of what is the preponderant opinion than the courts, and that the courts should not be allowed to reverse the political philosophy of the people."[24] To Taft, such raw "direct democracy" threatened to replace basic checks-and-balances safeguards with public opinion. He sized up Roosevelt's rhetoric, popularity, and personality as troubling indicators that a third-term TR might carry his fight for the "people" beyond constitutional boundaries. Undoubtedly, he feared an imperial presidency.

Others shared Taft's concerns about Roosevelt, including some of Roosevelt's closest friends. "I found myself confronted with the fact that I was opposed to your policies [regarding judicial recall]," confessed an unhappy Lodge. "During the last three or four years I have expressed my convictions, which are deep on these points, in several public speeches. I knew of course that you and I differed on some of these points but I had not realized that the difference was so wide."[25] In response to Massachusetts state senator Albert Apsey's request that he attack Roosevelt's record, however, Lodge demurred:

> The situation created by Mr. Roosevelt's candidacy was to me personally very trying indeed. I could not support him, of course, on the politics [of judicial review by popular decision] for which he declared in his Columbus Speech. I am utterly opposed to them and my convictions on the subject are deep; but Mr. Roosevelt has been my closest and most intimate friend entirely apart from politics, for nearly thirty years and nothing can exceed the devoted affection which he has shown to me and in every circumstance of life. If the situation in the country were such that taking an active part in the campaign was absolutely necessary for the sake of the country, I should of course sacrifice anything to do it, but there is no such need as that and if I should fight him personally for the nomination I should be guilty of a disloyalty in friendship which in my opinion ought to forfeit for me the respect of all decent men. I simply cannot do it.[26]

To another correspondent, Lodge argued that the 1912 election was nothing less than a fight for the soul of the GOP. As the two sides squared off, he stood firmly by the Old Guard. "I am . . . going to support [Taft] because I believe that with all its shortcomings the Republican party is the best instrument we have for intelligent government and I do not want to see it destroyed."[27]

The Adamses also watched Roosevelt's 1912 candidacy with a mixture of interest and regret. Henry's brother Brooks, a great believer of civilizational decline, thought TR's democratic pose pointed the way to an anarchic future: "I am very sorry for the breach between Roosevelt and his friends," he wrote, "for I am sure that Roosevelt is sincere, and I suspect that he represents what must be the prevailing side in the end." Henry offered a characteristically sardonic read of the situation. "Do not be alarmed about the election," he shrugged to Lodge's wife, Anna. "Whatever way it goes it is sure to go against us, so we might as well look on it with perfectly philosophical eyes. I see no one possible feature of it that can by any means within the range of imagination be of any good to us. That is such a consoling view that it dispenses me from thinking about it at all. I am somewhat more puzzled to know what satisfaction Theodore gets out of it, or will be likely to get out of it, and I have only one hope in regard to him, and that is that he will be firm on the point not to spend any of his own or of Edith's money on it. It is bad enough to ruin oneself and one's party too, without absolutely throwing away one's fortune."[28]

Having served with distinction in TR's cabinet as secretary of both war and state, Elihu Root now despaired of the new "radicalism" that had overtaken his old boss. "I have no doubt he thinks he believes what he says, but he doesn't. He has merely picked up certain ideas which were at hand as one might pick up a poker or chair with which to strike." Taft encouraged Root to enter the fray and denounce Roosevelt publicly. Like Lodge, Root judiciously held back. Caught between two old friends, he confined his criticism to private correspondence. "I am in favor of your nomination," he wrote Taft. "When, however, we come to questions as between the two administrations, and questions of Theodore's personal right or wrong conduct during his administration, and comparisons between his course and yours, the fact cannot be ignored that I was a member of his administration. . . . I could not enter upon a discussion of the matters to which I bore such a relation in an adverse attitude towards him without being subject, and I think justly subject, to the charge of betraying confidence and disloyalty. . . . I hope that you will pull through. I believe you will. I think it would be a great misfortune if you should not."[29]

Even without Root's aid, Taft moved confidently to keep Roosevelt from winning the nomination. As head of the party, he possessed enormous advantages nearly impossible to overcome; he planned to isolate TR politically, break his popularity among Republican regulars, and prevent his using the GOP as a private plaything. Controlling the nomination became for Taft an article of paramount importance. "I fear things are going to become very bitter before long," he wrote Butt. "But, Archie, I am going to defeat him at the Convention. He may defeat me for reëlection, and he probably will, but I think I will defeat him in the Convention."[30]

Presidential primaries were relatively new in 1912, and only thirteen states held them.[31] After winning nine primaries by generally wide margins, including one in Taft's Ohio, Roosevelt's supporters insisted upon their candidate's moral claim to the nomination. They were to be bitterly disappointed. For in the other states caucuses chose delegates, and these were susceptible to manipulation by professional politicians. Entering the GOP's national convention, a number of delegates remained contested. Clarence Kelsey, a Taft man from their Yale days, advised the president on how to handle the situation. The peremptory spirit of his counsel was followed more or less fully.

It seems that the fate of the Republican Party now rests in the hands of the National Committee and that if it handles the case with courage and determination it can save the day. It should not mince matters or temporize with Roosevelt or his claims, but should summarily throw out all his contests and force him out of the convention. No matter how much he howls or the press howls, or how unjudicial the Committee is accused of being, it should take the consequences and with certainty and speed install your delegates and take control of the convention. The giving of some of the delegates to him and giving him a chance to fight on the floor of the convention to win over enough more to give him a majority, will betray the party into his hands. Perhaps he will not be forced out of the convention anyway but no stone should be left unturned to drive him out of it. He has split the party in two but he should have to go off and form a new party and fight as an independent and not capture the old Republican party and go off with its good will and history as his own, because he has betrayed both.[32]

Taft assured his friend that matters were well in hand. "Never fear, old man, we are going to fight and, believe me, we are going to win."[33]

And he did—but victory came at an awful price. Days before the Chicago convention convened a pro-Taft Republican National Committee gathered to discuss the claims, challenges, and counterchallenges of 254 disputed delegates—nearly half of the 540 required. Roosevelt had earned 290 in the primaries with Taft (124) and La Follette (36) trailing far behind. Roosevelt believed that he could win the nomination by capturing the majority of these contested delegates, perhaps not on the first ballot but after it became apparent that Taft could not secure a majority. This wishful strategy succumbed to a stronger reality when the Republican National Committee awarded 235 of these delegates to Taft and only 19 to TR. Considering that caucuses, conventions, and state conventions loyal to Taft would choose the rest of the delegates, the committee's decision in effect handed the president the nomination. In protest a *Chicago Tribune* headline shouted, "THOU SHALT NOT STEAL!" Condemning the Old Guard's "steamroller" strategy, TR fulfilled the hopes of the professional politicians by leaving the party.

Taft rejoiced, believing Roosevelt to have passed the point of return. The convention, he adroitly wrote, "has made it impossible for him to become President this time, or at any other time in the history of the country. He is being driven so far from the Republican party as to make it impossible for him to be able to appeal to Republicans in the future as a standard bearer." Yet whatever satisfaction Taft might have mustered from Roosevelt's GOP exodus clashed with the inevitability of his own defeat. Sensitive to criticism, tired of TR's long shadow blanketing the electoral landscape, and genuinely concerned about the fate of the nation, he uncharacteristically descended to demonizing his former friend. "I look upon him," he informed Helen, "as I look upon a freak, almost, in the zoological garden, a kind of animal not often found." To another correspondent he damned Roosevelt as "the greatest menace to our institutions that we have had in a long time—indeed I don't remember one in our history so dangerous and so powerful."[34] It should be remembered that Taft's private attacks on Roosevelt arose in a heightened political atmosphere. Far from stirring up only GOP conservatives, TR, with his bold new rhetoric and controversial stand on the judiciary, pushed a good many moderates to the right.

By isolating TR and the insurgents, the standpatters hoped to return their party to its McKinley golden age. In the 1890s Republicans had combined to defeat "radical" reform in its Populistic and Bryan-Democratic permutations. Now the radicals resided within their own ranks. Accordingly, Taft stoically accepted the coming election as the centerpiece in a painful if necessary purging of ultraprogressives. No less than Roosevelt did he believe that "we stand at Armageddon." For an America with popular judicial recall, direct primaries, and a president more powerful than the Constitution, threatened, he argued, to overturn the legal restraints long the nation's source of strength. In this spirit of sacrifice Taft almost welcomed the coming rout. "The Republican party needs the discipline of defeat, and the great object that I have to carrying on this campaign is saving the parts of the party which can be saved, and making a solid disciplined force which will be ready to take advantage of the errors of our old time enemy the Democrats, and from which will have sloughed off, as members of importance, at least, these wild-eyed populists who insist on being Republicans, without obeying the rules of conformity that ought to obtain in a party which is to accomplish anything."[35]

Most important, Taft sought to stem a potential alliance of Democrats and Bull Moosers. Defeating the insurgents, he remarked just days before the election, "allows the Republican party to maintain its position as a balance wheel between the radicals of the progressive character, who numerically are not very great, and the colorless Democrats who are only looking about for some issue on which to get to power."[36] But in pushing for a business-as-usual GOP, Taftites ignored the set of historical forces that had brought their party to the forefront of American politics in the first place. More than a gathering of industrial interests, Republicanism in the 1850s combined farmers, mechanics, and abolitionists to form a great, even revolutionary league.

Taft's hostility to populistic politics antedated the 1912 election. In a 1903 letter to Roosevelt, he expressed a strong desire to see the Democratic Party force its Bryan faction from the field, and the communication doubles as an ironic prologue to his later attack on TR. "I sincerely wish that . . . a split [among Democrats] may come by which Bryan and his followers shall be relegated to the limbo of populism where they belong. Of course this would mean defeat in the next campaign; but were they to be united with the Populists, they would be defeated, and until they drive Bryan out of the party, they can never bring about a condition that will give them success." Taft clearly hoped that a purging of "extremists" within the two-party system might reinforce a conventional electoral culture informed by patronage rather than populism. "With the conservative element of the Democratic party in control," he advised Roosevelt, "we may have campaigns like those of the past, between Cleveland and Harrison, when, while the issues were important, it was known that the guaranties of social order and the rights of property would be sacredly observed under either." Now, nearly a decade later, Taft regarded Roosevelt as another Bryan. With a stinging defeat looming, he astonishingly looked to the pre-Populist 1880s as a template for the GOP future. "If Roosevelt beats me," he predicted, staring into the abyss, "it will be a serious disappointment and will present a somewhat dangerous situation for the conservatives of the country. We must keep him out of the Republican party at all hazards."[37]

In November Taft carried just two states and finished a distant third. "What I got," he said, facing the expected but unpleasant reality, "was the irreducible minimum of the Republican party." Though Roosevelt's sun had set, Taft foresaw imminent ideological challenges ahead. In a post-election press release he reprised the hazards of progressive politics while framing the GOP's future as on ongoing struggle against radicalism. "The vote for Mr. Roosevelt, the third party candidate, and for Mr. [Eugene] Debs, the Socialist candidate, is a warning that their propaganda in favor of fundamental change in our constitutional, representative government has formidable support. . . . It behooves Republicans to gather again to the party standard and pledge anew their faith in their party's principles and to organize again to defend the constitutional government handed down to us from our fathers." He then called upon Republicans and Democrats alike to isolate third- and fourth-party challenges. No doubt a painfully fresh electoral defeat informed his fears, and yet it is regrettable that such a capable thinker as Taft so unequivocally identified progressive politics outside the two-party consensus as a threat to the health and vitality of the nation. "We favor every step of progress toward more perfect equality of opportunity and the ridding society of injustice," he carefully observed, "but we know that all progress worth making is possible with our present form of government, and to sacrifice that which is of the highest value in our government structure for undefined and impossible reforms, is the wildest folly."[38]

And when that "folly" did come, new players had edged out the old. Taft returned to New Haven in 1913 as the Chancellor Kent Professor of Law and Legal History at Yale Law School. There he might have ended his days in a comfortable academic dotage had the Old Guard not returned to power in 1920. For the following year President Harding nominated Taft to replace deceased chief justice Edward Douglass White on the Supreme Court. At that moment it looked as though Taft's 1912 strategy had been vindicated in full. Along with Harding's historic victory—he captured the highest percentage of the popular vote by a GOP presidential candidate to that time—the party as a whole, under the stewardship of "regular" Republicanism, claimed large majorities in both the House and Senate. By any measure, it had been a marvelous year in what turned out to be a dominant decade for the GOP.

But then came the market crash and the Old Guard's inability to respond constructively to the economic crisis that followed. In that failure the settlement of 1912 came undone, and a new Roosevelt and a new insurgency loomed on the political horizon. Taft was spared this shock. Five weeks after retiring from the court in February 1930 his heart gave out; he would not live to see a second Roosevelt's constitutional revolution.

Franklin Delano Roosevelt himself embraced TR's progressive legacy as a precursor to his own presidency. In reply to one correspondent's claim that the Bull Moosers had anticipated the reforms of the 1930s, Roosevelt agreed without reservation: "I think you are entirely accurate in comparing the fight in the Republican Party against Cannonism and Aldrichism with the general principles and ideals of the New Deal." His adviser,

Felix Frankfurter, seconded this view in a 1934 letter to the president in which he complained that the same conservative interests that had moved "against T.R. . . . are now expressing themselves so violently and so sanctimoniously against your policies."[39] These ideas and programs secured for the Democratic Party leadership of the liberal activist state and put Republicanism on its heels. Caught between its Taft and TR wings, the GOP entered this difficult era of its history internally divided and unable to come to a consensus on how to proceed.

Part III **Pragmatists**

· ·

A new kind of central authority arose in the twentieth-century United States—the welfare-warfare republic. Pledged to a politics of prosperity, it offered both guns and butter, defending the "Free World" abroad while maintaining the reform spirit of the New Deal at home. For a generation this consensus made the Democratic Party the nation's dominant party. But its very success compromised its appeal. As blue-collar workers matriculated over the years into the middle-class, they sought to safeguard their gains by questioning the entitlement-state philosophy. Many of these new suburbanites joined a rising cohort of libertarians, cultural conservatives, and free-traders to challenge the standing liberal order. By the 1980s, they had forged a new consensus. Yet for all the talk of a "Reagan Revolution," pragmatic politics, that is to say, resistance to overtly ideological claims, remained in place. In fact, from 1981 to 2013, Democrats and Republicans battled to a relative congressional standoff. And in the 1990s, Clinton Democrats came to power by claiming the prevailing middle ground in a post–New Deal, post-Reagan political culture. In the new century's second decade, they occupy it still.

8 "Me-Too" Republicanism Meets the New Right
Henry Cabot Lodge Jr.

· — · · · ·

> What in God's name has happened to the Republican Party!
> —Henry Cabot Lodge Jr., 1964

In 1932, in the depths of the Great Depression, the long post–Civil War run of Republican Party rule came to an end. And with it expired the old American political tradition, defined by the historian Richard Hofstadter as "a belief in the rights of property, the philosophy of economic individualism, [and] the value of competition."[1] In a quintet of important and once solidly GOP states, growing support for social welfare programs challenged the once-sacred capitalist canons enumerated by Hofstadter. Excepting Theodore Roosevelt's aberrant Bull Moose candidacy in 1912, New York, Pennsylvania, Ohio, Michigan, and Illinois awarded a majority of their combined electoral votes to Republicans in every presidential contest between 1856 and 1928. Yet since 1928 Republicans have won a majority of these heavily populated, heavily industrialized states in only seven of twenty-one national campaigns. As this trend unfolded in the 1930s and 1940s, it produced heated and often bitter disputes within the GOP.

Republican traditionalists rejected New Deal liberalism as an American variation of European socialism. They stood instead for the return to a pre–welfare state politics. "The New Deal repudiation of democracy," observed former president Herbert Hoover in a 1936 speech, "has left the Republican Party alone the guardian of the Ark of the Covenant with its charter of freedom."[2] But this nostalgic call for a revival of "traditional reform-minded values" troubled moderate Republicans, who believed that a return to the Hoover 1920s doomed both their party and their country. They recognized that neither Franklin Roosevelt's far-reaching New Deal initiatives nor the nation's growing engagement in global affairs—another point of contention among isolationists on the right—could be wished away. Adopting a new identity, however, proved difficult. The centrist candidates put up by the GOP in the 1940s, Wendell Willkie and New York governor Thomas Dewey, were heckled by conservatives as "Me-Too" men, fellow travelers in the Roosevelt revolution. Their failure to win the presidency strengthened their in-party opposition.

Willkie, formerly a Democrat, captured the GOP nomination in 1940. A New York corporate lawyer born and educated in Indiana, he believed government intervention critical for resurrecting the moribund economy. Attending the 1932 Democratic National Convention, he briefly backed the favorite-son candidacy of former Cleveland mayor Newton D. Baker before jumping on the FDR bandwagon. Not long afterward, he jumped off. The president's Tennessee Valley Authority program, launched in 1933, pledged to bring flood control and low-cost electricity to the rural South. It also promised to compete against private power firms including the Commonwealth and Southern Corporation, a New York–based electric-utility holding company whose presidency Willkie had recently assumed. Failing to convince the New Dealers that the government-subsidized TVA threatened to put Commonwealth and Southern out of business, he sold the corporation to the TVA in 1939 for some $80 million—and switched parties with the idea of challenging Roosevelt the following year for the presidency. A qualified critic of the New Deal, Willkie acknowledged government's responsibility to provide services in those areas of the economy that private industry could not or would not. When "individuals cannot carry through large-scale social readjustments," he was quoted in *Life* magazine shortly before the election, "society owes an obligation to its members when it leads them up a blind alley."[3]

Though thrashed by FDR in the Electoral College (449 to 82), Willkie demonstrated moderate Republicanism's potential to revitalize American conservatism along progressive lines by polling more popular votes than Hoover did in 1928, indeed more than any previous Republican presidential candidate had. Still, the party remained fundamentally divided. With much of the world at war in 1940, a fierce debate arose in America between isolationists and internationalists. In his 1943 book, *One World*, Willkie called for greater U.S. overseas engagement while virtually damning the "America First" sentiment that appealed to many Republicans: "If our withdrawal from world affairs after the last war was a contributing factor to the present war and to the economic instability of the past twenty years," he wrote, "a withdrawal from the problems and responsibilities of the world after this war would be sheer disaster."[4] The most liberal Republican Party leader since Theodore Roosevelt, Willkie sought the GOP nomination again in 1944 but finished a distant fourth in the only primary he entered. Contemplating a Bull Moose–like breakaway, he made contacts with the newly organized Liberal Party of New York before his sudden death in October.

Dewey fared no better among Republican traditionalists. A midwesterner, he graduated from the University of Michigan before attending law school at Columbia University, after which a profitable Wall Street practice anchored him in Manhattan. Attracted to New York's crusade to clean up organized crime, he won plaudits as a special prosecutor for putting Dutch Schultz on trial and shutting down Lucky Luciano's prostitution ring. From there, he enjoyed a meteoric political rise. Elected district attorney of New York County (Manhattan) in 1937, Dewey, popular among the probusiness eastern establishment, captured GOP presidential nominations as a New Deal Republican in 1944 and 1948. But unlike previous "Me-Too" candidates, Generals William Henry Harrison and Zachary Taylor, antebellum Whig presidents chosen in part for their presumptive resemblances to the popular Andrew Jackson, Dewey lost. Frustrated, the Republican right called for a "real" conservative to head the ticket, and this meant a return to the party's pre-1932 positions.

Progressive Republicans considered this strategy suicidal. They had little doubt that average Americans accepted if not embraced Social Security, the G.I. Bill, and the surfeit of government programs that now impacted their lives. Rather than look to the past, GOP liberals advanced the candidacy of Dwight Eisenhower, an ideological centrist who accepted the social welfare state and supported the stationing of U.S. troops in Europe and Asia as the centerpiece of a new postwar collective-security arrangement. Old Guard Republicans, by contrast, never liked Ike. As with Theodore Roosevelt, they accepted his transitory leadership of the party (1952–60) while pining for a presidential candidate closer to their own convictions. Eisenhower returned the right's skepticism with his own doubts. "I had hoped that the first Republican national victory in twenty years would provide a strong, unifying influence within the party and among its representatives in the Senate and the House," he candidly observed once out of office. "But my hope for unanimity was quickly shattered. . . . Some Republican senators . . . had long been opponents of the mutual-security program, in which I believed implicitly. Others . . . wanted to reduce income taxes at once, regardless of Korean War costs and current deficits. . . . [A] few even hoped we could restore the Smoot-Hawley Tariff Act, a move which I knew would be ruinous."[5]

First days' difficulties between moderate and conservative Republicans were so pronounced that Eisenhower lingered lightly over the possibility of creating a new party. In March 1953 the president nominated the nonpartisan Charles Bohlen to head the U.S. embassy in Moscow. Present at the Yalta conference where, many on the right believed, FDR had consented to Soviet control of Eastern Europe, Bohlen was a controversial figure among anticommunists. Wisconsin senator Joseph McCarthy demanded that the FBI release its files on the would-be ambassador to the Senate before a confirmation vote was held.

Publicly, Eisenhower stated, "I have known Mr. Bohlen for some years. . . . I have listened to his philosophy. So far as I can see, he is the best-qualified man for that post that I could find." Privately, he wrote that if such red-baiting "were often repeated, it would give some weight to an argument that was [recently] presented to me. . . . It was that I should set quietly about the formation of a new party. The method would be to make a personal appeal to every member of the House and Senate; to every governor, and to every national committeeman whose general political philosophy and purpose seem to belong to that school known as 'the middle way.'" Bohlen was comfortably confirmed seventy-four to thirteen, but nearly every negative vote belonged to a member of the president's party. Afterward, Eisenhower recorded his hope for reconciliation: "If we can possibly bring about a greater solidarity among Republicans, if we can get them more deeply committed to teamwork and party responsibility, this will be much the better way." Yet he was willing to keep his options open—"It may come about that [leaving the GOP] will be forced upon us."[6]

· · · · ·

The Cabot-Lodge lineage offers a partial primer in American history. Its connections include a Mayflower voyager, ministerial divines, and a smattering of public officials. It also counted among its kin the high Brahmin Henry Cabot Lodge (1850–1924). Known today as the chief congressional critic of Woodrow Wilson's doomed League of Nations, Lodge began his public career as a reformer, thus offering his grandson, the senator, vice presidential candidate, and ambassador, Henry Cabot Lodge Jr. (1902–85), entry into the milieu of American progressive politics. Born in antebellum Boston, the senior Lodge enjoyed a privileged life. In adolescence he counted the cream of the Bay State's gentry as near and dear models of civic engagement. Daniel Webster and George Bancroft, Ralph Waldo Emerson and Oliver Wendell Holmes were among the cluster of greats who graced the family parlor. The impression they made proved lasting. Lodge belonged, as one Senate colleague recalled, to "that school of American youth who were trained and educated to possess a clear conception of duty, strong faith and pride in their ancestral and patriotic inheritance, and with a fixed resolve to succeed in life."[7]

At age eleven Lodge attended a private Latin school run by Epes Sargent Dixwell, descendent of a regicide judge who sat on the court that condemned Charles I. He later generalized these years as an endless chain of gray winter days packed with dull, uninspired lessons. "We had the old-fashioned classical curriculum, Latin, Greek, mathematics, a little classical history and geography, and exercises in declamation. The methods of teaching were largely mechanical: learning by rote." The leaden schedule, complete with weekly Bible instruction, was remembered by Lodge as "the serious Sundays" and molded the boy into a deliberate, careful, and conventional thinker. Not until he arrived at Harvard did Lodge find a dynamic intellectual model. There, he affectionately remembered Henry Adams's course in medieval history as the well-timed morning bell that "aroused my slumbering faculties."[8]

Beyond the classroom, Lodge observed in Cambridge the possibilities of a reformer-scholar profession. Working as Adams's unpaid assistant on the *North American Review,* he took note of his mentor's spirited, inspiring, and futile war on Grantism. Lodge's own youthful flirtation with liberal Republicanism soon followed. In May 1876 he served as secretary at the famous Fifth Avenue conference, an assemblage of reformers intent on making an impact on the upcoming presidential campaign. The attendees included William Graham Sumner, Carl Schurz, and Theodore Roosevelt Sr. Collectively, these independents issued an "address to the people" warning both parties to put up "clean" candidates if they hoped to win the support of the Best Men, and "re-establish the moral character of the government."[9] But come November, politics as usual won out. Many Fifth Avenue men meekly fell back in line and voted for the Republican Rutherford B. Hayes.

Not Lodge. For the only time in his life he supported a Democratic presidential candidate. "I believed that the Fifth Avenue conference meant what it said," he later explained, "&, Hayes being nominated, I did violence to every feeling & voted for Tilden to keep my pledge as I understood it. Very few did the same." Asked for his advice, Adams counseled a shaken Lodge to adopt his own strategy: drop politics for a "historico-literary" career. "Boston is running dry of literary authorities," he explained, "anyone who has the ability can enthrone himself here as a species of literary lion with ease, for there is no rival to contest the throne." Trying his hand, Lodge produced a spate of hagiographic political biographies of Hamilton, Washington, and Daniel Webster that lacked the depth, nuance, and irony so evident in Adams's work. These books are today unread.[10] But for Lodge there would be other worlds to conquer. Relegating 1876 to an unpleasant memory, he occupied a congressional seat for six years before a three-decade tenure in the U.S. Senate.

Lodge's son, George, broke decisively from the family's traditional occupational trajectory, politics or moneymaking. Boston born yet eager to enter Washington salons, Bay, as he was affectionately known, circulated in a social world laurelled by the likes of novelists Edith Wharton and Henry James, the self-proclaimed hedonist Alice Roosevelt, and the collector of Japanese art William Sturgis Bigelow. A voracious reader, Bay mastered French, German, and Italian before entering Harvard where he self-consciously adopted the pose of a poet bruised by American philistinism. Rejecting "proper" Boston, he became a "decadent" Brahmin. Along with Philip Savage, Hugh McCullough, and Trumbull Stickney, Bay is remembered in regional literary lore for his contribution to a minor school of verse writers known as the Harvard pessimists. All were destined to die young. Their friend, the philosopher-essayist George Santayana, blamed the parched cultural climate for their collective fate. They were "killed by the lack of air to breathe," he swore. "People individually were kind and appreciative to them . . . but the system was deadly, and they hadn't any alternative tradition . . . to fall back upon."[11] Darwinism, industrialism, and Grantism had robbed the American imagination of its romantic possibilities. There seemed nothing higher to live for.

After Harvard, Bay turned down an uncle's invitation to advantageously enter the corporate world. The graduate had other and more intensely personal plans. Privileged with wealth and connections, he set off for Europe in 1895 to study modern languages and medieval literature. There he cultivated the aesthetic of an "anarchist," that is, an antimodernist critical of the scientific-mechanical-commercial complex then coming to predominate in America. While in Paris, Bay recorded his alienation from American materialism in desperate if studied strokes: "The thing which tore me worst in all this mental struggle I have been going through was the continual thought of money and my crying inability to adapt myself to my time and to become a money-maker. I felt as if it was almost cowardly of me not to turn in and leave all the things I love and the world doesn't behind, and to adjust myself to my age, and try to take its ideals and live strongly and wholly in its spirit."[12]

Back in Washington, Bay lived a double and doubtful life. A bored bourgeois in his father's secretarial service, he sought inspiration as a nocturnal poet. Thinking over Bay's artistic aspirations during this delicate period, the senior Lodge judiciously withheld judgment, in itself a kind of judgment. "What he will come to I cannot guess," he informed Theodore Roosevelt. "He is struggling for utterance and when he gets command of his instrument we shall know whether he has anything to say."[13] In the midst of a prolonged ennui, Bay suddenly discovered inspiration in an unlikely source, the Spanish-American War. Descended from privateers and China traders, he looked upon the Cabot-Lodge line as an honorable antidote to counting house capitalism. In his poem "The Norsemen," Bay apotheosized its primitive promise:

These are the men!
The North has given them name,
The Children of God who dare . . .
These are the men!
In the strength of the primal song
As the increase world turned white
They descended and dwelt with the sea. . . .[14]

Off to war, Bay took a naval cadet post on board the USS *Dixie* captained by an uncle, Harry Davis. There, Bay commanded two gun crews and yearned to see action—"I only hope [the war] will last long enough to . . . give me one fight for my money." It did. A series of small assaults off the southern coast of Cuba elicited the following communication for family consumption: "We came down and on our way destroyed two blockhouses. . . . The next day we engaged a battery at a place called Trinidad, and yesterday we engaged the same battery, a gunboat in the harbor, and a gunboat that came out to us, and used them up pretty badly. So you see I am in it."[15]

After the war, Bay married Elizabeth Davis, granddaughter of the deceased New Jersey senator and former secretary of state Frederick Theodore Frelinghuysen. In 1902 their son, Henry Cabot Lodge Jr., was born; the child had only seven years with his father. The weak-hearted Bay contracted ptomaine poisoning in the late summer of 1909 and died at thirty-five. Ruminating on the young man's unfulfilled promise, an observant Wharton believed him, despite his war service, soft and spoiled. "He grew up in a hot-house of intensive culture, and was one of the most complete examples I have ever known of the young genius before whom an adoring family unites in smoothing the way. This kept him out of the struggle of life, and consequently out of its experiences, and to the end his intellectual precocity was combined with a boyishness of spirit at once delightful and pathetic." So great was this conspiracy of kindness that not even death could alter its course. Bay's modest exploits as a soldier and a poet were heroically recast so that he might join his kinsmen as an object lesson to the next generation. The ghosts of Essex County haunted their own. One relative advised young Henry with all the subtlety of a papal bull to "remember always that your father fought for his country in the Spanish War & that your grandfather whose name you bear & your ancestors on both sides for many generations have served your country in both war & peace. So you have an honorable tradition to maintain."[16]

· · · · ·

In youth, Lodge claimed an open intimacy with the politics and personalities that shaped pre–World War I Washington and expatriate Paris. The peerless Henry Adams ("Uncle Dordy") touched the boy directly—"Adams was extremely kind to me when I was a child. . . . I carry with me through life a definite and attractive picture of him." Wharton also made a distinct impression in her lovely Louis XIV hotel on the Rue de Varenne— "She was sometimes rather overpowering, but she liked the young and was always affectionate and most kind to me." Inescapably, Lodge's namesake made the deepest impress—"I remember long evenings spent in front of the fire alone with my grandfather. . . . He would talk to me at great length about public questions: the League of Nations, of course; but many other subjects as well, notably practical politics, local, state, and national."[17]

Following the inevitable Harvard education, Lodge made the inevitable European tour. Armed with a letter of introduction from President Calvin Coolidge, his itinerary included interviews with Mussolini, Austrian president Michael Hainisch, and French prime minister Raymond Poincare. In England he fell hard for Oxford and contemplated an extended stay to read romance languages. The proposal struck the senior Lodge, a frustrated observer of Bay's continental idleness, with an unwelcome ring of recognition. He advised otherwise: "You have worked hard . . . and I am very glad that you should have a vacation in Europe. I entirely sympathize with your taking one, but I have this to say. I must tell you what my opinion is. It must be a vacation; that is, a temporary and not overlong visit. I should be very sorry to see you undertake to live in Europe and I am sure you have no desire to do it. I should be sorry to see you go to Oxford for general and undefined study—a very pleasant thing. That is the way dilettantes are bred."[18] Duly apprised of his ancestral "duty," Lodge soon returned home. A few months later his grandfather—second father—died. On his own and in need of a suitable statesman-in-waiting apprenticeship, he passed time in the press corps writing for the *Boston Evening Transcript* and the Washington bureau of the *New York Herald Tribune*, the latter post offering convenient access to presidents and politicians. In 1932, just a dozen years out of prep school, Lodge won election to the Massachusetts legislature. Four years later he defeated Governor James Michael Curley for his grandfather's old Senate seat.

As a vital, constructive force in American politics, organized conservatism looked lost in 1936. Battered by the Depression and tainted by its association with Hoover, the GOP's presence in the Senate had shrunk to a meager sixteen seats in that year's elections, constituting the smallest percentage assemblage in the party's history. Days after the polls closed, renowned *Emporia (Kans.) Gazette* editor and informal spokesman for middle America, William Allen White, called the new welfare state liberalism "a political Johnstown flood" that had swept away its opposition. As the only Republican senator to replace a Democrat, and, at thirty-four, a rising star, Lodge looked ideally positioned to begin the arduous process of moving the American right to the center. When Republican National Committee chairman John Hamilton defensively called upon the GOP to act as a "militant and vigilant minority" in the dry days ahead, Lodge responded by questioning long-held conservative positions on financial, tariff, and taxation policies.[19] Out of step with party ideologues, he nevertheless anticipated more accurately than they the liberal swing of twentieth-century political economy.

Rejecting Hooverism, Lodge regarded the 1920s as the failed decade of the "new era" men. This class of private sector engineers, fresh off its triumphant turn coordinating the country's industrial output during World War I, claimed the organizational skills to create a harmonious business-labor stasis based on the promise of increased consumption. Lodge, looking over Wall Street's postcrash portfolio of broken promises, jumped off the engineers' bandwagon. Instead, he discarded the new-era model and entered the senate as a New Deal Republican. There, he pressed conservative irreconcilables to "go back to Abraham Lincoln and get some real liberality" to "become a party of the people."

Lodge's own liberality, it should be noted, went only so far. For if he saw acutely the need to revise conservative attitudes on domestic affairs, his pre–Pearl Harbor isolationism struck a more traditional chord. Despite Nazi Germany's growing threat to Europe, Lodge regarded the extension of U.S. commitments to Britain and France as a misplaced policy of propping up distant empires. His principled appeasement extended to the Pacific. Following Japan's 1937 invasion of coastal China, President Roosevelt called for a quarantine of aggressor countries. "If we are to have a world in which we can breathe freely and live in amity without fear," he argued, "then the peace-loving nations must make a concerned effort to uphold laws and principles on which alone peace can rest secure." Lodge countered the president's plea by urging Americans to "keep out of war by not taking sides in foreign quarrels." Not until March 1941, nine months after the fall of France, did he vote for material assistance to nations fighting Nazism.[20]

Despite his reluctance to involve U.S. armed forces overseas, Lodge had long been interested in military affairs. Just out of college he had joined the army reserves, in which he later struck up a friendship with General George S. Patton. In the summer of 1941 he shadowed the Second Armored Division for three weeks of maneuvers in northern Louisiana and East Texas; the following year he observed the ongoing North African campaign with U.S. tank crews as Rommel's forces pressed toward Tobruk in Libya. Not long afterward, he resigned from the Senate and entered active duty. With his facility for French and seemingly inexhaustible connections, Lieutenant Colonel Lodge served as a troubleshooter of sorts in the Western theater. It was for him a gentleman's war. He briefed Eisenhower, made acquaintances of Churchill and De Gaulle, and earned a host of honors: the Croix de Guerre, the Legion of Merit, and the Ordre National de la Légion d'Honneur. In the flush of victory hundreds of Moroccan Goumiers performed tribal dances and turned roasting sheep on spits for Lodge's disbanding Sixth Army Group. Returning home, he lost no time returning to the Senate.

Back in Washington, Lodge quickly dropped his old fortress America philosophy. Once heir to his grandfather's suspicion that collective security arrangements principally benefited Europe, he now believed that international cooperation had won the war and held the best hope for preventing future conflicts. Consequently, Cabot supported U.S. involvement in the United Nations and the Marshall Plan, programs partially designed to make Western Europe an adjunct of American anticommunism. To congressional veterans, watching a Lodge lead the charge to erect a European-centered alliance system made for rich political irony. Back in 1919, after all, Henry Cabot Lodge had successfully campaigned against American involvement in the League of Nations. Article 10 of its covenant, he had pointed out at the time, bound the United States to maintain the collective security of League members, a potentially open-ended commitment to conflict, which bypassed the war-making powers provided in the United States Constitution. Now, thirty years later, an American pledge to aid any NATO member combating external aggression effectively raised the specter of a revived article 10.

Of course, much had changed since the League battle. The senior Lodge's opposition to collective-security codicils harmonized with the nation's postwar mood, and his party went on to win the next three presidential elections. His grandson was no less receptive to public opinion and knew that a reflexive isolationism now doomed Republicans at the polls. He argued in a March 1949 address that America could no longer sit by and watch its Atlantic neighbors fall prey to aggressor powers. "I submit that if there was an armed attack on Western Europe that we would not, could not, and should not sit idly by. We would, I am sure, react and, I hope, react with effect." Lodge appealed to, even exploited, his countrymen's anticommunism (the Soviets, he insisted, were "determined to set up a godless world dictatorship") and emphasized the perils of a go-it-alone strategy ("We simply have not the manpower to carry the whole burden of a future war alone").[21] In July the Senate, with strong bipartisan support, ratified the North Atlantic Treaty eighty-two to thirteen.

• • • • •

Following FDR's death, Democrats looked with some trepidation toward the future. The Depression and war had reoriented American liberalism from a conventional capitalism to a modern social welfare state, but the economy's revival questioned the permanency of this exchange. In 1946 Republicans rolled up House and Senate majorities for the first time since the late 1920s. Fresh off this solid, hopeful victory, the GOP looked to 1948 with eager anticipation. After a generation bereft of power its leaders planned to capture the presidency, shrink the government, and bury the last twenty years.

Then the bottom fell out. Defying the polls, Truman carried the national election and Democrats reclaimed Congress. That week's copy of *Time* magazine made sport of Dewey's much anticipated landslide with the cutting headline, "Republicans: The Avalanche that Failed." Stunned and tremendously frustrated, the GOP once more engaged in a bout of ideological soul searching. Acting on behalf of disappointed Deweyites, Lodge moved aggressively to denounce those "regressive" colleagues who were calling for a philosophical return to the conservative principles of the 1920s. In a *Saturday Evening Post* essay, "Does the Republican Party have a Future?" he urged moderates to consider the election results "an opportunity to clean house, to discard archaic concepts, and to mold the party to greater conformity with the will and the aspirations of the American people."[22] He understood that many voters regarded the GOP as "a haven for reactionaries" or "a rich man's club" and conceded that this caricature fit a number of congressional peers who opposed the New Deal with "myopic fury." They resembled, he mischievously contended, nothing so much as the bloc of southern Jim Crow Democrats determined to repeal the twentieth century.

Drawing attention in his essay to the GOP's usable past, Lodge advised moderate Republicans to look to Lincoln and Theodore Roosevelt as they rebuilt their party. He made an intriguing if selective case for a conservative heritage resting less on its bond with business than its protectorship of producers. Republicans, he pointed out, had spearheaded the drive to secure constitutional rights for African Americans, gave Congress the power to collect income taxes, and expanded democracy's scope by providing for the popular election of U.S. senators. While Democrats extolled the New Deal as an unprecedented phase in reform politics, Lodge claimed the Reconstruction 1860s and 1870s and the Square Deal 1900s as the progressive backdrop to the FDR 1930s.

Parties that ran from reform, Lodge's *Post* piece continued, flirted with extinction. Whiggery collapsed in the 1850s after failing to take a strong stand against slavery's extension. Republicanism now faced a dilemma in some respects as self-alienating: it had antagonized organized labor, unpopularly questioned the government's right to provide a social safety net for its citizens, and hewed to an irrelevant isolationism. The growing insignificance of the GOP, Lodge argued, threatened to narrow ideological choice in America and weaken the country's Cold War claims to practicing a politics of pluralism with both a popular party in power and a viable opposition ready to regain power. "So great is the need for a living two-party system," he concluded, "so priceless are its benefits and so tragic are the consequences of not having it, that I have both faith and hope that we shall in Lincoln's words 'rise to the occasion.' "[23]

Lodge's print campaign prefaced a furious few years of concentrated house cleaning. He challenged Old Guard Republicans for leadership appointments in the Senate, put together a platform of positions detailing modern conservatism's role in the postwar world, and engaged in a prolonged and ultimately successful political courtship of Dwight Eisenhower. These years proved to be the most professionally constructive and personally satisfying of his career.

Lodge's first act of open defiance came shortly after Dewey's defeat, when he challenged the incumbent Robert Taft for Republican Policy Committee chairmanship in the Senate. A legislative discussion group created by act of Congress in 1946 to facilitate policy making between majority and minority parties, the committee analyzes bills and roll calls and conducts strategy sessions. In the wake of Truman's surprising victory the time seemed right to press, even symbolically, for fresh GOP leadership. "The Republicans had just lost the 1948 election," Lodge later recalled. "We thought that a basic cause was the feeling that the Republican Party was 'stand pat,' said 'no' to everything, opposed the Democrats blindly even when the Democrats were right, had no ideas and no program. A group of us believed that the time-honored and legitimate way to do something about this was to provide a choice between the so-called modern Republicans and the others headed by Senator Taft. . . . We felt this might crystallize public sentiment and give all the people in the country who felt as we did the feeling that there was some opportunity to bring about changes in the party. We knew, of course, that we could not possibly win." And win they did not. Taft, the conservative voice of the Senate, handily defeated Lodge twenty-eight to fourteen. Asked immediately after the vote by a reporter, "Do you and the other Republican liberals expect to keep up the fight inside the party?" Lodge replied, "We think it is our duty."[24]

Over the next four years Lodge and Taft engaged in an ideological struggle over the GOP's future. A revealing 1948 portrait by Richard Rovere illuminated the Ohio Senator's limitations. "It is surely a tragic circumstance that the ablest figure in American politics today, and in many ways the man of the firmest integrity and independence of mind is at the same time a man of impregnably parochial culture and of a personality even less beguiling, when viewed from a distance, than that of the late

Calvin Coolidge."[25] A member of the Midwest gentry, Taft bore a distinct resemblance to a composite of arid character types in a Sinclair Lewis novel. Balding, bespectacled, and horse-toothed, there was something of a gray banality about the man. His type once ruled the Senate floor but now stood on the verge of irrelevancy.

Beyond a sincere if sentimental faith in a redemptive free-enterprise republic, a mixture of nostalgia and fear informed Taft's politics. In the midst of the Depression he cleaved defensively to the competitive system while blaming New Deal income redistribution for undermining, as he put it, "the American ideal of opportunity and reward for ability and hard work."[26] His thinking in foreign affairs produced a tangle of contradictions. He condemned both international communism *and* efforts to limit Soviet expansion, he abused the proposed Marshall Plan only to reluctantly back it, and he voted against ratifying the NATO treaty even while acknowledging the critical importance of a free Western Europe. Taft's internal debate over the perils of internationalism all but paralyzed his decision-making capacities. It produced inconsistencies and intellectual confusion, causing a great many on both sides of the Atlantic to question the United States' security priorities. For Taft, no good alternatives existed. The kind of foreign policy "economization" he yearned for now proved impossible as the nation's expanding international profile prevented a return to a Fortress America mentality. Frustrated, he carried forth a well-intentioned opposition to interventionism much out of tune with the times.

Angling for the presidency, Taft laid out his vision of American foreign affairs in a two-and-a-half-hour January 1951 address before the Senate. It frightened a number of his colleagues. He condemned NATO as "a tremendous mistake," yet when asked by Oregon's Wayne Morse if he thought a Russian sphere of influence in Western Europe likely, he responded in the affirmative: "I share the point of view that they intend to take it over by Communist infiltration and persuasion." Illinois senator Paul Douglas broke in and questioned Taft about the United States' probable response to such a bleak scenario. Taft then casually replied that Soviet dominance in Western Europe would likely compel the United States to destroy through aerial bombing the continent's industrial facilities. A clearly taken-aback William Fulbright of Arkansas cut in: "It is a very shocking thing for Europeans to realize that we are willing to contemplate their destruction."[27]

Such ragged performances did little to enhance Taft's appeal beyond hard-core conservatives. A November 1951 Gallup poll revealed both the Ohio senator's control over the GOP and his inability to connect with the independent voters critical to victory. The survey asked more than 2,700 Republican county chairmen whom they favored in the following year's election. Of the 1,727 who replied, 1,027 preferred Taft; Eisenhower drew a distant second. Yet in a nationwide poll designed to record "general public sentiment," Eisenhower came in first, with Taft trailing behind Truman and Douglas MacArthur.[28]

Clearly the Ohio senator, long a national figure, had maximized his appeal. Party bosses in the Northeast accordingly dismissed his nomination as a nonstarter. As one Dewey supporter put it in early 1952, "I believe [Taft] would make a splendid President for a stable, prosperous country in an orderly world—say in 1925. I suspect, however, that, as has happened to many other able and patriotic men, his political serviceability has been repealed by World War II and the rise of the Third International." Even a good many Taftites began to align behind the inevitability of an Eisenhower candidacy. "I'm a Taft man," one delegate to a GOP convention in Bangor, Maine, proclaimed, "but you can't get away from it: we want to win next November more than anything else. I'm not sure that Taft could do it." Wall Street banker Prescott Bush, better known historically as the father and grandfather of presidents, wrote Taft a brief note explaining his path to moderate Republicanism. "I have been quite unhappy this past year, not supporting your candidacy. I did so in 1940, '44 and '48. But as I told you in New Haven, I backed Ike beginning a year ago because he seemed to me to be the most likely to win if nominated." And finally, Lodge predicted a political apocalypse if Taft took over the GOP: "The Republican party would either disintegrate completely or shrink into a small minority of extreme reactionaries."[29]

· · · · ·

As a rising senator in the 1930s, Lodge looked poised to make a serious run or two at the White House. But no more than Taft could he capture a partywide consensus. Formerly a king-in-waiting, in the 1950s he became a kingmaker. Eisenhower's presumptive ability to carry a national electorate factored heavily into Lodge's decision to court his candidacy, yet he also considered the party's future in decades to come. Republicans could claim two presidents, Lincoln and Roosevelt, whose reputations resonated throughout the nation. It needed now another unsullied icon; it needed a modern image for the ages. "Franklin D. Roosevelt's political activities," Lodge later observed, "had permanently strengthened the Democratic party and had made the word 'Democrat' a real political asset—of particular help to unpopular candidates. Eisenhower, I thought, could do the same for the word 'Republican.' "[30]

In June 1950 Lodge met privately in New York with Eisenhower, then president of Columbia University. He made the following appeal: as a popular career military officer the General uniquely connected with a postwar electorate eager for a moderate cabinet committed to keeping the best of the New Deal. Striking a deferential chord ("I know your great aversion to public office"), Lodge appealed to Eisenhower's concerns regarding America's international security commitments. As he later reported, "I . . . raised the possibility that a situation might very well occur in which the isolationist elements in the Republican party became so strong that the party would be on the verge of a definite turn in the wrong direction."[31] That was enough for now. A reluctant Eisenhower, cold to both parties' advances in 1948, would not be rushed.

The following summer Lodge flew to Paris to meet with Eisenhower, now supreme commander of NATO. Again he raised the issue of his host's candidacy. "Cabot, sitting in my NATO office," the General later recalled, "turned to the subject of the Republican Party itself and its problems in attempting to cope with the danger which faced our nation. He felt that the regular Republican leadership, cast in an opposition role for 20 long years, inescapably gave the country a negative impression. . . . He also said that in 1951 the opposition of that part of the Republican leadership known loosely as the Old Guard to the sending of U.S. troops to Europe to serve in NATO had made the party appear unaware of the realities of the modern world."[32] Following the meeting Eisenhower remained reticent, unsure whether he wanted to be president.

Lodge sensed that the General could be persuaded to run only if he felt certain of victory. Accordingly, in November he and a group of liberal Republicans made their move. Before a cluster of reporters in New York's Commodore Hotel, they announced a "Draft Ike" movement. In all, these were exhilarating if difficult months for Lodge. He had publicly supported a would-be nominee who refused to declare his candidacy or even voice interest in the presidency. Through a long winter, Lodge remembered, "We did not know what Eisenhower was going to say or do, we lacked money, and help was slow to come in. We had not fully realized, with all its implications, that the general would not return until a few short weeks before the convention and that army regulations would prevent his making any kind of politically helpful statement while he was abroad. We had not really faced up to the fact that, in every sense of the word, we would have to organize a draft."[33]

In the end, Lodge's instincts proved correct. Acting on his own initiative he entered Eisenhower's name on the New Hampshire primary ballot. Two months later, on 11 March, the General decisively defeated Taft, with 50 percent to 38 percent of the ballots cast. The following day Ike officially announced his candidacy. During the primary season Eisenhower and Taft traded victories, though the latter held a slight delegate edge as the Republican National Convention met in Chicago's International Amphitheater. Much of Taft's support came from the South. Derided by GOP liberals as "rotten boroughs," these old Dixie states rarely voted for Republican "Yankees" in the general election but formed, rather, a solid segregationist Democratic phalanx.[34] Of no practical use in November, they could, in a July convention, carry a conservative candidate over the top. As the Taft and Eisenhower forces struggled for advantage, it soon became apparent that the nomination might well be won or lost over the control of sixty-eight disputed but presumably solidly Taft delegates in Texas, Georgia, and Louisiana. Lodge led the charge to uncredential them and thus reduce the Ohio senator's support.

Following his lead, the convention refused by a 658-to-548 vote to allow the contested delegates to participate. This put Taft on the defensive since the roll call suggested that he had anticipated winning a first-ballot victory with dubious delegates. As the following day's *New York Times* put it, Taft's "steamroller is stopped."[35] The crack rudely called to mind another Taft at another convention. In 1912 reform Republicans had accused the Old Guard of "steamrolling" TR's supporters and denying their candidate the nomination. Now, in 1952, moderate Republicanism leveled the same charge against a new Old Guard. Conducting a floor vote on the legitimacy of contested delegates put the Taft team on its heels and it never recovered. Despite his long and distinguished service to the party, Taft lacked the support of a great many victory-starved Republicans who harbored grave doubts about his electability. Undoubtedly, this played a crucial role in the redistribution of some southern delegates in a manner favorable to Eisenhower. As the balloting began most of the drama had been drained. Eisenhower received 595 votes on the first roll call, just 9 shy of victory. Then, before the second poll, Minnesota switched 19 votes from favorite son Harold Stassen and put the

General over the top. Years of Old Guard efforts to revitalize American conservatism had come to naught. It took all of an hour. Taft secured an impressive 500 delegates, the most tallied by a defeated candidate. His infuriated supporters, beaten at yet another convention by yet another moderate, looked to Lodge as more enemy than friend.

· · · · ·

Massachusetts may count itself as the birthplace of American freedom, but political dynasties have rooted deeply in its democratic soil. Nearly continuously from 1893 to 2009 a Lodge or a Kennedy sat in the U.S. Senate. The former held court till 1952, then gave way completely. The weakening of Waspdom's hold in the Bay State goes some way in explaining the families' shifting political fortunes, but there is more here than meets the eye. For Lodge's midcentury fall from political grace is also part of a small but important skirmish in the broader conflict between moderate and conservative Republicans. Taftites in Massachusetts looked to avenge their candidate's convention defeat, and Lodge never sensed his political vulnerability. Rather, he presumed to pull off a political triple crown in 1952: engineer Eisenhower's nomination, serve as the General's campaign manager, and, in his spare time, win reelection. A Massachusetts Senate seat, after all, seemed a birthright.

But then along came John Kennedy and the considerable power and influence of his father, Joe. Blessed with enormous financial resources, a dynamic and highly motivated organization, and a terrific television personality, JFK proved to be, by any comparison, a formidable candidate worthy of all the energy an incumbent could muster. But Cabot had little to spare that year. No longer the rising wunderkind of the Senate, Lodge turned fifty in 1952, fifteen years older than Kennedy. The two candidates were competitively cordial to friendly acquaintances, respected one another, and found their political careers, despite the age difference, traveling parallel paths. They vied for the senate in 1952 and faced each other on competing national tickets in 1960, and Lodge served as U.S. ambassador to South Vietnam in the Kennedy administration. Their 1952 campaign both revived and anticipated future contests between the families. In 1916 Henry Cabot Lodge retained his Senate office, defeating Kennedy's grandfather, John Fitzgerald; in 1962 Edward Kennedy captured his brother's vacated senate seat by defeating Lodge's son, George.

On most domestic issues, Lodge and Kennedy accorded with moderate to liberal positions. Both supported expanding Social Security, increasing federal aid to education, and raising the minimum wage. "I don't see why we must choose between state socialism and no social progress at all," Lodge had remarked to a Massachusetts newspaper. "I don't see why we shouldn't use the power of the government to fill in the chinks that private enterprise can't fill for us." Kennedy was in some respects the more conservative candidate: he touted his anticommunism, accused Lodge of sustaining Truman's "appeasement" policy toward the Soviet Union, and retained a genial family friendship with Joseph McCarthy. Lodge, by contrast, cold-shouldered the Wisconsin senator. "Barriers of social class, ethnic background and personal temperament," as one scholar has put it, "stood in the way."[36]

Fallout from the Chicago convention gave every indication that Lodge was a marked man. Aside from a determined Democratic opposition, he faced resistance from Taft conservatives both in Massachusetts and beyond. In August, *Chicago Tribune* publisher Colonel Robert McCormick denounced the Eisenhower candidacy, called for Lodge's political scalp, and vowed never again to support another "Me-Too" Republican: "I swallowed Willkie in '40, Dewey twice in '44 and '48, candidates foisted upon the majority by sharp practice." Dismissing Eisenhower and his opponent Adlai Stevenson as ideologically interchangeable candidates, he urged the creation of an "American Party" to smash the moderate consensus. And looking to settle scores, he cast his eye East urging "every patriot [to] vote against [Lodge]."[37]

Basil Brewer, the influential editor of the *New Bedford (Mass.) Standard Times* and other New England newspapers, needed no encouragement. An Old Guard Republican and Taft's Massachusetts campaign manager, he considered the convention's handling of the Ohio senator disgraceful and made it his special mission to defeat Lodge. Their bad blood had been building for some time. Nearly a year before the nomination, in September 1951, Brewer had tried to compromise Lodge's then-clandestine courtship of Ike. "It is known you have stated you will support the General if he becomes a candidate for President. Specifically, however, are you heading up a group backing the General? Are you working for or do you intend to work for unpledged delegates in Massachusetts or elsewhere favorable to the General? And if you are personally not doing so or planning to, is anyone else authorized to do so on your behalf in Massachusetts or elsewhere? As I said to you some weeks ago, for your own sake I believe you should be neutral." Days later came Lodge's less-than-candid reply: "I have just received your letter . . . asking me whether I am 'heading up a group' backing General Eisenhower or whether I or someone else in my behalf is 'working for delegates in Massachusetts or elsewhere favorable to the General.' The answer to both questions is in the negative."[38]

Naturally Brewer published Lodge's response in his papers; one headline read "Lodge to Keep Hands off Delegate Race." He thought this put the issue to rest. "As I see it," he informed one correspondent, "Lodge will be compelled by necessity to stick to the promise he made and which we published. . . . I want to assure you now that we believe we have put Lodge in his corner." He also crowed to Taft at this time that an important page in Bay State politics had been turned: "Today I believe that the land of the Cabots and Cabot Lodges is pro-Taft."[39] Not long afterward, Lodge endorsed Eisenhower.

For Brewer, the situation went from bad to worse. In April, Eisenhower carried the Massachusetts primary by a wide margin. Then in July came the moderates' successful contestation of the sixty-eight disputed Taft delegates. "My motion," Lodge glibly wrote Brewer at the time, "aims solely to establish public confidence in the integrity of our procedures. We certainly cannot attack Democratic corruption if our own nomination rests on corruption." Brewer was livid. "I am absolutely opposed to any change of rules to fit your efforts to take over southern delegates," he upbraided Lodge. "Why don't you play the game according to the rules instead of trying to make up something special to suit your own plans and purposes? Why don't you . . . just be [a] Republican for once?"[40]

Coming out of the convention, a beaten Brewer promised to loyally support Eisenhower, a grace of party regularity he refused Lodge. "I would not be honest," he was quoted in the *Worcester (Mass.) Evening Post*, "if I did not say there are scars, deep ones, in the Republican Party as a result of the late primary campaign." His next move was predictable: at a 25 September news conference held at the Boston Sheraton Plaza Hotel, Brewer endorsed Kennedy. "We are not 'bolting' the Republican party," the publisher insisted, "for long ago Senator Lodge bolted his party by his votes for the Truman socialist New Deal."[41] Come November, Eisenhower won a sweeping victory against Illinois governor Adlai Stevenson, carrying thirty-nine states and a robust 55 percent of the popular vote. His campaign manager, however, suffered a painful loss. Out of more than 2.3 million votes cast, Kennedy bested Lodge by a plurality of 70,000.

Following the election, letters of regret piled up in Lodge's office. "Want to tell you how sick I am at your defeat," said one, "which was due, in my opinion, to the narrow-mindedness of a great many 'poor Taft losers' who put personal spite above 'welfare of the Nation.'" Another applauded the outgoing senator's stand against GOP irreconcilables. "Eisenhower's great personal victory, which you made possible at so high a personal sacrifice, can well be the dawning of a new era in this great land of ours under an enlightened Republican leadership." But in this contest Brewer got the final, angry word. In an open letter, "To the Voters," he wrote, "we rejoice, of course, at General Eisenhower's victory, restoring order, honesty, dignity—and a true sense of values to Washington. . . . But especially we rejoice at the wisdom of the voters of this state, who could, on the one hand vote overwhelmingly for Eisenhower and Nixon, Republican nominees—and at the same moment, with discrimination and solid sense, endorse John F. Kennedy, Democrat, against Senator Henry Cabot Lodge."[42]

It is tempting to say that, all things considered, Lodge got the better of Brewer in 1952. But this would not be true. In the years separating Taft's thwarted candidacy and Barry Goldwater's right-tilting 1964 presidential campaign, the Old Guard was bereft of compelling political leadership, and Republican modernizers had their best opportunity to liberalize their party. It came to nothing. The public regarded Eisenhower as a national rather than a partisan figure, and the GOP never enjoyed an "Ike" bounce to offset the Democrats' Roosevelt bounce. Republicans lost the House and Senate in 1954 and remained the minority party through the 1950s.

· · · · ·

Following the election, an appreciative Eisenhower appointed Lodge U.S. representative to the United Nations. These were years of Cold War high drama, and Lodge gravitated to center stage. He condemned the 1956 Soviet invasion of Hungary as "a body blow to Communism all over the world," responded to the U-2 spy plane crisis by displaying a KGB-bugged U.S. seal from the American Embassy in Moscow, and served as Nikita Khrushchev's personal representative of the president during the First Secretary's 1959 visit to the United States. A bemused Khrushchev took to calling Lodge "my capitalist."[43]

Though Lodge's confrontational style irritated some colleagues, it, along with his patrician demeanor and imposing physical presence, played well on television. As *Time* magazine fawningly reported in 1958, "With his strapping frame (6ft. 2 ¾ in.) and cinematically handsome face, Lodge even looks the part of the good guy of stage or screen who triumphs over the bad guys." The UN post kept Lodge in the public eye, and in 1960 he agreed to serve as running mate on the Nixon ticket. All did not go smoothly. Lodge's announcement in a Harlem speech pledging a new GOP administration to appoint the nation's first black cabinet member infuriated Nixonites. This forced Nixon, eager to win the support of southern whites, to publicly disavow the promise. "That murdered us in Texas," fumed Albert Fay of Texas's National Committee. In 1960, modern Republicanism never got off the ground.[44]

Following Kennedy's victory, Lodge accepted the directorship of the Atlantic Institute, an organization dedicated to facilitating public relations between the United States and its NATO allies. Then, in June 1963, Kennedy asked Lodge to head the U.S. embassy in Saigon. It was a brilliant move on the part of a president seeking bipartisan support—and, if necessary, blame—for his risky Vietnam venture. Conservatives denounced what they regarded as yet another moderate Republican betrayal. Ohio congresswoman Frances P. Bolton addressed Lodge directly: "I, with so many Republicans here on the hill, am deeply disturbed that you should have accepted the Ambassadorship to this terribly difficult spot in Southeast Asia. . . . Red China is determined to get a foothold in Southeast Asia and the best one for her purposes is South Viet-Nam. . . . Should this happen during your incumbency out there, you know what they would do to the Republican Party. We would be blamed!"[45]

On a personal level, serving in Saigon allowed Lodge the opportunity to overcome his foreign policy past. As a prewar noninterventionist turned postwar internationalist, he believed that the GOP's reluctance in the 1930s to contain fascism dogged it still. Perhaps now, in Vietnam, history could be rewritten and modern Republicanism might shake the noxious isolationist label that continued to linger about the party. With hindsight one might charge Lodge, like many of his generation, with careening from one foreign policy pole to another. He now adopted a reflexive, unimaginative cold warrior stance, determined to stop the march of communism. "If the Communist Chinese, using North Vietnam as a cover, were to take over South Vietnam, it would be interpreted among communist nations as a vindication of the militant Chinese policy," he wrote in *Life* magazine. "It would also be regarded as a reflection of U.S. inability or lack of will to prevent Communist aggression. . . . The loss of South Vietnam, with its weakening of the whole Free World position in Southeast Asia, would have a distressing effect, and many voices would be heard urging us to wash our hands of the world—to resign from it, to fall back onto our 'Fortress America.' "[46]

Despite his concern for the "free world position in Southeast Asia," Lodge did not stay long in Vietnam. Once again presidential politics, in this case the candidacy of the conservative Arizona senator Barry Goldwater, proved to be the catalyst of his concerns. After more than a generation of New Deal–fueled Democratic victories, here stood a rising Republican constituency looking to roll back the New Deal. This surprising Sunbelt-suburbia political phenomenon pointed to the failure of Lodge's new Republicanism, and from 10,000 miles away he fretted over his party's survival as a constructive force in American politics. "Goldwater's contention that the Federal Government should play no part in the civil rights problem," he wrote his son, George, a year before the election, "is not only monstrously bad government and bad Americanism and shows an ignorance of what the country and the Republican party stands for, but it will also lose us every Negro vote and the votes of millions of people in the population centers who descend from other than the old Anglo-Saxon stock. And yet, there appears to be nobody to beat him! We had a very similar situation with Senator Taft in 1952 (although Senator Taft was more intelligent than Goldwater), but a bunch of us were able to get together and promote General Eisenhower. Where is there such an equivalent today?"[47]

In the late autumn of 1963 Lodge still had reason to hope that Goldwater could be stopped. And while he had wondered out loud if an Eisenhower redux might be found, the fact could hardly have escaped his notice that he himself stood among the likeliest of candidates. Certainly others were aware. In December a Draft Lodge office opened in Washington, D.C.; the parallels to 1952 were striking. Like Eisenhower, Lodge held an overseas post that made it difficult to signal interest in contesting the nomination of what moderate conservatives regarded as an ultraconservative candidate. His January 1964 note to George could easily have been written by the General a dozen years earlier: "I am much complimented that people should want to run as delegates 'favorable' to me. I am also troubled because I do not want to give them any encouragement to think that I shall come back to campaign for the nomination, as I certainly have no intention whatever of doing so."[48]

In fact, a series of maneuvers and countermaneuvers transpired over anxious months as Lodge, eighteen years removed from his last electoral victory, assessed his chances of capturing the nomination. The following letter to George is indicative of the mixed signals he flashed. On the subject of the presidency: "I do not want it, I am not going to 'come back and slug it out' and I'm not going to hide behind childish talk that I can't do it because I have responsibilities in Viet-Nam. But I cannot honorably leave this job in Viet-Nam at the present time, and I'm not going to pretend I can when I can't. I know exactly what I want, and I do not want to be President." What could be clearer? But then came the following admission: "Of course, if a resolution were unanimously passed inviting me to be President, that would be something else, but there isn't a Chinaman's chance that that will happen." Less than a week later Lodge asked his son to "find out, discreetly" what state held the last primary before the convention. "It would be interesting to know what that state is and what the requirements are for entering." And ten days after that, having scrutinized a Draft Lodge statement penned by George, he replied, "I would only make one change—in paragraph 4 where you say I 'do not want the draft movement to stop.' I would say that I have no objection to the movement going on. . . . Of course you are right, under your point 6, that if the Convention were to choose me, I would run 'eagerly and enthusiastically'—considerably more so than in 1960 when I was number two."[49]

On 10 March Lodge won the New Hampshire primary. Though his name did not appear on the ballot he captured more than 33,000 votes, easily defeating Goldwater (20,692), New York governor Nelson Rockefeller (19,504), and Nixon (15,587). Over the next several weeks Lodge continued to poll well despite the considerable handicap of an undeclared candidacy. He swamped Goldwater in Massachusetts, took second in Pennsylvania behind favorite-son governor William Scranton, and followed that up with another second-place finish in Oregon. According to a May Gallup poll, 40 percent of independent voters favored Lodge compared with 20 percent for Nixon, 12 percent for Goldwater, and 10 percent for Rockefeller. But polls and beauty contest primaries meant little in the broader scheme of things. The Goldwater forces had already secured the commitments of numerous Republicans via conventions in several southern and midwestern states, "the game which Taft played in '51 and '52," Lodge complained from across the Pacific. With the delegate-rich California primary looming and Goldwater closing in on the nomination, Lodge predicted the worst, a November rout of epic proportions: "If Goldwater should get the nomination," he warned George, "it would be another disaster for the party. We would lose 30 or 40 congressmen at least. But Goldwater would certainly not take one step to conciliate those in the party who think the way you and I do. We could all go straight to hell as far as he is concerned."[50]

After capturing the crucial California primary on 1 June (the state prohibited write-in votes and Lodge was not a factor), Goldwater's path to the nomination looked clear. Only Governor Scranton remained in the field, but his youth and lack of a national profile inspired limited support. Progressive party leaders pleaded with Eisenhower to endorse Scranton, but he refused. Asked point-blank by Rockefeller to do so, the General replied that he hoped to "preserve his influence." "For What?" Rockefeller reportedly shot back. By this time Lodge had decided to return to America and searched for a suitable pretext. His frustration with Eisenhower surfaced in a communication to one supporter: "It [would not] be terribly good to say that I had come home because I want the Republican Party to 'go forward in the image of Ike'—particularly if Ike hasn't shown the slightest desire to have me come home and bring the Republican Party forward in his image."[51] Emphasizing concern for his wife's flagging health in the unrelieved Southeast Asian heat, Lodge resigned his position on 23 June. Twelve days later, he arrived in Harrisburg, Pennsylvania, ready to talk strategy with Scranton.

He might just as well have stayed abroad. All Lodge could do in America was watch with mounting frustration as the Goldwater forces rolled to victory. It didn't take long for a retaliatory sarcasm to creep into his commentary. After the Arizona senator suggested using low-yield A-bombs to expose the Ho Chi Minh trail, Lodge cracked that "using an atomic bomb to defoliate is like using an atomic bomb to light a cigarette. We use weed killer." Speaking in California, he warned his audience, "We must never countenance such a thing as a trigger-happy foreign policy which would negate everything we stand for and destroy everything we hope for—including life itself." On the domestic front, Lodge countered Goldwater's iconic cowboy individualism with a nod to the New Deal. "No one in his right mind would today argue that there is no place for the Federal government in the reawakening of America. Indeed, we need another Republican-sponsored Marshall Plan for our cities and schools."[52]

Considering the Sunbelt's new power in national politics, it seemed fitting that the Republicans assembled in San Francisco's storied Cow Palace to choose their nominee. It marked, after all, only the second time in its history that the GOP had met west of Kansas City. There, in the party's most raucous convention since Taft and Roosevelt locked horns,

Lodge's worst nightmare came true. His nearly thirty-year struggle to modernize the GOP had come to nothing—Goldwater seized the nomination on the first ballot. Lodge missed that moment, having flown out of town earlier in the day, in no mood to see "Mr. Conservative" crowned. Beaten, exhausted, and bewildered, he confined his campaign efforts to the Massachusetts state GOP ticket and his brother John's (unsuccessful) bid for a Connecticut senate seat. Weeks before the general election he confided to one correspondent, "I have stated publicly that I will not bolt the party and I shall not. Neither will I go back on the convictions of a lifetime. I consider myself a true conservative and I know that one cannot be a conservative if one is not willing to innovate. A conservative who simply is negative about everything very soon has nothing left to conserve."[53] In November, Goldwater suffered one of the greatest defeats in the history of presidential politics, earning less than 40 percent of the popular vote. Lodge's concern that "we would lose 30 or 40 congressmen" was fully born out. The GOP dropped thirty-six house seats and an additional two in the senate. Its thirty-two seats in the upper chamber marked Republicanism's lowest total in a generation.

Embittered and a little shell shocked, Goldwater's supporters lashed out at Lodge's unwillingness to back their man. Lodge offered no apologies. "As far as the election was concerned," he wrote, "I certainly did not stultify myself by paying lip service to ideas which I had opposed all my life and it would certainly not have helped Senator Goldwater if I had sacrificed principle to crass political expediency. Moreover, his acceptance speech in San Francisco [where the candidate had controversially declared 'extremism in the defense of liberty is no vice'] and later developments made it clear that the support of Republicans like me is not desired. I did not bolt the party. The more I think about my course of action; the more I think I did the right thing."[54]

·····

Lodge returned to South Vietnam in 1965, serving the Johnson administration for two difficult years. Afterward he briefly headed the U.S. embassy in West Germany (1968–69) before taking a lengthy turn as special envoy to the Vatican (1970–77). An impeccable patrician, he struck the Washington wise men as eminently suited for foreign service window-dressing stints in Europe. Indeed, he qualified as something of an aristocrat in his own right. In retirement Lodge lived out his final years in Essex

County, the ancestral home of the Junto that once drew his kin. There he died in 1985. Once, Lodge had asked with some imperiousness of the Old Guard Republicans, "They say there is this tremendous untapped 'conservative' vote. Let them produce it now."[55] In the last few quiet years of his life, in the ideological commotion of the "Reagan Revolution," "they" did just that.

9 West of Center

The Bushes

••

Texas would be new and exciting for a while.

—George H. W. Bush, 1948

From 1952 to 2009 three generations of Bushes wielded more influence over a longer period of time than any political family since the Adamses. Aside from a slew of sinecureships—chairman of the Republican National Committee, U.S. ambassador to the United Nations, director of Central Intelligence, and so on—they captured House and Senate seats, governed Electoral College leviathans Texas and Florida, and served as president or vice president for a combined twenty years. Timing, as much as talent, marked their success. The Bushes' rise to prominence paralleled a cultural sea change in American life. If post-1930s politics reflected the sensibilities of an urban, Keynesian, left-of-center nation, than post-1960s politics moved to the mannerisms of a suburban, supply-side, right-of-center constituency. A combination of forces catalyzed the conservative revival; the trail of oil, energy, population, and prosperity shifted power from the Kennedy Northeast to the Goldwater Southwest. The consequences were immense, but not unprecedented.

Back in 1803 not a few Federalists looked upon the Louisiana Purchase as the greatest evil to visit New England since the Salem witch trials. As George Cabot complained at that time, "It is so obvious that the influence of our part of the Union must be diminished by the acquisition of more weight at the other extremity."[1] And he was right. Between 1804 and 1832 southern slaveholders captured more popular votes than their opponents in every presidential election. Not until the later emergence of a new demographic exchange, aided considerably by the arrivals of Irish and German immigrants in the northern states, were Yankees able to wrest power from their Dixie neighbors. A civil war followed. In the 1960s a booming Sunbelt reprised among liberals the old Federalist fear of irrelevancy. Advances in the electronics and aeronautics industries, the capitalist call for nonunionized labor, and a sprawling defense industry energized a new conservatism. Their opponents feared the worst—and they were right. Between 1964 and 2004 a southerner or Californian won every presidential election.

Unlike the other historical actors observed in these pages, the Bushes avidly courted both sides of the conservative divide. Once fixtures of the moderate northeastern wing of Republicanism, they moved to the right, along with many of the party's voters. Exploring their shared political and geographic journey sheds a reflective light on the resurgence of free-market capitalism, the flight of the white middle class from the nation's urban centers, and the impact of Christian fundamentalism in the ideological arena. It offers, in other words, a family-tree familiarity with the peculiar set of circumstances that sustained four decades of Republican resurgence.

Henry Cabot Lodge was also a patrician, of course, but his career can tell us only so much. For both regional and generational reasons, he has little to say about the post-1960s migration of moderate politics from the GOP to the Democratic Party. A trio of Bushes, rather, helps to tell this story and in the process also brings together the modern presidential history of three regions. Ohio-born Prescott Bush left the Midwest in 1923 just as its long era of elevating favorite-son candidates to the White House (no fewer than seven between 1868 and 1920) had come to an end. Bush spent his formative professional years (1924–44) in New England, during a period in which northeastern candidates carried five of six presidential canvasses. In 1948 Prescott's son, George Herbert Walker Bush, migrated to Texas, thus establishing for himself and his eldest son, George W., a foothold in the political future. Anyway one looks at it, the family had a remarkable history of running with the winners.

The key figure here is George H. W. Bush. Temperamentally he never embraced the right, never lost sight of the old-money patrician backdrop that shaped his life. Mindful of the conservative renaissance in American politics, however, he courted this powerful constituency and briefly led his party. Even so, hardcore Reaganites never embraced him. Reflecting on Bush's tenure as president, the pugnacious Pat Buchanan undoubtedly spoke for many on the right when he declared, "Under the rubric of conservatism, the Republican party of Bush . . . has been reinventing itself into what conservatives would have once recognized as a Rockefeller [party] reciting Reaganite pieties."[2] For centrists like Bush, however, the party's real "reinvention" meant the dominance of men who had little use for Rockefeller—or for him.

In some respects this and the following chapter, which assays the ascendency of a moderate persuasion in the Democratic Party, offer multiple sides of the same story. For political centrism did not disappear with the onset of Goldwaterism and Reaganism; rather, it found a new home across the partisan aisle. The process proved to be long and involved, spanning two generations and numerous actors. In the interest of clarity, I offer concise treatments of this development by focusing on the major players in the major parties. As such, this chapter registers the protracted decline of moderation within the postwar GOP and the following charts the Democrats' hesitant migration from the reform liberalism once its bread and butter toward the political center. In full it is a cautionary and suggestive history. Since the 1980s the GOP can claim success in but two general elections—as the moderate party, Democrats have taken the rest. These chapters thus argue not simply for the existence of a moderate persuasion but rather for its critical importance in national campaigns. There are certainly moments in our history when moderates failed to make the difference in their party's capturing of the White House, but we are not living in such times.

· · · · ·

Prescott Bush's great-grandfather, Obadiah, anticipated his heirs' westward drift. A native Vermonter who helped garrison Buffalo's Fort Niagara during the War of 1812, he raised a large family and ran a prosperous general store in the booming canal town of Rochester. There he might have stayed, excepting the temptation, wanderlust, or just plain piratical compulsion to uproot in the name of fortune hunting. A bona fide forty-niner, he tramped across the unsettled continent in search of California gold, fruitlessly as things turned out. In 1851 he boarded a ship heading east with no more bullion, bars, or ingots than when he arrived, and promptly died at sea.[3]

Obadiah's eldest son, James, a Rochester lawyer, wed the year of his father's death. Eighteen months later, he buried his bride. The double blows suggest the occupational psychology of his next move, the abandonment of law for an Episcopal ordination and parish in Orange, New Jersey. There, he married Harriet Eleanor Fay, a native of Concord, Massachusetts, and relative of Samuel Prescott, reputed to have ridden with Paul Revere. Haunting his father's final travels, James took a pastorship in San Francisco, later returned to the East, and later still, near sixty, left the church. One associate believed James a latent freethinker no longer able to abide by the dry nineteenth-century pietism once central to his spirituality. "I discovered early in my acquaintance with Mr. Bush that his theological garments were outgrown. . . . We met often enough to get the flavor of each other's mind, and to raise the question with me, 'Where will he come out?' He was by nature and constitution a Liberal, but did not know it, until his own moral nature had grown strong enough to break the shell of automatic habit."[4] Turning inward, James retreated to Concord, Harriet's ancestral home and the hearth to many a nineteenth-century Elysian seeker. There he traversed its woods and ponds, preached on occasion, and, with the exception of a few months, lived out the remainder of his life in this ornate cradle of American transcendentalism.

James's son, Samuel Prescott, made the first Bush fortune. Born in 1863, he completed an engineering degree at New Jersey's Stevens Institute of Technology and joined the Pennsylvania Railroad; the job meant living in Columbus, Ohio. There, in 1908, he commenced a near twenty-year reign as the president of Buckeye Steel Castings, a major railroad equipment manufacturer. At Buckeye he succeeded Frank Rockefeller, John D.'s brother, and made important contacts with the Standard Oil empire as well as the Houses of Morgan and Harriman, whose locomotives were supplied with Samuel's couplings. Later, he directed the Federal Reserve Bank of Cleveland and served during World War I on the War Industries Board, a government agency established to encourage the mass production of war materials through standardization.[5]

Samuel's son, Prescott, born in 1895, brought his family closer into the rising military-industrial complex soon to scaffold the American Century. Though he recalled with fondness a plebian Ohio upbringing—"I went to the pubic schools in Columbus . . . and I've always looked back on that as a very good thing"—he was sent following the eighth grade to the elite St. George's School at Newport, Rhode Island. Next came Yale, where the eager-to-please Prescott (voted most versatile in the class of 1917) played baseball, sang baritone in the country's oldest collegiate a cappella group, and joined a small body of seniors tapped for Skull and Bones. Graduating into the Great War, he served as a field artillery captain in the Meuse Argonne offensive. "We were close enough to the enemy," he later recalled, "to see the sunlight glint off the barrels of their rifles."[6]

Mustered out in 1919, Prescott secured through family connections a position at the Simmons Hardware Company in St. Louis. There, he met and fell in love with Dorothy Walker. Her father, George Herbert Walker, had organized the 1904 St. Louis World's Fair, helped finance the city's

Democratic Party, and in 1920 joined W. A. Harriman & Company, one of the largest investment banking firms in the nation. Dorothy married Prescott in 1921. Five years later, Harriman & Company made Prescott a vice president.

In 1931 Harriman & Company merged with Brown Brothers & Company to create Brown Brothers Harriman & Company, a standout among the world's great private banks. Shuttling between Greenwich, Connecticut, and the money mines of Lower Manhattan, Prescott accrued a modest fortune while making financial and political connections crucial to his future and that of generations of Bushes. Aching for public office, he began the process of converting self-interest into political capital. Samuel's Federal Reserve and War Industries Board days had given the patina of romance to even the most mundane government work. "While [my father] never was active in connection with political life, except on the sidelines," Prescott later reported, "he was very actively interested in it . . . and he rather infiltrated me with this feeling that we have a public obligation and you should do all you can about it. He felt that everybody doesn't have an equal obligation. Some people have better opportunities than others to serve and better facilities, better equipment, and that one's obligation increased with the fact that you were—perhaps—better qualified or better able, for any reason, to do something about the public scene."[7]

Presumably armed with "better facilities, better equipment," Prescott adapted easily to the hail-fellow-well-met persona prized among the Greenwich public service set. His activities included membership in the county's Hospital Association, a trusteeship in the Episcopal Church Foundation of America, director of the Connecticut State Mental Hygiene Committee, and chairman of the United Negro College Fund. A great many other organizations claimed his time though none compromised his mandatory golf game. A one-time holder of the senior national record for a single round (an efficient 66), Prescott took a term as president of the United States Golf Association.

Early in his Brown Brothers Harriman & Company days, Bush entered local politics. Elected to Connecticut's representatives town meeting in 1933, he soon became its longstanding moderator. In 1946 the state's Republican fathers approached the popular Prescott to run for the House seat soon to be vacated by Clare Boothe Luce. A quick conference with his banking partners quashed the idea. As Bush later noted, "[They said] look, if this was the Senate we'd back you for it and we'd like to see you do it, but for the House, don't do it. We need you more here than the House needs you."[8]

To commandeer a Senate seat, Prescott faced the daunting task of appealing to a constituency suspicious of his Manhattan connections. So uncertain were his prospects that Bush, derided in some Connecticut corners as a Grand Central Station carpetbagger, later claimed to have no upper chamber ambitions. "Why it never crossed my mind as a possibility. I live in the wrong part of the state. Greenwich is known upstate as a commuter town. It would be hard for them to swallow a Greenwichite at the state level, for Governor or Senator. I'm a commuter. I'm an international banker."[9] In fact, Bush's Wall Street connections proved critical in promoting his political aspirations. Appointed chairman of the Connecticut Republican State Finance Committee in 1947, he kept its coffers full, receiving in kind the party's backing for senator in 1950. He lost that contest by fewer than 2,000 votes. But two years later, following the death of Connecticut's senior senator, Democrat Brian McMahon, Bush carried the special election to fill his seat. He was one of twelve new Republican senators in a political year dominated by Dwight Eisenhower's presidential candidacy.

According to one of his Capital Hill colleagues, Bush "looked more like a Senator than any Senator had the right."[10] His athletic 6-foot-4, 210-pound frame complimented a mouth full of teeth, a head of silver-grey hair, and a prominent Roman nose; tennis courts and golf links stood at the ready for his recreation. Renting the old Alexander Graham Bell estate in Georgetown, Bush bounced between the Armed Services, Bank and Currency, and Joint Economic Committees. A man in full, he enjoyed the senate, left little legislative legacy, but served with some consequence as a staunch supporter of the moderate conservatism favored by Eisenhower and Lodge. He championed, in other words, the kind of GOP later rejected by his son and grandson. As a "new" or "centrist" Republican, Bush hoped to maneuver his party back into the mainstream of American life. The agenda that conservatives had customarily ridden to power—advancing the fortunes of big business, ignoring organized labor, and identifying with the nation's Wasp cultural dominance—could no longer be counted on to capture a national constituency, something it had not done since 1928.

Regularly defeated in presidential elections, the GOP was further afflicted by an internal struggle over McCarthyism. Two years before Bush's election to the senate, Maine's Margaret Chase Smith had preceded him to the upper chamber, becoming the first woman to serve in both houses of Congress. On 1 June 1950, less than four months after Wisconsin senator Joseph McCarthy delivered his incautious "enemies from within" speech at Wheeling, West Virginia, Smith countered with an address critical of the slur and slander tactics employed by her colleague. Trembling slightly and with McCarthy sitting two rows behind her, she stood up and delivered a fifteen-minute speech entitled a "Declaration of Conscience."[11]

Identifying the rights to criticize, to protest, and to assert unwelcome views as basic American principles, Smith argued that "the Senate"—a catch-all for McCarthy and his supporters—threatened now to overturn the country's culture of open debate. "The exercise of these rights," she insisted,

> should not cost one single American citizen his reputation or his right to a livelihood nor should he be in danger of losing his reputation or livelihood merely because he happens to know some one who holds unpopular beliefs. . . . The American people are sick and tired of being afraid to speak their minds lest they be politically smeared as "Communists" or "Fascists" by their opponents. Freedom of speech is not what it used to be in America. . . . Today our country is being psychologically divided by the confusion and the suspicions that are bred in the United States Senate to spread like cancerous tentacles of "know nothing, suspect everything" attitudes. . . . I don't like the way the Senate has been made a rendezvous for vilification, for selfish political gain at the sacrifice of individual reputations and national unity.[12]

Recognizing that many in the GOP saw the anticommunist crusade as a way to reclaim the White House, Smith called this problematic strategy "political exploitation" and appealed to her colleagues' sense of fair play— "surely we Republicans aren't that desperate for victory." The speech went into the *Congressional Record* along with a "Statement of Seven Republican Senators" endorsing the address and chastising "certain elements of the Republican Party" for trying to garner "victory through the selfish political exploitation of fear, bigotry, ignorance, and intolerance." The seven included Smith and six GOP moderates, all of whom, excepting Wayne Morse of Oregon, quickly recanted under pressure. Morse would leave the Republican Party in 1952 in protest over Eisenhower's selection of running mate Richard Nixon. An independent until 1955, Morse then joined the Democrats.[13]

Victims of poor timing, Smith and her few and ephemeral Senate supporters (jeered at by McCarthy as "Snow White and the Six Dwarfs") got nowhere in 1950. Though newspaper coverage of the speech was generally favorable—the *Washington Post* praised Smith for saying what "desperately needed to be said for the salvation of the country," and former FDR adviser Bernard Baruch believed that "if a man had made the Declaration of Conscience, he would be the next President"—larger concerns quickly took over.[14] On 25 June, North Korean forces crossed the 38th parallel and the United States entered the Korean War. That autumn Republican candidates for public office were tempted as never before to campaign on the issue of anticommunism.

This was largely the political—and senatorial—climate that greeted Prescott Bush in 1952. Manifesting a New England reticence for McCarthyism's absence of diplomacy and fairness, he hoped, like Smith, to mute its impact, insisting on the campaign trail that to "justify support by the people" Republicans would have "to make a record in many other fields [than anticommunism]." Hardly were these words spoken when McCarthy himself arrived in Connecticut to speak at Bridgeport's Memorial Hall. Prodded by GOP officials to attend, Bush showed little enthusiasm: "Well, we get down there, and the place is packed, with standing room only. I never saw such a wild bunch of monkeys in any meeting that I've attended." The audience expected red meat, but Bush, sharing the stage with McCarthy, offered an innocuous comment or two before speaking from the heart: "I must in all candor say that some of us, while we admire his objectives in his fight against communism, we have very considerable reservations sometimes concerning the methods which he employs."[15] Not long after, the Senate voted to censure McCarthy on two counts relating to his conduct. Democrats lined up 45–0 for the condemnation of their colleague, and a divided GOP split evenly, 22–22. Bush supported the measure.

Three days after the censure ballot, Prescott outlined for the *New York Commercial and Financial Chronicle* his vision of a more inclusive Republican Party. "One hears criticism, of course, that [Eisenhower] doesn't take our [conservative] side strong enough. Well, our side has got to be good enough, I think if we are to survive in our philosophy . . . and I don't think we want the President to lose his grasp on the big middle section of the political thinkers in this country by getting too deep into the question of partisan politics." Hoping to convince the "big middle section" to give the GOP a chance, Bush worked diligently in his first term to revise Republicanism's prickly relationship with organized labor. The controversial 1947 Labor Management Relations Act, commonly known as Taft-Hartley, sought to restrain the power gained by unions during the New Deal. Passed over President Truman's veto, it banned the closed shop, forbade strikes by federal employees, and singled out union leaders to take loyalty oaths. In 1953 Bush moved to amend the offending legislation. These addendums included tossing out the prohibition against secondary boycotts and mandating that if employees had to file noncommunist affidavits, so did their employers.[16] Bush's moderate conservatism struck a responsive chord in Connecticut. Running for a full term in 1956 he handily defeated Congressman Thomas J. Dodd, a longtime assistant for various attorneys general who had made his name prosecuting Nazis at the Nuremburg trials.

Secure in his seat, Bush supported the moderate Californian Thomas Kuchel's bid for Republican whip because, as Prescott put it, "he belongs to what I call the progressive group of Republican Senators." Days before Kuchel's victory, Bush had called upon GOP reformers to take command of their party "if we are to . . . depart from the views of 30 or 40 years ago . . . [and] survive."[17] Looking to enlarge "modern" Republicanism, Bush canvassed for centrist senatorial candidates and sought accommodation with ethnic minorities and labor unions, two constituencies historically hostile to the Anglo-corporate entente.

For his efforts, Prescott soon found himself serving as something of a spokesman for the progressive wing of his party. While appearing on *Face the Nation*, William Hines, Sunday editor of the *Washington Star*, asked the senator, "What exactly is the GOP? Is it the party that is represented by people like yourself . . . or is it of people like [Utah] Governor [J. Bracken] Lee who says that Eisenhower has taken us farther to the left than any President in any two-year period?" Bush predictably denied a Republican identity crisis, yet his response tellingly fell upon the theme of difference. "Well, we've got a big Party," he replied, "and there is room in it for a lot of people of different persuasions and different ideas about different things." He then dismissed conservatism's recent Hoover-Taft-McCarthy past by pointing to its late-to-the-table peace with FDR's New Deal. In fact he went so far as to argue that the social welfare reforms of the 1930s now stood as a model for the modern GOP. "I think that the Republican Party of today, in its general philosophy, has taken . . . a big scoop out of the Democrat philosophy. So, under what I think we have done, under the Eisenhower conception of the Republican Party, is to take the best out of both of the Democrat and the Republican Party, and put them together in what the President calls the moderate progressivism of our new Republican Party." Did this "big scoop" approach blur party lines? his interlocutor followed up. "The blurring, so to speak," the senator evenly replied, "doesn't bother me."[18]

By promoting reform Republicanism, Bush sought to be part of a centrist party with an expanded constituency. Accordingly, he touted the presumed prolabor positions of party icons Lincoln and Theodore Roosevelt while attacking so called liberal New Dealers for harboring in their camp a formidable quasi-apartheid minority. "So long as Democrats control the Congress, the key positions of power will be in the hands of southern Democrats," he complained in a campaign swing across Connecticut. The Dixiecrats, he continued, "represent an area whose interests are often in conflict with our own; men whose views on issues affecting basic human rights clash with the more liberal and enlightened views we hold."[19] By routinely returning Democratic majorities to Capitol Hill, East Coasters, he concluded, solidified a backward-looking southern oligarchy in Washington and thus, in an emerging age of civil rights activism, inadvertently supported that region's segregationist practices.

Aside from the race issue, Bush self-interestedly pointed out that southern congressional control damaged the East economically. World War II had funneled an ocean of federal dollars to the Sunbelt where senior senators and congressmen enjoyed the committee oversight powers to capitalize on skyrocketing Cold War defense budgets. The "South and southwest," Bush observed, "are anxious to promote the economic growth of their own regions. We do not blame them for that. We hope that their regions will grow and prosper along with our own—just so long as their growth and prosperity is not made at our expense." But looking over the numbers, he was certain that they were. In his 1956 reelection campaign, Prescott singled out Texas for siphoning some 7,000 Connecticut jobs, thus enriching a state and section soon to empower a branch of the Bush dynasty dedicated to a less center-minded Republican Party. Throughout the late 1950s and early 1960s, Prescott worked diligently to oppose the "industrial pirating" that helped grow the new conservatism. In response to the 1961 Depressed Areas Bill, a War on Poverty forerunner designed to channel a $200,000,000 loan primarily to the South and Southwest, Bush teamed with Maine senator Edmund Muskie to limit the legislation's presumptive negative impact on the North. They included language in the law prohibiting the use of federal funds to aid in the relocation of businesses from one region to another.[20]

The following year Prescott left office. On 16 May 1962, one day after turning sixty-seven, he issued a brief press release stating, "I shall not be a candidate for reelection." Citing "the seven-day work week" of a busy senator and his concern with "hav[ing] the strength and vigor needed to do full justice to the duties of the campaign ahead," he looked forward to retirement. But that grandfatherly sentiment quickly passed. Time away from Washington clarified Prescott's relationship to a city and a Senate he soon missed. "I probably would [have] beat[en] anybody they could put up," he later told an interviewer. "So as I look back on it, having not been happy in retirement . . . and watching the [capital] scene . . . with great interest . . . I do regret it. . . . I've been awfully sorry many times, that I made that decision."[21]

One might fairly ask why. Aside from the satisfaction of senatorial dispensations, what did the future have in store for a moderate conservative like Prescott Bush? Barry Goldwater's 1964 candidacy offered a template for the Sunbelt strategies Nixon employed so effectively in 1968 and Reagan repeated in 1980. Republicans were on their way to dominating national elections by moving back to the future, taking up the 1920s as a model when GOP majorities went hand-in-hand with corporate-friendly tax cuts and a moral culture that sustained prohibition, fundamentalism, and nativism. The governing mandate sought by Eisenhower and his congressional lieutenants had expired. In more ways than one, Bush's 1972 death reflected the passing of a moderate East Coast persuasion in postwar Republicanism that had failed to capture a consensus. The South would now have its say.

· · · · ·

Millions of veterans and their families made the postwar pilgrimage to the suburbs, the strip malls, and the Sunbelt. Lionized in popular memory as "The Greatest Generation," this much-mythologized cohort's most representative product is, ironically, relegated to a polite purgatory and regarded as more mediocrity than pole star. Superficially dismissed as a "preppy" or a "wimp," George H. W. Bush in fact demonstrated a steely, unyielding tenacity to reach the presidency. Playing well the postcollegiate chess game of personal contacts, business deals, and a general willingness to bend personal principles for political advantage, he joined a small set of men who, in the 1970s and 1980s, could reasonably aspire to the Oval Office. Reared in the progressive Republican faith of his father, Bush matured politically in a country moving to the right. By recognizing the importance of this reformation, he reaped a grand reward for his Yankee exodus.

Born in Milton, Massachusetts, in 1924, Bush early on trailed conspicuously in Prescott's wake. Both father and son played first base at Yale, were "Bonesmen," and served in a world war. From there their paths diverged dramatically. In 1948 the younger Bush took his family to Texas's Permian Basin in search of oil wealth. "I wanted to do something on my own," he later explained, "I did not want to be in the shadow of this very powerful and respected man."[22] But even this decision begged parental comparison. For shortly after returning from active duty in 1919, Prescott left ancestral Ohio to start anew in St. Louis with the considerable aid of Bush-Walker money. Not long afterward he stormed Wall Street. A generation later George H. W. arrived in Odessa, Texas, to work for Dresser Industries, an oil service company on whose board of directors Prescott sat.

Life at Dresser was not easy. The firm transferred Bush in rapid succession from Odessa, a barren, blue-collar city, to a cluster of small California towns before returning him to Texas. In 1950 an emancipatory letter arrived. Citing "an urgent need to strengthen our staff in the younger age group," Brown Brothers Harriman & Company offered Bush a gift-wrapped opportunity: "It is our thought that you would come in here and learn the business." After taking several weeks to think the proposal over he replied that loyalty to Dresser prevented the move. A few months later, however, Bush resigned from Dresser, but not to return East. With $350,000 in start-up money collected by Uncle Herbert Walker and an additional $50,000 tossed in by Prescott, George H. W. cofounded the Bush-Overbey Oil Development Company. As partner John Overbey laconically put it, the venture "rocked along and made a few good deals and a few bad ones." Three years later Bush and new collaborator Hugh Lietke created Zapata Oil and not long after that its subsidiary Zapata Off-Shore, specializing in petroleum exploration in the Gulf of Mexico, the Caribbean, and the Central American Coast. After a decade in the dusty Permian the corporate upgrade meant relocating from isolated Midland to flourishing Houston. "He wasn't yet a full-fledged self-made millionaire," noted one commentator, "but for a thirty-five-year-old Yalie who had learned the oil business from scratch, he was doing very well."[23]

In hindsight it is plain that George H. W.'s Texas travels marked the transformative passage in his life. Interestingly, neither an impressive war record—he flew more than fifty combat missions and received the Navy's Distinguished Flying Cross—nor a prominent patrimony brought such clarity. Bush, after all, shared World War II with millions of uniformed men and women while the Greenwich–New York financial corridor belonged to Prescott. He hoped, however, to call Texas his own, feathered to be sure by Bush-Walker money, but George H. W. considered his spurs fairly earned. "By God's will," he once wrote, "I was born to a family of comfortable means and given many opportunities. I suppose this makes me one of the elite. But an 'elitist' is a person who wants to associate only with other elites; in other words, a snob. I assure you I would never have moved to the oil fields of west Texas if I were an 'elitist.' "[24]

And yet it was precisely Bush's "elitist" access to capital that made his Texas makeover such a success. His dependence on family networks to enter the oil industry mirrored Prescott's earlier admission into the closed club of investment banking. If anything, the son's timing proved more fortuitous than his father's. The transition from hot to cold war coincided with an exploding consumer culture reliant on petroleum-based products, and coming to Houston brought George Bush to the epicenter of an oil, natural gas, and aeronautics empire on the edge of phenomenal growth. A sleepy city of 44,000 in 1900, Houston suffered a devastating hurricane that year, which accelerated its efforts to construct a deep-water dock. One year later, the Spindletop oil field near Beaumont began gushing and the Texas petroleum industry took off. Bush's 1959 arrival overlapped with an astounding surge in Houston's population, which doubled from 600,000 at midcentury to 1,200,000 in just twenty years.

At the same time, the Lone Star state began to rethink its politics. Before supporting Eisenhower in 1952, Texas had sustained Democratic candidates in every presidential election in its history, excepting Hoover in 1928. Then came a revolution in party loyalties. A number of factors, including the antiregulatory attitude of the oilmen, the conservatism of the state's large military installations, and a rejection of the liberal 1960s, help to explain Texas's move to the Republican right. Since 1972 the state has backed GOP candidates in every general election excepting Carter in 1976. As a young conservative eager to forge a political career, Bush could hardly have chosen a better place than Houston to set down roots. "It's exciting to be a Republican in Harris County, Texas today," he wrote in the early 1960s. "The inevitability of our victory is clear. One only has to graph the vast Republican strides to see the picture. . . . If we act responsibly, if we make a principled appeal to all voters, and if we continue our program of basic political organization, we cannot help but become the dominant force in Texas politics."[25] Bush knew that in the previous presidential contest, John Kennedy had carried the state by a mere 46,000 votes and that Houston returned a Nixon plurality, the largest American city to do so. More generally, the former Confederate states were in the throes of political flux. Here Nixon had received nearly 5 million votes, only half a million fewer than Kennedy.

The outline for future GOP success was mapped out in a 1963 policy paper entitled "Political Realignment: A Big Gain for Republicans." Distributed to party chieftains, it observed that East Coast Democrats historically partnered with southern Democrats to win elections but once in office pursued liberal agendas that antagonized the South. The time had come, the bulletin argued, for conservatives of all stripes and sections to unite: "Should the . . . South in 1964 successfully switch its support from the Presidential nominee of the . . . Democrat party to the Republican presidential ticket, that step could produce an immediate, far-reaching and long overdue political realignment in presidential elections. The 'switch' could involve all of the South's 128 electoral votes in 1964, more than 47 percent of the 270 electoral votes required to elect a President. If effected, it could be the basis of a momentous expansion of the Republican party."[26]

By the early 1960s, the South trembled on the verge of political rebellion—again. In 1833 South Carolina had threatened to leave the Union over a disputed federal tariff; in 1850 delegates from nine southern states passed a resolution at the Nashville Convention demanding slavery's integration into western lands newly won from Mexico; secession came, of course, in 1861. Northern acquiescence of Jim Crow cooled southern fire-eaters for several decades, but the impact of postwar liberalism once more put the white South on the defensive. In 1948 Truman desegregated the U.S. Army, denounced poll taxes, and voiced his support for a Fair Employment Practices Commission. In response, Jim Crow hardliners formed the States' Rights Democratic Party, popularly called the Dixiecrats. Its membership had long simmered at the centralization of federal planning under the New Deal. Some southerners argued that a postwar version of the old and hated Yankee capitalists and carpetbaggers now sought a second "radical" Reconstruction. This brewing resentment erupted at the 1948 Democratic convention when Minneapolis mayor

Hubert Humphrey successfully urged party liberals to include in their platform an antisegregation plank. The irreconcilables among them bolted. Lining up behind South Carolina governor Strom Thurmond, the Dixiecrats took thirty-nine electoral votes away from Truman in that autumn's election. Had these ballots gone to the Republican Dewey, the president's plurality would have narrowed considerably. Conservatives took note, for in a close election future Dixiecrats—or whatever they might choose to call themselves, including "Republicans"—could make the difference.

The process of converting Texas Democrats was well under way by the time Bush entered politics. In this undertaking, the GOP enjoyed no greater ally than FDR and the New Dealers. In 1936 a coalition of northern liberals and midwestern progressives overturned the old two-thirds rule for nominating the party's national tickets. First used in the Jacksonian era, it had effectively given the minority South a veto over Democratic presidential candidates. The following year Roosevelt attempted to pack the Supreme Court with an additional justice for each sitting member over the age of seventy up to a maximum of six new positions. Many southerners denounced the president for "executive usurpation," fearing a liberal court's judicial war on segregation. Shortly after Roosevelt announced his plan, North Carolina senator Josiah Bailey complained to one correspondent that FDR "is determined to get the Negro vote, and I do not have to tell you what *this* means." Eager to topple his internal opposition, FDR conducted a "purge" campaign in 1938 against conservative congressional Democrats. He worked, unsuccessfully as matters turned out, to unseat sitting senators in Georgia, South Carolina, and Maryland.[27] And still later, Roosevelt's third and fourth terms revived Dixie's fears of an imperial presidency, while his successor's aforementioned commitment to desegregation inspired the Thurmond boom. More recently, Bush and his Houston colleagues could point to Kennedy's support for civil rights as yet another rebuke to states' rights.

And then suddenly the center of southern politics collapsed. In May 1961 Texas held a special election to fill the Senate seat vacated by Vice President Lyndon Johnson. By a razor thin 50.6 to 49.4 percent margin, John Tower became the state's first Republican senator since Reconstruction and only the third Republican senator from the former Confederacy since Reconstruction. Days before the polls opened, Bush sensed a realignment soon to shake the country. "Should Tower be elected," he wrote to a Bank of Texas official, "it will be a tremendously important step in establishing an active two party system in Texas. . . . In the face of extremely liberal control of the National Democratic party it seems to me the importance of a two party system cannot be under estimated."[28]

Bush's insights on Texas politics came through persistence and preparation rather than second nature. Never a "good old boy" and nothing more than a "Connecticut carpetbagger" in some Lone Star eyes, he struggled with the contrast between his patrician training and the realities of Harris County culture. In the summer of 1963 he received a letter from William Michels, an old-timer in Houston politics who was disturbed that Republicans in that city had, as Michels put it, established a "negro headquarters in a black district." Michels hoped to enlighten Bush, Harris County's GOP chairman, on the folly of such a move. "Back in 1920," he wrote, "I was Republican Precinct Committeeman for my Precinct. That was the year the negroes tried to take control of the Republican Party in the County. They were not successful and the Party has been white since that time." After establishing his "credentials," Michels then urged Bush to end his proposed courtship of black voters; he did so by way of a history lesson.

> Prior to 1932 negroes voted Republican. Since that time and Franklin D. Roosevelt, negroes the nation over have voted solidly Democratic. They voted for Kennedy solid in 1960 and they will vote for him again in 1964. The Republican Party cannot out-promise the Democrats and that is all the negroes are interested in. Those few negroes who claim to be Republicans are just playing both ends against the middle. How much money have negroes contributed to the Party in any recent campaign? Nine out of ten people in the United States are white, so why shouldn't the Republican Party cater to the white people? Should the leadership kick in the teeth of millions of white voters on the mere chance of getting a few negro votes? The Democratic Party is now known as the Black Democratic Party. Let it continue to be known that way.[29]

To many "practical" segregationists like Michels, Bush's Lone Star liberalism compromised Republican efforts to take over the state. Accordingly, Bush's future in Texas politics hinged on how convincingly he could appeal to the right. This imperative became more pronounced in 1964 when he ran for the U.S. Senate against Ralph Yarborough, a genuine southern progressive. In Texas's de facto one-party system, Yarborough represented the Democracy's reform wing, which vied with the more conservative politics of Lyndon Johnson and John Connally. During his tenure in the Senate (1957–71), Yarborough voted for every civil rights act that came before Congress, and he criticized the so-called Southern Manifesto, an angry response to the 1954 *Brown v. Board of Education* decision that, contra the Supreme Court's ruling, denounced the integration of public places. One hundred and one southern House and Senate members signed the pronouncement, all Democrats with the exception of two Virginia Republicans. A liberal populist, Yarborough once campaigned on the slogan, "Let's put the jam on the lower shelf so that the little people can reach it." Against Bush he made like the old Louisiana "King Fish," Huey Long and denounced his opponent as an outlander, a son of privilege, and a "tool of the Eastern Kingmakers."

Unable to "out-liberal" Yarborough, Bush hoped to "out-Texas" him. He opposed the 1964 Civil Rights Act, came out against a nuclear test-ban treaty, and sharply attacked the New Deal and its recent permutations. "I like Goldwater," he wrote to one correspondent. "I find him far more reasonable than one would believe from reading the newspapers about him. I think he will be a greater threat to Johnson than many people feel right now, particularly in the South and West." Bush ran a strong campaign against Yarborough and captured more votes than any Republican in a Texas Senate race to that time. He also lost decisively in what was an awful year for the GOP. Johnson crushed Goldwater, while Democrats secured a two-thirds majority in both wings of Congress, a feat since unmatched. For Bush, the sting of defeat called for a searching confession of ideological faith. "I took some far-right positions to get elected," he reportedly confessed to his Houston minister. "I hope I never do it again. I regret it."[30]

More broadly, Bush blamed the influence of ultraconservatism for the Republican debacle. In a letter to Richard Nixon he stressed the need to back away from the polarizing politics then circulating through the Southwest. "November 3rd has come and gone and we got whipped, and whipped soundly. . . . I have great respect for Barry Goldwater. In fact, most of his positions are totally acceptable to me. The only criticism is that his campaign, in many areas, in our state anyway, got taken over by a bunch of 'nuts' whose very presence at a rally would shake up a plain fellow coming in to make up his mind."[31] Though condemnatory of party yahoos, Bush's remark reveals a tinge of private desperation, for he had become a prisoner of Texas. The accruing of political capital in the Sunbelt came at a Faustian price—conversion to a strain of conservatism that never quite suited him. It speaks volumes about Bush's relationship with the Southwest that he won a national election yet never a state race.

In truth, Bush gave Texas Republicans—and later many right-leaning Republicans—reason to be wary. In 1980 he campaigned for the presidency as a prochoice candidate critical of Ronald Reagan's supply-side budget plan, which he ridiculed as "voodoo economics." But running again in 1988 he staked out a prolife position while lauding, despite spiraling deficits, Reaganomics. His 1991 decision as president to break a critical campaign promise and raise new taxes provoked a firestorm on the right. Ed Rollins, the national campaign director for the second Reagan-Bush campaign, called the decision "probably the most serious violation of any political pledge anybody has ever made."[32] For all of Bush's efforts, his decade in West Texas, his oilman's resume, and his promises to carry on the Reagan revolution, he could no more win the heart of his adopted state than he could the conservative movement.

He could, however, cultivate a political base in accommodating Harris County. In 1966 Bush handily captured the House seat for the Seventh Congressional District, a so-called carpetbagger district, and easily won reelection, even as he maneuvered for higher office. For a few weeks in the summer of 1968 speculation swirled around Nixon's choice for a running mate. Eager to erect a national profile, Bush audaciously encouraged a letter-writing campaign touting his credentials. After Nixon chose Maryland governor Spiro Agnew, he assured supporters that his fledgling veep run was given "very serious consideration."[33]

Loyal to Nixon and eager to pad his political portfolio, Bush took the president's advice in 1970 and left his safe house seat for a second Senate run against Yarborough. Bush looked like a lock. He captured the Republican primary with nearly 90 percent of the vote and, more important, Yarborough's brand of liberalism had fallen out of favor among Texans, who seemed willing to entertain the idea of having two Republican senators for the first time since Reconstruction. Then Bush's luck broke. In the Democratic primary former congressman Lloyd Bentsen upset Yarborough, and Bentsen wasn't a liberal. Consequently Bush (earning the dubious honor of John Kenneth Galbraith's endorsement, the kiss of death in Texas) lost whatever advantage he had. Running to his opponent's right, Bentsen accused Bush of supporting gun control, a guaranteed income for the indigent, and the federal Fair Housing Act, which moved to eliminate discrimination in the housing market. It was an uphill battle all the way, and Bush lost decisively 53 percent to 46 percent.

Since the Seventeenth Amendment first provided for the popular election of U.S. senators a century ago, every president who had previously vied for a senate seat claimed one, excepting Bush, who stumbled twice in six years. So much for Texas. Bush's political resurrection began appropriately enough in the liberal Northeast as United States ambassador to the United Nations. There in New York, as the city suffered through garbage strikes, escalating crime rates, and a brutal solvency crisis, the specter of urban breakdown reassured Bush of the "American" values he associated with the Sunbelt—in the process validating at middle-age his youthful decision to trade East for West. "I am continually impressed by how unrealistic a place New York is," he wrote while at the UN. "I find it very difficult to be polite when people ask me how I like New York. It is an unrepresentative city. There are tremendous host country problems. There are tremendous intensified urban problems that are not 'the real America.' . . . I am continually amazed at the arrogance of the intellectual elite in New York. They are so darn sure they are right on everything. It's unbelievable. Having lived in Texas for 23 years I had forgotten how concentrated this problem is, but it's sure there."[34]

Bush left New York in 1973 for a series of appointed posts, including chairman of the Republican National Committee, chief of the U.S. liaison office in the People's Republic of China, and director of the Central Intelligence Agency. Heading into the 1980 presidential campaign he could point to a long record as a Republican "cleanup" man, chairing the party during the Watergate debacle and taking over the CIA in the wake of devastating congressional findings that U.S. national security agencies were involved in various legal abuses, including attempts to assassinate foreign leaders. Still, he lacked a national audience. His major opponent, the former Hollywood actor Ronald Reagan, had a reputation for staring down Berkeley "radicals" during his tenure as California's governor. More important, conservatives embraced Reagan as one of their own. In a contest between Bush's accumulated political capital and Reagan's raw appeal, the "Great Communicator" captured the hearts and hopes of an increasingly right-turning Republican Party. In fact it was no contest at all; Reagan won forty-four primaries, including Texas's. As Reagan biographer Lou Cannon later noted, "Certainly, on paper Bush was better prepared than Reagan to be president. . . . But in some ways, the very breadth of his career counted against Bush, for his resume was seen in party circles as reflecting not only a devotion to duty but an inability to say no. To many Republicans, the whole of Bush was less than the sum of the parts."[35] Reagan seemed to agree with this assessment, and only after a Reagan–Gerald Ford "dream ticket" fell through did he hesitantly make Bush his running mate. This decision ultimately set in motion two GOP presidencies, the second clearly dependent upon the first in an electorally successful if ideologically strained political marriage that echoed William Howard Taft's reliance on Theodore Roosevelt.

If the 1980 campaign reflected the last gasp of moderate Republicanism, it was owing less to Bush's failed presidential pursuit than to that of John B. Anderson. A ten-term (1961–81) congressman from Illinois's Sixteenth District, Anderson moved ideologically in a different direction from Bush. A Goldwater supporter in 1964, he inched increasingly toward the political center after that election. Stirred by the civil rights movement, Anderson, though always a fiscal conservative, began to adopt moderate positions on a number of surfacing social issues, including women's rights, federal aid for education, and gun control. In 1974 he became the first house Republican to call for the Watergate-mired Nixon to resign from office—and no later than the mid-1970s had he aroused the ire of Illinois's rising right wing.

Seeking reelection in 1978, Anderson faced a difficult primary challenge from Don Lyon, a forty-six-year-old conservative evangelical known to many in the Sixteenth District as the longstanding host of *Quest for Life*, a locally aired religious television program. The contest quickly attracted attention beyond north central Illinois as money began to pour in to Lyon's campaign from around the country; the challenger spent nearly $300,000 in all, "an enormous amount by historical standards," wrote Anderson press secretary Mark Bisnow, "for an election in Rockford, Illinois." In response, Anderson, faced with his first primary struggle since 1960, was compelled to rely on Washington colleagues and Chicago businessmen to help him raise funds. As one student of the campaign has observed, "Anderson had never been forced to resort to calling on political friends for help in his own district. He felt humiliated."[36] Come March, Anderson carried the primary by a comfortable margin of nearly 16 percent, and this included the assistance of crossover independents and Democrats. In November he easily defeated his Democratic challenger and returned to Washington.

Asked after the bruising primary if he planned to reconcile with those conservatives who opposed him, Anderson balked at such a prospect. "Now that they've sunk their axes in my back?" he testily replied, "after they've publicly excoriated me? No, I don't plan any rapprochement with them." As the new congress assembled he soon learned that his colleagues on the right had yet to put their "axes" away. Habitually elected since 1969 to chair the House Republican Conference, he now had to beat back yet another challenge by a minority of more conservative members in his party. Anderson won, but, as with the free-spending primary skirmish, the contest rankled. When first elected to Congress in 1960 he entered a legislative body in which moderate voices were still prominent within the GOP. But the party was moving in an altogether different ideological direction, and the Lyon campaign made this unmistakably clear. Bill O'Donnell, an Anderson aide, later noted that the opposition the congressman faced from the right made him rethink what it meant to be a Republican. "He felt betrayed, blindsided. And that, coupled at the same time with the more conservative build-up within his party, just really alienated him."[37]

In 1980 Anderson took his alienation across the country, canvassing for the presidency first as a moderate Republican and then as an independent. Both decisions were born of a single strategy, to stem the GOP's right-moving momentum. Much of the media initially designated Bush as the "moderate" candidate of the coming primary season, but Anderson saw his GOP opponents as basically interchangeable in their ardor to court "ultra" conservatives. Believing that Republicans were "going down the wrong road . . . hopelessly wedded to policies that were appropriate to the past but not the future," he refused to make peace with his party, but instead launched a nonparty presidential campaign.[38] Anderson announced his candidacy in April following a series of primaries that saw him win more votes than Reagan in Massachusetts and more than Bush in Vermont, Illinois, and Kansas; in the conservative South, by contrast, his percentage of the vote failed to crack 10 percent.

His support nationwide peaking at 26 percent, Anderson attracted independents and college students, a number of prominent intellectuals, and Democrats disaffected with Jimmy Carter. Interestingly, moderate Republicans, among his earliest supporters, tapered off as the campaign season moved on. Sensing a big year for the GOP, they didn't want anything to spoil the party's success. Some spoke to Anderson about discontinuing his candidacy but he persisted, believing these emissaries failed to reckon beyond November. "It isn't that I didn't respect some of the people who made those interventions," he later observed, "but I thought the issue was larger than the issue that they could see.[39] At least one moderate, former Massachusetts senator Edward Brooke, remarked to Anderson that by running as an independent he was all but ensuring that other centrists within the GOP would now be ostracized and left without an effective voice within the party.

More than a footnote to the 1980 election, the Anderson campaign seemed to suggest the accuracy of Brooke's prophecy. And yet the influence of moderates within the GOP had been on the wane for a number of years. We might, in fact, see Anderson's long-shot presidential run as fitting within the framework of an era (1960–80) in which a number of centrists—including William Scranton and Nelson Rockefeller, George Romney and Howard Baker—failed to wrest control of their party from the right. One would-be centrist, George H. W. Bush, did of course reach the political summit, but only by deferring to the GOP's conservative wing.

·····

Having ridden the right to the White House, Bush tried to govern from the center. If Reaganomics celebrated a supply-side utopia anchored philosophically in the "creative destruction" of capitalism, Bush emphasized the need for, as he put it, a "kinder, gentler nation." Not that he wished to revive LBJ's ambitious if problematic Great Society ("programs administered by the incumbent few," he complained), but he did call for "a Good Society" that innocuously stressed "service, selflessness, [and] action." His beau ideal of a president came readily to mind. "A model, I think . . . would be Teddy Roosevelt. He comes out of the same elitist background that I do." The Roosevelt analogy is telling. Nearly a century earlier, TR hoped to assert the prerogatives of the patricians in a political culture dominated by party professionals. Now, Bush defended his own generation's "better sort," the sons of senators and industrialists, trained to rule but boxed in by the 1960s liberal left and the post-1960s cultural right. Addressing his Greenwich Country Day class reunion in 1997, Bush observed that "our parents taught us to care—and the faculty here seemed to be intent on inculcating into us the fact that we had an obligation to care, indeed that we have an obligation to help others. Our critics call it Noblesse Oblige. I was later to call it being one of a 1000 Points of Light."[40]

Ironically, the patrician prompting that failed to win Bush the White House proved critical to his greatest success while in it. Following the

August 1990 Iraqi invasion of Kuwait, the president, aided by a thick Rolodex of personal contacts, assembled a broad coalition of nations that successfully implemented operations Desert Shield and Desert Storm. Other foreign policy highlights marked the Bush presidency, including the rapid but peaceful unification of Germany, the break-up of the Soviet Union, and the end of the Cold War. Having "kicked," as Bush blithely put it, the nation's "Vietnam syndrome once and for all," American triumphalism briefly held court, but the moment did not last. Moving toward the 1992 campaign, economic and social concerns, Democratic issues, predominated. The sixty-eight-year-old incumbent was in for a tough fight, and that was before two challengers on the right emerged.

Patrick Buchanan, a former Nixon and Reagan speechwriter, regarded Bush as little more than a "Me-Too Republican," reminiscent of the moderate conservatives who dominated the party in the 1940s and 1950s. Scholars tend to agree with this assessment. As historian Michael Kazin has recently noted, "Although [Bush] portrayed himself as the consolidator of the 'Reagan Revolution,' his temperament and policies seemed closer to those of the then marginal but still despised 'Rockefeller Republicans' from the Northeast." A devotee of the "Reagan Revolution" and no fan of the moderate Bush, Buchanan had briefly considered running for the GOP nomination in 1988. After Bush went back on his campaign pledge not to raise taxes, Buchanan edged closer to a candidacy. "Like a lot of conservatives," he later said, "I felt [Bush had] broken the main commitment he'd made for us."[41] Bush's successful overseeing of the Persian Gulf War temporarily put Buchanan at bay, but the president's signing of the 1991 Civil Rights Act, a so-called quota bill designed to end employment discrimination by obligating employers to set aside jobs for minority applicants, combined with his fading postwar popularity in the face of a sharply declining economy, pushed Buchanan to challenge Bush for the nomination.

Buchanan's surprisingly strong showing in the New Hampshire primary (he took 37 percent of the vote) revealed a broader discontent with Bush than most analysts had realized. It further galvanized Buchanan's supporters to carry on a protracted campaign against the president that lasted several months and resulted in their candidate's securing 22 percent of the popular ballot in the primaries. Two of the previous three Republican incumbents, by contrast, ran virtually unopposed. In 1972 the conservative Ohio congressman John Ashbrook polled only 5 percent against Nixon, while Reagan captured nearly 99 percent of the votes cast in the 1984 GOP primaries. The third case, the hotly contested Ford-Reagan contest of 1976, was anomalous, with Ford being the only incumbent in the nation's history unelected to either the presidency or the vice presidency.

The plain-talking Texas businessman H. Ross Perot presented Bush with an even greater challenge. A self-made billionaire concerned with America's "decline," he promised to balance the federal budget, stem the outsourcing of U.S. jobs, and promote direct democracy through "electronic town halls." A charismatic and controversial figure, he entered the American popular imagination as a can-do maverick. During the Iranian Revolution, two of his Electronic Data Systems employees were arrested and jailed in Tehran. Frustrated at what he regarded as the State Department's blank response, Perot organized a successful rescue mission that spirited the two workers out of the country. Ken Follett's popular 1983 novel *On Wings of Eagles* dramatized the account, as did the 1986 television miniseries of the same name—Richard Crenna of *Rambo* fame played Perot. Recalling the outsider status of an Andrew Jackson, Perot emphasized his alienation from big government and faith in popular rule. For a while the public was willing to listen. In one June poll registering presidential preference, Perot—backed now by the newly formed Independence Party—led both Bush and the Democratic nominee, Bill Clinton.

Then things got strange. Reports began to circulate that ABC was about to release a story concerning a relationship that had taken place a decade earlier between Perot's daughter, Suzanne, and one of her Vanderbilt University professors. Supposedly Perot had put the couple under surveillance and, so the professor maintained, had approached him and said, "My daughter's never going to marry a Jew." Perot then announced that "digitally altered" photographs of his affianced younger daughter, Carolyn, would be released if his candidacy continued. "I received a report of a high-level Republican meeting," Perot told a Pittsburgh audience, "where they said: 'We have thrown everything we can make up on Perot and he just keeps on coming and keeps going up in the polls. Isn't this guy sensitive to anything?' And one person in the meeting—I'm thinking they said—'he adores his family.' I got a report on that, and I filed it away. A couple of weeks later I got a report that there was a plan to smear my daughter Carolyn, who was about to get married on August 23 and, believe it or not, disrupt the church service at her wedding."[42] Perot offered no proof to this allegation. Citing an obligation to protect his family, he pulled out of the race in July, only to reenter (at the behest of United We

Stand volunteers, he insisted) on 1 October. His campaign never recovered its summer momentum.

In August the 1992 Republican national convention met in Houston's Astrodome. Here was a final chance for Texas's flagship city to embrace its adopted son and, more important, give Bush a momentum-building send-off for the difficult campaign ahead. Instead, the convention disintegrated into one of the most brittle and divisive political gatherings in recent history. A longer lens reveals its resemblance to the 1912 and 1964 conventions, disastrous affairs that deepened the divisions between the party's moderate and conservative wings and led to November defeats. Despite the fact that some 9 million Americans were unemployed, the family-values wing of the GOP dominated the convention's messaging. This played into the polemical talents of Buchanan, a practiced hand at the art of inflammatory rhetoric. That he was given a prime-time audience following months of slashing attacks on Bush in the primaries attested to the belief among moderate Republicans that they could not win without the party's red-meat right in tow.

The fallout was predictably bad. Bush's acceptance speech, presumably the centerpiece of the convention, was overshadowed by Buchanan's polemical "culture war" address, which emphasized the centrality of social conservative issues among the Republican base. Throwing out such incendiary lines as "Bill Clinton and Al Gore represent the most pro-lesbian and pro-gay ticket in history," Buchanan drew a sharp division between two Americas. "There is a religious war going on in this country," he warned a chanting Buchanan Brigade, and unlike the Cold War, he continued, "this war is for the soul of America." As the convention opened, moderate Republicans were left to wonder at the rising intolerance of their party. Journalists Jack Germond and Jules Witcover reported that "the morning after Buchanan's speech, one longtime Bush supporter from the Farm Belt, a middle-aged woman who worked as a vice president of a major corporation, telephoned us to talk about it. 'It wasn't just the speech,' she said, 'it was the people all around me cheering while Buchanan was saying those things. What's happened to my party?' "[43] Come November, Bush earned the lowest voter percentage for an incumbent since Taft.

· · · · ·

The cultural dynamics within the GOP that helped bring down one Bush presidency produced another. The son of a Yankee patrician, George W. Bush made an easy ideological alliance with Sunbelt Republicanism. In contrast to his father's strained marriage of convenience with the GOP right, "W." more nearly embraced its platform of moral politics, privatized economics, and rhetorical war on big government. If he wasn't exactly Reagan, he wasn't exactly his father, either.

Perusing George W.'s resume one finds a path littered with conspicuous "Bush" signage. This includes attendance at an exclusive East Coast prep school (Phillips Academy), followed by the requisite Yale turn, a military interlude (the Texas Air National Guard), and a connection-laden entry into the business world. As important as these congruencies are, the contrasts are no less compelling. As Bush once put it, "I'm more like Ronald Reagan than my dad. The difference is, my dad was raised in the East, and I was raised in Texas." Liberated among the Lone Stars, Bush gravitated to a populistic persona spiritually and ideologically translated into an uncomplicated fundamentalism. While George H. W. described himself as "kind of an inward guy when it comes to religion," his son gravitated to an activist faith embodied in what he called the "passionate" preaching of the charismatic Texas evangelicals Tony Evans and T. D. Jakes. As David Farber has observed, W.'s walk to the cross had a profound impact on his political identity: "Bush found the core of his conservative values not in his readings in free-market economics or anticommunist treatises but, he said, in the words of God as revealed in the Bible. . . . [He] found his conservative anchor in his spiritual and not his intellectual life."[44]

George H. W., always a little Ivy League stiff among the Pentecostal types, nevertheless recognized their political value in the brewing post-1960s culture wars. He even claimed a selective identification with their concerns. Writing in 1982 to an old friend, Yale president A. Bartlett Giamatti, he defended the nation's growing reaction to liberalism: "We must understand that in our post–Viet Nam post-Watergate guilt, we have condoned things we should have condemned. Now a decade later a lot of people are concerned. Some of them are totally intolerant, but in my view most are not. . . . They are trying to stand up for things that fundamentally I believe in."[45]

For George W., the "come to Jesus" moment materialized much more naturally. A failed energy entrepreneur in the oil glut 1980s, a heavy social drinker practiced at the art of deflecting questions about past drug use with a glancing, "when I was young and irresponsible, I was young and irresponsible," he had approached forty in something of a funk. And then, as his father flirted with the Christian right for political reasons, he suddenly found his center. W. gave up alcohol and began attending Bible classes. He later remembered 1986 as "a year of change" even as he struggled to understand what had transpired—"when I look back at it . . . I really never have connected the dots all the way."[46]

Some made the linkage for him. In fact, more than a few Americans believed that God had gifted George W. the presidency. "Is this a reprieve?" one cyber writer asked in 2001. "Did God appoint him as leader to spare us the moral darkness of the Clinton years?" Distinct from his father, who hitched a ride on the Reagan bandwagon, W. came to office under the shadow of a bitterly contested election with Al Gore that ultimately found resolution in a split Supreme Court decision. Not long after that came the devastating 9/11 attacks. A number of fundamentalists interpreted this dark day as God's payback for America's secular lifestyle. As the televangelist Jerry Falwell coarsely put it, "I really believe that the pagans, and the abortionists, and the feminists, and the gays and the lesbians who are actively trying to make that an alternative lifestyle, the ACLU, People For the American Way, all of them who have tried to secularize America, I point the finger in their face and say 'you helped this happen.'" Though the president never touched that combustible rhetoric he remained in contact with Falwell over the years, described the televangelist as "a great friend of this administration," and sent a White House aide to the minister's 2007 funeral.[47]

Bush clearly regarded his reign as one grounded in the idea of a redemptive republic. In this sense, he was no Reaganite. "The Gipper," after all, had come to his conservatism by way of a critical reaction to the social welfare state, which he saw as antithetical to American capitalism. Reagan's eight-year turn (1954–62) as host of General Electric Theater served as an introduction to powerful business leaders as well as hundreds of Rotarian types eager to advance the free-market system. As a "corporate ambassador," Reagan not only represented GE on what he called the "mashed potato circuit," but he in turn proved receptive to the revolt against big government that he encountered on the road. Lou Cannon has perceptively written that "many of the questions asked [Reagan] by his corporate or service club audiences focused on government excesses. In responding to these questions, Reagan gradually became more critical of government. No one told him to do this, but Reagan paid attention to his audiences. Reagan was already a company man when he began his GE tours, but he was still a nominal Democrat who had been raised to be suspicious of Big Business. Over time, on tour for General Electric, these suspicions diminished and were replaced by distrust for Big Government."[48]

Bush, by contrast, arrived at his conservative convictions through a rejection of the cultural liberalism that had shaped the 1960s. These were demanding years for W., who self-consciously felt every bit the Texas outsider amid the petty prep snobbery he encountered in the Northeast. He found Phillips Academy in Andover, Massachusetts, "cold, distant and difficult," and in his freshman year at Yale he was embarrassed and angered when Yale chaplain and campus icon the Reverend William Sloane Coffin said to him, "I knew your father, and your father lost [the 1964 Texas senate election] to a better man." "You talk about a shattering blow," Barbara Bush told a *Washington Post* reporter several years later, "not only to George, but shattering to us. And it was a very awful thing for a chaplain to say to a freshman at college."[49]

Though he immersed himself in Yale's extracurricular culture—playing sports, joining a fraternity, and partying on the weekends—Bush, with his short hair, Texas twang, and support of the Vietnam War, stood akimbo to the superior pose struck by the school. Reagan, too, had been critical of America's cultural turn during this period and in fact launched his political career in 1966 by vowing to "clean up the mess at Berkeley," perhaps the most striking example of a postwar university in conflict with the military-industrial-academic complex. Yet for Reagan, the "Battle at Berkeley" was about containing the idealism of his opponents; Bush, by contrast, wrestled with a lack of idealism, a kind of privileged nihilism that he detected at Yale and may have later held accountable for the life drift that he experienced in his twenties and thirties. When later, as a policymaker, Bush grappled with free-enterprise issues, he inevitably filtered them through a Christian moral perspective absent in Reagan. "Economic growth can't solve all our problems," he insisted in his second inaugural address as Texas's governor. "In fact, we're now putting too much hope in economics, just as we once put too much hope in government. Reducing problems to economics is simply materialism."[50]

As president, Bush's domestic agenda was truncated by the 9/11 attacks and his 2003 decision to invade Iraq. He had campaigned as a "compassionate conservative," by which he meant that the nation's social problems would be better tackled by churches, charities, and corporations than by big government. An echo of his father's "thousand points of light" volunteerism—and Bill Clinton's 1990s emphasis on workfare over welfare—compassionate conservatism pursued the privatization of social services while emphasizing personal responsibility and self-reliance. In practice this philosophy yielded the No Child Left Behind Act (2001) and the Medicare Prescription Drug, Improvement, and Modernization Act (2003), both of which, ironically, expanded the purview of government oversight. Many on the right were critical of Bush on this score. Corporate executive and 2012 GOP presidential hopeful Herman Cain denounced compassionate conservatism as a "ruse," maintaining that it had "completely betrayed conservative voters and their decades of grassroots activism."[51]

Bush was on firmer ground with the Republican right on foreign affairs. Here the religious overtones in compassionate conservatism's tough-love moralism were echoed in the president's crusader-like response to 9/11. As the March 2003 invasion of Iraq gave way to a difficult occupation, Bush took solace in the conviction that a righteous people and a powerful military made for a just cause. After reading Richard Carwadine's biography *Lincoln: A Life of Purpose and Power*, "W." confessed a special connection to the sixteenth president through a shared faith in a redemptive republic: "This book talks about the constituency that Lincoln had. And one was religious people who were going through this Second Awakening, that loved Lincoln's position that all men are created equal: there is a God, and all men are created equal by that God, and so it's a moral position. And the military loved Lincoln. . . . There's a parallel here. And that's that our military understands this. . . . And they look to me—they want to *know* whether I've got the resolution necessary to see this though. And I do. I believe—I *know* we'll succeed."[52]

In this case, success meant redrawing the political map of the Near East by promoting democratic states in a region historically committed to nondemocratic regimes. Interestingly, the second Gulf War rested in large measure on the premise that the first Bush administration had failed to contain Saddam Hussein's plans to produce weapons of mass destruction. In essence, the son acted to correct the father's error. To do so, however, he needed public support, and that meant many months of overplaying the Iraqi risk, of saying, in effect, that George H. W.'s Gulf War decision to leave Saddam Hussein in office had been a large and potentially catastrophic mistake.

The senior Bush appears to have taken note. In August 2002 his former national security adviser, Brent Scowcroft, wrote a featured article in the *Wall Street Journal* questioning the second Bush administration's efforts to gin up a war against Iraq. A close personal friend of George H. W., Scowcroft had recently cowritten with the retired president *A World Transformed*, their reflections on the collapse of the Soviet Union, German reunification, and Operation Desert Storm. "We chose to focus on the most important events of the years 1989–1991," they wrote at the time, as these culminated "in the emergence of the United States as the preeminent power." Now that preeminence seemed threatened, perhaps less by the reach of international terrorism than by the reaction of George W.'s administration to international terrorism. Reading Scowcroft's article one receives the distinct impression that its author, while expressing his own views, served in some capacity as an amanuensis, passing the sentiments of one Bush president to another. As Robert Gates, formerly Scowcroft's deputy at the National Security Council put it, "What makes [Scowcroft's criticisms] even more awkward is the suspicion that he's speaking not just for himself."[53]

While conceding Saddam Hussein's potential as a global irritant, Scowcroft rejected the new Bush team's claims that the United States stood in imminent danger. "Saddam is a familiar dictatorial aggressor, with traditional goals for his aggression," he wrote. "There is little evidence to indicate that the United States itself is an object of his aggression." Scant proof of Iraqi ties to international terrorism existed, nor did Hussein appear likely to ferry phantom weapons of mass destruction around the region. Rather, regime change in Iraq threatened the U.S.'s global antiterrorist efforts, for "a military campaign very likely would have to be followed by a large-scale, long-term military occupation." Scowcroft called for a vigorous war against terrorism, and no war against Saddam Hussein.[54]

· · · · ·

Bush left office in January 2009 with a disapproval rating that could only be described as Nixonesque. Even on the right resided a host of critics, many of whom regarded his presidency as insufficiently Reaganesque. On the foreign policy front, traditional conservatives attacked his global crusading, asking if the country's two prolonged wars in the Near East had in fact ensured America's safety. More mainstream conservatives denounced "W." for growing government and leaving the nation with a soaring federal budget deficit. These observations from the right form part of a broader argument that Bush, like his father, was never really the conservative that "real" conservatives imagined. The actions of his

Democratic successor have only begged a surprising comparison. *New York Times* columnist Ross Douthat claimed in 2013 that "the continuities between Bush and Obama on civil liberties, presidential power and the war on terror make the same point: To critique Bushism appropriately, you need to recognize that on many, many issues, his presidency was much more centrist and establishment than it was radical or right-wing."[55] Taken on these terms, "W." was perhaps not so far removed from the moderate governing instincts of his father and grandfather. But he governed in different times and, thinking of Prescott's midcentury GOP, a much different party.

Turning away from particular criticisms of the Bush presidency, a broader question could be raised as to how "W." "failed" as a conservative. One answer is to see his presidency as the concluding act of the Sunbelt conservatism that mastered American politics for nearly half a century. It was during Bush's tenure in office that the founding fathers of the modern political, economic, evangelical, and intellectual right all passed from the scene. The deaths of Reagan (2004), Milton Friedman (2006), Jerry Falwell (2007), and William F. Buckley Jr. (2008) suggested a torch passing of sorts. This perception of the right in retrenchment took on added import in light of consecutive national electoral defeats to Obama in 2008 and 2012, the first successful non-Sunbelt candidate since Kennedy in 1960.

Should Bush represent the last stand of late twentieth-century conservatism, one could be excused for seeing a fitting arc in the affair. From Prescott to the present day, the family has made itself amenable to those strongest currents within the GOP. But if the party's right wing can no longer carry national candidates to November triumphs, the Bushes, and more broadly center-minded Republicans, will have no more reason to remain under its ideological spell. Their opposition's successful move to the middle, the subject of the following and final chapter, offers perhaps the key to the GOP's political future.

10 After Liberalism

Carter, Clinton, Obama

. . . .

In many cases I feel more at home with the conservative Democratic and Republican members of Congress than I do with the others.

—Jimmy Carter, 1978

All Americans, without regard to party, know that our welfare system is broken, that it teaches the wrong values, rewards the wrong choices, hurts those it was meant to help.

—Bill Clinton, 1996

Reagan offered Americans a sense of a common purpose that liberals seemed no longer able to muster.

—Barack Obama, 2006

In the last decades of the twentieth century the Democratic Party struggled to honor its still-resonant FDR past without losing its future. Born in reaction to the old pre–market crash consensus, modern liberalism comprised a formidable coalition of interest groups linking progressive elites with mass constituencies. An ambitious, transformative politics, it helped shape the American Century, bringing together organized labor and the civil rights movement to promote economic equality, advance social justice, and expand the country's middle class. Sensitive to criticisms that "soft-hearted" reformers made for poor cold warriors—and eager to avoid the accusatory gaze of red-baiters and far-righters—postwar progressives struck a hawkish pose in foreign affairs. For years the Democratic Party promised both guns and butter, plenty at home and security abroad. Master of the welfare-warfare state, champion of "relief, recovery, and reform," it won election after election.

By the late 1960s this formula was coming undone. The civil rights movement combined with the "new immigration" from Africa, Latin America, and Asia to fundamentally transform the bases of both the Democratic and Republican Parties. Along the way many of the blue-collar constituencies long essential to Democratic political success had migrated to the nation's suburbs; a relative affluence and desire to protect their economic gains aroused a reaction against the redistributive policies of big government. As a result, the party of FDR moved closer to the middle. While recognizing its longtime liberal support with progressive judicial appointments and promises to extend health care coverage, Democrats began to embrace balanced budgets, champion welfare reform, and renounce the politics of entitlement. Trending centrist, they have reaped a king's ransom. After dropping five of six presidential contests between 1968 and 1988 as "liberal" Democrats, they have popularly outpolled their opponents in five of the six post-1988 campaigns as New Democrats.

The emblematic figures in this transformation are Jimmy Carter, Bill Clinton, and Barack Obama. The first two came from the South, a region particularly dissatisfied with the expansion of the postwar welfare state. In the 1970s and 1980s they rose to prominence within a party moving slowly if decidedly toward the political center. In Clinton's pragmatic Third Way positioning, a synthesis of conservative economic and liberal social policies, Democrats once again became competitive in national elections. While the simplified version of American politics remained stuck in a generic "Roosevelt versus Ronald Reagan" backdrop, the electorate had moved on. As Obama put it, the categories "of 'conservative' and 'liberal' . . . were inadequate to address the problems we faced."[1] In tandem, these three leaders represented various stages in the development of the moderate New Democrats. Before considering their contributions, however, we should first address the historical circumstances that prepared their ascent.

The Democratic Party's march to the middle began as a reaction to the sudden collapse of the postwar liberal order. In late August 1968, with the Vietnam War, a culture-rending generation gap, and a painful spate of high-profile political assassinations providing a tinderbox setting, the Democratic National Convention then meeting in Chicago succumbed to chaos. While thousands of police and antiwar protesters clashed outside in the city's Grant Park, astonished politicians and delegates inside the International Amphitheater struggled to respond. Addressing the convention, Connecticut senator Abraham Ribicoff denounced what he called the "Gestapo tactics" of the local law enforcement; incensed by this attack on his handling of the demonstrators, Chicago's mayor, Richard J. Daley, stood in Ribicoff's sightline shouting, "Fuck you you Jew son of a bitch you lousy motherfucker go home[!]"[2] NBC News carried all of this live. Viewers were left with the vivid imagery of a divided party in meltdown. The New Deal consensus—a combination of urban machines, labor unions, farmers, minorities, and southerners—was under attack from within. Many among its younger cohort, unimpressed by their political elders nostalgia for the FDR 1930s, denounced the party's long collaboration with American capitalism, imperialism, and racism. Sixty-eight days after the convention, Nixon defeated Hubert Humphrey, the establishment liberal pol par excellence, in a tight race.

The following year Democrats set out to ensure there would be no more Chicagos. The Democratic National Committee chairman, Senator Fred Harris, oversaw the creation of the Commission on Party Structure and Delegate Selection. Its twenty-eight-member panel, headed first by Senator George McGovern and, later, Congressman Donald Fraser, sought to establish a more open nominating process that reflected the values, interests, and expectations of Democratic voters. On all accounts, reforming and expanding the presidential primaries looked to be the key. In 1968 only fourteen states held primaries; antiwar senators Eugene McCarthy of Minnesota and Robert Kennedy of New York captured ten of these contests. Vice President Humphrey refused to enter a single race but claimed the nomination by dint of delegates won in nonprimary states where political bosses controlled the conventions. "Several factors worked to Humphrey's advantage," writes biographer Carl Solberg. "Kennedy and McCarthy were locked in fierce man-to-man primary contention, while Humphrey was free to concentrate on bagging the far more numerous delegates from non-primary contests." And these delegates, Solberg continues, were susceptible to the reach, pressure, and persuasion of the vice president: "In Maryland . . . a few parliamentary maneuvers and some brisk arm-twisting got the state committee to deliver all [of its] 49 votes to Humphrey under the unit rule. Delaware's delegation came over in a body after the Humphreyites chartered a plane and airlifted all 22 delegates and their spouses to Washington for a convivial evening that included a chat for each with the vice-president."[3] Scholars have long debated whether the popular Kennedy could have won the nomination over the objections of the party's power brokers, but this seems unlikely. Killed after carrying the California primary, Kennedy still lagged far behind Humphrey in the delegate count, 561 to 393. In Chicago, Humphrey, with legions of long-sewn-up delegates, crushed McCarthy 1,759 to 601.

Dismayed at the "undemocratic" pattern of picking party leaders, the McGovern-Fraser Commission drafted a new nominating structure. It drew up rules to tear down the boss/delegate relationship, made the process of selecting convention electors transparent, and gave a greater voice to female, minority, and younger voters. More specifically, the reformers barred party potentates from choosing delegates in secret and established quotas to ensure that electors stood in proportion to the population of the states they represented. Primaries and caucuses—not state conventions—would now dole out the bulk of the delegates. Issued in the spring of 1970, the commission's report, *Mandate for Reform*, argued that without change, the Democratic Party risked irrelevancy: "We believe that popular participation is more than a proud heritage of our party, more than a first principle. We believe that popular control of the Democratic Party is necessary for its survival. . . . If we are not an open party; if we do not represent the demands of change, then the danger is not that people will go to the Republican Party; it is that there will no longer be a way for people committed to orderly change to fulfill their needs and desires within our traditional political system. It is that they will turn to third and fourth party politics or the anti-politics of the street."[4] True to the commission's intent, the innovations it established neutralized the old interest-group blocks; more, they reduced the importance of national conventions—once indispensable pieces of party identity—to mere coronations.

The McGovern-Fraser structure may have produced a fairer system, but what Democrats really wanted was a winning system, and that they did not get. In 1972 George McGovern claimed the nomination (giving rise to criticism that he used the commission to advance his own presidential aspirations). Yet his appeal to affluent liberals and reputed ties to the "amnesty, abortion, and acid" left alienated some traditional Democratic constituencies. Come November, he suffered one of the greatest defeats in American political history; Nixon took forty-nine states and captured a staggering 96 percent of the electoral votes, a sum exceeded only by James Monroe's 98 percent in 1820 and Franklin Roosevelt's 98 percent in 1936. Aside from cementing the South, Nixon captured more Catholic support than McGovern and made inroads into the Jewish and African American vote. He even won over many old New Dealers. Texas governor John Connally headed the Democrats for Nixon campaign, asserting before the election that the McGovern-Fraser rules had turned the Democratic Party into "an ideological machine closed to millions who have been [its] most loyal and steadfast members."[5] Connally hoped to encourage 20 million Democrats to cross over for Nixon. Many did. In Pennsylvania, West Virginia, New Jersey, Indiana, and Ohio—traditional blue-collar states—McGovern captured less than 40 percent of the popular vote. Eight years before Reagan Democrats shook the electoral landscape, Nixon Democrats had already shown the way.

In essence, the reformers practiced a politics of the heart. They sought to shut the Vietnam War down, push for affirmative action, and back an emerging environmental movement. In McGovern, they discovered a candidate who took seriously their concerns and gave voice to their resentments. Although this connection energized certain constituencies on the left, it angered others nearer to the center. Choice McGovernisms, such as "Mr. Nixon has spent . . . $60 billion of your taxes to kill human beings in Asia" and "This [Senate] chamber reeks of blood" sounded more self-righteous than presidential. These kinds of raw, alienating remarks quickly became a point of interest among the major media outlets unaccustomed to moral crusading among liberals. In a caustic *Newsweek* profile published just days before the election, Richard Stout and Peter Goldman tore into McGovern's political fundamentalism: "George Stanley McGovern, in the waning weeks of his campaign, has turned more furiously evangelical than any major-party candidate since William Jennings Bryan. . . . He is, in a sense, the preacher's boy from Mitchell, S.D., come home in the end to the politics of rectitude. . . . With his polls stubbornly low . . . he has returned more and more to the old moral absolutes—and to the harshest rhetoric of any campaign in memory."[6]

Journalists were not the only ones turned off. McGovern's "conscience of the party" candidacy clashed badly with longstanding Democratic constituencies. The New Deal coalition emerged, after all, partly as a reaction to the piety politics practiced by Republicans in the 1920s. That decade's evangelistic call for prohibition and immigration restriction and its attack on the teaching of evolution in the schools struck many Depression-era Americans as an attempt by cultural conservatives to "impose" a Waspish tone on public and private life. Now, many of them were no more enamored with the efforts of McGovern-Fraser liberals to "impose" a pro-choice, pro-busing agenda on public and private life. That's not what they had signed up for in 1932. The old FDR alliance, rather, stressed a pragmatic politics of economic need and worked this formula to a generation of electoral victories.

But this was part of the problem. By the 1970s the success of the New Deal had brought millions of Americans into the middle class. Accordingly, the old farm-labor-ethnic bloc saw its numbers and thus political power decrease. An autoworker in, say, 1936 might well have been the beneficiary of government programs; whereas in, say, 1966 that same autoworker might instead complain of the high taxes he paid to subsidize the recipients of government programs. "Basic middle-class issues," argued Stuart Eizenstat, chief domestic policy adviser to President Carter, had come to dominate Democratic constituencies. "Jews and Catholics and so forth don't feel that they're outside the mainstream the way they did in the 1930s and 1940s and perhaps even in the '50s." And agribusiness, Eizenstat pointed out, had long ago replaced the family back forty. "Those farmers who are left are essentially corporate farmers, so they're gone. . . . The only ones who still vote over 85 percent Democratic are the ones who are still largely outside the mainstream and still view the government as essential to bring them in." But this population, mainly minorities, could scarcely cover for those leaving.[7]

Thus by the mid-1970s Democrats faced perhaps their greatest internal struggle since the 1920s. Divided between McGovernites and New Dealers, the party threatened to slip into paralysis. The old guard, under whose watch the liberal center had not held, looked particularly lost. Despite the Watergate scandal and the advantage of challenging Nixon's unelected successor Gerald Ford for the presidency, Senators Kennedy, Humphrey, and Edmund Muskie declined to make the race. The timing seemed right for a new kind of candidate to come forward, one associated with neither the establishment politics of 1968 nor the reform wing of 1972.

· · · · ·

Enter Jimmy Carter. Born and raised in the southern Georgia hamlet of Plains, Carter pursued the presidency as an avowed Washington outsider. In the wake of the Watergate wars public suspicion of Beltway politicians soared, and what might have passed for a thin political resume—two terms in the state senate and a single term as governor (1971–75)—became instead a real asset. Ideologically, the New Deal could make few claims to Carter. His early memories were of familial resistance to FDR's Agricultural Adjustment Act, a controversial program to rationalize the farming economy by sharply cutting production. "My father, Earl Carter, often said that he . . . had been a strong supporter of Franklin Roosevelt in

1932," Carter later remembered, "but Daddy fiercely opposed Roosevelt's subsequent imposition of controls on cotton acreage and his limitation on the number of hogs being prepared for market. When Daddy was forced to plow up knee-high cotton and to slaughter some of his growing pigs, he was deeply embittered and never again voted for the Democratic president."[8] Instead, Earl Carter joined the 36 percent of Americans who cast ballots for Alf Landon in 1936. Although the New Deal brought rural electrification, low-interest farming loans, Social Security, and so on to the South, it never impacted the region's identity in quite the way it did the urban North. The kind of united liberal-labor complex that stretched from New England into the Midwest scarcely touched Carter's Georgia; nor did many of the ethnic interest-group constituencies that shaped Democratic politics outside the South.

Carter's from-the-crib suspicion of big government circa 1935 neatly prefaced his dim view of big government circa 1975. Thus when liberals asked themselves whether Carter shared their politics, many unsurprisingly answered no. Tired of listening to Carter run down the "Washington establishment," Humphrey, himself a symbol of that establishment, cut into the presidential aspirant: "Candidates who make an attack on Washington are making an attack on government programs, on blacks, on minorities, on the cities. It's a disguised new form of racism, a disguised new form of conservatism." On the question of race, Humphrey was wrong. Carter owned an admirable civil rights record; in 1965 he supported the opening of his own church to blacks, advocated the integration of Georgia's schools as a state senator, and used his gubernatorial inaugural address to call for an end to residual segregation. On the question of Carter's conservatism, however, Humphrey's charge hit home. Though he stood to the left of his party's Dixiecrat irreconcilables, Carter occupied an ideological place to the right of its more powerful liberal wing. No FDR acolyte, he aspired to be a transitional figure in a post–New Deal Democratic Party anxious to jettison both its ancient states' rights fixation and its more recent special-interest "pandering."[9]

Resisting ideological labels came naturally to Carter. He received a technical education at the U.S. Naval Academy, operated a successful seed, fertilizer, and insurance agribusiness, and from the statehouse emphasized practical problem solving over politics as usual. Asked by reporters in 1966 if he was a liberal, conservative, or moderate, Carter brushed the inquest aside: "I am a more complicated person than that." Ten years later, while pursuing the presidency, the question persisted, much to the candidate's annoyance. "When forced to answer," he later remarked, "I would say that I was a fiscal conservative but quite liberal on such issues as civil rights, environmental quality, and helping people overcome handicaps to lead fruitful lives. My reply did not satisfy [news reporters], and sometimes they accused me of being evasive, but it was the most accurate answer I could give in a few words." This ecumenical response—liberal on environmental and social justice concerns, conservative on matters relating to fiscal responsibility and government growth—also annoyed the prevailing branch of the Democratic Party that was still fiercely proud of its social welfare past. It did, however, appeal to moderates within the party. Most of these men and women were young, resided in suburbs, and looked upon FDR as a historical figure rather than as a contemporary political model. One of their number, Colorado's junior senator, Gary Hart, remarked to the *Denver Post* a month before Carter defeated Ford, "The New Deal has run its course. The party is over. The pie cannot continue to expand forever."[10]

Carter interpreted his narrow victory (a 297–240 triumph; Ford carried twenty-seven states, the most ever by a losing candidate) as an endorsement for the new—beyond left and right—politics. His chief pollster, Patrick Caddell, quickly fired off a postelection memorandum to the president-elect that disparaged Ted Kennedy and other old-line liberals as "traditional Democrats . . . in many ways . . . as antiquated and anachronistic a group as are conservative Republicans." Caddell counseled Carter to move beyond "traditional ideology" and pursue a third path between liberalism and conservatism. The incoming president pronounced the assessment "excellent." Putting plan to practice, Carter proceeded to alienate important Democratic constituencies. Among the complainants, organized labor chafed against the president's refusal to back a robust increase in the nation's minimum wage and reproached his unwillingness to battle, à la Roosevelt and Lyndon B. Johnson, for social and economic justice by lavishly funding government programs. A dismayed McGovern accused Carter of attempting "to balance the budget on the backs of the poor."[11]

Carter dismissed such criticisms as evidence of the old guard's failure to feel the pulse of a changing electorate. "I wish some of you could have sat in on some of our leadership meetings and just seen the stricken expression on the faces of those Democratic leaders when I was talking about balancing the budget," Carter told an interviewer. "John Brademas and Shirley Chisholm and Tip O'Neill, even Jim Wright. I mean it was anathema to them to be talking about balancing the budget. That wasn't something a Democratic President was supposed to do." This disconnect between Carter and his party's powerbrokers extended well beyond policy meetings to include a broader philosophical disagreement over the legacy of modern liberalism.

This point was driven home shortly after Carter took office, when some 750 Democrats gathered at Washington's Mayflower Hotel to celebrate the forty-fourth anniversary of FDR's first inauguration. While former Roosevelt adviser Ben Cohen's keynote address, "The New Deal Looks Forward," optimistically assumed Carter's loyalty to their cause, others were less sure. West Virginia senator Jennings Randolph related that evening how, as a thirty-year-old representative, he had observed FDR overcome conservative congressional critics. "I still can see . . . his knuckles getting white. Roosevelt [said], 'but gentlemen, do you realize that we must act now. By acting now we will make mistakes, but if we do not act now, we may not have another opportunity to act at all.'" Here, Randolph hinted strongly, was an example of the forceful liberal leadership he hoped to see under the new Democratic administration. Might 1977 revisit 1933? Carter thought not and kept his distance, both literally and politically, from any talk of a Roosevelt redux. He neither attended the Mayflower fete (just five blocks north of the White House) nor sent even a cursory acknowledgement to its attendees. Columnist Marquis Childs, the evening's master of ceremonies, took Carter's silence as a slight, observing accurately enough, "This is a clean break between the past and the present."[12]

Nine months later another Democratic constituency, the Democratic Socialist Organizing Committee, gathered at the Mayflower Hotel, and rather than commemorate past achievements it looked to the future. Before some 2,000 attendees, Michael Harrington, author of *The Other America*, a groundbreaking study of poverty in the United States, called in his keynote address for full employment, environmental legislation, and an increase in foreign aid. Outlining an aggressive Democratic agenda, he declared, "We have to go as far beyond Roosevelt as Roosevelt went beyond Hoover." Financed primarily by union money and dedicated to moving the party toward a European style of social democracy, the conference called for a revitalized welfare state much at odds with Carter's economic conservatism. Indeed, the president was on his way to deregulating the airline and trucking industries, reducing government services, and preparing a $25 billion tax reduction bill, which, he later acknowledged, "was unbalanced in favor of the rich and did not include the basic tax reforms I had requested." Republican senator Howard Baker crowed at the time, "We've got a Democratic President singing a Republican song!"[13]

Carter's efforts to shrink the reach of the federal government were prompted by the alarming convergence of low economic growth, sharp declines in manufacturing, and spikes in both inflation and unemployment. With the nation reeling from its greatest economic crisis since the Depression, many Democrats, and not simply the Socialist Organizing Committee kind, called for a new New Deal. But Carter, fearing inflation above all else, refused to plow government savings into the economy. Instead, he took a page from the GOP, opting for budget cuts and credit curbs. In the throes of fiscal restraint, he seemed reconciled to writing off the welfare state as a relic of the past. Notably, he anticipated Reagan's famous insistence that "government is not the solution to our problem, government is the problem" by asserting in his 1978 State of the Union Address that "government cannot solve our problems, it can't set our goals, it cannot define our vision. Government cannot eliminate poverty or provide a bountiful economy or reduce inflation or save our cities or cure illiteracy or provide energy." Several months later, Carter unveiled a plan to attack inflation by attacking big government. His critics called it an "austerity" package; Vice President Walter Mondale said it made the administration "look heartless."[14]

But Carter, armed with a dizzying array of spreadsheets and budgetary reports, moved forward promising to "concentrate my [economic recovery] efforts within the government. We know that government is not the only cause of inflation. But it is one of the causes, and government does set an example. Therefore, it must take the lead in fiscal restraint. We are going to hold down government spending, reduce the budget deficit, and eliminate government waste. We will slash Federal hiring and cut the Federal work force. We will eliminate needless regulations. We will bring more competition back to our economy. And we will oppose any further reduction in Federal income taxes until we have convincing prospects that inflation will be controlled."[15] Carter subsequently called for a combined $3 billion reduction in social services, Social Security, and school lunches; the following year he proposed shrinking various programs, including food stamps and job training for the low-income and longtime unemployed.

And what, to offset the federal retreat, did Carter have to offer the aggrieved liberal wing of his party? Essentially nothing. When his chief speechwriter, Hendrik Hertzberg, trotted out the idea of a "New Founda-tion" for the 1979 State of the Union Address, the president showed little enthusiasm, arguing that catchwords were notoriously "simplistic and misleading." But Hertzberg kept prodding. "The slogan is some-thing to rally around and it's something to take a lot of [ideas] and group them together, so that people think of them as being consistent," he later explained. "The New Deal was a wonderful slogan because it suggested that what we needed was some kind of redistribution of power in our society . . . and [the] Fair Deal was the same way. And the New Frontier . . . because it suggested youthful vigor and a kind of adven-turous spirit. The Great Society was a terrific slogan . . . because it sug-gested this kind of vast ambition for a neo-Roman magnificence and beneficence." And the "New Foundation"? Hertzberg understood that under Carter no expansive public works programs were in the offing. Rather, he proposed renovation over revolution: "The New Foundation [was] . . . very much the idea of . . . not putting big new wings on the house, but patching up the leaks in the basement." Yet even this stripped down version of Democratic DNA failed to meet with Carter's approval. Though "New Foundation" did make it into the State of the Union Ad-dress, the president quickly walked away from it. "He was asked in [his] first press conference after giving that speech, well, is this your slogan or isn't it," Herzberg recalled. "And basically, he disavowed it. . . . It was really just for one speech. . . . He wasn't ready to say that it described his program. So, he shot it down himself."[16]

While liberal Democrats denounced Carter's centrism, they almost cer-tainly expected too much from him. The end of the great postwar boom had yet to sink in, and their anticipation of an activist administration shepherding heroic social welfare legislation through Congress clashed with prevailing economic realities. These critics stood on firmer ground, however, in their claim that liberal organizing and liberal votes had made Carter president. In a tight election his crossover appeal had been slight—there were few Carter Republicans. Traditional Democratic constituen-cies, rather—the South, organized labor, and urban voters—had eased him over the finish line. When Carter announced early in his campaign, "I owe the special interests nothing. I owe the people everything," he in-dulged in a bit of political naiveté that prefaced a rocky relationship with the base of his party.[17]

And by 1978 that base was inching toward open rebellion. At that year's Democratic midterm convention in Memphis, Edward Kennedy gave a ringing address to some 4,000 delegates that flayed Carter's economizing. Pounding the podium, he endorsed a broadening of the nation's health care system that clashed with the president's budgetary conservatism: "I want every delegate at this convention to understand that as long as I have a vote, and as long as I have a voice in the United States Senate, it's going to be for that Democratic platform plank that provides decent quality health care, North and South, East and West, for all Americans as a matter of right and not of privilege!" Carter, by contrast, used his midterm convention address to throw cold water on the idea of employing government programs to alleviate economic distress: "It is an illusion to believe we can preserve a commitment to compassionate, progressive government if we fail to bring inflation under control."[18]

Many in Memphis disagreed with this analysis—and some of them wanted the president to know it. "The Carter family moved between workshops [at the midterm convention], which allowed an unprecedented degree of contact between a sitting president and angry party activists," writes historian Timothy Stanley. "The contact was not always friendly. Although some activists were thrilled at the chance to meet the president, those that the [farther-to-the-left] Democratic Agenda [organization] had brought along were made of more militant stuff. These people were a mixture of social workers, single-issue campaigners, and union members. They were not cheerleaders for the administration but rather guardians of ideological purity. When the Agenda's people met the president, they were tough and uncompromising, even disrespectful." At least Carter showed up. The list of liberal luminaries and vote getters who, disenchanted with the president, boycotted the Memphis convention included Senator Muskie, California governor Jerry Brown, and AFL-CIO secretary-treasurer Lane Kirkland. Democratic National Committee issues coordinator Elaine Kamarck conceded, "Our turndown list reads like a *Who's Who* of American politics." *Time* reported that "beneath the session's cheer, there was an undercurrent of feeling among many Democratic factions that Carter is not really their President. Black leaders have been particularly vocal in their discontent, but it is shared by others: labor, Jews, intellectuals, farmers, urban leaders and old-line machine politicians feel a wariness about the man."[19]

If liberals left Memphis hoping for a better 1979, they were to be sorely disappointed. In July Carter delivered his (in)famous "malaise" speech before some 100 million American television viewers. Shaken by the energy shortage, long gas lines, and inflation angst, a confused audience looked for assurance and relief. Instead, the president offered a searching and pessimistic appraisal of the nation's predicament. "I want to talk to you right now about a fundamental threat to American democracy," he said. "The threat is nearly invisible in ordinary ways. It is a crisis of confidence. It is a crisis that strikes at the very heart and soul and spirit of our national will. We can see this crisis in the growing doubt about the meaning of our own lives and in the loss of a unity of purpose for our nation. The erosion of our confidence in the future is threatening to destroy the social and the political fabric of America." As a Jeremiah, Carter offered a thoughtful critique of American consumerism while calling for sacrifice, limits, and humility. It was not, however, what the public wanted to hear. Nor what Edward Kennedy expected, either. "I watched the televised talk with mounting incredulousness and outrage," he later recalled. "This message was contrary to—it was in conflict with—all the ideals of the Democratic Party that I cherished. It was in conflict with what the country was about. I tried to imagine President Kennedy or Bobby Kennedy ever abandoning their optimism in the face of adversity and giving vent to sentiments remotely as melancholy. . . . It was in the aftershocks of this speech that I began thinking seriously about running for the presidency in 1980. . . . I recognized that Jimmy Carter, although he was of my own party, held an inherently different view of America from mine."[20]

And so Kennedy, as well as Governor Brown, challenged Carter for the Democratic nomination in 1980. It proved to be a difficult battle for the incumbent; in victory he lost a dozen primaries and carried a bare majority (51 percent) of the popular vote. This struggle merely prefaced Carter's inability to connect with core Democratic constituencies in the general election. His landslide loss to Reagan, in which he took only 49 electoral votes and 41 percent of the popular vote (the smallest percentage for an incumbent since Herbert Hoover), indicated that many alienated liberals sat the contest out. "I spent a major portion of my time [during the campaign] trying to recruit back the Democratic constituency that should have been naturally supportive—Jews, Hispanics, blacks, the poor, labor, and so forth," a frustrated Carter later reported.[21] Many obviously either stayed at home or crossed over.

The Democratic debacle of 1980 pointed to liberalism's unresolved and unclear future. The reform wing still constituted the heart of the party but could no longer win national elections. Its historical reliance on special interest groups and more recent inability to attract middle-class voters had become a distinct problem. Underperforming as a party leader,

Carter failed to impose his policies of fiscal restraint and economic deregulation upon the progressives. As he left office, most Democrats still viewed American political history through the prism of the New Deal. It would take more political defeats to create a moderate coalition capable of capturing a governing consensus.

· · · · ·

In the 1980s three groups vied for Democratic Party preeminence: traditional (Kennedy) liberals, moderate (Carter) liberals, and McGovern-Fraser liberals. The latter two agreed that the New Deal could no longer serve as the centerpiece for future electoral success, but for different reasons. McGovern-Fraser Democrats responded positively to the social justice crusades that shaped the 1960s, the civil rights and antiwar movements as well as the broader "rights revolution" coming increasingly to inform modern American jurisprudence and culture. Many of them dismissed the Age of Roosevelt (1932–68) for failing to remedy group-based inequities based on race, class, and gender. While the New Deal emphasized equal opportunity, they called for equality of outcome.

Moderate Democrats also sought to move the party beyond the New Deal—not because they thought its legacy fundamentally unjust but because they thought its mission now fundamentally irrelevant. Millions of blue-collar workers who had stormed the suburbs were looking now to conserve their gains, and many of them believed they could do that best by voting Republican. As liberalism evolved in the 1960s from broad special-interest group politics—the ideological arm of family farms, organized labor, and old-age pensions—to more narrow special-interest group politics, millions of alienated Democrats jumped ship. Political strategist Stanley Greenberg analyzed the history and implications of this change in his classic 1985 study of Macomb County, Michigan, home to the kind of white ethnics and unionized autoworkers once the backbone of the New Deal coalition. "In the 1960s," Greenberg explained, "this was the most Democratic suburb in the nation, but the riots, the anti-busing battles, and the transformation of the Democratic party changed all that. The residents of Macomb felt betrayed and voted en masse for Ronald Reagan."[22] These "Reagan Democrats" were reluctant Republicans, Greenberg noted, yet tacked right when they came to believe that liberals no longer identified with the interests of the working class.

Ironically, Democratic decline in Macomb was born of Democratic success. By the 1960s the county's residents could afford good housing, a couple of cars in the garage, and perhaps even a boat or a swimming pool. A certain dynamic of taking from the rich and giving to the poor had once broadened FDR's coalition, but a growing number of Americans were coming to believe that Robin Hood now worked for the Crown. Clark Clifford, a Washington wise man who served four Democratic presidents, reflected in the early 1980s on the predicament his party faced.

> The tenor and the attitude of the country was changing because the people had advanced so generally and so steadily during these decades that the old concept of what was needed—to help the great mass of our citizens who were out of work and were doing badly—did not really exist in the same fashion that it did before. . . . The New Deal and the Fair Deal in my opinion were so basically successful in restoring prosperity to the country that they pretty well sounded their own death knell. [Entering the 1970s] we still had the poor, maybe not as many as we had before, [and] we had a much higher level of income and a much better living standard in the country. [As a consequence taxpayers] became much more conscious of taxes. They began to get concerned too about the cost of government, and they got concerned about the question of whether the government was taking care of the people they need not take care of. So a whole new philosophy developed in the country, a more conservative philosophy.[23]

As the 1970s gave way to a new decade, a group of congressional southern moderates, concerned with their party's slide toward irrelevancy, published *Rebuilding the Road to Opportunity* (1981), a book of policy planning designed to win back America's Macombs. The group's leader, Gillis Long of Louisiana, wrote, "In these papers, we renew our commitment to the fundamental principles of the Democratic party—to equal opportunity, to economic growth and full employment, and to a strong national defense."[24] Eager to try out their ideas on the national stage, Long and his collaborators looked hopefully to 1984.

With no incumbent, that year's Democratic primaries shaped up into a fractious three-way race. Mondale represented the party's fast-fading FDR past, the civil rights activist Jesse Jackson sat further to the left, and New Democrat Gary Hart appealed to suburban and independent voters. The battle for the nomination quickly narrowed to an ideological struggle between liberals and moderates. In one Tampa speech, a frustrated

Mondale (dismissed by Hart as an "old fashioned" New Dealer) all but called his in-house critics Republicans: "We are about to decide whether we are a generous party and a caring nation or whether we're not. . . . We will decide whether we will be a party that follows the polls or is led by principle."[25] In fact, Mondale lost the Florida primary and several others. In the end he captured the nomination by taking only 38 percent of the vote and twenty-two states compared with Hart's 35 percent and twenty-six. In defeat the New Democrats gained momentum, and come November, Mondale's landslide loss to Reagan strengthened their hand.

Following Long's January 1985 death, Al From, previously executive director of the House Democratic Caucus, took his place. He had little doubt that the exhaustion of New Deal liberalism had combined with the unpopularity of special-interest liberalism to neutralize Democrats in the Reagan years. Seeking a fresh approach, From and several like-minded colleagues created the Democratic Leadership Council, a meetinghouse of southern moderates that included Governor Charles Robb of Virginia, Senator Sam Nunn of Georgia, and Representative Richard Gephardt of Missouri. Its membership stood at a fledgling forty-one, including a smattering of senators, congressmen, and governors, but no women and only two African Americans.

On economic issues, the DLC recognized that the nation's declining manufacturing centers—the Rustbelt—would have to undergo dramatic change if they were to thrive in the future. The information/computer age had birthed a nimble, dynamic, and decentralized economy that was here to stay, no matter what organized labor thought. Accordingly, the council challenged the founding principle of FDR's electoral juggernaut: the Keynesian idea that sustained GNP growth required central state oversight. Social issues mattered as well, of course, and the DLC came out tough on crime, skeptical of entitlement programs, and receptive to majority complaints of minority privileges.

The DLC's insistence on a party makeover gained momentum in 1988 after the GOP captured a third straight national election. It wasn't simply that another Democrat had lost (in this instance Massachusetts governor Michael Dukakis), it was the way in which the Republicans successfully demonized the word "liberal." Under, say, Harry Truman, "fighting liberalism" meant positive government intervention on the side of the little guy. But Dukakis was dubbed a "card carrying member of the ACLU," and that meant, in the sloppy pseudo-McCarthyism of the day, a liberal weak on crime, dubious on national defense, and out of touch with mainstream values. Kamarck later remembered the election as a critical moment in the party's history. "After '88 we really needed a second look on the part of the voters, because in '80 and '84, everybody chalked it up to 'Oh, Ronald Reagan, he's so charismatic.' But George Bush wasn't so charismatic at all, and he beat us. And we needed substance behind that second look. We realized after the 1984 campaign that the New Deal way of looking at the electorate was dead, and the 1984 Mondale campaign was really the end of the New Deal coalition."[26]

But to win on the national level, New Democrats had to first win over their own party. They planned to do this by repeating rather than making history. "Make no mistake about it," From wrote to council board members in 1989, "What we hope to accomplish with the DLC is a bloodless revolution in our party. It is not unlike what the conservatives accomplished in the Republican Party during the 1960s and 1970s. By building their movement, nurturing it with ideas from conservative think tanks, and with Ronald Reagan as their standard bearer, they were able to nominate their candidate for President and elect him, and in the process, redefine both the Republican Party and the national pubic policy agenda."[27] With its information-age itinerary and centrist views on social issues, the DLC mapped out a plausible formula for success. All it needed now was a candidate capable of winning the electorate's confidence.

From already had someone in mind. In January 1990 he asked Arkansas governor Bill Clinton to take over as DLC chair. It was no secret that Clinton harbored presidential ambitions, and From knew that by heading the council the presumptive candidate could crisscross the country gauging the political winds. In making his pitch to Clinton, he explained, "We need a charismatic leader willing to get on the road himself and equally important willing to ask other DLC leaders to do so, as well. And in my view, it would be very helpful if our next chairman were from outside Washington. A political movement needs to be built out in the country, and it's hard to excite the rank and file Democrats when playing within the constraints of the Congressional caucuses." Appreciating the advantages outlined by From, Clinton accepted. "I was convinced," he later recalled, that "the group's ideas on welfare reform, criminal justice, education, and economic growth were crucial to the future of the Democratic Party and the nation." His decision would have a major impact on post–Cold War politics in America. Under Clinton's leadership the DLC drafted at its 1990 conference the New Orleans Declaration, a detailed statement of centrist policy positions. It bore little resemblance to the

Democratic platforms of the past. Reflecting the views of moderate liberals, the Declaration took positions on a range of issues that sounded positively GOP-ish: government aid should be attended by personal accountability; the free market is the best guarantor of economic growth; the welfare system needed to be rethought; America's military must remain vigilant following the Soviet Empire's collapse; criminals ought to be punished rather than coddled; rights are diminished without responsibility. Reagan couldn't have said it better—and that was the point.[28]

The following year Clinton announced his presidential candidacy. Naturally he planned to run as a New Democrat, and this meant taking a page from the old Republican playbook, appealing to a middle class that felt fleeced, disrespected, and taken for granted by the ruling party. In what became a standard stump speech, Clinton accused the Reagan-Bush era of ushering in a new Gilded Age on the backs of the nation's working class. "Through it all," he said, "millions of decent, ordinary people who worked hard, played by the rules and took responsibility for their own actions were falling behind, living a life of struggle without reward or security." He even evoked Nixon's memorable 1968 call to liberalism's discontents—"the forgotten Americans"—in his assertion that "for 12 years, these forgotten middle class Americans have watched their economic interests ignored and their values literally ground into the ground."[29]

And what did the DLC's standard-bearer offer the Democratic Party? Not a New Deal but rather, as Clinton put it, a "New Covenant." By this he meant smaller government, support for free enterprise, and empowerment over entitlement. But weren't these, like the New Orleans planks, Republican positions? Progressive Democrats certainly thought so. Historian Arthur Schlesinger Jr., author of several books extolling the virtues of the FDR and Kennedy presidencies, called the DLC "a quasi-Reaganite formation"; Jesse Jackson deadpanned that DLC stood for "Democrats for the Leisure Class." In 1990 Ohio senator Howard Metzenbaum, "tired," as he put it to *Washington Post* writer David Broder, "of seeing more and more of my colleagues become shadow Republicans," used $50,000 in leftover funds from his 1988 campaign to create a liberal counterweight to the DLC: the Coalition for Democratic Values. With a roster that included fellow senators Kennedy, Tom Daschle, Alan Cranston, Christopher Dodd, and Paul Simon, the coalition sought to cut short its party's deep bow to the right. "The future of the Democratic Party does not lie in fine-tuning of Reaganism," one of its manifestoes avowed.[30] In place of Clinton's New Covenant, coalition members remained committed to the party's old covenant: standing by organized labor, increasing taxes on the well-to-do, and growing social service programs. They never gained traction.

· · · · ·

Under Clinton's leadership, Democrats again became a party in full, capable of capturing national elections even in a conservative age. To do so, however, meant looking decidedly more Eisenhower than LBJ. Self-conscious converts, New Democrats dressed up their retreat from liberalism as a bold advance toward a fresh politics. The party's 1992 platform torpedoed Reaganism and Rooseveltism alike: "We reject both the do-nothing government of the past twelve years and the big government theory that says we can hamstring business and tax and spend our way to prosperity. Instead we offer a third way." But was this really a new way? Carter had also rejected the tired liberal/conservative dichotomy in his attempt to govern as something of a centrist. Then Clinton was a Carterite? Not quite: Carter's crises-filled presidency—energy, hostage, confidence—made him a modern Herbert Hoover, the man his party ran from. Instead, Democratic messaging in the 1992 campaign wiped the slate clean, claiming for its candidates a kind of ideological virgin birth. "They're a new generation of Democrats, Bill Clinton and Al Gore," one campaign commercial enthused as sunlit images of farmers, police officers, and American flags filled the screen, "and they don't think the way the old Democratic Party did. They've called for an end to welfare as we know it, so welfare can be a second chance, not a way of life. They've sent a strong signal to criminals, by supporting the death penalty. And they've rejected the old tax-and-spend politics: Clinton's balanced twelve budgets, and they've proposed a new plan investing in people, detailing a hundred and forty billion dollars in spending cuts they'd make right now."[31] Come November, America elected its first DLC president.

Or perhaps not just yet. Early in his tenure Clinton took liberal positions on two "culture war" issues, repealing the prohibition on abortion counseling at federally financed clinics and challenging the ban on gays in the military. One of Clinton's campaign advisers later complained that by contesting the military's restriction rule against gays, the president had confused party moderates: "It sent precisely the wrong message. I'm not saying he shouldn't have taken that position. But as the first thing he did? It was exactly the sort of 'liberal elitist' issue that we'd been trying to submerge throughout the campaign. It sent the signal that he was going to govern differently from the way he campaigned—as an 'Old Democrat.' "[32]

But this and other fraternal objections were relatively minor compared with the storm Clinton set off over his support for a universal health care plan. A slew of critics, including conservatives, libertarians, and small-business owners, raised the ghost of big-state social engineering run amuck. The Health Insurance Association of America spent millions on a series of scare television ads featuring white suburban forty-somethings Harry and Louise brooding over the bureaucratic nightmare they faced if "Clinton Care" became law. A number of respected news outlets, including *Time*, CNN, and the *Wall Street Journal,* questioned the president's critical premise that a health care crisis even existed. Did hitting the health care barricades mean that Clinton was a closet capital "L" liberal after all? Hardly. Yet having thrown his support behind major DLC initiatives—the North American Free Trade Agreement and a deficit-shrinking budget—he wanted badly to recognize the traditional Democratic base. "We must have something for the common man," he said to one health insurance working group. "At least we'll have health care to give them, if we can't give them anything else."[33] But in the end he couldn't give them even this. A health reform bill died in the senate without ever coming to a vote.

Stung by a string of setbacks to his administration, Clinton brought in political consultant and former Reagan White House director of communications David Gergen for a fresh perspective. "He was very reflective," Gergen later recalled. "He thought that the administration was way out of position politically. That he had intended to come as a New Democrat and he was perceived as being way off to the left and he had to get back to the center and he had to get back to working with Republicans and he thought I could be a potential bridge to help get back to the center where he wanted to govern. . . . Well, I told him that he was terribly out of position and that he had lurched to the left when he came in and it sent signals to people like me, who thought he was going to be a centrist Democrat, that he had lost his moorings."[34]

And for losing his moorings, Clinton and his party paid a heavy price. The 1994 congressional elections produced GOP majorities in both the House and Senate for the first time in decades. No one had to tell Oklahoma congressman Dave McCurdy that something big had just happened. The outgoing DLC chairman was one of November's more conspicuous casualties. Defeated for an open Senate seat, McCurdy watched his candidacy turn to ashes when Sooner Republicans aired ads of his seconding Clinton's nomination at the 1992 Democratic Convention. A few weeks after the election, at the DLC's annual conference, McCurdy warned his colleagues, "While Bill Clinton has the mind of a New Democrat, he retains the heart of an Old Democrat. The result is an administration that has pursued elements of a moderate and liberal agenda at the same time, to the great confusion of the American people." Months later, McCurdy more colloquially reiterated his disenchantment with Clinton's look to the left: "Those of us in the center," he told a reporter, "we got screwed."[35]

The fallout of the 1994 elections fashioned talk of a revolt among party moderates. In a December *Wall Street Journal* article, Joel Kotkin, a senior fellow at the Progressive Policy Institute, called for New Democrats to support another candidate in the next cycle of presidential primaries. Some DLCers who had hoped that Clinton might be their Eisenhower now wondered if in fact retired four-star Army general Colin Powell could play the role more convincingly. He wasn't interested; rather than move Democrats to the right, he planned to encourage Republicans to step a little to the left. At the GOP's August 1996 national convention in San Diego he stated before a skeptical audience, "I became a Republican because I want to help fill the big tent that our party has raised to attract all Americans. You all know that I believe in a woman's right to choose abortion. And I strongly support affirmative action. And I was invited here by my party to share my views with you because we are a big enough party and big enough people to disagree on individual issues and still work together for our common goal: restoring the American dream."[36] Abortion? Affirmative action? One wonders if Powell would have proved too liberal even for the DLC.

Just weeks after the GOP's resounding 1994 congressional victories, Clinton began his march to the middle. Countering the Republican's "Contract with America," the budget-trimming brainchild of incoming House Speaker Newt Gingrich, Clinton responded with a "Middle-Class Bill of Rights." This omnibus offered tax cuts for medium-income Americans, a proposal to make college tuition tax deductible, and a promise to prune federal programs. Unveiled in January's State of the Union Address, even many liberals, aghast at the specter of a "Gingrich revolution," were more or less on board. One critic, civil rights scholar Taylor Branch, was at that time secretly working with Clinton on a history of his presidency. During a New Year's night taping session, Clinton asked Branch for his "true re-action" to the Middle-Class Bill of Rights. Branch hedged, "I said it did not strike me as one of his better efforts," but when pressed he offered a less varnished assessment. "I said, well, it was a sugar-daddy speech. He was seducing voters to feel good by running down the government." According to Branch, Clinton "erupted." In a retort thick with sarcasm, he pointed out that the electorate wanted tax cuts and didn't care if they came from Democrats or Republicans. "The voters were sovereign," Clinton told Branch, "they were the boss. He would give them what they wanted, even if it was stupid."[37]

And what they really wanted was a New Democrat. This Clinton would now give them in full. Criticize recent GOP cuts in Social Security? He didn't do it. Run as a tax-and-entitlement liberal? His 1996 budget proposal called for spending cuts of more than $1 trillion over ten years—and a tax cut to boot. But what about cultural issues? Clinton supported the school uniform option, questioned gratuitous violence on television, and signed legislation designed to curb illegal immigration. He rolled this momentum into the election year signing the Personal Responsibility and Work Opportunity Reconciliation Act of 1996, more commonly known as "welfare reform." More than anything Clinton did as president, this legislation broke the longstanding idea that Democrats would always work to provide a social safety net for impoverished Americans. Indeed, that year's Chicago convention served as a coronation of New Democratic power, the antithesis of the violent 1968 Chicago convention. Education and the environment were on the plank, but so were assurances of balanced budgets, tougher crime laws, and deficit reduction. With a November victory in sight, the platform conspicuously spurned the activist state: "We need a smaller, more effective, more efficient, less bureaucratic government that reflects our time-honored values. The American people do not want big government solutions and they do not want empty promises. They want a government that is for them, not against them; that doesn't interfere with their lives but enhances their quality of life."[38] The party's past triumphs and grand visions were neatly tucked away as Clinton won reelection handily on the strength of the North American Fee Trade Agreement, welfare reform, tax cuts, and budget reduction. Labor, progressives, and minorities—the heartbeat of the party—were safely taken for granted.

And there was little that liberals could do about it. Over the years this tension within Democratic politics divided, if one might put it in such a way, DLCers and "dreamers," the latter remaining faithful to the possibilities of government paternalism. Former secretary of labor Robert Reich called one Clinton budget "staggeringly bad when the country is so wealthy." Where, in a prosperous nation with a federal budget *surplus*, was the next New Deal? The next New Frontier? "To make debt elimination a new goal is to put a straightjacket on any future public ambitions," Reich complained. On the same stymied note, House minority leader Richard Gephardt protested that Clinton had too often settled for "small ideas that nibble around the edges of big problems." And in his 2009 memoir, *True Compass*, Ted Kennedy recalled the 1990s as a dark decade in Democratic Party history: "A conviction took hold that the electorate had embraced the conservative cause. This became a settled truth for many pundits, other opinion-makers, and sadly, for many Democratic leaders as well. I never accepted this. The Democratic *Party* may have lurched to the right in response to the [1994] elections. The Democratic Leadership Council and, I feared, President Clinton were moving in that direction. But I believed they were chasing a phantom. As I'd put it in remarks to the National Press Club [shortly after the election] 'If the Democrats run for cover, if we become pale carbon copies of the opposition, we will lose—and deserve to lose.'"[39]

But most Democrats denied their party's incorporation into the Reagan Revolution. They saw their brand of Third Way politics as center-left not center-right, and they charged it with the task of advancing a reformed welfare state funded by a restructured market economy. Hardly an American idea, Third Way governments ruled Australia in the 1980s and 1990s while the "Neue Mitte," Polder Model, and Liberal Party shaped politics in Germany, the Netherlands, and Canada. British prime minister Harold Macmillan was an early adherent of the idea. His 1938 study *The Middle Way* advocated a mixed private-planned approach that included both free enterprise and enough state oversight to bring about a "minimum standard of life." In more recent decades, sociologist Anthony Giddens has revisited Third Way strategies. His 1994 book *Beyond Left and Right* makes the case for a post–Cold War "market socialism" that embraces government-backed risk-insurance policies designed to enlarge medical and unemployment options.

The welfare debate that drew Giddens's attention became the centerpiece of Anglo-American Third Way politics in the 1990s. Even so, in both Britain and the United States, liberal-minded leaders were forced to the middle and thus far from the market socialism to which they may have aspired. As Clinton made peace with the Reagan Revolution, Labour Party prime minister Tony Blair looked for a path between the democratic socialism that long defined his party and the free-market Thatcherism of more recent vintage. In November 1997, six months after assuming power, he convened with Clintonites at Chequers, the official country residence of British prime ministers since the 1920s. There, writes Clinton adviser Sidney Blumenthal, "Blair said about our respective political parties: 'The similarities are more striking than not. But something is missing from the picture. We win power, but not the battle of ideas. . . . Unless we define our new type of politics, people will become disillusioned with us. They apply the wrong tests to us.'" Rather than be judged by the old left-right standards, Blair grandly if somewhat vacuously called for "a different world, economy, and political contest." The catchwords were "opportunity," "responsibility," and "community." Clinton warmed to the theme, and in his final State of the Union Address he somewhat dubiously declared Third Way politics the real winner of the Cold War: "We restored the vital center, replacing outdated ideologies with a new vision." Liberal Democrats called this a compromised victory at best; conservatives, watching as the Age of Reagan stretched toward the twenty-first century, must have thought that Blair had come closer to the truth in his tart observation that "the right wins even though they're not in power."[40]

On the subject of Third Way theory, as with so many of the issues and challenges facing the Clinton presidency, Hillary Clinton largely shared her husband's ideological instincts. Though a shade further to the left, she too came to believe in the importance of a new kind of governing philosophy, one that moved beyond the old liberal-versus-conservative, communism-versus-capitalism categories that had long shaped postwar politics. Of course there were notable differences between the two. Unlike Bill Clinton, Hillary had grown up in a Republican household and in 1964, as a Goldwater Girl, canvassed minority Chicago neighborhoods checking on the registration status of voters—a tiny part of the GOP's efforts to tamp down Democratic ballots in a Democratic city. A high school senior at the time, Hillary had fallen under the spell of her history teacher Paul Carlson, an ardent anticommunist known to play his students selections of Douglas MacArthur's farewell address to Congress. As Hillary later recalled, "Mr. Carlson encouraged me to read Senator Barry Goldwater's recently published book, *The Conscience of a Conservative*. That inspired me to write my term paper on the American conservative movement, which I dedicated 'To my parents, who have always taught me to be an individual.'" Despite Carlson's best efforts, however, another ideological influence competed for Hillary's attention. Donald Jones, a young Methodist minister trained at Drew University Seminary, became something of a spiritual mentor to Hillary at the First United Methodist Church of Park Ridge (Illinois). A devotee of Dietrich Bonhoeffer and Reinhold Niebuhr, theologian-ethicists interested in actively promoting social justice, Jones took a decidedly liberal line. Naturally Hillary struggled to find a place between the poles of Carlson's realism and Jones's idealism, a struggle emblematic of her generation's searching transition from 1950s consensus to 1960s clash. As she later noted, "I now see the conflict between Don Jones and Paul Carlson as an early indication of the cultural, political, and religious fault lines that developed across America in the last forty years."[41]

Leaving her native Midwest to attend Wellesley College, Hillary began an ideological pilgrimage made by many of her peers. Influenced in the East by the civil rights crusade, the women's movement, and opposition to the Vietnam War, she abandoned her father's rock-ribbed midwestern Republicanism, and when the GOP gave its presidential nomination to Richard Nixon in 1968, she knew there was no going back. The anointing of Nixon, she observed some years later, "cemented the ascendance of a conservative over a moderate ideology within the Republican Party, a dominance that has only grown more pronounced over the years as the party has continued its move to the right and moderates have dwindled in numbers and influence. I sometimes think that I didn't leave the Republican Party as much as it left me."[42] One can well imagine a number of circa-1968 GOP centrists, including such notables as Henry Cabot Lodge Jr., George Romney, Margaret Chase Smith, and Prescott Bush, having, in their own ways, similarly acidic reactions to the deepening relationship between Republicanism and the New Right.

While serving as first lady, Hillary joined her husband in prodding Democrats toward a less ideological liberalism. In effect, this alienated the party's more progressive wing while winning her no friends on the other side of the aisle. Indeed, many conservatives regarded her efforts to provide universal health care for all Americans ("HillaryCare") as evidence of their architect's "socialistic" leanings. Accordingly, they all but ignored her support for welfare reform and, more broadly, her doubts about the future of big government. The 1996 welfare act, for example, fixed federal welfare benefits to a five-year lifetime limit, reduced assistance to legal immigrants, and more strictly monitored food stamps eligibility. In response, old-line liberals erupted. "Bill's decision, and my endorsement of it," Hillary later remembered, "outraged some of our most loyal supporters . . . [who] hoped I would oppose the measure." Why didn't she? Perhaps foremost because of a firm conviction that, as she put it, "the system desperately required reform," and by not finding common ground with the GOP on this by now overripe issue, there was very little her husband's administration could hope to accomplish in a second term. In this case realism had trumped idealism. Hillary subsequently wrote of her nonofficeholding liberal critics, "They were not bound to compromise, and unlike Bill, they didn't have to negotiate with Newt Gingrich and Bob Dole or worry about maintaining a political balance in Congress. I remembered all too well the defeat of our health care reform effort, which may have happened in part because of a lack of give-and-take."[43]

Beyond a pragmatic stance on the welfare question, Hillary more generally sought during her tenure as first lady to reimagine the Democratic Party. Liberalism's "modern" DNA began with the New Deal and traced along a golden arc that included fighting fascism, containing communism, and codifying the civil rights revolution into law. And yet these real achievements were, by the 1990s, dated and unable to give focus and direction to the future. What, in other words, should the twenty-first-century Democratic Party advocate? And how would it forge itself into an electoral giant, going beyond its liberal base to win back the blue-collar Reagan Democrats it had lost in the 1980s? Hillary, like her husband in the aftermath of the bruising 1994 elections, had no illusions concerning the long-term viability of the old liberalism but sought rather, as she hazily put it, "to craft a 'dynamic center'" sensitive to "changing patterns of work and family in American life."[44]

Since leaving the White House, Hillary's attempts to reach across the partisan divide have continued. After claiming a senate seat in 2000 she immediately sought to establish a working relationship with Republicans, some of whom had voted in December 1998 to impeach her husband for lying about, as he put it, an "inappropriate" relationship with former White House intern Monica Lewinsky. This included cosponsoring legislation with dozens of GOP colleagues and participating in a Senate prayer group that counted among its membership a number of social conservatives. In fact, some of her sharpest critics have been liberals. Her 2002 vote supporting the authorization of military action against Iraq and opposition as a presidential candidate in 2008 to same-sex marriages were particular points of contention. But to what avail? The old Democratic liberal base has lost considerable ground in recent decades, and one can see in the Clinton "copresidency" and its aftermath a recognition of this truism. From college-age organizers working on George McGovern's doomed 1972 presidential bid to New Democrat occupants of 1600 Pennsylvania Avenue a generation later, Bill and Hillary's ideological trajectory tells us much about liberalism's difficult path in the past century's final decades.

· · · · ·

Today it is Barack Obama who wears the crown of Democratic centrism. Disdainful of "right" and "left" labeling, he ascended to the presidency as a pragmatist interested more in ideas than in ideologies. If this sounds quintessentially Clintonesque, some small qualification is in order. While Clinton embraced the DLC, Obama, more sensitive to liberal sympathies, once kept a respectful if not altogether convincing detachment from the council's agenda. His mixed-mindedness was captured in a June 2003 communication with *The Black Commentator*. While the then Illinois state senator stated firmly, "I am not currently, nor have I ever been, a member of the DLC," one might have wondered, "Why not?" In a series of carefully qualified statements, Obama indicated various degrees of support for both the North American Free Trade Agreement and union workers critical of affirmative action. He also objected to "the misogyny and materialism of much of rap culture," which some took as his "Sister Souljah Moment," a reprise of Clinton's 1992 critique of the rapper Sister Souljah in what appeared to be a calculated effort to distance himself from a "special interest" that many Americans viewed with disdain. In closing his *Commentator* open letter, Obama acknowledged that party progressives would see his flirtation with the DLC as something of a dance with the devil—"To some, this approach may appear naïve; to others, it may appear that I'm headed down a path of dangerous compromise"—though he believed that with a sound "moral compass" he could keep both body and soul intact.[45]

Impressed with Obama's political inclusiveness, Al From anointed the Illinois senator a child of the Third Way. "What he has done is he has certainly taken a good part of the strategy we have articulated over the years. Which is to not polarize, but try to unite and build a coalition that understands that a Democratic victory is a coalition." And no one built a better coalition in 2008 than Obama. True, Republicans were reeling from the twin albatrosses of imperial overreach and the late summer collapse of the nation's housing and mortgage markets, yet Obama was topping his opponent, Arizona senator John McCain, in most polls leading up to the financial crisis. Pulling together women, minorities, blue-collar workers, upscale professionals, and independents he captured 53 percent of the popular vote, the highest percentage for a Democratic presidential candidate since Lyndon Johnson in 1964. This ecumenical alliance completed the Democrats' return to relevancy, though it was no more now the party of FDR than the party of FDR had been the party of Jefferson and Jackson. Shortly after taking the presidential oath of office, Obama, addressing a group of congressional conservative liberals, owned up to one of Washington's worst-kept secrets: "I am a New Democrat."[46]

Of course anyone who read Obama's 2006 presidential campaign coming-out book, *The Audacity of Hope*, knew that. An unusually reflective political autobiography, it ruminated on spirituality, race, culture, and the American condition at the beginning of the new century in a way that appealed to readers eager to engage in a post–culture war politics. Searching for the center, Obama denounced the corrosive course that partisanship had taken in recent decades. "You don't need a poll to know," he wrote, "that the vast majority of Americans—Republican, Democrat, and independent—are weary of the dead zone that politics has become, in which narrow interests [what he elsewhere called "radical conservatism"] vie for advantage and ideological minorities [what he elsewhere called "perverse liberalism"] seek to impose their own version of absolute truth." Taken selectively, one might read *Audacity of Hope* as a reaffirmation of DLC principles. The book echoes, after all, Clinton's call for "a new kind of politics" and denounces the dilemma of defending either "an oppressive, government-run economy" or "a chaotic and unforgiving capitalism."[47] The overlap is more than incidental, for Obama shares Clinton's old quandary: he is a liberal constrained by the ideological cage of modern American politics. His middle course reflects less a new departure than continuity within the post-1988 Democratic Party to seek a moderate consensus.

Frankly, many expected more than this. Sensing history in the making, a host of pundits, politicos, and public intellectuals interpreted the 2008 campaign as a "paradigm shift" in American politics—the collapse of Reaganism. In what might prove to be a premature obituary, *New York Times Book Review* editor, Sam Tanenhaus wrote, "We stand on the threshold of a new era that has decisively declared the end of an old one. In the shorthand of the moment this abandoned era is often called the Reagan Revolution. In fact it is something larger and of much longer duration: movement conservatism, the orthodoxy that has been a vital force in our political life for more than half a century and the dominant one during the past thirty years, vanquishing all other rival political creeds until it was itself vanquished in the election of 2008."[48]

Historian David Farber agreed with this postmortem, writing, "In 2009, liberals, after many years out of power, would have their chance, again, to craft a political order. . . . The modern conservative movement had fallen." And the title of Democratic strategist James Carville's postelection book, *40 More Years: How the Democrats Will Rule the Next Generation*, announced the GOP's sudden post–Iraq War, post–financial crisis, post–culture war irrelevance. Obama, by contrast, was far more circumspect about the election's "meaning." When asked by journalists Dan Balz and Haynes Johnson if his victory signaled the end of Reaganism, Obama observed, "What Reagan ushered in was a skepticism toward government solutions to every problem. . . . I don't think that has changed. I think that's a lasting legacy of the Reagan era and the conservative movement." Scarcely a new theme for Obama, Reaganism's impact could be read throughout *The Audacity of Hope*. The "overly bureaucratic" social welfare system, he wrote, produced a "conservative revolution" whose criticism's of liberal tax-and-spend policies "contained a good deal of truth." Other cautiously worded if choice admissions in the book such as, "I believe in the free market, competition, and entrepreneurship" and "I reject a politics that is based solely on racial identity, gender identity, sexual orientation, or victimhood generally" and "conservatives— and Bill Clinton—were right about welfare as it was previously structured," indicated the extent to which Obama had mastered a modern Democratic idiom.[49]

Unlike, say, Bill Clinton circa 1993, Obama was not tempted in 2008 by favorable election results into pushing for an unusually progressive agenda. Some of his followers, however, pointing to impressive Democratic majorities in both house (257 to 178) and senate (57 to 41), wanted him to do just that. Thinking historically they sought a revisitation of FDR's famous "Hundred Days" of reform or a replay of Johnson's Great Society. In both cases, Democrats had rolled up large congressional majorities that paved the way for legislation that enlarged the nation's middle-class. But 2008 was neither 1932 nor 1964; there was little outcry to build a new liberal order.

To be sure there were progressive parts to Obama's first term, including the passage of a health care reform bill, the appointment of two liberal justices to the Supreme Court (Sonia Sotomayor and Elena Kagan), and the critical bailout of Chrysler and General Motors, which propped up the American automobile industry and its subsidiaries. And yet Obama's stimulus package bail out of Wall Street in the wake of the Great Recession, inability to close the deal on immigration reform, and failure to shut down the infamous Guantanamo Bay detention camp provoked criticism on the left. In May 2011, the prominent African American intellectual Cornel West called Obama "a black mascot of Wall Street oligarchs and a black puppet of corporate plutocrats." He further denounced the Democratic Party as "milquetoast and spineless" and insisted that liberal-minded Americans should begin "to think seriously of third-party candidates, third formations, [and] third parties." More broadly, there came from the left a minor boomlet of books condemning Obama's centrism. These included former *Harper's Magazine* editor Roger D. Hodge's *The Mendacity of Hope: Barack Obama and the Betrayal of American Liberalism,* which attacked equally the president and the New Democratic philosophy that propelled him into power.[50] One might fairly say that as Obama sought reelection in 2012 his two great antagonists were the American right and the left wing of his own base.

In any case, that year's presidential campaign seemed something of a comedown after the grand hopes of 2008. Some had wanted to enshrine the earlier campaign as a "critical election" akin to the coming to power of the Jeffersonians, the ascendancy of free labor under Lincoln, and the emergence of the social welfare state under FDR. One might argue, however, that for both Obama and America the critical election was really 2012. Though it did not result in the rise of a new liberalism (the dashed hopes of 2008), it did suggest the staying power of the centrist approach favored by New Democrats. In 2012 after all, Obama became the second of this relatively recent political genus in sixteen years to win reelection.

But where, beyond 2012 and a brief line of New Democratic leadership, does Obama fit into the broad scope of American political history? Who are his allies and antecedents? Although we are attentive to the intriguing range of his references—a Kenyan father, an Indonesian preadolescence, and a post-boomer backdrop—we might be diverting ourselves in a stubborn insistence on "difference." Absent the exotica, we will come nearer to the heart of his presidency if we see him less as a paradigm shifter and more as a consensus-driven realist. In this context Obama becomes an instantly recognizable historical figure. More than a New Democrat, he is linked to a longer line of moderates angling under various prods, pressures, and convictions toward the center of the ever-evolving American political tradition.

Conclusion
Holding the Center

· ·

Never again can the Republican Party simply write off entire segments of our entire society because we assume our principles have limited appeal. . . . We need to be larger than that.

—Jeb Bush, 2013

The Democratic Party's successful run in recent national elections raises the question: Can Republicans advance a fresh agenda that beats with the pulse of the culture and is still amenable to the GOP's clashing wings? Can it, in other words, meld the dissonant voices of the party's moralizers and modernizers into a coherent whole? Historically speaking, stranger things have happened. Reinvention, after all, in response to any number of game changers, including wars, economic downturns, or demographic shifts, is perhaps the cardinal creed of our political system. How else can we explain the winding and at times head-scratching paths of partisanship so evident throughout the country's development? As agrarian-oriented Jeffersonians, Democrats long defended the interests of southern slaveholders, but as urban-oriented New Dealers they incorporated African Americans into a coalition dominated by the industrial North. As "radicals," antebellum Republicans were the free-labor champions of Main Street, and yet postbellum Republicans became known as the conservative advocates of Wall Street.

Today the GOP finds itself at a political crossroads: Will it continue promoting a platform alienating to many independent voters (now some 40 percent of the electorate), or will it edge to the middle on issues ranging from immigration reform to same-sex marriage to climate change? Henry Cabot Lodge Jr. thought the recipe for success rather simple, even as he sometimes puzzled over his party's inability to follow it. "A good way to destroy yourself politically," he put the matter in retirement, "is to insist that everyone agree with you. If our parties ever become ideological parties, they are condemned to certain defeat."[1] Lodge's observation is worth remembering today. For recent presidential election cycles suggest strongly that the old Sunbelt consensus has come undone and that the GOP faces now the possibility of slipping into a longstanding minority status.

Demography need not be destiny, but the numbers look to be on the wrong side of the right. According to the 2010 census, minorities, strong supporters of the Democratic Party, accounted for 35 percent of the population, up 5 percent from 2000; in California minorities make up some 70 percent of those under the age of fifteen; and four states—California, Texas, New Mexico, and Hawaii—have majority minority populations. They, along with the District of Columbia (65 percent minority), currently account for nearly 39 percent of the electoral votes needed to capture a national election. The GOP, by comparison, can point to no comparable expanding cohort. Sifting over the census returns, *National Review Online* editor-at-large Jonah Goldberg soberly noted, "The core Republican coalition of culturally or religiously conservative whites is comparatively shrinking."[2]

At least since Roosevelt's epic 1912 battle with Taft have Republicans been at odds over their party's future. More recently, the contraction of the GOP core in recent decades has only sharpened the terms of debate. Looking toward the 2016 general election, this center-versus-right struggle has shown no signs of letting up. In January 2015 Senator Ted Cruz of Texas, speaking at the South Carolina Tea Party Convention in Myrtle Beach, called for his fellow Republicans to avoid choosing a presidential candidate from "the mushy middle." Insisting that a moderate candidate would alienate conservatives, Cruz said, "The same people who stayed home in 2008 and 2012 will stay home in 2016 and the Democrats will win again. There is a better way." A few days later Kentucky senator Rand Paul chimed in, acknowledging the GOP's divided house and wondering, like Cruz, if the party's right wing might now be able to press successfully for a "real" conservative nominee. "I think one of the biggest debates we will see is: Do we want the leader of our party to be a moderate or a conservative? I think many times in the past, conservatives have [split] the vote, and we've wound up with a moderate. The question is whether conservatives in the party are now strong enough to unite and elect a conservative. I think that will be a big debate."[3]

The senators share the view that GOP defeats in recent general elections are attributable less to the public's perception that their party is too far to the right than to its self-defeating caving in to the aforementioned "mushy middle." By nominating Robert Dole (1996), John McCain (2008), and Mitt Romney (2012), the argument goes, Republicans put up compromise candidates who could neither energize the party nor attract sufficient independent and crossover appeal to win. This is hardly a new argument; the GOP right made a similar claim in the era of New Deal liberalism (1932–68), denouncing the likes of Wendell Willkie, Thomas Dewey, and Nelson Rockefeller. And yet the most consequential Republican leader during this period, Dwight Eisenhower, was a moderate, and when given the opportunity to run a candidate that excited the right— Barry Goldwater—the party reaped an electoral disaster.

Today we should once again be suspicious of claims that the GOP need only rediscover its inner Reagan to win the White House. In 2012 a host of conservative candidates, including Newt Gingrich, Ron Paul, Herman Cain, Rick Santorum, Rick Perry, and Michele Bachmann, failed to compete effectively in the primaries. In a walkover, Romney captured the popular vote in forty-two states and won nearly 75 percent of the delegates. This was nothing new. Since the 1980s candidates on the right have shown no hint of being able to carry a national campaign, in fact they can't even carry their own party. The most popular hard conservative running in the presidential primaries is routinely trounced. In 1992 and 1996 Buchanan won 22 and 20 percent, respectively, of the popular vote, Alan Keyes could eke out only 5 percent in 2000, Mike Huckabee plateaued at 20 percent in 2008, a sum matched by Santorum in 2012. As for the argument that centrist candidates don't energize the electorate, we should keep in mind that Romney's percentage of the vote in the 2012 election (47.2) nearly equaled that of the victorious Bush in 2000 (47.9)—and that Romney's total of 60 million votes exceeded Bush's by more than 10 million.

Shy of collecting a few more electoral cycle results, we will require some years before being able to sufficiently assess the Republican response to its current, as some pundits have put it, intraparty civil war. The path it chooses from this point on may well determine whether it will be able to nominate presidential candidates capable of claiming coast-to-coast coalitions or instead limit its reach to state and congressional contests. As a work of history this study has no rooting interest in that outcome, nor has it, I hope, overstated the moderate style in American politics or been blind to its shortcomings. Clearly there have been critical periods in our past, say the emancipatory year of 1863 or the famous first hundred days of FDR's New Deal, when more radical measures proved both necessary and successful. It is equally evident that on occasion moderates have simply echoed their opposition (think Lodge and company's Me-Too Republicanism) while struggling to make sense of organized conservatism's place in a liberal period. And finally, moderates have on occasion flat out failed, as any student of Henry Adams's ineffectual scholar-in-politics efforts to upend Grantism can attest.

I have attempted, rather, to offer a wider purview of our partisan past than the old liberal-conservative consensus allows, arguing instead for a distinctively moderate leadership line. Read in such a way, the centuries-long sequence reaching from John Adams to Barack Obama takes on added nuance and understanding. More than merely Whigs or Republicans, Democrats or Progressives, those occupying the pragmatic center have constituted a separate force in American politics, and one that continues to both inform and give substance to our ideological choices. In a 2013 interview with ABC's Diane Sawyer and George Stephanopoulos, Colin Powell called for his party to "drift a little bit back [to the center]. Not because it's just good to be a moderate, but because that's where the American people are."[4] Taking Powell's observation a step further, there is good reason to believe that America is in the midst of a moderate era. For all its noise, the hard right can command only selective support, while there is no electoral left to speak of.

Before lamenting the loss of our individual pet ideologies, we might remember that at one time Americans embraced the political middle as part of a compromise tradition that served the Union well. A few irreconcilables to the contrary, a spirit of open-eyed conciliation informed the Constitutional Convention and did much to impart a pragmatic tone on the nation's emerging partisan system. Reflecting on the virtues of concession making, Hezekiah Niles, editor of *Niles' Register* (1811–49), an influential national political newsweekly praised by such disparate pols as Adams, Jefferson, and Jackson, argued that in public life, "Gentlemen must give way a little. It does not become a republican to say, 'I will not submit to this,' or 'I will have that,'—his great duty is to regard the general good and suffer the majority to govern."[5] For Niles, in other words, to be a republican citizen meant that, by definition, *one was a moderate*—willing, that is, to moderate one's views, positions, and votes on the great and often contentious public issues of the day. The very nature of democratic governance called for no less. Perhaps a king or a pope might claim a kind of divine right to rule, but popularly elected representatives operated under far different assumptions and in a far more open arena of debate.

Some two centuries on, we continue to govern within the same federal structure as in Niles's day. As such, the question of compromise remains vital to our politics and sense of a shared republic. Despite this truism, we are invariably drawn to, and in many cases distracted by, those left-liberal and right-conservative wings whose more incendiary offerings bounce about the blogosphere in a news cycle contest for sound-bite supremacy. The result is often more confusion than clarity. A genuinely mystified Rush Limbaugh grumbled not so long ago, "By definition, moderates can't be brave—they don't have opinions! . . . I mean, brave moderates? 'Great Moderates in American History?' Show me that book."[6] I have argued in these pages ("that book"), by contrast, that the center has its own distinct history and that within the framework of the American story it deserves both our critical attention and careful consideration. Ideologues may come and go, but as long as the republic persists, the prevailing tradition trends moderate.

Notes

Introduction

1. Brinkley, "Problem of American Conservatism," 409; Phillips-Fein, "Conservatism," 724.

2. Knupfer, *Union As It Is*, 211.

3. Cooper, *Warrior and the Priest*, 154.

4. Lengell, "Limbaugh More Loyal than Powell."

5. "Jeb Bush."

6. Blake, "Jeb Bush."

7. Sewell, *Ballots for Freedom*, 310; Donald, *Lincoln Reconsidered*, 133.

8. The 1936 elections were a crushing blow to the GOP. Its presidential nominee, the genial if colorless Kansan Alf Landon, was trounced by FDR in the Electoral College 523 to 8 and received less than 37 percent of the vote, the lowest percentage for a Republican nominee in a primarily two person contest in the party's history. The situation in the new Congress was equally desperate; the GOP claimed only 20 percent of the House and 17 percent of the Senate.

9. The five contests I refer to are the 1992, 1996, 2000, 2008 and 2012 elections. In the 2000 race Al Gore, though defeated in the Electoral College, captured a higher percentage of the popular vote (48.4) than George W. Bush (47.9).

10. Klein, "Obama Revealed."

11. Swanson, "Obama Says"; Dunkley, "Obama Would Have Been a 'Moderate Republican.'"

12. "Cruz, South Carolina Tea Party Convention."

Chapter 1

1. Parrington, *Colonial Mind*, 312.

2. C. F. Adams, *Works of John Adams*, 6:484; Peterson, *Portable Thomas Jefferson*, 465.

3. Butterfield, *Diary and Autobiography*, 3:256.

4. Grant, *John Adams*, 19–20.

5. Cappon, *Adams-Jefferson Letters*, 375, 374.

6. Peterson, *Portable Thomas Jefferson*, 217; Franklin, *Autobiography*, 43.

7. John Adams, *A Defence of the Constitutions of the United States of America*, in Diggins, *Portable John Adams*, 292.

8. Morris, *Forging of the Union*, 157.

9. Niebuhr, *Moral Man & Immoral Society*, xxvi.

10. Butterfield, *Diary and Autobiography*, 1:41.

11. Butterfield, *Adams Family Correspondence*, 5; Butterfield, *Diary and Autobiography*, 3:260.

12. McCullough, *John Adams*, 64; Butterfield, *Diary and Autobiography*, 2:59.

13. Banning, *Jeffersonian Persuasion*, 34.

14. Butterfield, *Diary and Autobiography*, 1:324.

15. McDonald, *Alexander Hamilton*, 214.

16. Koch and Peden, *Selected Writings*, 149.

17. Ibid., 162, 163; Cappon, *Adams-Jefferson Letters*, 401–2.

18. Diggins, *Portable John Adams*, 352.

19. Cappon, *Adams-Jefferson Letters*, 551. On this theme, the social scientist Daniel Bell wrote in the 1970s, "The Protestant ethic and the Puritan temper, as social facts, were eroded long ago. . . . The breakup of the traditional bourgeois value system, in fact, was brought about by the bourgeois economic system—by the free market, to be precise. This is the source of the contradiction of capitalism in American life." Bell, *Cultural Contradictions of Capitalism*, 55.

20. Nagel, *Descent from Glory*, 16; Diggins, *John Adams*, 151.

21. Cappon, *Adams-Jefferson Letters*, 297, 355.

22. Ibid., 357.

23. Ibid., 587–88.

24. Foner, *Tom Paine*, 123; Butterfield, *Diary and Autobiography*, 3:333; Ferguson, *American Enlightenment*, 117.

25. Cappon, *Adams-Jefferson Letters*, 358.

26. Diggins, *Portable John Adams*, 381. On Adams's conjecture that education encouraged a not altogether salutary competition among rising classes, the case of Alexander Hamilton may be instructive. There are several opinions as to why Hamilton met Aaron Burr in their deadly "affair of honor." One school suggests that the duel brought to an end a contentious rivalry between two men who had long circulated in a constricted Manhattan legal-political milieu. Buckner F. Melton Jr. has written, "Each was brilliant. Each was in ambition's grip. And New York was too small to hold two such men. In every contest, one of them had to lose." See Melton, *Aaron Burr*, 24.

27. Gross, *Oxford Book of Essays*, 286.

28. Veblen, *Theory of the Leisure Class*, 223.

29. Foucault, *Madness and Civilization*, 65.

30. Diggins, *Portable John Adams*, 381–82.

31. Peterson, *Portable Thomas Jefferson*, 534; Diggins, *Portable John Adams*, 430, 431.

32. Diggins, *Portable John Adams*, 421.

33. Plumb, *Origins of Political Stability*, 19, 1.

34. Hofstadter, *Idea of a Party System*, 21.

35. Koch and Peden, *Selected Writings*, 144.

36. Miller, *Federalist Era*, 201.

37. McDonald, *Alexander Hamilton*, 328.

38. Miller, *Federalist Era*, 232, 237.

39. Cappon, *Adams-Jefferson Letters*, 329.

40. Weisberger, *America Afire*, 233–34.

41. H. Adams, *History of the United States of America during the Administrations of Thomas Jefferson*, 1240, 1245; Wilentz, *Rise of American Democracy*, 396–97.

42. Adams and Cunningham, *Correspondence*, 181.

43. Kraus and Joyce, *Writing of American History*, 68; Koch and Peden, *Selected Writings*, 161.

44. Hogan and Taylor, *My Dearest Friend*, 431.

45. Ibid., 340.

46. Cappon, *Adams-Jefferson Letters*, 270.

47. Ibid., 271, 273, 274.

48. Ibid., 275, 276, 281, 282.

Chapter 2

1. H. Adams, *Documents Relating to New England Federalism*, 338.

2. H. Adams, *History of the United States during the Administrations of Thomas Jefferson*, 154, 175–76, 210.

3. Fischer, *Revolution in American Conservatism*, 2.

4. Pickering has attracted little monographic attention from modern scholars. For a critical account see Clarfield, *Timothy Pickering*; for a more sympathetic reading see the relevant passages in Wills's *"Negro President."*

5. Arrington, *Municipal History of Essex County*, 1. For a recent history of economic decline in Essex's entrepot see Booth, *Death of Empire*.

6. Lodge, *Life and Letters*, 18.

7. Peterson, *Portable Thomas Jefferson*, 456; Cabot to Dear Sir, 5 May 1791, Reel 127, HCLP.

8. Slaughter, *Whiskey Rebellion*, 131.

9. Cabot to Dear Sir, 12 August 1794, Reel 127, HCLP.

10. Peterson, *Portable Thomas Jefferson*, 464–65; Lodge, *Life and Letters*, 180.

11. Ammon, *James Monroe*, 145; Cabot to King, 2 August 1793, Reel 127, HCLP.

12. Miller, *Federalist Era*, 243; C. F. Adams, *Works of John Adams*, 10:130.

13. Cabot to Pickering, 31 and 16 October 1799, Reel 127, HCLP.

14. Cabot to Wolcott, 20 July 1800, Reel 128, HCLP.

15. Syrett, *Papers of Alexander Hamilton*, 171–72.

16. Ibid., 186; Lodge, *Life and Letters*, 300.

17. Cabot to Hamilton, 21 August 1800, Reel 128, HCLP.

18. Banner, *To the Hartford Convention*, 270–71; Lodge, *Life and Letters*, 341.

19. H. Adams, *Documents Relating to New England Federalism*, 352.

20. Ibid., 339, 341.

21. Ibid., 345, 341, 342.

22. Ibid., 346.

23. Ibid., 347.

24. Lodge, *Life and Letters*, 345, 348.

25. Isenberg, *Fallen Founder*, 257, 258.

26. Malone, *Jefferson and His Time*, 5:483.

27. Zall, *Jefferson on Jefferson,* 15; Peterson, *Portable Thomas Jefferson*, 8, 10.

28. Peterson, *Portable Thomas Jefferson*, 9.

29. McDonald, *Presidency of Thomas Jefferson*, 149; Levy, *Jefferson and Civil Liberties*, 107.

30. Cabot to Pickering, 12 March 1808, Reel 128, HCLP.

31. Taylor, *William Cooper's Town*, 355; Wilentz, *Chants Democratic*, 24.

32. Banner, *To the Hartford Convention*, 295–96.

33. Cabot to Otis, 14 August 1808, Reel 127, HCLP.

34. Ibid.

35. Ibid.

36. Rutland, *Presidency of James Madison*, 4; H. Adams, *Documents Relating to New England Federalism*, 373.

37. This and the next few paragraphs hue closely to Banner's observations in *To the Hartford Convention*, see especially pages 294–350.

38. Ibid., 305.

39. Peterson, *Thomas Jefferson*, 915.

40. Madison, "War Message to Congress."

41. Banner, *To the Hartford Convention*, 306–7; Lodge, *Life and Letters*, 408–9.

42. H. Adams, *History of the United States of America during the Administrations of James Madison*, 581.

43. Taylor, *Civil War of 1812*, 415; Goodrich, *Recollections of a Lifetime*, 31.

44. Lodge, *Life and Letters of George Cabot*, 519.

45. Goodrich, *Recollections of a Lifetime*, 36–37.

46. McDonald, *Select Documents*, 199.

47. Ibid., 200.

48. Miller, *Federalist Era,* 276.

Chapter 3

1. Schlesinger, *Age of Jackson*, 12, 35.

2. Howe, *Political Culture of the American Whigs*, 3. Howe has updated his argument in *What Hath God Wrought*. See particularly chapter 15, "The Whigs and Their Age."

3. Nagel, *John Quincy Adams*, 328.

4. Nagel, *Descent from Glory*, 28; Butterfield, *Adams Family Correspondence*, 1:388.

5. Unger, *John Quincy Adams*, 22. "Every Thing in Life should be done with Reflection, and Judgment," the future president counseled the future president, "even the most insignificant Amusements." Butterfield, *Adams Family Correspondence*, 4:56.

6. Adams to Brooks Adams, 18 February 1909, Reel 34, HAP; C. F. Adams, *Memoirs of John Quincy Adams*, 9:442.

7. C. F. Adams, *Memoirs of John Quincy Adams*, 1:282–83.

8. H. Adams, *Documents Relating to New England Federalism,* 148.

9. Wheelan, *Mr. Adams's Last Crusade*, 21.

10. H. Adams, *Documents Relating to New England Federalism*, 366–67; J. Q. Adams, *Parties in the United States*, 67.

11. C. F. Adams, *Memoirs of John Quincy Adams*, 1:510.

12. Ibid., 374–75.

13. Ibid., 1:497.

14. Ford, *Writings of John Quincy Adams*, 236–37.

15. Hofstadter, *Idea of a Party System*, 195–96.

16. Bemis, *John Quincy Adams*, 340.

17. Howe, *Political Culture of the American Whigs*, 47.

18. Adams to Brooks Adams, 18 February and 13 March 1909, Reel 34, HAP.

19. Adams to Brooks Adams, 13 March 1909, Reel 34, HAP.

20. J. Q. Adams, "Inaugural Address."

21. Watson, *Liberty and Power*, 151, 138; Lunt, *Discourse*, 57.

22. C. F. Adams, *Memoirs of John Quincy Adams*, 8:100.

23. Wheelan, *Mr. Adams's Last Crusade*, xii, xiii; C. F. Adams, *Memoirs of John Quincy Adams*, 8:247.

24. Stewart, *Holy Warriors*, 83; Wheelan, *Mr. Adams's Last Crusade*, 99.

25. C. F. Adams, *Memoirs of John Quincy Adams*, 12:80, 10:345.

26. Wheelan, *Mr. Adams's Last Crusade*, 106.

27. Ibid., 192–99.

28. Lovejoy and Lovejoy, *Memoir of the Reverend Elijah P. Lovejoy*, 11–12.

29. J. Q. Adams, *Argument of John Quincy Adams*, 135.

30. Miller, *Arguing about Slavery*, 144; Wheelan, *Mr. Adams's Last Crusade*, 107.

31. Niven, *John C. Calhoun*, 54.

32. Bemis, *John Quincy Adams*, 419.

33. Wheelan, *Mr. Adams's Last Crusade*, 212.

34. C. F. Adams, *Memoirs of John Quincy Adams*, 11:86, 10:454.

35. Wheelan, *Mr. Adams's Last Crusade*, 147.

Chapter 4

1. Wood, *Radicalism of the American Revolution*, 369.

2. Torget and Ayers, *Two Communities in the Civil War*, 110. That Republican newspaper, the *Franklin (Pa.) Repository*, is not altogether in error. In 1778

Jefferson drafted a Virginia law prohibiting the importation of enslaved Africans; six years later he proposed an ordinance banning slavery in the Northwest Territory, and he was known to be a supporter of gradual emancipation. It was after 1789, historian David Brion Davis argues, that Jefferson exhibited an "immense silence" on the subject. See Davis, *Problem of Slavery in the Age of Revolution*, 179.

3. Hopkins and Hay, *Papers of Henry Clay*, 2:479; Richardson, *Compilation of the Messages and Papers of the Presidents*, 2:298.

4. Rakove, *James Madison*, 171; Peterson, *Portable Thomas Jefferson*, 549.

5. C. F. Adams, *Memoirs of John Quincy Adams*, 76; Currie, *Constitution in Congress*, 4n9; Washington, *Writings of Thomas Jefferson*, 387.

6. H. Adams, *Writings of Albert Gallatin*, 289; Hamilton, *Writings of James Monroe*, 196.

7. Weaver, *Correspondence of James K. Polk*, 381; Malone, *Jefferson and His Time*, 6:302.

8. Clay, "His Attack on Jackson."

9. Hopkins and Hay, *Papers of Henry Clay*, 10:50.

10. McKitrick, *Slavery Defended*, 9; Wish, *Ante-bellum*, 57.

11. Risjord, *Old Republicans*, 47; Bruce, *John Randolph of Roanoke*, 372.

12. Genovese, *Southern Tradition*, 23–26; Fox-Genovese and Genovese, *Mind of the Master Class*, 482, 587.

13. Richardson, *Compilation of Messages and Papers*, 4:657–58.

14. Silbey, *Party over Section*, 68.

15. Earle, *Jacksonian Antislavery*, 142, 5.

16. Ibid., 2.

17. See the fifth chapter of Potter's *Impending Crisis*.

18. Howe, *Political Culture of the American Whigs*, 278.

19. Holt, *Political Parties and American Political Development*, 69.

20. Lincoln, "First Political Announcement."

21. Basler, *Collected Works of Abraham Lincoln*, 2:111.

22. Swain, *Life and Speeches of Henry Clay*, 39.

23. Holt, *Rise and Fall of the American Whig Party*, 341.

24. Riddle, *Life of Benjamin F. Wade*, 65.

25. "Republican Platform of 1856."

26. Wood, *Empire of Liberty*, 171.

27. Lincoln, "Letter to Henry L. Pierce."

28. Ball, *Lincoln*, 64.

29. Basler, *Collected Works of Abraham Lincoln*, 3:375.

30. Lincoln, "Letter to Owen Lovejoy."

31. Wilentz, "Abraham Lincoln and Jacksonian Democracy," 63.

32. Basler, *Collected Works of Abraham Lincoln*, 3:339 and 2:391.

33. Sewell, *Ballots for Freedom*, 310.

Chapter 5

1. Chernow, *Titan*, 326.

2. H. Adams, *Education of Henry Adams*, 4.

3. Levenson, *Letters of Henry Adams*, 6:480. Adams's grave concerns for industrialization's impact on republican government captured only part of his era's struggles to create a workable democracy. Another part, the assimilation of several million African Americans into the country's social, political, and economic systems, failed to earn his interest. And in warring on Grantism he attacked a presidential administration more liberal on the race question than the Liberal Republican Party he more generally supported. For a discussion of this topic, see Simpson's *Political Education of Henry Adams*, 25–26.

4. Levenson, *Letters of Henry Adams*, 1:315.

5. On the impact of political "extremism" in the 1850s, see Menand's *Metaphysical Club*, particularly the first three chapters.

6. H. Adams, "New York Gold Conspiracy," 365.

7. Ibid., 325, 332, 326; emphasis added.

8. Levenson, *Letters of Henry Adams*, 2:86.

9. Julian, *Political Recollections*, 337.

10. Downey, "Horace Greeley and the Politicians," 731.

11. Duberman, *Charles Francis Adams*, 357, 358; Samuels, *Young Henry Adams*, 227. A few weeks after the general election, but before the Electoral College met to cast its ballots, Greeley died. Subsequently, four different candidates received electoral votes from Greeley electors.

12. Levenson, *Letters of Henry Adams*, 2:226, 2:247

13. Ibid., 2:251.

14. Holt, *By One Vote*, 78.

15. Hochfield, *Great Secession Winter*, 308, 293; Levenson, *Letters*, 2:287.

16. Holt, *By One Vote*, 37.

17. H. Adams, *Democracy*, 13, 185. On Adams's idolization in the novel of "women as the incorruptible, arbiters of morality," see Simpson's *Political Education of Henry Adams*, 111–12.

18. H. Adams, *History of the United States of America during the Administrations of Thomas Jefferson*, 62.

19. H. Adams, *History of the United States of America during the Administrations of James Madison*, 1252.

20. Samuels, *Henry Adams*, 355.

21. H. Adams, *Mont-Saint-Michel and Chartres*, 32, 205.

22. H. Adams, *Education of Henry Adams*, 21; H.Adams, *Democracy*, 49.

23. Levenson, *Letters of Henry Adams*, 5:88.

24. H. Adams, *Education of Henry Adams*, 389; Levenson, *Letters of Henry Adams*, 5:418, 4:644.

25. H. Adams, *Education of Henry Adams*, 69.

26. Ibid., 345, 380.

27. Ford, *Cycle of Adams Letters*, 237–40.

28. On the progressive side of the populist movement, see Postel, *Populist Vision*.

Chapter 6

1. F. D. Roosevelt, *Continuing Struggle for Liberalism*, 38.

2. Dallek, *An Unfinished Life*, 373–74.

3. Hawley, *Theodore Roosevelt*, 147–48.

4. Robinson, *My Brother Theodore Roosevelt*, 3–4; T. Roosevelt, *Theodore Roosevelt*, 7. For a full history of the family see Schriftgiesser's *Amazing Roosevelt Family*.

5. Robinson, *My Brother Theodore Roosevelt*, 10; Morris, *Rise of Theodore Roosevelt*, 5; Dalton, *Theodore Roosevelt*, 171.

6. T. Roosevelt, *Theodore Roosevelt*, 95.

7. Morison, *Letters of Theodore Roosevelt*, 3:57.

8. Ibid., 3:102; Brands, *TR*, 170.

9. T. Roosevelt, *Theodore Roosevelt*, 88.

10. Brands, *TR*, 177; T. Roosevelt, *Theodore Roosevelt*, 150.

11. Morison, *Letters of Theodore Roosevelt*, 7:251. "TR was sentimental enough about Lincoln," Dalton notes, "to have boxwood cuttings from Lincoln's home planted at [his] Sagamore Hill [home]." Dalton, *Theodore Roosevelt*, 207.

12. Morison, *Letters of Theodore Roosevelt*, 5:101.

13. Ibid. The deaths were unconnected. Martha Roosevelt died of typhoid fever. Roosevelt's first wife, Alice Lee Roosevelt, died of Bright's disease just two days after giving birth to their daughter.

14. T. Roosevelt, *Theodore Roosevelt*, 210.

15. Morison, *Letters of Theodore Roosevelt*, 1:535–36.

16. Robinson, *My Brother Theodore Roosevelt*, 177.

17. Brands, *TR*, 357.

18. T. Roosevelt, *Theodore Roosevelt*, 499; Brands, *TR*, 397.

19. Brands, *TR*, 541.

20. Morison, *Letters of Theodore Roosevelt*, 1:237 and 2:1087.

21. Ibid., 6:1089.

22. Ibid., 7:34.

23. Pinchot, *Breaking New Ground*, 499–500; Morison, *Letters of Theodore Roosevelt*, 7:50n1.

24. Morison, *Letters of Theodore Roosevelt*, 7:51 and 7:80–81.

25. Brands, *Selected Letters*, 537.

26. Garraty, *Henry Cabot Lodge*, 293; Levenson, *Letters of Henry Adams*, 6:519.

27. Hawley, *Theodore Roosevelt*, 233.

28. Milkis, *Theodore Roosevelt,* 186, 182; Morison, *Letters of Theodore Roosevelt,* 7:594n2.

29. Chessman, *Theodore Roosevelt,* 184.

30. Morison, *Letters of Theodore Roosevelt,* 7:598.

Chapter 7

1. The Taft dynasty includes Alphonso Taft, secretary of war (1876) and attorney general (1876–77); William Howard Taft, president (1909–13) and chief justice of the U.S. Supreme Court (1921–30); Robert Alphonso Taft, U.S. senator (1939–53); Robert Taft Jr., U.S. senator (1971–76); and Robert Alphonso Taft III, governor of Ohio (1999–2007).

2. Ross, *An American Family,* 6–7; Pringle, *Life and Times of William Howard Taft,* 8–9.

3. Leonard, *Life of Alphonso Taft,* 71.

4. Ross, *An American Family,* 38.

5. Ibid., 47.

6. Harz, "Alphonso Taft."

7. Ross, *An American Family,* 62.

8. Foner, *Reconstruction,* 580.

9. Ross, *An American Family,* 110.

10. Pringle, *Life and Times of William Howard Taft,* 57–8; Ross, *An American Family,* 97.

11. Taft to Roosevelt, 7 November 1908, Reel 321, WHTP; Anderson, *William Howard Taft,* 14. Nellie Taft's biographer has emphasized the competitive relationship between Roosevelt and Mrs. Taft. "Certainly Roosevelt saw for himself just how formidable Nellie's power was over Will. In that sense she could be a potential challenge to his own effort to shape Will's speeches and his stand on the issues and, if he became President, policies. The extent to which Roosevelt could influence a potential President Taft would always be filtered through Nellie." Anthony, *Nellie Taft,* 189.

12. Coletta, *Presidency of William Howard Taft,* 46.

13. Ross, *An American Family,* 180–81.

14. Pringle, *Life and Times of William Howard Taft,* 128.

15. Anderson, *William Howard Taft,* 26.

16. Gould, *William Howard Taft Presidency,* 57, 51.

17. Gould, *Presidency of Theodore Roosevelt,* 205.

18. Gould, *William Howard Taft Presidency,* 167.

19. Smelser, *Democratic Republic,* 182.

20. Burner, *Politics of Provincialism,* 97, 125; Murray, *103rd Ballot,* 206.

21. "Cheer Taft Urging Canal Fortification," *New York Times,* 22 January 1911.

22. La Follette, *La Follette's Autobiography,* 212.

23. Butt, *Taft and Roosevelt*, 794; Taft to Mrs. William A. Edwards, 20 February 1912, Reel 455, WHTP.

24. T. Roosevelt, "Right of the People to Rule," 620.

25. Roosevelt and Lodge, *Selections from the Correspondence*, 423–24.

26. Lodge to Apsey, 4 March 1912, Reel 37, HCLP.

27. Lodge to John Morse, 11 October 1912, Reel 37, HCLP. Lodge informed Taft that he would campaign in 1912 for the GOP but avoid attacks on Roosevelt: "I shall not enter upon any personalities, for I think we have had too many of those in this campaign already and it seems to me high time that we should devote ourselves to the principles of the Republican party and say something about its character and traditions and what it means at the present day." Lodge to Taft, 6 September 1912, Reel 38, HCLP.

28. Brooks Adams to Henry Cabot Lodge, 10 March 1912, Reel 37, HCLP; Levenson, *Letters of Henry Adams*, 6:546.

29. Hofstadter, *American Political Tradition*, 229; Root to Taft, 5 May 1912, Reel 455, WHTP.

30. Butt, *Taft and Roosevelt*, 814.

31. In 1910 Oregon became the first state to hold a binding presidential primary, which required its delegates to the national nominating convention to support the winner of that primary. Before that, and beginning in the 1830s, delegates to the nominating conventions were nearly always selected by state nominating assemblies. These conventions were often dominated by political bosses and thus, by the turn of a new century, incurred the wrath of progressives.

32. Kelsey to Taft, 1 June 1912, Reel 455, WHTP.

33. William Howard Taft to "My Dear Kels," 4 June 1912, Reel 455, WHTP.

34. Taft to Mrs. Buckner R. Wallingford, 14 July 1912, Reel 513, WHTP; Coletta, *Presidency of William Howard Taft*, 242.

35. Taft to Mrs. Buckner R. Wallingford, 14 July 1912, Reel 513, WHTP.

36. Taft to Horace Taft, 29 October 1912, Reel 515, WHTP.

37. Taft to Roosevelt, 9 May 1903, Reel 319, WHTP; Taft to Horace Taft, 1 November 1912, Reel 515, WHTP.

38. Anderson, *Taft*, 247; "Statement given to the press by the President, in Cincinnati," 5 November 1912, Reel 515, WHTP.

39. Hechler, *Insurgency*, 226; Freedman, *Roosevelt and Frankfurter*, 218–19. FDR's private secretary Grace Tully wrote, "Teddy Roosevelt had once divided American Presidents into 'Buchanan' and 'Lincoln' types—the first being those who remained inactive in a national crisis and let the Congress whittle away the executive power; the second being those who had used their constitutional powers to the hilt in order to do what the nation expected of them. Franklin Roosevelt had T.R.'s division in mind when he appraised Herbert Hoover." Tully, *F.D.R.*, 59.

Chapter 8

1. Hofstadter, *American Political Tradition*, viii.

2. Hoover, *Addresses upon the American Road*, 218.

3. "Story of Elwood," 37.

4. Willkie, *One World*, 145–46. The America First Committee was a noninterventionist organization opposed to U.S. entry into World War II. Begun in 1940 and counting among its members future president Gerald Ford, the novelist Sinclair Lewis, film producer Walt Disney, and aviation hero Charles Lindbergh, it collapsed following the Japanese attack on Pearl Harbor.

5. Eisenhower, *Mandate for Change*, 195. Kim Phillips-Fein has recently argued, "Eisenhower believed that the old Republican faith in laissez-faire needed to be updated to reflect the realities of modern capitalism. Government should, he thought, 'prevent or correct abuses springing from the unregulated practice of a private economy.' . . . While [Eisenhower] welcomed businessmen into his administration . . . he mistrusted the shortsighted or selfish demands of business nearly as much as those of labor unions." Phillips-Fein, *Invisible Hands*, 57.

6. Ambrose, *President*, 60; Ferrell, *Eisenhower Diaries*, 234.

7. Lodge, *Henry Cabot Lodge*, 9.

8. Lodge, *Early Memories*, 186.

9. Sproat, *Best Men*, 92.

10. Garraty, *Henry Cabot Lodge*, 50; Levenson, *Letters of Henry Adams*, 2:138–39. "It is difficult to give a quick estimate of Lodge as a historian," wrote Nathan Schachner in 1948, himself a Hamilton biographer. "The best I can say is that he was pretty inaccurate in his research, and intensely partisan in his writing. His life of Hamilton is a bit of special pleading, with definite concealments of what he must have known or could easily have found out. . . . His editing of letters was sloppy. Dates and attributions are wrong in too many instances; he omitted sections of letters that in some cases might be interpreted to the detriment of his hero. . . . It was the early nineteenth century pietistic type of editing rather than sound modern practice." Schachner to John Garraty, 28 April, 1948, b39, HCLJP.

11. Crowley, *George Cabot Lodge*, 24; Corey, *Letters of George Santayana*, 306.

12. Adams, *Life of George Cabot Lodge*, 33–34.

13. Roosevelt and Lodge, *Selections from the Correspondence*, 185–86.

14. Miller, *Henry Cabot Lodge*, 6.

15. Adams, *Life of George Cabot Lodge*, 75; Miller, *Henry Cabot Lodge*, 18.

16. Wharton, *Backward Glance*, 150; Miller, *Henry Cabot Lodge*, 29.

17. "Memorandum Regarding the 'Letters of Henry Adams,'" edited by Harold Dean Cater," b39, HCLJP; internal evidence suggests July 1947. Lodge, *Storm Has Many Eyes*, 23, 26.

18. Lodge to Lodge Jr., 8 December 1923, b39, HCLJP.

19. "The Presidency: Triumph," *Time*, 16 November 1936, 23; "Hamilton Pledges Militant Minority," *New York Times*, 4 November 1936.

20. Hofstadter and Hofstadter, *Great Issues in American History*, 381; Miller, *Henry Cabot Lodge*, 138, 139.

21. Lodge, "Military Aid to Western Europe," 395–96.

22. Miller, *Henry Cabot Lodge*, 200.

23. Ibid., 201.

24. Lodge to William J. Miller, 17 March 1964, b11, HCLP; "Senator Lodge's Statement Re: Policy Chairmanship," 3 January 1949, f157, BBP.

25. On Taft, the best biographical treatment remains James Patterson's *Mr. Republican*. For a briefer but incisive treatment, see Alonzo Hamby, "The Crisis and Regeneration of Republican Conservatism: Dwight D. Eisenhower, Robert A. Taft, and Joseph R. McCarthy," in his *Liberalism and Its Challengers*; and for a more recent appraisal of Taft's place in modern American conservatism see David Farber's chapter "Robert Taft: The Gray Men of Modern Conservatism and the Rights of Property," in his *Rise and Fall of Modern American Conservatism*.

26. Wunderlin, *Papers of Robert A. Taft*, 1:509.

27. "National Affairs," *Time*, 15 January 1951, 12.

28. "Political Notes," *Time*, 19 November 1951, 23.

29. Patterson, *Mr. Republican*, 560; "National Affairs," *Time*, 7 April 1952, 22; Wunderlin, *Papers of Robert A. Taft*, 4:406n2; Lodge, *Storm Has Many Eyes*, 76.

30. Lodge, *As It Was*, 56.

31. Lodge, *Storm Has Many Eyes*, 77.

32. Miller, *Henry Cabot Lodge*, 216–17.

33. Lodge, *Storm Has Many Eyes*, 85–86.

34. A "rotten borough" was slang for a parliamentary constituency in England that enjoyed representation even when there were exceedingly few constituents to represent.

35. "Taft Effort Fails," *New York Times,* 8 July 1952.

36. Whalen, *Kennedy versus Lodge*, 55, 142.

37. "The American Party," *Chicago Sunday Tribune*, 24 August 1952.

38. Brewer to Lodge, 18 September 1951, f318, BBP; Lodge to Brewer, 20 September 1951, f319, BBP.

39. Brewer to Kenneth Hutchins, 13 Oct 1951, f321, BBP; Brewer to Taft, 8 October 1951, f321, BBP.

40. Lodge to Brewer, 1 July 1952, f319, BBP; Brewer to Lodge, 2 July 1952, f374, BBP.

41. "This I Have Seen," *Worcester (Mass.) Evening Post*, 12 July 1952; "Lodge, Morse—and Ike!," *Boston (Mass.) Post*, 26 September 1952.

42. Dwight Waring to Lodge, 6 November 1952, Carton 6, HCLJP; Denholm M. Jacobs to "Cabot," 7 November 1952, Carton 6, HCLJP; "To the Voters," *Cape Cod (Mass.) Standard-Times*, 5 November 1952.

43. Miller, *Henry Cabot Lodge*, 278.

44. "National Affairs," *Time*, 11 August 1958, 11; "The Nation," *Time*, 15 May 1964, 35. Lodge had his own take on what ailed the GOP ticket in 1960: "If Dick

Nixon . . . had not gone into the television studio in agony because of his knee," he wrote his son, "he would not have made the television appearance which undoubtedly cost him the election." Lodge to Dearest Georgie, 31 December 1963, b11, HCLJP. An injured knee had kept Nixon in the hospital for the two weeks before his debate with Kennedy, and some thought his televised appearance pasty.

45. Miller, *Henry Cabot Lodge*, 336.

46. "How the World's Hottest Spot Looks to Me," *Life*, 17 April, 1964.

47. Lodge to George Lodge, 18 October 1963, b12, HCLJP.

48. Lodge to George Lodge, 25 January 1964, b11, HCLJP.

49. Lodge to George Lodge, 31 December 1963, 6 January 1964, and 16 January 1964, b11, HCLJP.

50. Lodge to George Lodge, 22 February 1964, b12, HCLJP; Lodge to George Lodge, 2 April 1964, b11, HCLP.

51. Theodore H. White, *Making of the President, 1964*, 158; Lodge to Paul Grindle, 14 May 1964, b11, HCLJP.

52. "The Nation," *Time*, 10 July 1964, 25; "The Nation," *Time*, 17 July 1964, 19; Miller, *Henry Cabot Lodge*, 366.

53. Lodge to Mrs. Thomas J. Drake, 25 September 1964, b12, HCLJP.

54. Lodge to Frank M. Adams, 18 February 1965, b12, HCLJP.

55. Lodge to George Lodge, 12 June 1964, b11, HCLJP.

Chapter 9

1. Lodge, *Life and Letters of George Cabot*, 334.

2. Buchanan, *Where the Right Went Wrong*, 234.

3. Herskowitz, *Duty, Honor, Country*, 16–17.

4. Ibid., 22.

5. Phillips, *American Dynasty*, 21.

6. RPSB, 6; Herskowitz, *Duty, Honor, Country*, 37.

7. RPSB, 48–49.

8. Ibid., 54.

9. Ibid., 52.

10. "Interview Script" by Dave Clarke, internal evidence suggests 1962, b19, PBP.

11. Wallace, *Politics of Conscience*, 106.

12. U.S. Congress, Senate, *Congressional Record*, 81st Congress, 2d sess., 621.

13. Ibid., 623.

14. Wallace, *Politics of Conscience*, 107–8.

15. RPSB, 100.

16. *New York Commercial and Financial Chronicle*, 5 December 1954; press release, 9 April 1953, b3, PBP.

17. WHAY interview, 30 December 1958, b2, PBP; *Bridgeport (Conn.) Post*, 15 December 1958.

18. *Face the Nation,* 15 January 1955, b5, PBP.

19. "Basic Speech," 1956, b6, PBP.

20. Ibid.; "News Release," 8 May 1961, b11, PBP.

21. Press release, 16 May 1962, b11, PBP; RPSB, 437–38.

22. Herskowitz, *Duty, Honor, Country,* 87.

23. Tom McCance to Poppy, 4 May 1950, Zapata Oil File, Personal Alphabetical File, b4, GBP; Parmet, *George Bush,* 81, 85.

24. Bush, *All the Best,* 294.

25. Untitled article written by George Bush, internal evidence suggests 1963, Zapata Oil File, Personal Alphabetical File, b1, GBP.

26. "Political Realignment: A Big Gain for Republicans," 16 July 1963, Zapata Oil File, Political Alphabetical File, b4, GBP.

27. Shogan, *Backlash,* 126; Leuchtenburg, *Franklin D. Roosevelt and the New Deal,* 267.

28. Bush to Leslie Coleman, internal evidence suggests spring 1961, Zapata Oil File, Political Alphabetical File, b1, GBP.

29. Michels to Bush, 25 July 1963, Political Correspondence Files, 1957–64, b1, GBP. Bush replied to Michels: "We have contacted certain responsible leaders, negroes who have been Republicans for a long time and who own their own businesses. These men believe strongly in economic conservatism, freedom of the individual and in general in all the things that you and I believe in. I do not think that we can leave 30,000–50,000 votes unsolicited in this county." Bush to Michels, 29 July 1963, Political Correspondence Files, 1957–64, b1, GBP.

30. Bush, *All the Best,* 87; Wicker, *George Herbert Walker Bush,* 18.

31. Bush to Richard Nixon, 10 November 1964, Congressional File—General-Personal, b1, GBP.

32. Germond and Witcover, *Mad as Hell,* 35.

33. Bush to Bob Connery, 20 August 1968, Congressional File—General, b1, GBP.

34. The year after leaving the UN, Bush fired off a similar broadside to his sons. "There is an arrogance about some Ivy League connections that is bad," he wrote. "Thank God, George, you got the best from Yale but you retained a fundamental conviction that a lot of good happens for America south and west of Woolsey Hall." Bush, *All the Best,* 142, 182.

35. Cannon, *Governor Reagan,* 468.

36. Bisnow, *Diary of a Dark Horse,* 16; Mason, *No Holding Back,* 34–35.

37. Bisnow, *Diary of a Dark Horse,* 17; Mason, *No Holding Back,* 37.

38. Kabaservice, *Rule and Ruin,* 359.

39. Mason, *No Holding Back,* 246.

40. McGrath, *Heartbeat,* 57; Bush, *All the Best,* 603.

41. Kazin, "From Hubris to Despair," 291; Germond and Witcover, *Mad as Hell,* 131.

42. Germond and Witcover, *Mad as Hell,* 366; "The 1992 Campaign; Excerpts from Speech by Perot," *New York Times,* 26 October 1992.

43. Buchanan, "Speech to the 1992 Republican National Convention"; Germond and Witcover, *Mad as Hell*, 413.

44. Draper, *Dead Certain*, 110; Farber, *Rise and Fall of Modern Conservatism*, 212.

45. Bush, *All the Best*, 320.

46. Mitchell, *W*, 198.

47. "George Bush Is President"; "Falwell Apologizes."

48. Cannon, *Governor Reagan*, 108–9.

49. Mitchell, *W*, 87.

50. Lyman, "Bush Blends Optimism and Challenge."

51. Cain, "Compassionate Conservatism Lost."

52. Draper, *Dead Certain*, xiv–xv.

53. Bush and Scowcroft, *World Transformed*, xi; Goldberg, "Breaking Ranks."

54. Scowcroft, "Don't Attack Saddam," *Wall Street Journal*, 15 August 2002. If doubtful of Iraq's nuclear capabilities in 2002, the senior Bush had earlier predicted that terrorism and weapons of mass destruction would in fact threaten the United States. "Over the next few years," he stated in a 1976 speech, "governments such as ours are likely to find terrorism the most urgent, and least tractable, international threat with which they have to cope. Whatever be its actual or alleged motivation, the concrete results of this terrorism are likely to be acts of mindless, disruptive violence including bombings, the taking of hostages, and the kidnapping or murder of civilian and military government officials. These terrorist acts, which will be almost impossible to prevent, will exploit the vulnerability of complex, interdependent societies such as ours to severe disruptions by the acts of small numbers of fanatics who care little for human lives, including their own. At some point within the next decade, the terrorist problem will probably take a quantum jump in severity and complexity by acquiring a nuclear dimension." George Bush, Kansas City Speech, 26 April 1976, b1, Events and Appearances Files, GBP.

55. Douthat, "Bush in Hindsight."

Chapter 10

1. Obama, *Audacity of Hope*, 34.

2. Gitlin, *Sixties*, 334.

3. Carl Solberg, *Hubert Humphrey*, 335–36, 337.

4. McGovern, *Grassroots*, 151.

5. "Connally Sets Up Panel of Democrats for Nixon," *New York Times*, 19 August 1972.

6. Miroff, *Liberals' Moment*, 109, 114; Perlstein, *Nixonland*, 522.

7. Leuchtenburg, "Jimmy Carter and the Post–New Deal Presidency," 18. As early as 1952 the literary critic Alfred Kazin observed the defensive tone of the new middle class. He wrote in November of that year, just after Eisenhower's election, "America in a conservative mood: the generation brought up under

Roosevelt wants to keep what it has—and, I suppose, deny it to others." Cook, *Alfred Kazin's Journals*, 169.

8. Carter, *Turning Point*, 5.

9. Fink and Graham, *Carter Presidency*, 11.

10. Zelizer, *Jimmy Carter*, 19; Carter, *Keeping Faith*, 73; Fink and Graham, *Carter Presidency*, 18.

11. Fink and Graham, *Carter Presidency*, 12.

12. Ibid., 13; Leuchtenburg, *Shadow of FDR*, 192.

13. Meyerson, "Ghost of Democratic Agenda"; Carter, *Keeping Faith*, 108.

14. Carter, "State of the Union Address"; Gillon, *Democrats' Dilemma*, 287.

15. Carter, "Anti-Inflation Speech."

16. Hertzberg, "Exit Interview." In 2009, President Obama used the phrase "new foundation" in a number of speeches. Conservative pundits pounced on the slogan as a case of Carter-itis. Undaunted, the president periodically drew upon it as late as October 2011. It did not catch on. Baker, "Familiar Obama Phrase Being Groomed as Slogan," *New York Times*, 15 May 2009.

17. Zelizer, *Jimmy Carter*, 46. Timothy Stanley writes, "Jimmy Carter had been elected by a renewed liberal coalition committed to the passage of a number of ambitious programs. The Democratic National Committee's private postelection polling found that the public generally regarded Carter as an economic liberal on the basis of the party's platform. . . . It was therefore logical for liberals to assume that Carter was bound by his word and electoral necessity to implement their platform." Stanley, *Kennedy vs. Carter*, 30.

18. Sandbrook, *Mad as Hell*, 237; Zelizer, *Jimmy Carter*, 86.

19. Stanley, *Kennedy vs. Carter*, 83; "Jimmy's Party in Memphis," *Time*, 18 December 1978, 22.

20. Carter, "Crisis of Confidence Speech"; Kennedy, *True Compass*, 367. For assessments of Carter's address and its political and cultural fallouts, see Mattson, *"What the Heck Are You Up to Mr. President?,"* and Horowitz, *The Anxieties of Affluence*.

21. Carter, *Keeping Faith*, 569.

22. Greenberg, *Middle Class Dreams*, 22, 31.

23. Germond and Witcover, *Wake Us When It's Over*, 22–23.

24. Baer, *Reinventing Democrats*, 43.

25. Germond and Witcover, *Wake Us When It's Over*, 175–76.

26. Witcover, *Party of the People*, 643.

27. Greenberg, *Middle Class Dreams*, 204.

28. Ibid., 205; B. Clinton, *My Life*, 357.

29. B. Clinton, "New Covenant."

30. Baer, *Reinventing Democrats*, 81; Broder, "Hill Liberals Launch Democratic Coalition," *Washington Post*, 14 May 1990; Diemer, *Fighting the Unbeatable Foe*, 199.

31. Romano, *Clinton and Blair*, 2; Schafer, *State of American Politics*, 32.

32. Klein, *Natural*, 45.

33. Woodward, *Agenda*, 165.

34. Gergen, "Interview."

35. Baer, *Reinventing Democrats*, 242.

36. DeYoung, *Soldier*, 281.

37. Branch, *Clinton Tapes*, 222–23.

38. Democratic Party Platform of 1996.

39. Berman, *From the Center to the Edge*, 109, 78; Kennedy, *True Compass*, 458–59. Presumably Kennedy would have found hollow Clinton's claim that "Bobby Kennedy became the first New Democrat, before Jimmy Carter, before the Democratic Leadership Council . . . and before my campaign in 1992." B. Clinton, *My Life*, 122.

40. Blumenthal, *Clinton Wars*, 308; Berman, *From the Center to the Edge,* 107.

41. H. R. Clinton, *Living History*, 21, 23.

42. Ibid., 36. One of Hillary's Wellesley classmates later remembered her as "never truly left" but rather "very much a moderate, very much a facilitator." Bernstein, *Woman in Charge*, 104.

43. H. R. Clinton, *Living History*, 369, 367.

44. Ibid., 424.

45. "Obama to Have Name Removed."

46. Horowitz, "Barack Obama"; Reed, "Yes He Is."

47. Obama, *Audacity of Hope*, 8–9, 24, 158.

48. Tanenhaus, *Death of Conservatism*, 4.

49. Farber, *Rise and Fall of Modern American Conservatism*, 256; Carville, *40 More Years*; Balz and Johnson, "Political Odyssey," *Washington Post*, 2 August 2009; Obama, *Audacity of Hope*, 156–57, 10, 11, 256. On Obama's pragmatic political education, see Kloppenberg, *Reading Obama*.

50. Hedges, "Obama Deception." Other studies critical of Obama's centrism include Paul Street's *The Empire's New Clothes: Barack Obama in the Real World of Power*, Tariq Ali's *The Obama Syndrome: Surrender at Home, War Abroad*, and Jeffrey St. Clair and Joshua Frank's *Hopeless: Barack Obama and the Politics of Illusion*.

Conclusion

1. *Danvers (Mass.) North Shore*, 13 November 1977.

2. Goldberg, "Post-Census Party-Pooping."

3. "Ted Cruz Says"; Boyle, "Rand Paul at 38,000 Feet."

4. Falcone, "Colin Powell Slams 'Idiot Presentations.'"

5. Knupfer, *Union as It Is*, 56.

6. Kabaservice, *Rule and Ruin*, 398.

Bibliography

Archival Sources

Boston, Mass.
    Henry Adams Papers, Massachusetts Historical Society
    Henry Cabot Lodge Papers, Massachusetts Historical Society
    Henry Cabot Lodge Jr. Papers, Massachusetts Historical Society
College Station, Tex.
    George Herbert Walker Bush Papers, The George Bush Presidential Library
        and Museum, Texas A&M University
    Prescott Bush Papers, The George Bush Presidential Library and Museum,
        Texas A&M University
Columbia, Mo.
    Basil Brewer Papers, State Historical Society of Missouri, Ellis Library,
        University of Missouri–Columbia
New York, N.Y.
    Reminiscences of Prescott Sheldon Bush, Columbia University Center for
        Oral History, Butler Library, Columbia University
Washington, D.C.
    William Howard Taft Papers, Library of Congress

Books, Articles, and Online Sources

Adams, Charles Francis, ed. *The Works of John Adams, Second President of the United States: With a Life of the Author.* 10 vols. Boston: Charles C. Little and James Brown, 1850–56.

——, ed. *Memoirs of John Quincy Adams: Comprising Portions of His Diary from 1795 to 1848.* 12 vols. Philadelphia: J. B. Lippincott and Company, 1874–77.

Adams, Charles Francis, Jr. *Charles Francis Adams, 1835–1915: An Autobiography.* Boston: Houghton Mifflin, 1916.

Adams, Henry, ed. *Documents Relating to New England Federalism, 1800–15.* Boston: Little, Brown, and Company, 1877.

——, ed. *The Writings of Albert Gallatin.* Vol. 2. Philadelphia: J. B. Lippincott and Company, 1879.

——. "The New York Gold Conspiracy." In *Historical Essays.* New York: Charles Scribner's Sons, 1891.

——. *The Life of George Cabot Lodge.* Boston: Houghton Mifflin, 1911.

———. *Democracy: An American Novel*. New York: Library of America, 1983.

———. *History of the United States of America during the Administrations of James Madison*. New York: Library of America, 1986.

———. *History of the United States of America during the Administrations of Thomas Jefferson*. New York: Library of America, 1986.

———. *Mont-Saint-Michel and Chartres*. New York: Penguin Books, 1986.

———. *The Education of Henry Adams*. New York: The Modern Library, 1999.

Adams, John, and William Cunningham. *Correspondence between the Hon. John Adams, Late President of the United States, and the late Wm. Cunningham, Esq.: Beginning in 1803 and Ending in 1812*. Boston: E. M. Cunningham, 1823.

Adams, John Quincy. *Argument of John Quincy Adams, before the Supreme Court of the United States, in the Case of the United States, Appellants, vs. Cinque, and Others, Africans, Captured in the Schooner Amistad, by Lieut. Gedney, Delivered on the 24th of February and 1st of March, 1841*. New York: S. W. Benedict, 1841.

———. *Parties in the United States*. New York: Greenberg, 1941.

———. "Inaugural Address." March 4, 1825. http://www.bartleby.com/124/pres22.html, January 8, 2015.

Ali, Tariq. *The Obama Syndrome: Surrender at Home, War Abroad*. London: Verso, 2010.

Alter, Jonathan. *The Center Holds: Obama and His Enemies*. New York: Simon and Schuster, 2013.

Ambrose, Stephen E. *The President*. Vol. 2 of *Eisenhower*. New York: Simon and Schuster, 1984.

Ammon, Harry. *James Monroe: The Quest for National Identity*. New York: McGraw-Hill, 1971.

Anderson, Judith Icke. *William Howard Taft: An Intimate History*. New York: W. W. Norton, 1981.

Anthony, Carl Sferrazza. *Nellie Taft: The Unconventional First Lady of the Ragtime Era*. New York: William Morrow, 2005.

Appleby, Joyce. *Capitalism and a New Social Order: The Republican Vision of the 1790s*. New York: New York University Press, 1984.

———. *Inheriting the Revolution: The First Generation of Americans*. Cambridge, Mass.: Harvard University Press, 2000.

Arrington, Benjamin F., ed. *Municipal History of Essex County in Massachusetts*. Vol. 1. New York: Lewis Historical Publishing Company, 1922.

Baer, Kenneth S. *Reinventing Democrats: The Politics of Liberalism from Reagan to Clinton*. Lawrence: University Press of Kansas, 2000.

Ball, Terence, ed., *Lincoln: Political Writings and Speeches*. New York: Cambridge University Press, 2013.

Banner, James M., Jr. *To the Hartford Convention: The Federalists and the Origins of Party Politics in Massachusetts, 1789–1815*. New York: Knopf, 1969.

Banning, Lance. *The Jeffersonian Persuasion: Evolution of a Party Ideology.*
 Ithaca: Cornell University Press, 1978.

Basler, Roy P., ed. *The Collected Works of Abraham Lincoln.* 9 vols. New
 Brunswick: Rutgers University Press, 1953–55.

Beard, Adrian. *The Language of Politics.* New York: Routledge, 2000.

Bell, Daniel. *The Cultural Contradictions of Capitalism.* New York: Basic Books,
 1996.

Bemis, Samuel Flagg. *John Quincy Adams and the Foundations of American
 Foreign Policy.* New York: Knopf, 1949.

Berman, William C. *From the Center to the Edge: The Politics and Policies of the
 Clinton Presidency.* Lanham.: Roman & Littlefield Publishers, 2001.

Bernstein, Carl. *A Woman in Charge: The Life of Hillary Rodham Clinton.* New
 York: Knopf, 2007.

Bisnow, Mark. *Diary of a Dark Horse: The 1980 Anderson Presidential Campaign.*
 Carbondale: Southern Illinois University Press, 1983.

Blake, Aaron. "Jeb Bush: GOP Needs to Stop Being the 'Anti' Party." *Washington
 Post,* 15 March 2013, http://www.washingtonpost.com/blogs/post-politics
 /wp/2013/03/15/jeb-bush-gop-needs-to-stop-being-the-anti-party/.
 5 January 2015.

Blumenthal, Sydney. *The Clinton Wars.* New York: Farrar, Straus and Giroux, 2003.

Booth, Robert. *Death of Empire: The Rise and Murderous Fall of Salem, America's
 Richest City.* New York: Thomas Dunne Books, 2011.

Boyle, Matthew. "Rand Paul at 38,000 Feet: GOP Needs Conservative, Not a
 Moderate as 2016 Nominee." *Breitbart News Network,* 30 January 2015,
 http://www.breitbart.com/big-government/2015/01/30/exclusive-rand-paul
 -at-38000-feet-gop-needs-conservative-not-a-moderate-as-2016-nominee/.
 7 February 2016.

Branch, Taylor. *The Clinton Tapes: Wrestling History with the President.* New
 York: Simon and Schuster, 2009.

Brands, H. W. *TR: The Last Romantic.* New York: Basic Books, 1997.

——, ed. *The Selected Letters of Theodore Roosevelt.* New York: Cooper Square
 Press, 2001.

Brick, Howard. *Age of Contradiction: American Thought and Culture in the
 1960s.* New York: Twayne Publishers, 1998.

Brinkley, Alan. "The Problem of American Conservatism." *American Historical
 Review* 99 (April 1994): 409–29.

——. *Liberalism and Its Discontents.* Cambridge, Mass.: Harvard University
 Press, 1998.

Bruce, William Cabell. *John Randolph of Roanoke, 1773–1833.* Vol. 1. New York:
 G. P. Putnam's Sons, 1922.

Buchanan, Pat. "Speech to the 1992 Republican National Convention."
 17 August 1992, http://livefromthetrail.com/about-the-book/speeches
 /chapter-19/pat-buchanan. 3 February 2015.

——. *Where the Right Went Wrong: How Neoconservatives Subverted the Reagan Revolution and Hijacked the Bush Presidency.* New York: Thomas Dunne Books, 2004.

Burner, David. *The Politics of Provincialism: The Democratic Party in Transition, 1918–1932.* New York: Knopf, 1968.

"Bush: 'God Told Me to End the Tyranny in Iraq." 7 October 2005, http://www .theguardian.com/world/2005/oct/07/iraq.usa. 3 February 2015.

Bush, George. *All the Best: My Life in Letters and Other Writings.* New York: Scribner, 1999.

——. *Heartbeat: George Bush in His Own Words.* New York: Scribner, 2002.

Bush, George W. *A Charge to Keep: My Journey to the White House.* New York: Perennial, 2001.

Bush, George, and Brent Scowcroft. *A World Transformed: The Collapse of the Soviet Empire, the Unification of Germany, Tiananmen Square, the Gulf War.* New York: Knopf, 1998.

Butler, Leslie. *Critical Americans: Victorian Intellectuals and Transatlantic Liberal Reform.* Chapel Hill: University of North Carolina Press, 2007.

Butt, Archibald. *Taft and Roosevelt: The Intimate Letters of Archie Butt.* Vol. 2. Garden City, N.Y.: Doubleday, Doran & Company, 1930.

Butterfield, L. H., ed. *Diary and Autobiography of John Adams.* 4 vols. Cambridge, Mass.: Harvard University Press, 1961.

——, ed. *Adams Family Correspondence.* Vol. 1. Cambridge, Mass.: Harvard University Press, 1963.

Cain, Herman. "Compassionate Conservatism Lost." *Human Events*, 13 November 2006, http://humanevents.com/2006/11/13/compassionate -conservatism-lost/. 3 February 2015.

Campbell, Colin, and Bert A. Rockman, eds. *The Clinton Legacy.* Chatham, U.K.: Chatham House, 2000.

Cannon, Lou. *Governor Reagan: His Rise to Power.* New York: PublicAffairs, 2003.

Cappon, Lester J., ed. *The Adams-Jefferson Letters: The Complete Correspondence between Thomas Jefferson and Abigail and John Adams.* Chapel Hill: University of North Carolina Press, 1987.

Carter, Jimmy. "The State of the Union Address," 19 January 1978, http://www .presidency.ucsb.edu/ws/index.php?pid=30856axzz106RVq7pf. 5 February 2015.

——. "Anti-Inflation Speech," 24 October 1978, http://www.pbs.org/wgbh /americanexperience/features/primary-resources/carter-anti-inflation/. 5 February 2015.

——. "Crisis of Confidence Speech," 15 July 1979, http://www.pbs.org/wgbh /americanexperience/features/primary-resources/carter-crisis/. 5 February 2015.

——. *Keeping Faith: Memoirs of a President.* New York: Bantam Books, 1982.

———. *Turning Point: A Candidate, a State, and a Nation Come of Age.* New York: Times Books, 1992.

Carville, James. *40 More Years: How the Democrats Will Rule the Next Generation.* New York: Simon and Schuster, 2009.

Chace, James. *1912: Wilson, Roosevelt, Taft & Debs; The Election That Changed the Country.* New York: Simon and Schuster, 2004.

Chernow, Ron. *Titan: The Life of John D. Rockefeller Sr.* New York: Random House, 1998.

Chessman, G. Wallace. *Theodore Roosevelt and the Politics of Power.* Boston: Little, Brown, 1969.

Clarfield, Gerard H. *Timothy Pickering and the American Republic.* Pittsburgh: University of Pittsburgh Press, 1980.

Clay, Henry. "His Attack on Jackson." http://www.bartleby.com/268/9/6.html. 9 January 2015.

Clinton, Bill. "The New Covenant," 23 October 1991, http://www.ibiblio.org /pub/academic/political-science/speeches/clinton.dir/c57.txtp, 5 February 2015.

———. *My Life.* New York: Knopf, 2004.

Clinton, Hillary Rodham. *Living History.* New York: Simon and Schuster, 2003.

Cohen, Lizabeth. *A Consumers' Republic: The Politics of Mass Consumption in Postwar America.* New York: Vintage Books, 2003.

Coletta, Paolo E. *The Presidency of William Howard Taft.* Lawrence: University Press of Kansas, 1973.

Cook, James F. *The Governors of Georgia, 1754–2004.* Macon, Ga.: Mercer University Press, 2005.

Cook, Richard M., ed. *Alfred Kazin's Journals.* New Haven: Yale University Press, 2011.

Cooper, John Milton, Jr. *The Warrior and the Priest: Woodrow Wilson and Theodore Roosevelt.* Cambridge, Mass.: Harvard University Press, 1983.

Cory, Daniel, ed. *The Letters of George Santayana.* New York: Charles Scribner's Sons, 1955.

Crowley, John W. *George Cabot Lodge.* Boston: Twayne Publishers, 1976.

Cruz, Ted. "Address to South Carolina Tea Party Convention." 18 January 2015, https://www.youtube.com/watch?v=sONGWZjIf9s. 11 December 2015.

Currie, David P. *The Constitution in Congress: Democrats and Whigs, 1829–1861.* Chicago: University of Chicago Press, 2005.

Dallek, Robert. *An Unfinished Life: John F. Kennedy, 1917–1963.* Boston: Little, Brown, and Company, 2003.

Dalton, Kathleen. *Theodore Roosevelt: A Strenuous Life.* New York: Knopf, 2002.

Darling, Arthur B. *Political Changes in Massachusetts, 1824–1848: A Study of Liberal Movements in Politics.* New Haven: Yale University Press, 1925.

Davis, David Brion. *The Problem of Slavery in the Age of Revolution, 1770–1823.* Ithaca: Cornell University Press, 1975.

Dawidoff, Robert. *The Education of John Randolph.* New York: W. W. Norton, 1979.

Democratic Party Platform of 1996, 26 August 1996, http://www.presidency .ucsb.edu/ws/?pid=29611. 7 August 2015.

DeYoung, Karen. *Soldier: The Life of Colin Powell.* New York: Knopf, 2006.

Diemer, Tom. *Fighting the Unbeatable Foe: Howard Metzenbaum of Ohio, the Washington Years.* Kent, Ohio: Kent State University Press, 2008.

Diggins, John Patrick. *John Adams.* New York: Henry Holt and Company, 2003.

——, ed., *The Portable John Adams.* New York: Penguin Books, 2004.

Donald, David Herbert. *Lincoln Reconsidered: Essays on the Civil War Era.* New York: Knopf, 1956.

——. *Lincoln.* New York: Simon and Schuster, 1995.

Douglass, John Aubrey. "The Carnegie Commission and Council of Higher Education: A Retrospective." Research and Occasional Paper Series, Center for Studies in Higher Education, Berkeley, Calif., 2005.

Douthat, Ross. "George W. Bush in Hindsight." *New York Times, Opinionator,* 25 April 2013, http://douthat.blogs.nytimes.com/2013/04/25/george-w-bush -in-hindsight/?_r=0. 3 August 2015.

Downey, Matthew T. "Horace Greeley and the Politicians: The Liberal Republican Convention in 1872." *Journal of American History* 53 (March 1967): 727–50.

Draper, Robert. *Dead Certain: The Presidency of George W. Bush.* New York: Free Press, 2007.

Duberman, Martin B. *Charles Francis Adams, 1807–1886.* Boston: Houghton Mifflin, 1961.

Dunkley, Gabrielle. "Noam Chomsky: Obama Would Have Been a 'Moderate Republican' Several Decades Ago." *Huffington Post,* 1 February 2013, http://www.huffingtonpost.com/2013/02/01/noam-chomsky-obama_n _2599622.html. 5 January 2015.

Earle, Jonathan H. *Jacksonian Antislavery and the Politics of Free Soil, 1824–1854.* Chapel Hill: University of North Carolina Press, 2004.

Eisenhower, Dwight D. *Mandate for Change, 1953–1956: The White House Years.* New York: Doubleday, 1963.

Elkins, Stanley, and Eric McKitrick. *The Age of Federalism: The Early American Republic, 1788–1800.* New York: Oxford University Press, 1993.

Ellis, Joseph J. *Passionate Sage: The Character of and Legacy of John Adams.* New York: W. W. Norton, 1993.

——. *American Sphinx: The Character of Thomas Jefferson.* New York: Knopf, 1997.

Falcone, Michael. "Colin Powell Slams 'Idiot Presentations' by Some Republicans, Urges GOP Leaders to 'Speak Out.'" ABC News, 21 January 2013, http://abcnews.go.com/blogs/politics/2013/01/colin-powell-slams-idiot

-presentations-by-some-republicans-urges-gop-leaders-to-speak-out-2/. 7 February 2015.

"Falwell Apologizes to Gays, Feminists, Lesbians." CNN.com, 14 September 2001, http://www.cnn.com/2001/US/09/14/Falwell.apology/. 2 February 2015.

Farber, David. *The Rise and Fall of Modern American Conservatism: A Short History*. Princeton: Princeton University Press, 2010.

Fehrenbacher, Don E. *The Slaveholding Republic: An Account of the United States Government's Relations to Slavery*. Completed and edited by Ward M. McAfee. New York: Oxford University Press, 2001.

Ferguson, Robert A. *The American Enlightenment, 1750–1820*. Cambridge, Mass.: Harvard University Press, 1994.

Ferrell, Robert H., ed. *The Eisenhower Diaries*. New York: W. W. Norton, 1981.

Fink, Gary, and Hugh Davis Graham, eds. *The Carter Presidency: Policy Choices in the Post–New Deal Era*. Lawrence: University Press of Kansas, 1998.

Fischer, David Hackett. *The Revolution of American Conservatism: The Federalist Party in the Era of Jeffersonian Democracy*. New York: Harper and Row, 1965.

Foner, Eric. *Reconstruction: America's Unfinished Revolution, 1863–1877*. New York: Harper and Row, 1988.

———. *Tom Paine and Revolutionary America*. New York: Oxford University Press, 2005.

———, ed. *Our Lincoln: New Perspectives on Lincoln and His World*. New York: W. W. Norton, 2008.

———. *The Fiery Trial: Abraham Lincoln and American Slavery*. New York: W. W. Norton, 2010.

Ford, Worthington Chauncey, ed. *Writings of John Quincy Adams*. Vol. 3. New York: Macmillan, 1914.

———, ed. *A Cycle of Adams Letters, 1861–1865*. Vol. 2. Boston: Houghton Mifflin, 1920.

Foucault, Michel. *Madness and Civilization: A History of Insanity in the Age of Reason*. New York: Vintage, 1988.

Fox-Genovese, Elizabeth, and Eugene D. Genovese. *The Mind of the Master Class: History and Faith in the Southern Slaveholder's Worldview*. Cambridge: Cambridge University Press, 2005.

Franklin, Benjamin. *The Autobiography of Benjamin Franklin*. New Haven: Yale University Press, 2003.

Freedman, Max, ed., *Roosevelt and Frankfurter: Their Correspondence, 1928–1945*. Boston: Little, Brown, 1967.

Freeman, Joanne B. *Affairs of Honor: National Politics in the New Republic*. New Haven: Yale University Press, 2001.

Garraty, John A. *Henry Cabot Lodge: A Biography*. New York: Knopf, 1953.

Genovese, Eugene D. *The Southern Tradition: The Achievement and Limitations of an American Conservatism*. Cambridge, Mass.: Harvard University Press, 1994.

"George Bush Is President." Duty Is Ours, Results Are God's, http://dutyisours
.com/gwbush.htm. 2 February 2015.

Gergen, David. "Interview." *Frontline*, June 2000, http://www.pbs.org/wgbh
/pages/frontline/shows/clinton/interviews/gergen.html. 5 February 2015.

Germond, Jack W., and Jules Witcover. *Blue Smoke and Mirrors: How Reagan
Won and Why Carter Lost the Election of 1980*. New York: Viking, 1981.

———. *Wake Us When It's Over: Presidential Politics of 1984*. New York:
Macmillan, 1985.

———. *Whose Broad Stripes and Bright Stars? The Trivial Pursuit of the
Presidency, 1988*. New York: Warner Books, 1989.

———. *Mad as Hell: Revolt at the Ballot Box, 1992*. New York: Warner Books, 1993.

Giddens, Anthony. *Beyond Left and Right: The Future of Radical Politics*. Palo
Alto, Calif.: Stanford University Press, 1994.

Gillon, Steven M. *The Democrats' Dilemma: Walter F. Mondale and the Liberal
Legacy*. New York: Columbia University Press, 1992.

Gitlin, Todd. *The Sixties: Years of Hope, Days of Rage*. New York: Bantam Books,
1987.

Goldberg, Jeffrey. "Breaking Ranks." *New Yorker*, 31 October 2005, http://www
.newyorker.com/magazine/2005/10/31/breaking-ranks. 3 February 2015.

Goldberg, Jonah. "Post-Census Party-Pooping." *National Review Online*,
24 December 2010, http://www.nationalreview.com/articles/255923/post
-census-party-pooping-jonah-goldberg. 7 February 2015.

Goodrich, Samuel G. *Recollections of a Lifetime or Men and Things I have Seen:
In a Series of Familiar Letters to a Friend*. Vol. 2. New York: Miller, Orton, and
Mulligan, 1857.

Gould, Lewis L. *The William Howard Taft Presidency*. Lawrence: University
Press of Kansas, 2009.

———. *The Presidency of Theodore Roosevelt*. Lawrence: University Press of
Kansas, 2011.

Grant, James. *John Adams: Party of One*. New York: Farrar, Straus and Giroux,
2005.

Greenberg, Amy S. *A Wicked War: Polk, Clay, Lincoln, and the 1846 U.S. Invasion
of Mexico*. New York: Knopf, 2012.

Greenberg, Stanley B. *Middle Class Dreams: The Politics and Power of the New
American Majority*. New York: Times Books, 1995.

Gross, John, ed. *The Oxford Book of Essays*. New York: Oxford University Press,
1991.

Hamby, Alonzo L. *Liberalism and Its Challengers: From F.D.R. to Reagan*. New
York: Oxford University Press, 1985.

Hamilton, Stanislaus Murray, ed. *The Writings of James Monroe*. Vol. 7. New
York: G. P. Putnam's Sons, 1903.

Haraszti, Zoltán. *John Adams and the Prophets of Progress*. Cambridge, Mass.:
Harvard University Press, 1952.

Harrington, James. *The Commonwealth of Oceana and a System of Politics.*
J. G. A. Pocock, ed. 1656. Reprint, Cambridge: Cambridge University Press,
1992.

Harz, Walter. "Alphonso Taft." 27 January 2007, http://uudb.org/articles
/alphonsotaft.html. 23 January 2015.

Hawley, Joshua. *Theodore Roosevelt: Preacher of Righteousness.* New Haven:
Yale University Press, 2008.

Hechler, Kenneth W. *Insurgency: Personalities and Politics of the Taft Era.* New
York: Russell and Russell, 1964.

Hedges, Chris. "The Obama Deception: Why Cornel West Went Ballistic." *Truth
Dig,* 16 May 2011, http://www.truthdig.com/report/print/the_obama
_deception_why_cornel_west_went_ballistic_20110516. 5 February 2015.

Heilemann, John, and Mark Halperin. *Game Change: Obama and the Clintons,
McCain and Palin, and the Race of a Lifetime.* New York: Harper, 2010.

Herskowitz, Mickey. *Duty, Honor, Country: The Life and Legacy of Prescott Bush.*
Nashville, Tenn.: Rutledge Hill Press, 2003.

Hertzberg, Rick. "Exit Interview of Rick Hertzberg." Jimmy Carter Library,
10 December 1980, http://www.jimmycarterlibrary.gov/library/exitInt
/Hertzberg.pdf. 5 February 2015.

Hochfield, George, ed. *The Great Secession Winter of 1860-61 and Other Essays.*
New York: Sagamore Press, 1958.

Hofstadter, Richard. *The American Political Tradition and the Men Who Made It.*
New York: Knopf, 1948.

——. *The Idea of a Party System: The Rise of Legitimate Opposition in the United
States, 1780–1840.* Berkeley: University of California Press, 1969.

Hofstadter, Richard, and Beatrice K. Hofstadter. *Great Issues in American
History: From Reconstruction to the Present Day, 1864–1981.* New York:
Vintage Books, 1982.

Hogan, Margaret A., and C. James Taylor, eds. *My Dearest Friend: Letters of
Abigail and John Adams.* Cambridge, Mass.: Harvard University Press, 2007.

Holt, Michael F. *Political Parties and American Political Development: From the
Age of Jackson to the Age of Lincoln.* Baton Rouge: Louisiana State University
Press, 1992.

——. *The Rise and Fall of the American Whig Party: Jacksonian Politics and the
Onset of the Civil War.* New York: Oxford University Press, 1999.

——. *By One Vote: The Disputed Presidential Election of 1876.* Lawrence:
University Press of Kansas, 2008.

Hoover, Herbert. *Addresses upon the American Road.* New York: Charles
Scribner's Sons, 1938.

Hopkins, James F., and Melba Porter Hay, eds. *The Papers of Henry Clay.* 10
vols. Lexington: University of Kentucky Press, 1959–92.

Horowitz, Daniel. *The Anxieties of Affluence: Critiques of American Consumer
Culture, 1939–1979.* Amherst: University of Massachusetts Press, 2004.

Horowitz, Jason. "Barack Obama, D.L.C. Clintonite?" *Observer*, 4 March 2008, http://observer.com/2008/03/barack-obama-dlc-clintonite/. 5 February 2015.

Howe, Daniel Walker. *The Political Culture of the American Whigs*. Chicago: University of Chicago Press, 1979

———. *What Hath God Wrought: The Transformation of America, 1815–1848*. New York: Oxford University Press, 2007.

Hunt, Gaillard, ed. *The Writings of James Madison*. Vol. 8. New York: G. P. Putnam's Sons, 1908.

Isenberg, Nancy. *Fallen Founder: The Life of Aaron Burr*. New York: Penguin Books, 2007.

"Jeb Bush: No Place for Father, Reagan in Today's GOP." BuzzFeed, 11 June 2012, http://www.buzzfeed.com/buzzfeedpolitics/jeb-bush-no-place-for-father -reagan-in-today39.icREYGlWg. 5 January 2015.

Julian, George W. *Political Recollections, 1840–1872*. Chicago: Jansen McClurg, 1884.

Kabaservice, Geoffrey. *Rule and Ruin: The Downfall of Moderation and the Destruction of the Republican Party, from Eisenhower to the Tea Party*. New York: Oxford University Press, 2012.

Kaufman, Burton I. *The Presidency of James Earl Carter, Jr.* Lawrence: University Press of Kansas, 1993.

Kazin, Michael. "From Hubris to Despair: George W. Bush and the Conservative Movement." In *The Presidency of George W. Bush: A First Historical Assessment*, edited by Julian E. Zelizer, 282–302. Princeton: Princeton University Press, 2010.

Kennedy, Edward M. *True Compass: A Memoir*. New York: Twelve, 2009.

Kirk, Russell. *John Randolph of Roanoke: A Study in American Politics, with Selected Speeches and Letters*. Chicago: Henry Regnery Company, 1964.

Klein, Ezra. "Obama Revealed: A Moderate Republican." *Washington Post*, 25 April 2011, http://www.washingtonpost.com/business/economy/obama -revealed-a-moderate-republican/2011/04/25/AFPrGfkE_story.html. 5 January 2015.

Klein, Joe. *The Natural: The Misunderstood Presidency of Bill Clinton*. New York: Doubleday, 2002.

Kloppenberg, James T. *Reading Obama: Dreams, Hope, and the American Political Tradition*. Princeton: Princeton University Press, 2010.

Knupfer, Peter B. *The Union As It Is: Constitutional Unionism and Sectional Compromise, 1787–1861*. Chapel Hill: University of North Carolina Press, 1991.

Koch, Adrienne, and William Peden, eds. *The Selected Writings of John and John Quincy Adams*. New York: Knopf, 1946.

Kohl, Lawrence Frederick. *The Politics of Individualism: Parties and the American Character in the Jacksonian Era*. New York: Oxford University Press, 1989.

Kraus, Michael, and Davis D. Joyce. *The Writing of American History*. Norman: University of Oklahoma Press, 1985.

La Follette, Robert M. *La Follette's Autobiography: A Personal Narrative of Political Experiences*. Madison: University of Wisconsin Press, 1960.

LaFeber, Walter, ed. *John Quincy Adams and American Continental Empire*. Chicago: Quadrangle Books, 1965.

Lears, T. J. Jackson. *No Place of Grace: Antimodernism and the Transformation of American Culture, 1880–1920*. Chicago: University of Chicago Press, 1981.

Lengell, Sean. "Cheney: Limbaugh More Loyal than Powell." *Washington Times*, 11 May 2011, http://www.washingtontimes.com/news/2009/may/11/cheney -limbaugh-more-loyal-than-powell. 5 January 2015.

Leonard, Lewis Alexander. *Life of Alphonso Taft*. New York: Hawke Publishing, 1920.

Leuchtenburg, William E. *Franklin D. Roosevelt and the New Deal, 1932–1940*. New York: Harper and Row, 1963.

——. *In the Shadow of FDR: From Harry Truman to Ronald Reagan*. Ithaca: Cornell University Press, 1983.

——. *The FDR Years: On Roosevelt and His Legacy*. New York: Columbia University Press, 1995.

——. "Jimmy Carter and the Post–New Deal Presidency." In *The Carter Presidency*, edited by Gary Fink and Hugh Davis Graham, 7–28. Lawrence: University Press of Kansas, 1998.

Levenson, J. C., et al., eds. *The Letters of Henry Adams*. 6 vols. Cambridge, Mass.: Harvard University Press, 1982–88.

Levy, Leonard W. *Jefferson and Civil Liberties: The Darker Side*. Cambridge, Mass.: Harvard University Press, 1963.

Lincoln, Abraham. "First Political Announcement." 9 March 1932, http://www .abrahamlincolnonline.org/lincoln/speeches/1832.htm. 9 January 2015.

——. "Letter to Henry L. Pierce and Others." 6 April, 1859, http://www .abrahamlincolnonline.org/lincoln/speeches/pierce.htm. 9 January 2015.

——. "Letter to Owen Lovejoy." 11 August 1855, http://quod.lib.umich.edu/l /lincoln/lincoln2/1:334.1?rgn=div2;view=fulltext. 9 January 2015.

——. "Temperance Address." 22 February 1842, http://www .abrahamlincolnonline.org/lincoln/speeches/temperance.htm. 9 January 2015.

Lipsky, George A. *John Quincy Adams: His Theory and Ideas*. New York: Thomas Y. Crowell, 1950.

Lodge, Henry Cabot, ed. *Life and Letters of George Cabot*. Boston: Little, Brown and Company, 1878.

——. *Early Memories*. New York: Charles Scribner's Sons, 1913.

——. *Henry Cabot Lodge: Memorial Addresses Delivered in the Senate and House of Representatives*. Washington, D.C.: Government Printing Office, 1925.

Lodge, Henry Cabot, Jr. "Military Aid to Western Europe." *Vital Speeches of the Day*, New York: The City News Publishing Company, March 1949.

———. *The Storm Has Many Eyes: A Personal Narrative*. New York: W. W. Norton, 1973.

———. *As It Was: An Inside View of Politics and Power in the '50s and '60s*. New York: W. W. Norton, 1976.

Lovejoy, Joseph C., and Owen Lovejoy. *Memoir of the Reverend Elijah P. Lovejoy: Who was Murdered in Defence of the Liberty of the Press, at Alton, Illinois, November 7, 1837*. New York: John S. Taylor, 1838.

Lunt, William P. *A Discourse Delivered in Quincy, March 11, 1848, at the Internment of John Quincy Adams, Sixth President of the United States*. Boston: Charles C. Little and James Brown, 1848.

Lyman, Rick. "Bush Blends Optimism and Challenge in Texas Inaugural." *New York Times*, 20 January 1999, http://www.nytimes.com/1999/01/20/us/bush -blends-optimism-and-challenge-in-texas-inaugural.html. 12 August 2015.

Madison, James. "War Message to Congress." June 1812, http://www.presidential rhetoric.com/historicspeeches/madison/warmessage.html. 7 January 2015.

Malone, Dumas. *Jefferson and His Time*. 6 vols. Boston: Little, Brown and Company, 1948–81.

Martin, William. *With God on Our Side: The Rise of the Religious Right in America*. New York: Broadway Books, 2005.

Mason, Jim. *No Holding Back: The 1980 John B. Anderson Presidential Campaign*. Lanham: University Press of America, 2011.

Mattson, Kevin. *"What the Heck Are You Up to Mr. President?" Jimmy Carter, America's "Malaise," and the Speech That Should Have Changed the Country*. New York: Bloomsbury, 2009.

Mayo, Bernard, ed. *Jefferson Himself: The Personal Narrative of a Many-Sided American*. Charlottesville: University Press of Virginia, 1942.

McCullough, David. *John Adams*. New York: Simon and Schuster, 2001.

McDonald, Forrest. *The Presidency of Thomas Jefferson*. Lawrence: University Press of Kansas, 1976.

———. *Alexander Hamilton: A Biography*. New York: W. W. Norton, 1979.

McDonald, William, ed. *Select Documents: Illustrative History of the United States, 1776–1861*. New York: Macmillan, 1901.

McGirr, Lisa. *Suburban Warriors: The Origins of the New American Right*. Princeton: Princeton University Press, 2001.

McGovern, George. *Grassroots: The Autobiography of George McGovern*. New York: Random House, 1977.

McGrath, Jim, ed. *Heartbeat: George Bush, in His Own Words*. New York: Scribner, 2001.

McKitrick, Eric L., ed. *Slavery Defended: The Views of the Old South*. Englewood Cliffs: Prentice-Hall, 1963.

Melton, Buckner F., Jr. *Aaron Burr: Conspiracy to Treason*. New York: Wiley, 2002.

Menand, Louis. *The Metaphysical Club: A Story of Ideas in America*. New York: Farrar, Straus and Giroux, 2001.

Meyerson, Harold. "The Ghost of Democratic Agenda." *American Prospect*, 13 February 2009, http://prospect.org/article/ghost-democratic-agenda. 5 February 2015.

Micklethwait, John, and Adrian Wooldridge. *The Right Nation: Conservative Power in America*. New York: Penguin Press, 2004.

Milkis, Sidney M. *Theodore Roosevelt, the Progressive Party, and the Transformation of American Democracy*. Lawrence: University Press of Kansas, 2009.

Miller, John C. *The Federalist Era, 1789–1801*. New York: Harper and Row, 1960.

Miller, William J. *Henry Cabot Lodge*. New York: Heinemann, 1967.

Miller, William Lee. *Arguing about Slavery: The Great Battle in the United States Congress*. New York, Knopf, 1996.

Minutaglio, Bill. *First Son: George W. Bush and the Bush Family Dynasty*. New York: Times Books, 1999.

Miroff, Bruce. *The Liberals' Moment: The McGovern Insurgency and the Identity Crisis of the Democratic Party*. Lawrence: University Press of Kansas, 2007.

Mitchell, Elizabeth. *W: Revenge of the Bush Dynasty*. New York: Hyperion, 2000.

Morison, Elting E. ed. *The Letters of Theodore Roosevelt*. 8 vols. Cambridge, Mass.: Harvard University Press, 1951–54.

Morris, Edmund. *The Rise of Theodore Roosevelt*. New York: Coward, McCann, and Geoghegan, 1979.

Morris, Richard B. *The Forging of the Union, 1781–1789*. New York: Harper and Row, 1987.

Murray, Robert. K. *The 103rd Ballot: Democrats and the Disaster in Madison Square Garden*. New York: Harper and Row, 1976.

Nagel, Paul C. *Descent from Glory: Four Generations of the John Adams Family*. New York: Oxford University Press, 1983.

———. *John Quincy Adams: A Public Life, a Private Life*. New York: Knopf, 1997.

Nevins, Allan, ed. *The Diary of John Quincy Adams, 1794–1845: American Diplomacy, and Political, Social, and Intellectual Life from Washington to Polk*. New York: F. Ungar Publishing, 1969.

Niebuhr, Reinhold. *Moral Man and Immoral Society: A Study in Ethics and Politics*. Louisville: Westminster John Knox Press, 2001.

Niven, John. *John C. Calhoun and the Price of Union: A Biography*. Baton Rouge: Louisiana State University Press, 1988.

Obama, Barack. *The Audacity of Hope: Thoughts on Reclaiming the American Dream*. New York: Crown Publishers, 2006.

"Obama to Have Name Removed from DLC List." *Black Commentator*, 19 June 2003, http://www.blackcommentator.com/48/48_cover_pr.html. 5 February 2015.

Paine, Thomas. *Common Sense and other Writings*. Edited by J. M. Opal. New York: W. W. Norton, 2011.

Parmet, Herbert S. *George Bush: The Life of a Lone Star Yankee*. New York: Scribner, 1997.

Parrington, Vernon P. *The Colonial Mind*. Vol. 1 of *Main Currents in American Thought*. New York: Harcourt, Brace & World, 1927.

Patterson, James T. *Mr. Republican: A Biography of Robert A. Taft*. Boston: Houghton Mifflin, 1972.

Perlstein, Rick. *Before the Storm: Barry Goldwater and the Unmaking of the American Consensus*. New York: Hill and Wang, 2001.

———. *Nixonland: The Rise of a President and the Fracturing of America*. New York: Scribner, 2008.

———. *The Invisible Bridge: The Fall of Nixon and the Rise of Reagan*. New York: Simon and Schuster, 2014.

Peterson, Merrill D. *Thomas Jefferson and the New Nation: A Biography*. New York: Oxford University Press, 1970.

———, ed. *The Portable Thomas Jefferson*. New York: Penguin Press, 1975.

Phillips, Kevin. *American Dynasty: Aristocracy, Fortune, and the Politics of Deceit in the House of Bush*. New York: Viking, 2004.

Phillips-Fein, Kim. *Invisible Hands: The Making of the Conservative Movement from the New Deal to Reagan*. New York: W. W. Norton, 2009.

———. "Conservatism: A State of the Field." *Journal of American History* 98 (December 2011): 723–43.

Pinchot, Gifford. *Breaking New Ground*. Washington, D.C.: Island Press, 1998.

Plumb, J. H. *The Origins of Political Stability: England, 1675–1725*. Boston: Houghton Mifflin, 1967.

Postel, Charles. *The Populist Vision*. New York: Oxford University Press, 2007.

Potter, David. *The Impending Crisis, 1848–1861*. Completed and edited by Don E. Fehrenbacher. New York: Harper and Row, 1976.

Pringle, Henry. *The Life and Times of William Howard Taft: A Biography*. Vol. 1. New York: Farrar and Rinehart, 1939.

Rakove, Jack. *James Madison and the Creation of the American Republic*. New York: Harper Collins, 1990.

Randolph, Thomas Jefferson, ed. *Memoir, Correspondence, and Miscellanies from the Papers of Thomas Jefferson*. Vol. 4. Charlottesville, Va.: F. Carr and Company, 1829.

Reed, Bruce. "Yes He Is: Obama Calls Himself a New Democrat and Shows What It Means." *Slate*, 11 March 2009, http://www.slate.com/articles/news_and _politics/the_hasbeen/2009/03/yes_he_is.html. 5 February 2015.

Remini, Robert V. *Andrew Jackson and the Course of American Empire, 1767–1821.* New York: Harper and Row, 1977.

"Republican Platform of 1856." USHistory.org, http://www.ushistory.org/gop /convention_1856republicanplatform.htm. 9 January 2015.

Richardson, James D., ed. *A Compilation of the Messages and Papers of the Presidents, 1789–1897.* 10 vols. Washington, D.C.: Government Printing Office, 1896–99.

Riddle, A. G. *The Life of Benjamin F. Wade.* Cleveland: Williams Publishing, 1888.

Risjord, Norman K. *The Old Republicans: Southern Conservatism in the Age of Jefferson.* New York: Columbia University Press, 1965.

Robinson, Corinne Roosevelt. *My Brother Theodore Roosevelt.* New York: Charles Scribner's Sons, 1921.

Rodgers, Daniel T. *Age of Fracture.* Cambridge, Mass.: Harvard University Press, 2011.

Romano, Flavio. *Clinton and Blair: The Political Economy of the Third Way.* New York: Routledge, 2006.

Roosevelt, Franklin D. *The Continuing Struggle for Liberalism.* Vol. 7 of *The Public Papers and Addresses of Franklin D. Roosevelt.* New York: Macmillan, 1941.

Roosevelt, Theodore. "Right of the People to Rule." *Outlook: A Weekly Newspaper,* vol. C (January–April 1912). New York: Outlook Company, 1912.

——. *Theodore Roosevelt: An Autobiography.* New York: Da Capo, 1985.

Roosevelt, Theodore, and Henry Cabot Lodge. *Selections from the Correspondence of Theodore Roosevelt and Henry Cabot Lodge, 1884–1918.* Vol. 2. New York: Charles Scribner's Sons, 1925.

Ross, Earle Dudley. *The Liberal Republican Movement.* New York: Henry Holt and Company, 1919.

Ross, Ishbel. *An American Family: The Tafts, 1678–1964.* Cleveland: World Publishing, 1964.

Rovere, Richard H. "Taft: Is This the Best We've Got?" *Harper's Magazine,* April 1948, 289.

Rutland, Robert Allen. *The Presidency of James Madison.* Lawrence: University Press of Kansas, 1990.

Samuels, Ernest. *The Young Henry Adams.* Cambridge, Mass.: Harvard University Press, 1948.

——. *Henry Adams: The Middle Years.* Cambridge, Mass.: Harvard University Press, 1958.

——. *Henry Adams: The Major Phase.* Cambridge, Mass.: Harvard University Press, 1964.

Sandbrook, Dominic. *Mad as Hell: The Crisis of the 1870s and the Rise of the Populist Right.* New York: Knopf, 2011.

Schafer, Byron E., ed. *The State of American Politics*. New York: Roman & Littlefield Publishers, 2002.

Schlesinger, Arthur, Jr. *The Age of Jackson*. Boston: Little, Brown and Company, 1945.

Schriftgiesser, Karl. *The Amazing Roosevelt Family, 1613–1942*. New York: Wilfred Funk, 1942.

Schutz, John A., and Douglass Adair, eds. *The Spur of Fame: Dialogues of John Adams and Benjamin Rush, 1805–1813*. San Marino, Calif.: Huntington Library, 1966.

Sewell, Richard H. *Ballots for Freedom: Antislavery Politics in the United States, 1837–1860*. New York: Oxford University Press, 1976.

Shaw, Peter. *The Character of John Adams*. Chapel Hill: University of North Carolina Press, 1976.

Shogan, Robert. *Backlash: The Killing of the New Deal*. Chicago: Ivan R. Dee, 2006.

Silbey, Joel H. *Party over Section: The Rough and Ready Presidential Election of 1848*. Lawrence: University Press of Kansas, 2009.

Simpson, Brooks D. *The Political Education of Henry Adams*. Columbia: University of South Carolina Press, 1996.

Slaughter, Thomas P. *The Whiskey Rebellion: Frontier Epilogue to the American Revolution*. New York: Oxford University Press, 1986.

Smelser, Marshall. *The Democratic Republic, 1801–1815*. New York: Harper and Row, 1968.

Smith, Margaret Chase. *Declaration of Conscience*. Edited by William C. Lewis Jr. Garden City: Doubleday, 1972.

Smith, Richard Norton. *On His Own Terms: A Life of Nelson Rockefeller*. New York: Random House, 2014.

Solberg, Carl. *Hubert Humphrey: A Biography*. New York: W. W. Norton, 1984.

Sprout, John G. *"The Best Men": Liberal Reformers in the Gilded Age*. New York: Oxford University Press, 1968.

St. Clair, Jeffrey, and Joshua Frank, eds. *Hopeless: Barack Obama and the Politics of Illusion*. Oakland: AK Press, 2012.

Stampp, Kenneth M. *America in 1857: A Nation on the Brink*. New York: Oxford University Press, 1990.

Stanley, Timothy. *Kennedy vs. Carter: The 1980 Battle for the Democratic Party's Soul*. Lawrence: University Press of Kansas, 2010.

Stewart, James Brewer. *Holy Warriors: The Abolitionists and American Slavery*. New York: Hill and Wang, 1996.

"'The Story of Elwood Is the Story of America.'" *Life*, August 12, 1940, 36–44.

Street, Paul. *The Empire's New Clothes: Barack Obama in the Real World of Power*. Boulder: Paradigm Publishers, 2010.

Swain, James Barrett, ed. *The Life and Speeches of Henry Clay*. Vol. 2. New York: Greeley and McElrath, 1843.

Swanson, Ian. "Obama Says He'd Be Seen as Moderate Republican in 1980s." *The Hill,* 14 December 2012, http://thehill.com/policy/finance/272957 -obama-says-his-economic-policies-so-mainstream-hed-be-seen-as-moderate -republican-in-1980s. 5 January 2015.

Syrett, Harold C., ed. *The Papers of Alexander Hamilton.* Vol. 25. New York: Columbia University Press, 1977.

Tanenhaus, Sam. *The Death of Conservatism: A Movement and Its Consequences.* New York: Random House, 2009.

Taylor, Alan. *William Cooper's Town: Power and Persuasion on the Frontier of the Early American Republic.* New York: Knopf, 1995.

——. *The Civil War of 1812: American Citizens, British Subjects, Irish Rebels, and Indian Allies.* New York: Knopf, 2010.

"Ted Cruz Says 'Democrats Will Win Again' If GOP Picks Moderate Candidate in 2016." Fox News, FoxNews.com, 19 January 2015, http://www.foxnews.com /politics/2015/01/19/ted-cruz-says-democrats-will-win-again-if-gop-picks -moderate-candidate-in-2016/. 7 February 2015.

Torget, Andrew J., and Edward L. Ayers. *Two Communities in the Civil War.* New York: W. W. Norton, 2007.

Troy, Gil. *Leading from the Center: Why Moderates Make the Best Presidents.* New York: Basic Books, 2008.

Tully, Grace. *F.D.R.: My Boss.* New York: Charles Scribner's Sons, 1949.

Unger, Harlow Giles. *John Quincy Adams.* Boston: Da Capo Press, 2012.

Veblen, Thorstein. *The Theory of the Leisure Class.* New York: Penguin, 1967.

Waddan, Alex. *Clinton's Legacy? A New Democrat in Governance.* New York: Palgrave, 2002.

Wallace, Patricia Ward. *Politics of Conscience: A Biography of Margaret Chase Smith.* Westport, Conn.: Praeger, 1995.

Washington, H. A. ed. *The Writings of Thomas Jefferson.* Vol. 7. New York: J. C. Riker, 1855.

Watson, Harry L. *Liberty and Power: The Politics of Jacksonian America.* New York: Hill and Wang, 1990.

Weaver, Herbert, ed. *The Correspondence of James K. Polk.* Vol. 2. Nashville: Vanderbilt University Press, 1972.

Weisberger, Bernard A. *America Afire: Jefferson, Adams, and the First Contested Election.* New York: William Morrow and Company, 2000.

Whalen, Thomas J. *Kennedy versus Lodge: The 1952 Massachusetts Senate Race.* Boston: Northeastern University Press, 2000.

Wharton, Edith. "George Cabot Lodge." *Scribner's Magazine,* February 1910, 236–39.

——. *A Backward Glance.* New York: D. Appleton-Century, 1934.

Wheelan, Joseph. *Mr. Adams's Last Crusade: John Quincy Adams's Extraordinary Post-Presidential Life in Congress.* New York: PublicAffairs, 2008.

White, Theodore H. *The Making of the President, 1964.* New York: Atheneum Publishers, 1965.

Wicker, Tom. *George Herbert Walker Bush.* New York: Penguin, 2004.

Widenor, William C. *Henry Cabot Lodge and the Search for an American Foreign Policy.* Berkeley: University of California Press, 1980.

Wilentz, Sean. *Chants Democratic: New York City and the Rise of the American Working Class, 1788–1850.* New York: Oxford University Press, 1984.

———. *The Rise of American Democracy: Jefferson to Lincoln.* New York: W. W. Norton, 2005.

———. "Abraham Lincoln and Jacksonian Democracy." In *Our Lincoln: New Perspectives on Lincoln and His World,* edited by Eric Foner, 63. New York: W. W. Norton, 2008.

———. *The Age of Reagan: A History, 1974–2008.* New York: Harper, 2008.

Willkie, Wendell L. *One World.* New York: Simon and Schuster, 1943.

Wills, Garry. *"Negro President": Jefferson and the Slave Power.* Boston: Houghton Mifflin, 2003.

———. *Henry Adams and the Making of America.* Boston: Houghton Mifflin, 2005.

Wiltse, Charles M., and Harold D. Moser, eds. *The Papers of Daniel Webster.* Vol. 1. Hanover, N.H.: University Press of New England, 1974.

Wish, Harvey, ed., *Ante-bellum: Writings of George Fitzhugh and Hinton Rowan Helper on Slavery.* New York: Capricorn Books, 1960.

Witcover, Jules. *Party of the People: A History of the Democrats.* New York: Random House, 2003.

Wood, Gordon S. *The Radicalism of the American Revolution: How a Revolution Transformed a Monarchical Society into a Democratic One Unlike Any That Had Ever Existed.* New York: Knopf, 1992.

———. *Revolutionary Characters: What Made the Founders Different.* New York: Penguin Press, 2006.

———. *Empire of Liberty: A History of the Early Republic, 1789–1815.* New York: Oxford University Press, 2009.

Woodward, Bob. *The Agenda: Inside the Clinton White House.* New York: Simon and Schuster, 1994.

Wunderlin, Clarence E., Jr., ed. *The Papers of Robert A. Taft.* 4 vols. Kent, Ohio: Kent State University Press, 1997–2006.

Zall, Paul M., ed. *Jefferson on Jefferson*: Lexington: University Press of Kentucky, 2002.

Zelizer, Julian E. *Jimmy Carter.* New York: Times Books, 2010.

Index

Adams, John Quincy, 44, 50, 70–90, 115, 125, 129, 136; H. Adams view of, 127; American System and, 70–71, 81–82, 83, 85, 90, 92, 93; antislavery of, 72, 80–82, 84, 86–89, 91; background/childhood of, 15–17, 73; centrism of, 111; collapse and death of, 89; congressional career of, 70, 74, 80–82, 83–84, 89; diplomatic posts of, 72, 73, 74, 78–79; grandson Henry's appraisal of, 80–81; historians' reappraisal of, 71–72; Jacksonian false portrayal of, 90; moral outlook of, 84–85; political partisanship and, 74–75, 94; presidential election of, 79–80; presidential second-term defeat of, 71, 82, 83; temperament of, 73–74, 83

Adams, Samuel, 46

Adams family, 15–16, 26, 46, 151, 202; alcoholism and, 72–73, 116; late nineteenth-century politics and, 121; political decline of, 126; privilege and, 116

Adams National Historical Park, 26

Adams-Onis (Transcontinental) Treaty (1819), 79

Addams, Jane, 147–48

Adorno, Theodor, 30

Affirmative action, 237, 253, 259

African Americans, 72, 186, 197, 264; Carter policies and, 244; enslavement of (see Slavery); party affiliation of, 197, 217. See also Civil rights movement; Segregation

Age of Jackson, The (Schlesinger), 71

Age of Lincoln (1848–65), 110–11

Age of Reason. See Enlightenment

Age of Reform (1890–1940), 117–18

Age of Roosevelt (1932–68), 246

Agnew, Spiro, 219

Agrarianism, 5, 6, 24, 38, 48, 70, 97, 98; Jeffersonian Republicans and, 17, 92, 106–7. See also Farmers

Agribusiness, 238

Agricultural Adjustment Act (1933), 238–39

Agriculture. See Farmers

Airline deregulation, 241

Alabama, CSS, 135

Albany (N.Y.) Register, 55

Alcohol. See Prohibition

Aldrich, Nelson A., 151, 171

Alien and Sedition Acts (1798), 6, 35, 36, 38, 40

Alliance, Treaty of (1778), 35

America Aurora (Jeffersonian newspaper), 36

America First Committee, 176, 279 (n. 4)

American Anti-Slavery Society, 84

American Civil Liberties Union, 248–49

American colonies, 22, 56–57, 58

American Colonization Society, 84, 104

American Missionary Association, 84

American pragmatic tradition, 7. See also Moderates

American Revolution, 26, 28, 45, 46, 56–57, 73; French aid to, 35; Jay Treaty and, 49

American System, 81–82, 83, 85, 90, 92, 93, 98, 104; description of, 71; southern fears of, 98

Ames, Fisher, 45

Amistad case (1841), 87

Amity, Commerce, and Navigation Treaty (1794). See Jay Treaty

Anarchiad (heroic verse), 19

Anderson, John B., 221–23

Anticommunism, 178, 185, 193, 207–9, 256

Anti-Masons, 74, 161

5–6; customary agenda of, 207; deaths of modern founders of, 232; defeat in 1936 election of, 183; Democratic centrist tilt toward, 240, 255; dominance since 1980 of, 261 (*see also* Reagan Revolution); Federalist wing and, 45, 60, 61; future of, 232; Goldwater "ultra-conservative" campaign and, 8, 195, 197–98, 256; late antebellum rising middle class and, 91; New Right and, 257; Reagan and (*see* Reagan Revolution); Republicans and, 3, 132, 145, 146, 209, 222, 245, 249, 257, 265–66 (*see also* Old Guard Republicans); revival post–1960s of, 202–3; T. Roosevelt brand of, 143; social issues of, 212, 226; social welfare model vs., 9; southern Democrats and, 186, 211, 215–16, 239; Sunbelt and, 72, 197, 199, 212

Conservative Political Action Conference, 5

Conspicuous consumption, 30

Constitutional Convention (1787), 3, 47, 267

Consumer protection, 132

Containment policy, 58

Continental Army, 45

Continental Congress, 57

Contract with America, 253

Coolidge, Calvin, 132, 163, 182, 188

Cooper, Charles D., 55

Cooper, John Milton, 3–4

Copperhead Democrats, 140

Corporations, 24, 143; H. Adams critique of, 119; power of, 119, 150; Reagan as ambassador of, 228; Republican Party and, 9, 113, 116, 207, 212; rise of, 110; taxation of, 4, 212. *See also* Trusts

Corruption. *See* Political corruption; Spoils system

Cotton Belt, 85

Cotton Whigs, 109, 111, 141

Country ideology, 21–23, 41

Courts. *See* Judiciary; Supreme Court

Cox, Jacob D., 121–22

Cranston, Alan, 250

Crawford, William, 80

Credit, 14, 18–19, 22, 23, 95, 98

Crenna, Richard, 225

Crime laws, 254

Crittenden Compromise (1860), 111

Cross of Gold speech (Bryan, 1896), 24

Cruz, Ted, 10, 265

Cuba, 150

Cultural conservatives, 173, 226–29, 237, 251; Democratic centrists and, 254, 259

Cultural liberalism, 229

Curley, James Michael, 183

Currency, 137; bimetallism and, 25; hard, 72, 90, 95, 102; paper, 18–19, 22, 98; uniform, 14

Currency Acts (1764), 22

Czolgosz, Leon, 142

Dakota Territory, 136, 139

Daley, Richard J., 234–35

Daschle, Tom, 250

Davis, David (judge), 121

Davis, David Brion (historian), 274 (n. 2)

Davis, Elizabeth (Mrs. George Cabot), 181

Davis, Harry, 181

Davis, John W., 163

Deal making, art of, 3

Debs, Eugene, 139, 170–71

Debtors. *See* Credit

Declaration of Independence, 57, 80, 106

Dixiecrats, 186, 211, 215–16, 239
Dixwell, Epes Sargent, 179
DLC. *See* Democratic Leadership Council
Dodd, Christopher, 250
Dodd, Thomas J., 210
Dole, Bob, 258, 265
Donald, David Herbert, 7
Douglas, Paul, 188
Douglas, Stephen, 101, 110
Douthat, Ross, 232
Downey, Matthew T., 120
Dred Scott decision (1857), 7, 96, 102, 108
Dresser Industries, 213
Duane, William, 95
Duer, William, 25
Dukakis, Michael, 9, 248
Dwight, Timothy, 60

Earle, Jonathan H., 100
East India Company, 56
Easy Plan for a Militia, An (Pickering), 45
Economic crisis. *See* Financial crisis; Great Depression
Economic development: centrist Democrats and, 250; Federalist and Whig emphasis on, 106; Hamilton vs. Adams and, 23. *See also* American System
Economic individualism, 175
Economic policy: Carter and, 241–42; New Deal and, 248; Reagan and, 4–5, 202, 219, 223. *See also* Fiscal policy
Edmunds, George, 137
Education: G. W. Bush legislation, 230; evolution theory teaching restrictions and, 237; federal aid to, 193, 221, 242; "Ph.D. Octopus" (W. James term) and, 29–30; promotion of public schools and, 93, 102; Protestant practices and, 154; school desegregation and, 218; universities and, 118
Education of Henry Adams, The (H. Adams), 128–29
Edwards, Frances Taft, 165
Egalitarianism. *See* Equality
Eisenhower, Dwight D., 8, 177–78, 184, 187, 189–95, 199, 207, 214; conservative critics of, 210, 211; "Draft Ike" movement and, 190–91, 197; expired mandate of, 212; moderate Republicanism and, 210, 211, 266; Nixon as running mate, 208–9
Eizenstat, Stuart, 238
Elections. *See* Primary elections; Suffrage; *and Presidential election headings*
Electoral College: election of 1800 and, 40, 52, 59, 106; election of 1824 and, 74; election of 1876 and, 155; election of 1936 and, 236; election of 1980 and, 245; election of 2000 and, 269 (n. 9); record winners in, 236; Republican dominance of, 175; slaveholding states' advantage in, 53
Electoral Commission Act (1877), 155–56
Eliot, Charles, 140
Embargo of 1807, 6–7, 37, 56, 57–58, 60, 97; J. Q. Adams and, 78; economic effects of, 59; Federalist challenge to, 62–63; repeal of, 63
Emerson, Ralph Waldo, 85, 178–79
Emerson, William, 85
Employment discrimination, 215, 224
Emporia (Kans.) Gazette, 183
Endicott, John, 46
Energy crisis (1977–79), 244, 251
Enforcement Acts (1870–71), 58, 62–63
England. *See* Great Britain

Iraq war (1990–91). *See* Persian Gulf War

Irish-Americans, 163, 202

Isolationism, 5, 6, 175, 176, 184, 185, 186, 190, 279 (n. 4)

Jackson, Andrew, 25, 37–38, 85–86, 144, 177, 225, 267; J. Q. Adams centrism vs., 111; as "common man" champion, 71; Democratic Party and, 24, 71, 72, 90, 94–95, 98, 99–100, 102, 161; disputed 1824 election and, 74, 80; imperial presidency of, 106; Jefferson's dislike of, 94; military achievements of, 68; pocket veto and, 38; policies of, 37–38, 71, 72, 82, 89–90, 94–95; Senate censure of, 95

Jackson, Jesse, 247, 250

Jacobinism, 26–27, 43, 51, 58; J. Adams rejection of, 33, 35; Jeffersonian Republicans and, 42, 48–49, 50

Jakes, T. D., 227

James, Henry, 180

James, William, 29–30

James II (king of England), 21

Jay, John, 47

Jay Treaty (1794), 49

Jefferson, Mary ("Polly"), 39

Jefferson, Thomas, 6, 7–8, 23, 25, 33, 77–78, 94, 97, 102, 104, 267; A. Adams correspondence with, 39–40; J. Adams late-life correspondence with, 27, 29, 31, 35–36, 73–74; agrarianism and, 6, 17, 59, 92, 106–7; American Revolution and, 57; British-French conflict and, 37, 76; Burr vice presidency and, 40, 55; democracy and, 13, 45, 54; French Revolution support by, 38, 48–49; frontier supporters of, 106; internal improvements and, 93–94; Louisiana Purchase (1803) by, 52; Madison presidential candidacy and, 55, 58–59, 60–61; national banks and, 95; nationalism and, 93; *Notes on the State of Virginia*, 17; partisanship of, 44, 47; political outlook of, 13, 14, 31; political patronage and, 60; presidential election of, 37, 40, 52; presidential reelection of, 56; slavery and, 92, 98–99, 100, 102, 273–74 (n. 2); *A Summary View of the Rights of British America*, 57; vice presidency of, 34

Jeffersonian Republicans, 5, 6–7, 13, 19–20, 28, 32, 106, 262; H. Adams historical perspective on, 125; J. Adams centrism and, 111, 117; J. Q. Adams and, 74–75, 77–78, 125; agrarian supporters of, 49, 70, 92, 106–7; Alien and Sedition Acts response by, 35; Cabot's centrism and, 111; congressional seats of, 63; Enlightenment ideals of, 1, 13, 23, 95, 100, 102; Era of Good Feelings and, 79; factors in demise of, 5; Federalist secessionists and, 44; formation of, 33; Hartford Convention itemized indictments of, 67; ideological center and, 79; internal dissent and, 96, 161–62; Jackson rejection by, 94–96; Lockean liberalism and, 24; Northerners and, 58, 60, 61, 62–63, 64, 69, 77, 96; policies of, 14–15, 27, 36, 38, 102; popular success of, 42; populist strain of, 68, 96; presidential election successes of, 62; reasons for success of, 68; Republican Party (1850s) origins in, 91, 92, 106–8; Southerners and, 61, 68, 69, 95, 96–99; War of 1812 and, 65, 97. *See also* Democratic Party

presidential election (1968) of, 224, 235, 236–37; resignation from presidency of, 221; Sunbelt strategy of, 212

No Child Left Behind Act (2001), 230

Non-Intercourse Act (1809), 53

"Norsemen, The" (G. Lodge), 181

North African campaign (World War II), 184

North American Free Trade Agreement, 252, 254, 259

North American Review, 122, 123–24, 179

North Atlantic Treaty, 185, 188. *See also* NATO

North Korea. *See* Korean War

North Vietnam. *See* Vietnam War

Northwest Ordinance (1787), 100, 106; slavery ban, 108, 274 (n. 2)

Notes on the State of Virginia (Jefferson), 17

Nova Scotia, 53

Nuclear Test Ban Treaty (1963), 218

Nunc Age (H. Adams term), 116

Nunn, Sam, 248

Obama, Barack, 234, 259–63, 267; *The Audacity of Hope,* 260, 261; election successes of, 232, 260; moderate policies of, 3, 9–10, 260–63; pragmatism of, 259; on Reagan, 233

O'Connor, Sandra Day, 5

Odessa (Tex.), 213

O'Donnell, Bill, 222

Ohio, 105, 151, 167; Bush family background and, 203, 213, 305; Jacksonian Democrats and, 99; Republican dominant electoral votes and, 175; Taft family and, 153, 156, 158

Oil business, 213

Old Guard Republicans, 142, 147, 148, 159, 163, 166, 168, 172, 177; P. Bush's

moderate views and, 210; collapse of, 150, 152; failed 1952 presidential election attempt by, 181–92, 195; isolationism and, 190; Lodge, Jr. challenge to, 186–87, 189–94; Reagan Revolution and, 201; return to power (1920s) of, 171, 172

Old Republicans (Jeffersonian faction), 161

O'Neill, Tip, 240–41

1000 Points of Light (G.H.W. Bush program), 223

One World (Willkie), 176

On Wings of Eagles (Follett novel/TV miniseries), 225

Operation Desert Shield, 224

Operation Desert Storm, 224, 231

Ordinance of 1787, 108

Oregon, 106, 155, 278 (n. 31)

Organized crime, 177

Organized labor. *See* Labor unions

Other America, The (M. Harrington), 241

Otis, Harrison Gray, 59, 60

Overbey, John, 213

Oxford English Dictionary, 104

Oxford University, 182, 183

Pacific Northwest, 72

Pacific possessions, 137, 141, 142

Paine, Thomas, 28, 139; *Common Sense,* 27

Panama Canal, 164

Panic of 1837, 81, 82, 144

Panic of 1873, 124

Paper money, 18–19, 22, 98

Paris Exhibition (1900), 129

Parish, Elijah, 64

Paris Peace Treaty (1898), 128

Parliament, 21, 56

Parrington, Vernon, 13–14, 115

Parson, Theophilus, 45

Party system. *See* Political parties

appointments to, 262; presidential 2000 election decision by, 228; Reagan appointments to, 5; F.D. Roosevelt packing attempt, 216; W. H. Taft as chief justice, 156, 158, 171
Swedenborgianism, 98
Swift, Lucius B., 145

Taft, Alphonso, 152–56, 157, 277 (n. 1)
Taft, Charles, 158
Taft, Helen ("Nellie"), 157, 169
Taft, Louise Torrey, 153
Taft, Robert, 5, 187–88, 189, 191, 193, 194, 195, 197, 198, 210, 277 (n. 1)
Taft, Robert, Jr., 277 (n. 1)
Taft, Robert, III, 277 (n. 1)
Taft, William Howard, 145, 147, 148, 150–72, 277 (n. 1); assessment of, 159; death (1930) of, 171; family background of, 152–56; father's professional interests and, 156; legal and political career of, 156–57, 158; personality of, 158, 159; political outlook of, 158–59; post-presidency career of, 171; presidency of, 150, 152, 159, 164–65; presidential second-term defeat of, 168, 169, 170; on T. Roosevelt, 150; T. Roosevelt relationship with, 144, 160, 165–66, 167, 168–69, 170, 265; as T. Roosevelt's designated successor, 144, 157, 221; as Supreme Court chief justice, 156, 158, 171; trust-busting and, 159; unraveling of presidency of, 164–65
Taft dynasty, 277 (n. 1)
Taft-Hartley Act (1947): provisions of, 210
Talleyrand, Charles-Maurice de, 36–37
Tanenhaus, Sam, 260–61
Taney, Roger, 95
Tariff, 97, 137, 177; constitutionality of, 3; Payne-Aldrich, 159, 160, 161, 164; protective, 88, 93; Smoot-Hawley, 177

Tariff of 1833, 44, 215
Taxes, 36, 146, 247, 254; British colonies and, 22, 56, 57; G.H.W. Bush raising of, 219, 224; Carter reduction bill, 241–42; B. Clinton reduction of, 253, 254; corporate cuts in, 212; corporate raises in, 4; Democratic coalition and, 9–10; Republican policies and, 212; Whiskey Rebellion against, 47–48, 51. See also Income tax; Poll taxes
Tax Reform Act (1986), 4
Taylor, John, 31–32, 56
Taylor, Zachary, 99, 177
Tea Party (1773). See Boston Tea Party
Tea Party conservatives (contemporary), 10, 265
Tennessee, 106
Tennessee Coal and Iron Company, 160
Tennessee Valley Authority, 176
Terrorism, 228, 231, 232, 283 (n. 54)
Tertium quid (Jeffersonian faction), 161
Texas: annexation of, 85; Bush family and, 203, 213–14, 217–20, 226, 227, 229; conservative Republicans and, 191, 214–15; de facto one-party system of, 217–18; economic power of, 211; expansion of slavery to, 72; majority minority population, 265; oil wealth and, 213; statehood and, 85–86, 89, 98; Taft Republicans and, 191
Texas Air National Guard, 227
Texas War for Independence, 85
Textile trade, 109
Theory of the Leisure Class, The (Veblen), 30
Third parties, 145–48, 170–71, 175, 178, 221–23, 225–26; Dixiecrats and, 186, 211, 215–16, 239
Third Way, 234, 240, 251, 255–56; British policies and, 256; Obama and, 259, 260–61